Contemporary International Issues

Contemporary International Issues

Contending Perspectives

edited by
Steven L. Lamy

Lynne Rienner Publishers ◆ Boulder & London

Published in the United States of America in 1988 by
Lynne Rienner Publishers, Inc.
948 North Street, Boulder, Colorado 80302

and in the United Kingdom by
Lynne Rienner Publishers, Inc.
3 Henrietta Street, Covent Garden, London WC2E 8LU

Library of Congress Cataloging-in-Publication Data

Contemporary international issues.

  Bibliography: p.
  Includes index.
  1. World politics—1945-   . I. Lamy, Steven L.
D849.C583 1988   327′.09′04   88-18281
ISBN 1-55587-016-3 (alk. paper)

British Library Cataloguing in Publication Data
A Cataloguing in Publication record for this book
is available from the British Library.

Printed and bound in the United States of America

The paper used in this publication meets the requirements
of the American National Standard for Permanence of Paper
for Printed Library Materials Z39.48-1984. ⊗

To our students

Contents

Exhibits

Preface

This book has its origin in a series of discussions that I inevitably have with students in my introductory international relations courses as we explore contending interpretations of complex and controversial international issues. I find that a significant number of my students have never been encouraged to think critically about why they see the world a certain way and why their perception of issues and events and their attending policy prescriptions may not be universally shared. Thus, the students and I spend a significant amount of time considering the assumptions and beliefs that make up their worldview, and then exploring its limits by comparing and contrasting that worldview with those held by others in the international system.

Not surprisingly, I find that many of my colleagues face similar challenges in their efforts to involve students in this process of critical analysis. The challenge, in both research and teaching, is to develop within our students a sense of the importance of being able to identify and then to examine the assumptions behind contending worldviews.

Addressing that challenge, this text was written by university scholars who teach introductory courses in international relations or related subject areas. Each chapter was written with a specific learning objective in mind: to prepare our students for living and working in a world that is not defined solely by the students' interests and concerns. In our courses, we try to prepare students to assess issues and events competently, and then to appreciate how their lives are inextricably linked with the welfare of citizens throughout the world. Our goal is not to overwhelm our students with accounts of poverty, conflict, and other such problems. Instead, it is to inform, and enable them to become innovative and creative participants in world affairs. It is in this spirit that this book provides readers with an opportunity to explore several important international and regional issues and to compare different perceptions of the issues being discussed. As students of international relations, we discover more about the world by critically reviewing the assumptions and values that lie *behind* each worldview.

I have incurred a number of debts in the preparation of this volume. First, I would like to thank the Danforth Foundation and the Immaculate Heart College Center for their support of discussions and seminars. The staff of the Center for Public Education in International Affairs contributed significantly to the preparation of the manuscript; in particular, I would like to thank Julie Zimmerman, Erin Rowe, Natalie Pipitone, Teresa Hudock, Rosanne DeBenedetti, and Cheryl Crow. In addition, the staff at Lynne Rienner Publishers has been helpful, supportive, and patient. All of these contributions are greatly appreciated.

—*Steven L. Lamy*

About the Authors

Laurien Alexandre is director of global studies at Immaculate Heart College Center. Dr. Alexandre's research focuses primarily on the role of media in international relations. Her book, *The Voice of America: From Detente to the Reagan Doctrine*, examines the relationship of U.S. government broadcasting and foreign policy.

Donald K. Alper is associate professor of political science at Western Washington University. He has published articles on Canadian-U.S. relations in *Candian Public Policy/Analyse de Politiques* and the *American Review of Canadian Studies*.

Farrokh Jhabvala is professor of international relations at Florida International University. He has published widely on international law and human rights.

Ann Kelleher, assosciate professor of political science at Pacific Lutheran University, was formerly director of the university's Office of International Education. Dr. Kelleher's current teaching and research interests include Third World debt, change in the Arab world, and women in developing countries.

Steven L. Lamy is associate professor in the University of Southern California's School of International Relations, and director of the Center for Public Education in International Affairs. He is currently working on a comparative study of foreign policy processes. Dr. Lamy has served as a consultant for international affairs education in over twenty states and several foreign countries and was special consultant for the Danforth Foundation in 1988.

Deborah Anne Palmieri, assistant dean of the Graduate School at the University of Southern California, is a specialist on Soviet foreign policy and economic relations between the Soviet Union and the industrialized West. Dr. Palmieri is currently working on a history of Soviet global political economy from Stalin to Gorbachev.

Steve Smith is director of the Centre for Public Choice Studies, and senior lecturer in international relations at the University of East Anglia (England). He has written extensively on nuclear weapons/arms control and foreign policy theory.

John F. Stack, Jr., is professor of political science at Florida International University. He is the author of many publications about ethnicity and world politics and is now working on a study of ethnic relations in Miami.

Roger Tooze, principal lecturer in the Department of International Relations, North Staffordshire Polytechnic (England), has published widely in the field of international political economy. His latest book, edited with John MacLean, is *The International Political Economy of Knowledge and Information.*

William Tow is assistant professor in the School of International Relations, University of Southern California. He has coedited three books and is currently working on a study of extended deterrence issues in the Asian Pacific.

Susan Waltz, assistant professor of international relations at Florida International University, is a specialist in North African politics. She has twice been appointed a U.S. delegate to Amnesty International's International Council Meeting and is currently researching the development of indigenous human rights groups in North Africa.

Carl Anthony Watson is a doctoral candidate in international relations at the University of Southern California. His fields of study include diplomatic history and military and strategic affairs.

Donald C. Wilson is associate professor in the Department of Social and Educational Studies, the University of British Columbia (Canada). Active in Canadian studies programs in both the United States and Canada, he is the author of *Teaching Public Issues in a Canadian Context* and co-editor of *Communication Canada: Issues in Broadcasting and New Technologies.*

Robert B. Woyach is a member of the senior faculty of Ohio State University's Mershon Center and an adjunct assistant professor in the Department of Political Science. Dr. Woyach has written or edited nine volumes of curriculum material for secondary schools, including *Making Decisions: Our Global Connection, National Security and World History* and a *Global History Resource Book.* His most recent edited book is an analysis of five *Approaches to World Studies*, designed for use by curriculum planners.

Contemporary International Issues

1

Worldviews Analysis of International Issues

STEVEN L. LAMY

This book explores thirteen international issues. These issues are complex, affecting both public and private actors throughout the international system, and are not easily resolved by the actions of a single government, private corporation, or individual. These same issues are controversial: Those affected by them often disagree over definitions of the problems, explanations of their origins, and how best to respond to the challenges they present.

Part 1 discusses wide-ranging and persistent policy issues, such as nuclear- and conventional-arms races, international inequality, global resources and growth, human rights, and the ideological battle between the United States and the Soviet Union.

The mistrust and geopolitical competition that has shaped relations between the United States and the Soviet Union is a good example of this kind of policy issue. Each of the superpowers has devoted significant resources to efforts aimed at controlling and perhaps overcoming the other superpower. They have involved the entire world community in their strategic chess game for over forty years. Soviet and U.S. policy actions have had a significant impact on international and regional institutions established to maintain global order and stability. Additionally, in an effort to maintain positions as a friend or foe in this global struggle and to protect their national interests, both large and small states have allocated a substantial amount of their resources to defense and strategic policy programs.

Part 2 discusses tension areas or conflict regions in the international system. Most of the conflict situations discussed in this volume have significant geopolitical implications that directly involve the United States and the Soviet Union. The chapters on Southern Africa and Central America focus on areas in which both superpowers are providing diplomatic support, technical services, non-military goods, and military assistance to adversaries.

Not all conflicts in international affairs involve the use of military force. It is important for students of international affairs to understand the political, economic, and cultural dimensions of conflict situations, as well as the military and geopolitical aspects. For example, this section of the volume includes a chapter that explores the conflict between rich and poor states over the control of information production and dissemination agencies. This conflict is not being played out on a battlefield. Diplomats, media experts, scientists, and corporate leaders debate this issue and explore possible solutions at conferences and seminars sponsored by the United Nations and by more specialized international institutions as well.

It is also important for students of international affairs to realize that conflicts over policy issues also cause problems among allies. A review of Canadian-U.S. relations illustrates some of the problems faced by traditional allies whose leaders are attempting to reconcile national interests with regional or international priorities in a competitive international environment.

Each author of the chapters in this book was asked to organize his or her assessment of a particularly controversial international issue or event within an analytical framework that encourages the comparisons of contending worldviews. These different worldviews offer divergent descriptions, competing explanations, contrast in predictions, and a wide range of policy solutions. For purposes of this analytical framework, a *worldview* is defined as a set of assumptions, core beliefs, and values, which individuals use to interpret the world around them. Individuals use their worldview as a lens to analyze and evaluate events, actions of other individuals or nation-states, and conditions having a long-term or passing effect on people or societies (e.g., a national disaster or the image one ethnic community has about a second ethnic community). It is important to note that this lens creates an image of reality that may not be universally shared. There are many ways of seeing the world around us, and it is extremely important for students of international relations to realize the limits of their interpretations.

In attempting to understand controversial international issues, a multiple-perspective or contending-worldviews analytical approach is critical. This approach does not assume that all actors in the system have similar policy goals and objectives. It does assume that cultural factors, ideology, and traditional processes of socialization (e.g., the media, schools, and the family) will create different values and priorities. Individuals in leadership positions will make decisions that are consistent with their worldviews. Not all political leaders will support policies aimed at maintaining the status quo, in terms of the distribution of power and influence in the international system. Those who want change in the system may seek incremental reforms or radical transformations. Thus, a comprehensive understanding of issues that affect societies throughout the world will require an examination of worldviews in three categories: those of *system maintainers, system reformers, and system transformers.*

This book is aimed at students, scholars, and teachers interested in exploring the views of the significant actors in a given international-issue area. The worldviews-analytical framework provides the student of international affairs with a method for organizing research and the identification and analysis of contending theories and policy issues. This approach is particularly useful when an individual is trying to understand or teach about especially controversial international issues.

This is an introductory text that does not assume an in-depth awareness of the issues discussed in each chapter. The authors have sought to raise questions that might encourage further research. The text is not meant to stand alone. Each author encourages the reader to seek out additional empirical studies representing the theoretical and policy debates that define each worldview category.

The chapters presented in this volume do not present a single perspective or a particularly U.S. worldview. Clearly, the choice of issues and conflict areas that are addressed in this study reflects a U.S. foreign-policy agenda. However, the worldviews-analytical approach helps overcome the limits normally imposed by the cultural, ideological, and situational factors that usually influence the content of classes and the methods of instruction. The emphasis on encouraging a more pluralistic, in terms of worldviews, assessment of world issues makes this an important contribution to any discussion or lecture in which students are wrestling with complex and distant issues. Students often accept a specific explanation or analysis of an international event because of the difficulty associated with finding alternative interpretations of these same issues or events. The worldviews-analytical framework presented in this book is not foolproof, and its proper application requires careful and thoughtful research. Its strength is that it presents the reader with a way of thinking and teaching about world politics that recognizes the existence of multiple interpretations of reality. This method of analysis is essential for effective policymaking in the international system.

A WORLDVIEW AND ISSUE APPROACH

First, it is important to emphasize that any approach or method of analysis reflects a particular view of the world. The authors of this book were asked to examine international issues from three worldview categories: those of *system maintainers, system reformers, and system transformers.*[1] In these categories, "system" refers to the international system. The international system is defined by the interactions among state and non-state actors and the resulting processes of decisionmaking and arrangements of power and influence.

Since the end of World War II, the international system has been shaped by significant transformations. Each has had some impact on the structure of the international system. These are not just changes that influence activities within units. These transformations are significant because they each have an impact at the international-system level. Many theorists concerned with understanding international relations suggest that change or transformation is insignificant unless the event changes the "arrangement of the parts of the system" or the order of the structure. For example, *an event or a series of decisions that move the international system from anarchy to a more centralized power structure is an example of a significant change or transformation*. (Waltz 1979, 88–97)

A second definitional characteristic of the international system relates to specific functions of actors within the system. According to Kenneth Waltz (1979), nation-states are like units and are not significantly different in the functions that each unit performs. While it is true that nation-states may have different resources, and thus different capabilities, they generally perform similar functions in the international system. Consequently, *a significant transformation in the international system would result in a differentiation of functions among state actors*. This could mean that larger, more powerful states would play a more custodial role in certain policy areas (e.g., the control of nuclear arms) and weaker states would be expected to play a role in regional affairs (e.g., New Zealand's role as a stabilizing force in the Pacific Islands region) or as leaders in multilateral policy organizations (e.g., the Netherlands as a major proponent of development-assistance programs in the Organization of Economic Cooperation and Development [OECD] and the United Nations [UN]).

One may also recognize the role played by non-state actors (e.g., the Roman Catholic Church, Amnesty International, and the Exxon Corporation) and international or regional governmental organizations (e.g., the UN and the Organization of African Unity) in the international-policy arena. However, these non-state actors are generally considered to be subservient to the policy interests of state actors.

The international system is defined also by the distribution of power and influence in that system. Accordingly, *any significant shift in power which changes the order of states in the system must be considered a delimiting transformation*. For example, the economic collapse of a major power or the emergence of a new nuclear military force would undoubtedly influence the distribution of power and influence throughout the international system. (Waltz 1979, 97)

These three characteristics describe the traditional view of the international system. From this viewpoint, the international system is seen as competitive and anarchic (i.e., no central authority exists to maintain order) with the principal powers being nation-states. Those states with power are the rule makers in the international system. Leaders in every state select policies aimed at furthering their national interests. The strategy of self-help is critical for survival in an international system with only minimal rules of behavior. Furthermore, a traditional view of the international system supports the notion that a nation-state's leaders must be prepared to use force or the threat of force in their efforts to promulgate policies aimed at securing the national interest.

Those political leaders and international-affairs experts who adhere to this traditionalist view recognize that changes have occurred within the system since 1945. For example, Japan has gone from a devastated and defeated Asian power to a major global economic power. Most see these changes as part of the maturation of the system. Changes such as the increase in the number of nation-states and the increase in transactions between states are seen as influencing attributes within the countries; however, these changes or transformations are not recognized as having a major influence on the order within the system, the functions of nation-states, or the fungibility of certain capabilities, such as nuclear arms, in determining the rules in the international system.

Traditionalists maintain that although the priorities and actions of states may have to change because of the emergence of new states in Africa or the shift of economic power toward East Asian states, the basic rules of the international system remain the same. Those states with significant power, the ability to mobilize political, economic, and military resources to convince another country to act in a manner that supports their interests, continue to define the rules. Thus, in spite of new developments in the international system, the United States and the USSR remain as the directors of their respective spheres of influence.

The Contemporary International System

The authors contributing to this volume were asked to consider an alternative to this traditional view of the international system. This alternative interpretation of the contemporary international system recognizes the continuance of certain traditional characteristics, such as the persistence of conflict and the primacy of state actors. However, this alternative view accepts the notion that transformations since 1945 have created a less anarchic and more pluralistic international system. This view suggests that these transformations have changed the distribution of power and have resulted in the establishment of international rules and regulations that have moved the system further away from a system without governance. There are numerous transformations that have affected the structure and order of the international system. Perhaps the most significant transformations are:

1. The emergence of new state actors and the tremendous growth in the number and salience of non-state actors (e.g., transnational enterprises and international non-governmental actors)
2. Changes in the distribution of power and the increasing importance of non-force policy options (e.g., economic policies aimed at furthering national interests)
3. The exponential increase in international transactions linking public and private actors throughout the international system

These three transformations represent characteristics of the contemporary international system that differentiate it from a more traditional system. A closer examination of these three transformations suggests clear differences between the international system that existed prior to World War II and the contemporary system. For one, it is quite clear that the contemporary system is still developing in terms of power distributions and the patterns of interaction between state and non-state actors within the system.

The Emergence of New Nation-States and Non-State Actors
The first major transformation that has played a role in shaping the international affairs agenda in the contemporary world is the emergence of new nation-states (i.e., state actors) and non-state actors. As a result of the decolonization process after World War II, over eighty new countries have joined the international community. These developing states have brought new interests, priorities, and needs to the economic- and security-policy debates at both bilateral (i.e., country-to-country) and multilateral (i.e., international organizations) levels. These countries enjoy equal legal status as sovereign states; however, few of these states have the economic, military, or political resources that would give them parity with the more advanced industrial states of the West. Thus, these states play a different role in the international system. The majority of new states is dependent upon political, economic, and security assistance from larger, more powerful states. These dependencies make new states vulnerable to superpower competition and increase the chances of instability within the international system. The "politics of survival" in many of these countries require that their leaders either accept the continuance of a dependency relationship with wealthier and more powerful states or support strategies aimed at dissociation from the present international system. A few of these leaders are seeking a more self-reliant path of development; however, most accept the need to reform or significantly change existing international economic and political structures. Consequently, the leadership in many of these states has willingly transferred sovereignty and authority to multilateral efforts aimed at restructuring the international economic system. Although the primary motivation is still self-interest, the weaker states in the international system seem to be supporting either collective unilateral policies (e.g., the Organization of Petroleum Exporting Countries' [OPEC's] oil embargo) or collective multilateral efforts, such as special sessions sponsored by the United Nations, which focus on global crises. Support for collective or multilateral organizations challenges the state-centric view of international politics. It may also suggest a differentiation of political strategies and policy orientations among state actors. Weaker states, unable to represent their interests unilaterally, have begun to look to international institutions and other multilateral forums as their primary political arena and as primary representatives of their national interests.

A second aspect of this "actor" transformation in the international system is the increase in the number of and the commensurate acceleration of activities of non-state actors such as transnational enterprises (TNEs) and not-for-profit organizations within and between nation-states. Minimally, this means increased involvement with state actors; maximally, this means an increase in the power of non-state actors vis-à-vis nation-states. There have always been non-state actors participating with nation-states in the international system. These non-state actors work as pressure groups in the international-affairs policy arena, and as the interests and concerns of domestic groups become more international, the activities of these groups increase commensurately. To date, these groups have not replaced nation-states as centers of power and authority or the focus of citizen identity and loyalty. Corporations such as IBM and private organizations such as Church World Services must abide by the laws of local and national governments. Their activities are usually controlled by states; if these non-state actors pursue policies that challenge the interests of indigenous elites who control power, they will be asked to leave. However, these non-state actors do play a very important role in the policymaking processes of most states. For example, the leaders of the Catholic Church continue to advocate political change in those Latin American countries where dictators persist in their support of policies aimed at denying basic human rights within their societies. TNEs provide local employment, loans, technology, and other economic resources. These large corporations can make or break a government with their decision to invest or build a new production facility. It is obvious that the economic resources and investment capabilities held by TNEs could challenge the traditional authorities of the state.

This is not to say that TNEs will supplant the nation-state. Instead, these actors might work with states with similar interests, challenge those they cannot afford to leave or those they feel can be influenced, and exit from those states who push them too far. The role of U.S.-based corporations in the overthrow of the Allende government in Chile provides an example of the flag and the dollar working to influence domestic and foreign policy. As countries continue to compete for markets and resources, the role of TNEs is bound to increase. Likewise, if citizens find their government to be ineffective or unconcerned about a problem or issue, they may work with a non-governmental organization to represent their interests. A brief glimpse at a current debate in U.S. foreign policy provides a useful example of this point.

A traditional view of the international system suggests that when confronted with challenges to its national interests, a state will use its power to counter those challenges. Leaders act rationally in these situations, selecting policies that maximize benefits and minimize costs. Thus, a powerful state could easily discourage the activities of less powerful states encroaching on its interests by using or threatening force. In the traditional view, leaders of states are rarely challenged in the foreign-policy arena. To illustrate: U.S. foreign-policy leaders, acting rationally, should be free to use the power of the United States to deter and counter Soviet-backed aggression in Central America. However, many U.S. citizens belong to groups opposed to U.S. military action in Central America. As the U.S. congressional debates on Contra funding have shown, these groups do have some influence on U.S. foreign-policy activities. If these interest groups opposed to U.S. military activity in Central America succeed in their efforts to change the direction of U.S. foreign policy, their success will have an effect on other conflict situations (e.g., South Africa) where the United States has been directly or indirectly involved. Furthermore, any change in the foreign-policy priorities of the United States will have an immediate impact on other actors in the system.

Thus, the activities of non-state actors could result in more formal and informal rules governing the behavior of both state and non-state actors. More importantly, as the non-state actors provide citizens with access to decision-makers, they will be more frequently used by individuals interested in shaping the policy agenda. Loyalty once reserved for national governments could be shifted to private non-state actors. This "privatization" of foreign-policy activities has the potential to influence significantly the structure of the international system by challenging the primacy of states and by changing the rules of the game. Consequently, the reliance on international and regional fora and the support for multilateral organizations by new states, and the dramatic increase of non-state-actor policy activity has moved the international system further away from an anarchic environment.

Changing Options for Power and Influence
A second major transformation defining the contemporary system relates to the changes in the distribution of power and influence in the system. This involves the increasing salience of non-force options and the inappropriateness of military tools of statecraft for resolving many international disputes. The countries of the world spend over $300 billion a year on both nuclear and conventional arms and related military programs. There are at present five major nuclear powers—the United States, China, the Soviet Union, France, and Great Britain. An additional six countries are thought to possess nuclear power capabilities—Brazil, South Africa, Argentina, Israel, Pakistan, and India. The global arms culture also includes an extensive proliferation of conventional arms, which has increased superpower involvement throughout the world. The United States and the Soviet Union use arms-trade and military-assistance programs to further their political and security interests among their allies and in many developing countries. In a similar fashion, regional powers or adventurist weak states often use military advantages to control or coerce other states in their efforts to extend their power and prestige or divert attention from major domestic problems. The proliferation of both conventional and nuclear arms has dramatically increased the chances for a regional conflict or war occurring and developing into a major global confrontation. This situation has changed the nature of international statecraft and certainly has changed public attitudes toward war. Leaders are confronted with policy dilemmas that require non-military responses (e.g., trade wars) or situations in which the use of force might cause a major escalation of the conflict.

These changes in military dimensions of power are accompanied by significant shifts in economic capacities of power and influence. The United States no longer enjoys a predominant position in the world economy. Japan, the "newly industrializing" countries of Taiwan, Brazil, and South Korea, and the European Economic Community (EEC) have effectively used trade, investment, and assistance programs and processes, initiated by the United States after World War II, to build viable and extremely effective economic systems. U.S. trade deficits reflect the increasing number of U.S. product, service, and commodity dependencies in the international economy.

The shift from a world in which the United States was the economic hegemon, immediately following World War II, to a more pluralistic world in which it is a major actor, is seen by some theorists to be the result of the proper development of the political and economic system designed and implemented by the United States. (Calleo 1982) However, these changes in the dimensions both of political power and influence and of economic strength have created new dependencies for the United States and other wealthy states, unaccustomed to the restrictions and frustrations which accompanying a shift in status and power. For example, U.S. dependence on strategic minerals imported from South Africa clearly influenced the Reagan administration's choice to pursue a policy of "constructive engagement," which encourages the maintenance of trade linkages, rather than a policy of economic divestment. Trade dependencies affect the independence and flexibility of weak and strong states alike.

The complexities of international affairs in the contemporary system have also limited the effectiveness of many traditional tools of foreign policy; namely, the implementation of military solutions in crisis situations. Conflicts with Japan about trade issues or boycotts by commodity cartels (e.g., OPEC's oil embargo) are not effectively resolved by bombs or military invasions. Non-force options seem to be more effective in an international system in which economic and sociocultural issues are now defined and accepted as national-security concerns. This suggests a need to rethink the traditional view of how states represent their interests in a competitive and anarchic international system. A traditional geopolitical view emphasizes military strength as the guarantor of sovereignty. Although military strength is certainly still an important tool of statecraft, changes in power distributions suggest a need for states to develop more effective non-force tools aimed at securing a state's interest in a more pluralistic international system.

The need for new tools of statecraft is also emphasized by the expansion of the international-policy agenda. Foreign-policy experts must now carefully consider public-policy issues that were previously considered local or national problems or were simply non-issues. As governments have extended their responsibilities into private-sector areas, the list of "public issues" has expanded. Coincidentally, and in part because of the tremendous increase in international linkages, domestic-policy concerns such as pollution, labor laws, banking regulations, zoning rules, criminal-justice activities, educational policies, and consumer-protection laws are affected by international issues and events. In turn, these policy areas are now addressed by both foreign and domestic policymakers. These relatively new areas of international concern are not usually recognized as major national-security issues. Thus, there is a tendency to place these issues on a secondary or "low-politics-issue" agenda. However, it is clear that each of these issues has some bearing on the quality-of-life conditions and the protection of a way of life. To many individuals and groups, these are national-security issues.

The increasing salience of these new national-security issues has resulted in more public pressure for government intervention. The worse things get, the more citizens turn to government to do something about the problem. Many of these issues, such as air pollution, require cooperative responses. Dirty air does not stop at a country's boundary; thus, governments must work together and, in some cases, transfer policymaking authority to a potentially more effective supranational authority. Incrementally, these policy challenges are threatening the traditional notion of state sovereignty and the monopoly states have had in the area of public authority. In addition, in many policy areas, the international system now operates much like a domestic-policy arena, in which public and private organizations bargain and compete for public goods and services. As suggested earlier, more and more interest groups are now operating locally, nationally, and internationally to influence the actions of governments. A recent study on "local foreign policies" indicated that over $18 million was spent by individual states in the United States in an effort to promote exports, and an additional $8.5 million was allocated to programs aimed at encouraging foreign investment in their areas. (Shuman 1986–87)

In summary, changes in the distribution of power and influence and the expansion of the public-policy domain have had some impact on how nation-states interact with each other. Powerful states, in the traditionalist view, find themselves competing with and at times "losing out" to weaker states in the international system. Coalition politics (e.g., the use of cartels), trade restrictions and incentives, development assistance, and communication and technological resources are becoming important tools of statecraft. In some cases, these policies can be used in lieu of military force and are more effective. These tools have enabled small and middle states, and great powers to share policymaking roles in many issue areas. This challenges the traditional view, which suggests that the international-policy arena will be controlled almost exclusively by the major powers, more specifically the United States and the USSR.

Increased Interstate and Intrastate Transactions
The third area of transformation that differentiates the contemporary international system from those of previous eras involves the substantial increase in the volume of interstate and intrastate transactions. It is true that states have always traded products, exchanged art and music, and maintained political-security alliances. However, the depth and breadth of these economic, political, and cultural transactions have increased dramatically since the end of World War II. These linkages have increased the dependencies of nation-states; that usually results in an increase in a country's vulnerability. It is clear that nation-states

have become more dependent on other countries and on various non-state actors to provide essential goods and services. When countries are bound together in either symmetrical or asymmetrical interdependent relations, there will inevitably be national-security implications. Similarly, these connections will have a measurable impact on foreign-policy behavior. For example, a country with a significant dependency on strategic minerals, food, or military assistance may be limited in its capacity to define and implement an independent foreign-policy agenda. Likewise, a dependent state could be constrained in its ability to maintain order and prosperity at home if supplies of these strategic goods (e.g., oil) cannot be obtained from external suppliers.

There are costs and benefits associated with increasing economic, political, and cultural linkages. It would be difficult to identify a single country that has the capacity to produce domestically all of the goods and services essential for the maintenance of the "way of life" its society aspires to provide. The interdependent and dependent relations these linkages create have transformed how states behave with friends and enemies. The United States and the Soviet Union are ideological and military rivals, yet the Soviet Union trades for grain from the United States and the United States depends on the Soviet Union for strategic minerals and as a market for its agricultural surpluses.

These three transformations are examples of systemwide changes which serve to define the contemporary international system. These conditions have had an impact on the functions of actors, the power distribution, and the status of order within the international system. The existence of multilateral organizations with specific authority to regulate international transactions and to enforce certain rules suggests a change from anarchy. The existence of regulatory and enforcement regimes in some policy areas, and the increasing linkages between nation-states have changed the status of order within the system. National interests may still motivate the actions of policymakers; however, the complex nature of problems facing national leaders and the dramatic increase in international activities linking state and non-state actors has increased the cost and reduced the benefits of unilateral action.

The Distribution of Power
These significant transformations in the international system have had an impact on the functions of states. The distribution of power and influence has shifted rather significantly since the end of World War II. Consequently, many states considered weak or small in military terms have emerged as powerful actors in economic areas (e.g., Japan and South Korea) or influential forces due to their level of activity and normative behavior in international institutions like the UN (e.g., the Netherlands or Scandinavian countries). Power has also shifted to nation-states which support change-oriented policies (e.g., the members of OPEC). These policies threaten the advantages enjoyed by the dominant nation-states as rule makers in the international system. Consequently, middle-power nation-states have found themselves playing a major role as conciliators

or bridge builders in the system. Countries such as Canada and the Netherlands are playing important mediating roles in arms and security debates between the superpowers and in discussions between rich and poor states. As the international system matures and becomes more complex, nation-states seem to be assuming different roles and responsibilities.

Finally, these transformations have resulted in a change in the distribution of power within and between nation-states. The stability in the system that has been guaranteed by the nuclear-power balance, and facilitated by the emergence of both formal and informal rules of economic behavior, has contributed to the emergence of new economic powers such as Japan, Taiwan, and West Germany. The persistence of inequality within Third World nation-states and the continuing power struggle between the United States and the USSR, which is played out in the developing areas of the world, have also had a profound impact on power dimensions. Obviously, as citizens and their leaders accept a broader definition of national security, including military, economic, political, and socio-cultural dimensions, the definitions of power and influence will also change. This will also mean a change in the hierarchical structure of the system.

The need for international awareness is greatly increased in this more pluralistic contemporary international system. With an expanded policy agenda, a greater number of actors competing for resources and opportunities, and a more extensive decisionmaking process, the chances for controversy and disagreement increase appreciably. An informed decision in a policy area requires a more comprehensive understanding of the issues. In the case of the United States, it is very difficult for leaders and citizens alike to accept the change in status from that of hegemon to that of one of several principal powers. One reaction is to continue acting like a hegemon, disregarding changes in the international system and acting unilaterally to further U.S. interests over the interests of others. This policy attitude will not benefit the United States in the long run. A long-term strategy suggests the need to develop an informed response, which carefully and critically assesses the arguments presented by actors throughout the system. This is the basis for advocating a *worldviews approach* to the analysis and evaluation of controversial international issues. The assumption is that there is not only a U.S. or Soviet perspective on the issues. A thoughtful student of international affairs must consider the interests and ideas of weak and powerful actors alike. Similarly, political leaders will find it increasingly difficult to represent their constituencies and secure their national interests without reference to competing interests and alternative perspectives. It is in this spirit that the authors of this volume have been asked to develop their chapters around the dimensions of the worldviews analytical framework.

THE WORLDVIEWS ANALYTICAL FRAMEWORK

Earlier in this introductory chapter, a worldview was defined as a set of values, assumptions, and core beliefs that individuals use to interpret the world around them. This is the lens that individuals use to *describe* and *explain* issues, events, and conditions within the international system. Understanding worldviews also plays a major role in *predicting* how an individual might *respond* in a crisis situation or the type of program he or she might advocate in response to a social problem. When applied to international issues, the worldviews analytical framework encourages the student to compare and contrast descriptions, explanations, predictions, and policy prescriptions from three worldview categories. An outline of the analytical framework is provided in Exhibit 1. The three worldview categories, from which more specific worldviews emerge, are described more completely in the following pages.

The System-Maintainer Worldview

Out of civil states, there is always war of everyone against everyone.

—Thomas Hobbes, *Leviathan,* Chapter 13

The core assumptions of the traditional "realist" perspective in international affairs best describe the core beliefs of the system-maintainer worldview. Individuals who share this worldview see the state as the principal actor in world affairs. The international system is seen as anarchic and competitive. If men live in this international society without a common power or state to control their activities, war and violence is a constant condition. Leaders of states must therefore always prepare for war as a means of preventing war. A state that is strong militarily and possesses the will to use its force if necessary is the best deterrent against aggressive behavior.

System maintainers believe there are only minimal rules governing state behavior in the international system. Self-interest is the primary motivation in the international system. State leaders who act in a rational manner always attempt to select policies that further their national interests. A simple cost-benefit analysis, rather than morality and reason, often motivates policies.

System maintainers are generally skeptical about the chances for reform in the international system. Their Hobbesian view of humankind and the role of the state suggests that humans are by nature imperfect and competitive. The state, if properly endowed with power and authority, will provide order and stability in the international system. States use or threaten force to achieve their interests. Other tools of statecraft, such as development assistance, trade policies, and cultural activities, are also used to further a state's interests. Since there is no reliable and effective means for resolving interstate rivalries in an anarchic system, foreign policies tend to emphasize self-help options. The

Exhibit 1.1 Outline of the Worldviews Analytical Framework

Descriptions

1. What does this worldview define as the basic characteristics of the problem or issue?

2. What kind of world does this worldview see being created under present conditions?

3. What actors does this worldview see playing critical roles in a particular issue area?

4. How do these actors participate?

5. What priorities does this worldview assume actors have?

6. What structures and processes of decisionmaking does this worldview see as being involved?

Explanations

1. What relevant theories does this worldview advance to explain the development of this issue or problem?

2. How does this worldview account for persistence of this problem or issue?

3. How does this worldview explain the behavior of state or non-state actors in this policy arena?

Predictions

1. What does this worldview posit as possible scenarios for the future?

2. What will a future policy agenda governed by the assumptions and values of this worldview look like?

3. In this issue area, does this worldview predict that states will act unilaterally or multilaterally?

4. What role does this worldview predict that non-state actors will play?

5. Does this worldview predict that problems will persist?

6. What does this worldview predict will prevent the resolution of conflicts or policy disagreements in this issue area?

Prescriptions

1. What policy strategies does this worldview believe should be advocated by different actors involved in this situation?

2. What are the strengths and weaknesses of each set of solutions prescribed by this worldview?

---

realist view of the international system recognizes a general lack of commitment to a common good—a multilateral agenda for improving the system. Essentially, a system maintainer believes that no state can make its survival dependent upon the potential goodwill of other states.

The system-maintainer perspective is generally supportive of the status quo. This worldview embraces the belief that the present state-centric system provides opportunities for all states, rich and poor. The success of a nation-state depends upon how well a state's leaders use the present system to further their national interests. The system maintainer believes that those who seek changes in the system, either reforms or major transformations, have simply failed to use properly the opportunities that the major powers provide by maintaining order and stability in the international system. System maintainers see advocates of reform or transformation as leaders who want to change the rules rather than spend the time to develop the capacities to further their interests under the present rules of international behavior.

In summary, the core beliefs of the system-maintainer worldview are:

1. The international system is not defined by enforceable rules of behavior, rather it is an anarchic system.
2. Conflict is endemic among actors in the system.
3. Nation-states are the major actors in the system.
4. State leaders act rationally—selecting policies that maximize benefits and minimize costs. Codes of morality governing individual behavior cannot be used to judge states.
5. War is an inevitable feature of a system in which power is emphasized. States seek power to further their national interests and extend their influence over other state and non-state actors.
6. There is only minimal commitment to a common good in the international system.

The System-Reformer Worldview

The system-reformer perspective recognizes the need for some modifications in the international system, partially because of the increasing interdependence and dependence in economic relations, political affairs, communications, and human ambitions. Reformers also realize that injustices and other problems persist and that those who are disadvantaged are demanding changes. Rather than accept a radical transformation in the system, reformers seek *cooperative multilateral* efforts aimed at responding to inequities in the system.

An appropriate model for cooperation is provided by the gradual integration of public-policymaking authority in Western Europe, which resulted in the EEC. The EEC began as a cooperative effort between the coal and steel industries, then moved toward a customs union, and now provides a forum for cooperation in a variety of social, economic, and political areas. The best strategy for resolving international problems, in a system-reformer worldview, is to invest resources in multilateral institutions (such as the various functionally oriented organizations of the UN and other international or regional organizations). If these cooperative efforts are successful, system reformers believe that national leaders will be more inclined to support additional multilateral actions and might eventually accept a multilateral strategy as the most effective means of achieving their national objectives.

System reformers see the world quite differently than do system maintainers. An essential difference is the system reformers' view of the role of the state and their rejection of the anarchic view of the international system. First, system reformers recognize that both state and non-state actors are connected or linked in a "web of interdependence." Secondly, system reformers believe that individuals and groups who seek to influence public policy nationally or internationally have a variety of avenues open to them. In short, individuals or groups have numerous options for participating in the international system. This suggests that the state is not the only representative of individuals or interest groups working to secure resources and opportunities in the international system. A third characteristic of the system-reformer worldview is the attitude toward power in the international system. Power, according to system reformers, is defined in terms of power over outcomes and not as the use of force to subjugate, control, or coerce others. Nation-states are thus required to use a variety of tools of statecraft—not just military tools. A fourth system-reformer view recognizes that nation-states have established rules of behavior and regulatory institutions in an effort to manage their international interactions. These rules of behavior and the corresponding institutions do not fade away. As these *regimes* develop, according to a system reformer, patterns of practice encouraging cooperative behavior begin to define the interactions between state and non-state actors in the international system. The existence of regulatory and enforcement regimes suggests that states do not act in an anarchic system. Instead, these regimes operate to regulate activities and enforce certain rules of behavior.

A fifth characteristic of the system-reformer worldview is the support for transferring national authority or sovereignty to multilateral institutions in certain policy areas. Successful cooperative endeavors will create an atmosphere of support for additional multilateral activities. The system reformer believes that state leaders will realize that the most appropriate method for securing national interests in a complex and interdependent world is to work with other states in either regional (e.g., the Organization of American States) or international institutions (e.g., the UN) that have been established to manage and regulate international transactions. If leaders of states are able to maintain their power at home and more efficiently respond to the demands of their citizenry, their commitment to multilateralism and cooperative strategies will spill over into other policy areas. Eventually, the system reformer contends, the international system will be composed of a variety of multilateral policy institutions or regimes.

The system reformer suggests that the contemporary international system is defined by "common crisis" situations which threaten global stability (e.g., the world debt crisis, poverty, and environmental deterioration). Nation-states acting unilaterally will not be as successful as those working with other nation-states, international organizations, and TNEs to manage the linkages within and between societies and to set the agenda for future cooperative policymaking situations. (Keohane and Nye 1985) System reformers are not utopians advocating the establishment of a world government. The state will not wither away; however, the ability of leaders to respond to the needs of their citizens will require some rethinking about how states define their policy agenda and how these same states go about implementing policies. For example, many states seem to maintain a competitive zero-sum attitude (i.e., what is mine is mine and what is yours is mine) in their relations with other states and in their responses to policy problems.

The "trade wars" between states present an example of the policy attitude of system reformers. Countries often respond to their inability to compete with other producing countries by initiating protectionist policies (e.g., quotas or tariffs). The state that is the target of these actions usually responds with restrictions of its own. The conflict spiral created by the actions and reactions of the two states benefits few, and usually contributes to animosities in other policy areas. The system reformer prescribes policies aimed at encouraging joint economic ventures (e.g., Toyota's and General Motors' cooperative production of cars) and economic planning between states aimed at benefitting workers and owners throughout the international market. It is generally believed that in responding to a wide range of common crises, unilateral policies are less effective and, in an age of nuclear weapons, potentially catastrophic.

The essential beliefs of the system-reformer worldview are summarized below:

1. The international system is comprised of state and non-state actors linked in a complex web of interdependence.
2. Conflict is inevitable; however, most conflict situations are manageable through international institutions and regimes.
3. Nation-states are not the only actors participating in international affairs. Citizens may gain access to policy arenas through international or regional organizations and non-state actors such as TNEs and not-for-profit organizations.
4. National security interests cannot always be secured by military force. In many issue areas, the interdependence of actors prevents the use of military force. Thus, nation-states must use other tools of statecraft (e.g., economic or humanitarian assistance).
5. Power is broadly defined in terms of control or power over policy outcomes.

6. The majority of the issue areas which threaten global stability are common crisis situations. Nation-states must cooperate by sharing resources and expertise and, when appropriate, reform existing international institutions to increase their effectiveness. This reform might include the actual transfer of policymaking authority to regional or international institutions.

7. There is a momentum to this collaborative activity. As multilateral institutions become more effective, support for this type of response will increase and spill over into other policy areas.

The System-Transformer Worldview

The system transformer represents the third worldview category in the analytical framework. There are three very different categories of system transformers. Each will be explained in some detail in the next few pages. It is important for the reader to note that there are diverse opinions within each of these worldview categories. The differences, in terms of core beliefs and assumptions, are most obvious in the system-transformation category. There is very obvious disagreement over the preferred strategy for transformation and the view of the ideal state of affairs.

The Alternative Left

The first worldview within this transformation category believes that conflicts and policy problems that plague societies within the international system will continue unless the priorities of nation-states change and the international state-centric system is transformed. These system transformers have been described as idealists or utopians because of their desire to create a world in which national interests succumb to more universal human interests. Historically, the prescriptions from individuals holding this worldview have advocated the establishment of more decentralized decisionmaking authorities within an international or regional federalist structure. This would involve giving individuals more power locally and nationally, while simultaneously providing a structure to resolve regional (e.g., North American) or international problems. Representation and participation in these newly created decisionmaking units would not necessarily be determined by traditional rules of citizenship. For example, educators might vote for a delegate to a North American assembly to represent their interests and work for more spending on education and less on defense. This type of representative political system would challenge the status quo in many states.

For the purposes of this study this worldview will be called an alternative-left perspective. "Alternative" refers to the presentation of a set of goals that challenges the status quo. "Left" suggests a strong bias toward a government that is social-welfare oriented; it is assumed that government will intervene in the private sector to provide resources and opportunities for those who may be disadvantaged. Furthermore, alternative-left transformers seek to establish governments that provide a general environment of stability and prosperity for all. Some alternative-left transformers advocate an international system that will work to make everyone equal and others advocate the creation of an international "caring society." The caring society would provide public support for those who are in need and programs aimed at providing resources and opportunities for those more able to participate and contribute to the global society.

Usually those who represent the alternative left advocate the restructuring of the system based on specific values and priorities. These might include values such as peace, social justice, ecological balance, and cultural identity. The significant contributions made by the scholars who work within the World Order Models Project (WOMP) represent the best of the prescriptive literature in the field of international relations. Essays on inequality, disarmament, human rights, and theoretical treatises outlining and supporting plans for a new international order have been produced by WOMP scholars from around the world. Their goal is to convince citizens and their leaders to work toward the creation of a world where human interest, not national interest, motivates policymaking.

Generally, alternative-left system transformers see human nature as basically good. They believe that conflicts and other problems emerge from inappropriate and ineffective governmental institutions. Furthermore, those who hold this position feel that war and inequality should not be accepted as an inevitable by-product of the interactions of states. This idealist or utopian version of system transformation suggests that when individuals are left to their own devices, they will create decentralized and democratic institutions locally, and multilateral institutions that encourage cooperation and power sharing at regional and international levels. These system transformers see value in creating regional and international institutions with the authority to intervene and respond to crises that may threaten stability or adversely affect the quality of life in a specific geographic region. The alternative-left worldview believes that collective-security mechanisms and sophisticated arms-control policies are essential for global peace. Those with this worldview suggest that emphasis on national interest rather than human interest is the major cause of conflict within and between states. The nationalism and parochialism that accompany the present structure of the international system can only be overcome by educational programs and a commitment to restructuring decisionmaking institutions. From this worldview perspective, a new power structure that gives all citizens access to decisionmaking, and is *not* designed to unfairly advantage or disadvantage any individual, interest group, or state, is the anodyne.

The Alternative Right

A second transformation worldview must also be considered an "idealist" perspective. Individuals who adhere to this worldview have a view of world affairs similar to that of the system maintainer. However, these supporters of systemic transformation seek to create a more powerful authoritarian system of governance. The advocates of this position go beyond the Hobbesian view that government is the protector of individuals and should be endowed with sufficient power. Advocates of the alternative-right ("right" referring to the centralization of power) transformation worldview seek to establish a paternalistic and non-democratic system, which is built around an ideal state in which an individual's freedoms are limited and behavior challenging the views of those who hold power is proscribed by the state. The values and assumptions defining the core beliefs of this worldview usually reflect specific religious principles or an individual's evangelical interpretations of life. Hitler's fascism provides an appropriate example of this type of system-transformation model. The creation of an authoritarian system and the congruence of very prescriptive values with the interests of the state are the objectives of individuals who ascribe to this worldview. The nation-state plays a critical role in the socialization of citizens. Divergent worldviews are not openly tolerated in this sort of system. Once in control, these religious zealots or ideological purists often support an adventurous foreign policy, in which they seek to extend their influence by actual territorial expansion or the conversion of other nation-states to their evangelical ideals.

The Dependencia *Worldview*
The third worldview within the system-transformation category generally reflects the interests and priorities of the most disadvantaged nation-states. Some leaders and citizens in these poor states have given up on the present system because of the persistence of poverty in their societies and their inability to end their dependency on the rich and powerful actors in the international system. Those who ascribe to this worldview see the present international system as highly stratified; relations between rich and poor nation-states are based on exploitation, not mutual interest. These transformation advocates do not interpret interdependence as being beneficial or as creating a global community bound together in a symmetrical web of complex interdependence. The web of interdependence is seen as providing more advantages to the rich nation-states. In addition, the "free-trade" system established by the United States and its Western allies at the end of World War II is seen as a system that provides only limited opportunities for the poor states. The system is seen as neocolonial, one in which the poor states are considered suppliers of cheap labor, raw materials, and markets for manufactured goods and investments from the rich countries. The economic system is seen as unequal and inequitable. Furthermore, those with wealth use their military power and their economic resources to co-opt elites within the poor states. This usually means that elites within rich states support authoritarian regimes in poor states, and discourage democratic reforms in an effort to increase their profits in these countries and maintain their power in the international system.

Those who seek radical changes in the international system as a solution to these injustices and patterns of maldistribution recognize that this dependency condition is more than economic. The poor states find themselves politically and culturally dependent on the rich or core states. This *dependencia* worldview advocates a system transformation that will result in a more equitable distribution of global resources and opportunities. The *dependencia* worldview recognizes the need for more public (i.e., government) intervention in the international free market to reduce inequality and to promote social justice. Furthermore, advocates of this position support the creation of new regional and international institutions, in which voting power will be determined by the one-state-one-vote principle and not by a system of quotas based on economic or political power. Their general goal is the creation of an international system in which all citizens have the opportunity to live with dignity, and will be protected against any attempt to abridge their inalienable rights as citizens of a state and members of the global community.

All three worldview categories present ideal types. In their application in real world politics, there is often a significant gap between theory and reality. For example, those individuals who advocate the creation of interventionist political systems (e.g., social-welfare states) as a solution to the persistence of debilitating dependencies in the poor states, often fail to create effective and democratic social-welfare systems. Instead, many transformers who work to effect radical change in unequal systems and are successful in their efforts to gain power never follow through with their promises to change the structures of power. Once in power, they either continue their predecessors' policies or become even more authoritarian. Unless these transformers are successful in their efforts totally to dissociate from the present international system and create an alternative to the status quo, the new leaders' survival might necessitate rejoining the system. The transformer then becomes a junior member of the palace guard (a system maintainer) or an advocate of incremental reform.

The pragmatics of politics suggest that mere survival in a competitive international system requires flexibility as one attempts to translate ideals into policy actions. The student of international relations should be aware of how individuals from each worldview category see the world and how their assumptions about the world translate into policy actions. A summary of the general assumptions of each worldview category is presented in Exhibit 1.2.

THE ISSUES

The choice of issues to be examined in this volume reflects the interests of U.S. scholars. However, it would not be unfair to assume that most international-relations scholars are convinced of the importance of the issues discussed in this book. In his important study, *Theory of International Politics* (1979), Kenneth Waltz suggests that the international-policy agenda is defined by four critical issues—pollution, poverty, population, and proliferation. These seem to be issues that relate to the primary problems of war and inequality in the international system.

Exhibit 1.2 General Assumptions of the Three Worldviews

	System Maintainer	System Reformer	System Transformer (WOMP)	System Transformer (Dependencia)
Principal actors in world affairs	Nation-states (the more powerful, the more important)	Nation-states, international and regional organizations, and non-governmental organizations	Nation-states, international and regional organizations, and non-governmental organizations	Nation-states, regional and international organizations based upon the principle of one state, one vote
Primary concern of leaders	Maintaining power relative to other states	International security broadly defined to include economic, political, and sociocultural concerns	The implementation of policies generally reflective of specific human-centric ideals, such as social justice, economic well-being, and ecological balance	Addressing the problem of inequality and human misery by changing the world's economic system and finding a way out of the power struggle between the United States and the USSR
Policy behavior used to secure policy goals	Self-help (unilateral policies)	Cooperative (multilateral) behavior through international or regional institutions	Locally, decentralized power structures with an emphasis on individual participation and the promotion of human-centric goals and ideals; internationally, multilateral institutions where participation is not limited to states	Multilateral efforts aimed at presenting the rich states with an impression that the poor states are united and cooperate to create a more equitable system

Source of power and influence	Military, economic, and political resources and capabilities	Expertise and capabilities within regional and international institutions (e.g., agenda setting); specific strength in a particular issue area (e.g., trade)	Ability to gain confidence of citizens by providing for their basic human needs and insuring order and stability	Ability to use international fora to influence the policy actions of rich states; control of commodities (e.g., oil)
View of relations with other states	Zero-sum competition is the norm; cooperative behavior possible but national interest still rules	Nation-states coordinate their activities and cooperate in specific policy areas; the challenge of common crisis situations requires multilateral efforts	Nation-states act according to specific international norms guaranteed by multilateral enforcement institutions	Poor states are exploited by rich states. The core states control the international policy agenda and use the poor states to enhance their position in the international hierarchy. The poor states must work together to change the international system. This cooperation is hindered by the tendency for the global powers to create spheres of influence and encourage regional differences.
Preferred world future	The best the world can hope for is a balance of power where stability is guaranteed by deterrence and numerous alliances	A community of nation-states, not unlike the European Community, where state members encourage the integration of policymaking authority in specific issue areas; these institutions would encourage cooperative behavior and multilateral efforts aimed at protecting the welfare of citizens throughout the world	A global federation based on human-centric interests, not national interests	A more equitable international economic system and a global political system in which all countries, regardless of size, cultural composition, or ideological orientation enjoy equal access to decisionmaking institutions

This book also includes several studies of regional tension areas. These chapters focus on a system of relationships within a particular region. It is important to note that the power and position of relevant political actors might be different in regional-problem areas. For example, the United States is generally a supporter of the status quo—a system maintainer—in world affairs. Yet, in some policy arenas the United States might support a change-oriented position because a change in a particular region might strengthen the international position of the United States vis-à-vis its principal adversary, the Soviet Union. This suggests that a student of international affairs must take care not to apply these worldview categories broadly without a thorough consideration of various dimensions of an issue area. Similarly, students of international affairs should not reify these categories by suggesting that particular individuals represent "ideal types," though these individuals might appear consistently to select policies that reflect a given worldview. The policy outcomes in most societies reflect the interests, priorities, and values (i.e., worldviews) of a variety of individuals. These policy interests are influenced by national attributes (e.g., societal traditions, the characteristics of a country's political and economic system, and its resource base) and conditions that define the international system (e.g., level of conflict, number of actors, and the policies of those actors). All of these variables must be considered in an analysis of international issues.

What follows is an application of the worldviews analytical framework in seven international issue areas and five regional tension or conflict areas. The authors have done their best to demonstrate how the model can be used effectively as a method for comparing contending images of complex and controversial issues. The worldviews analytical model is particularly useful for scholars and teachers concerned with encouraging their students to think critically about the issues that will shape their futures. Most of the authors have used their chapters in the classroom. Most of them have learned that as a teaching and discovery approach the analytical model is quite effective. Perhaps more importantly, the contributors continue to discuss the intellectual strengths and weaknesses of this approach. It is in this spirit of building knowledge that this book is presented for critical review by students of international affairs.

NOTE

1. The terms system-maintainer, system-reformer, and system-transformer were first used extensively by Richard Falk and his colleagues involved in the World Order Models Project (WOMP). Professor Falk used the concepts to distinguish three distinctive approaches to world order. For further discussion, see his chapter, "Contending Approaches to World Order," in Falk, Kim, and Mendlovitz, *Toward A Just World Order* (1982).

REFERENCES

Calleo, David. *The Imperious Economy.* Cambridge, MA: Harvard University Press, 1982.

Falk, Richard, S. Kim, and S. Mendolvitz, editors. *Toward a Just World Order.* Boulder, CO: Westview Press, 1982.

Galtung, Johan. *The True Worlds: A Transnational Perspective.* New York: The Free Press, 1980.

Hobbes, Thomas. *Leviathan.* London: Andrew Crooke, 1651.

Keohane, Robert O. and Nye, Joseph S. *Power and Interdependence.* Boston: Little, Brown, 1977.

————. "Two Cheers for Multilateralism." *Foreign Policy* 60 (Fall 1985):148–167.

Shuman, Michael. "Dateline Main Street: Local Foreign Policies." *Foreign Policy* 65 (Winter 1986–1987):154–174.

Waltz, Kenneth. *Man, the State and War.* New York: Columbia University Press, 1959.

————. *Theory of International Politics.* Reading, MA: Addison-Wesley, 1979.

1

INTERNATIONAL POLICY ISSUES

2

National Security and Conventional Arms Trade

CARL ANTHONY WATSON

Depending on one's counting criteria, there are roughly a score of ongoing wars and major military engagements in the world today. The Soviet Union is winding down a nine-year conventional war against the Mujahadeen in Afghanistan that has cost thousands of lives. Nearby, Iraq and Iran are engaged in a brutal regional war for dominance of the Persian Gulf. There is insurgency in El Salvador, Nicaragua, the Western Sahara, and the Philippines, among other places, while civil wars rage in Chad and Lebanon. Israel exists in a permanent state of quasi war with many of the Arab states of the Middle East. (See Exhibit 2.1 for a short list of current conventional wars.)

The "general peace" that has prevailed in the world since 1945 may not have been shattered in the manner in which the two world wars of this century shocked and disrupted the system; however, this peace has certainly been challenged by a series of regional conflicts. Almost half the world's states have engaged in some sort of military action since 1970; most of the countries considered superpowers or Great Powers have been involved in one or more conflicts or military actions since 1945. War, that most sanguine of the riders of the apocalypse, is no stranger to the contemporary international system.

Simultaneously, expenditures on arms continue to rise in all states. Coincidentally, military organizations and interest groups involved in the production and distribution of arms are growing larger and more powerful. Conventional weapons steadily increase in sophistication, destructiveness, and cost. The arms trade is burgeoning. Traffic in military technology and armaments form an important part of international trade, while defense expenditures make up an impressive portion of the budgets of many states.

Progress toward peace and economic well-being has been signficant since the end of World War II; yet the modern world system remains violent. Conflict, atavistic or political, is oftentimes resolved by force of arms. Fortunately, nu-

Exhibit 2.1 Selected Current Conventional Wars

War	Participants	Year Started	Battle Deaths
Lebanese Civil War	Druze, Shiites, Syria vs. Maronites, Israel	1975	125,000
Afghanistan	USSR, Government vs. Mujahadeen rebels	1979	300,000
Persian Gulf War	Iraq vs. Iran	1981	427,000
Chadian Civil War	Rebels, Libya vs. Government	1980	2,000
El Salvadoran Civil War	Rebels vs. Government	1979	55,000
Nicaragua	Sandinistas vs. Contras	1981	12,000

Sources: Participants: James F. Dunnigan and Austin Bay, *A Quick and Dirty Guide to War*. New York: Morrow and Co., 1985. Battle Deaths: Ruth Leger Sivard, *World Military and Social Expenditures*. Washington: World Priorities, 1985, pp. 10-11.

These figures represent estimates and are in many cases based on incomplete information.

clear weapons have been used on only two occasions. However, there has been no holiday for conventional warfare; it remains a constant feature of the modern world.

THEORETICAL EXPLANATIONS

War and Systemic Change

War has been an all too common aspect of the history of the international system. States of war, hot or cold, actual or potential, have played an important role in shaping and defining the international system. Some philosophers and theorists have gone so far as to take the very pessimistic view that war is the natural condition for an anarchical international system and peace the abnormality.

One explanation for the prevalence of conflict is the efficacy of war as an instrument of policy: Diplomacy and negotiation may ameliorate issues and foster compromise, but war offers the chance to settle disputes in a more definitive manner. While some conflicts end in stalemate, or the issues they were fought to resolve persist once the fighting ends, those who advance the notion that war does not settle anything should be reminded of the fate of Carthage after the Third Punic War in 146 B.C. (for an extreme example) or how profoundly the denouement of World War II shaped the history of the second half of the twentieth century.

As Clausewitz (1976) suggests, in disputes between nations, war remains the final appeal. In the shadows behind diplomacy is the threat of war, even if that threat is never voiced. In a world that lacks collective measures for resolving differences and addressing the interests and needs of individual states, warfare is often the unsurprising result. Kenneth Waltz (1954, 238) points out in his book, *Man, the State and War*: "Each state pursues its own interests, however defined, in ways it judges best. Force is a means of achieving the external ends of states because there exists no consistent, reliable process of reconciling the conflicts of interest that inevitably arise among similar units in a condition of anarchy."

Resort to force of arms is an option for sovereign states; it is almost implicit in the definition of sovereignty. The viability of that option is, of course, something to be carefully considered at the time it is contemplated; however, the continued existence of sovereign states possessing the means to fight implies the continued existence of war as an instrument of policy.

Assuming a reasonable degree of rationality on the part of state leaders who decide for war, the employment of military force is in the pursuit of political goals. Warfare may prove to be a utilitarian, albeit brutal, tool of statecraft used to change a situation which is judged unacceptable by those who initiate the conflict. As the European historian Bela Kiraly has said, "War, if reason prevails, is waged to obtain a better peace than that which existed prior to the hostilities."

In the past, states have used war as a means of shifting the prevailing status quo in their favor. States dissatisfied with the existing international structure, and the distribution of political, economic, and prestige benefits resulting from the international hierarchy, have sometimes sought to redress the situation through the employment of military might. The international system is and has been hierarchical in nature. State actors are ranked, and at times states have challenged the given hierarchy in an effort to replace it with one in which their power and capabilities are recognized, a new order more favorable to themselves. (Gilpin 1981 and Organski and Kugler 1980)

One common explanation for World War II posits that Germany, Italy, and Japan were unwilling to continue to countenance a status quo that benefited the former Western Allies of World War I, chiefly France, Britain, and the United States. The Axis states believed that the existing system held their economic and political ambitions in check. Thus, they chose to challenge and reshape that status quo with the means judged most efficacious—military conflict. Similarly, the Napoleonic wars of the late nineteenth and early twentieth centuries can be explained as a French effort to change the existing international system, in which France was a Great Power arrayed in rough equilibrium with other Great Powers, to one in which France was the hegemon of the system. Such explanations need not be limited to large, systemic wars; one could similarly explain the Falklands/Malvinas War, in which Argentina attempted to change the existing status quo in the South Atlantic vis-à-vis Britain, or the 1973 Arab-Israeli War, wherein a coalition of Arab states challenged the growing power of Israel.[1]

Large, systemic wars, involving most of the major powers, have provided convenient historical benchmarks for students of diplomacy to divide the raw material of history into systemically distinct sections. This is not merely an arbitrary separation of time into manageable units, but a reflection of the transition from one manifestation of the system to another. The dates 1648, 1715, 1815, 1919, and 1945 all mark the conclusions of major systemic wars and the transitions from one international system to another. In each case, war served as the agent of change, an extremely rapid catalyst when compared to many other historical events that contribute to systemic transformation.

For example, the conclusion of World War II marked a decided change in the nature of the system. The former multipolar arrangement of powers, centered on the great European states, such as Great Britain, Germany, and France, gave way to bipolarity, to a world centered on two states outside Western Europe—the United States and the Soviet Union. A new international organization, the United Nations (UN), was introduced as a way to control the anarchy between states. Similarly, a new international economic order was instituted to provide stability to trade relations and to stave off a repetition of the Great Depression and possible trade disputes among the major economic powers.

The international system is a constantly evolving entity, subject to ongoing change in all of its aspects. However, the impact of war on this process of transfiguration is profound; wide-sweeping and sudden changes in the basic structures, especially the political structure, of the system seem to be the results of the upheaval caused by systemic war. Large-scale war disrupts and tears down existing orders and regimes. In most cases, a new structure, largely the construct of the victors, is created to replace the old.

Technology and War

The history of civilization and the history of the international system are both closely related to the developing nature of warfare and conflict. Advancements in science and technology, manifested in the areas of applied physics and mechanics, communications, and information gathering, have changed the nature of warfare and the potential impact it can have on the system. This is not a new phenomenon, but rather has always been the case, from the discovery of iron as material for weapons, to the advent of mechanized warfare on land, sea, and air. What is different is the rapidity of technological change and its subsequent impact on military affairs. It seems clear that the development of nuclear weapons created a sudden and profound advance in the destructive power and implications of war. This represents a quantum change in how states define their national security and how they organize their resources to protect their societies. Although conventional warfare had become increasingly destructive, nuclear weapons would come to threaten not only individual states within the system, but the continued existence of the system itself. Two effects of this phenomenon are important for our purposes.

First, a distinction was drawn between what are called *conventional forces,* the naval, ground, and air forces intended to defend and take traditional military objects as well as to punish the enemy through destruction of property, population, and trade; and *nuclear forces,* atomic warheads on bombs or atop missiles, capable solely of mass destruction. Conventional forces had been used in World War II to launch punishing attacks with the goal of weakening the enemy by destroying cities, people, and productive capacity. The firebombings of Tokyo and Dresden and the V-2 attacks are cases in point. But by and large, conventional forces were used for conventional purposes: seizing and defending military objectives. The purpose of atomic weapons is destruction. A war fought with such weapons could only have the subjugation of the enemy by destruction as its goal. Bomber and missile forces armed with atomic weapons could not take and defend objectives, they could only destroy them. Similarly, they could not conquer an enemy, only obliterate the target society.

The second change in the character of war brought on by the introduction of nuclear weapons relates to the systemic effects of a potential nuclear conflict. Where major systemic war had previously resulted in changes in the system, such a conflict fought with atomic weapons would most likely destroy the international system. Systemic wars had been total wars, where the major combatants used all of their considerable resources to prevail over one another. Total war in the post-1945 era implies the use of nuclear weapons and as long as they exist, that possibility will shadow any war. It could be argued then that the effect of nuclear weapons has been to restrain the resort to major systemic war, since the rationality of that enterprise as a means of creating a new, more favorable, situation is in doubt. As long as a rough parity in nuclear forces exists, so does "the balance of terror," in which the two superpowers are mutually deterred from attacking one another. Nuclear weapons provide the very real prospect that the next systemic war will not just change the ranking of the players within the system, but simply destroy the system itself. The new order could be no order at all.

Conventional War in the Modern System

The advent of nuclear weapons has not made war outmoded or a bootless pursuit. While nuclear weapons have made major war between the dominant powers irrational and pointless it is still a terrifying prospect. Furthermore, nuclear weapons have not marked the end or even the decline of conventional armed conflict. There is a continuity in the wars of the first half of the century and the conventional conflicts since 1945, especially in the manner in which military operations are conducted. Many strategic and tactical concepts endure, as does the basic structure and form of the military forces themselves.

The nature of modern conventional warfare today is conditioned by at least four factors that make this kind of warfare different from conflicts in previous eras. These include: (1) the influence of superpower bipolarity; (2) the shift in fighting from the industrialized North to the developing South; (3) the change in the nature and measure of power; and (4) the increasing cost of weaponry and troops.

The Influence of Superpower Bipolarity

The continued rivalry between the United States and Soviet Union in the postwar era has had a tremendous impact on the nature of warfare. This superpower competition is likely to remain a factor in the next century. The contemporary system, unlike that of at least 300 years before it, is a bipolar system; the superpowers are the major players on the world scene, and their competition is global in scope. Each is capable of confronting the other almost anywhere, and this "power projection" (i.e., extension of military power) includes air, land, and especially naval forces. Both maintain large navies and have bases in friendly countries throughout the world. In addition, the superpowers are the main source of financial and material support for the wars fought by lesser powers. It is rare to find a conflict in the developing world where one or (usually) both of the superpowers are not involved. Political conflicts within and between less developed countries very often take on the mantle of superpower competition. These smaller states seek patrons able and willing to supply arms, military training, and other support; in return, the two large states seek clients in an effort to extend their spheres of influence.

The Shift in Fighting from the North to the South
Another salient change from previous history is the shift in the locus of conflict from developed areas of the world, especially Europe, to the developing regions. Given the violent record of Europe's past and that both systemic wars in this century had the struggle for domination of Europe at their center, the peace that has existed on that continent for the last forty years is unprecedented. Previous long-term rivals, such as France and Germany, have been allies for forty years; the prospect of war between Germany and Great Britain is as inconceivable as war between the United States and Canada. Surely, rivalry, competition, and issues of disagreement exist between these states, but war is an unlikely option. Europe has been transformed from the seat of conflict that has spilled over to the world at large, to a continent between the two superpowers. Thus, European states benefit from the armed peace between the Soviets and the United States. The potential for a great and terrible war exists in Europe, should conflict break out between the North Atlantic Treaty Organization (NATO) and Warsaw Pact alliances, but the fearsome prospects of such a war contribute to a condition of peace in the region.

This condition of armed peace does not extend throughout the world. The developing, or Third World, states have become the new centers of conflict. Regional power conflicts and long-standing national and subnational rivalries, and the problems associated with political and economic development often create a rich seedbed for war. Poverty, which is accentuated by ineffective political systems and fierce competition for societal goods and services among ethnic groups, is a common cause for conflict. These tensions are usually manipulated by regional powers, former colonial powers, or the United States and the USSR.

After World War II, some of the colonial powers attempted to re-establish or retain their overseas holdings in the face of independence movements and growing nationalism. The results were wars like the bitter and ultimately unsuccessful French involvements in Indochina and Algeria, or the British efforts in Palestine, Aden, Borneo, and Cyprus. In other cases, the withdrawal of colonial powers left situations of anarchy, which provided opportunities for internal power struggles or external interventions. For example, after Great Britain's withdrawal from the Indian subcontinent, the region split along ethnic-religious lines; India fought two wars with Pakistan in 1965 and 1971 and a short border war with China in 1962. In some situations, the withdrawal of the colonial power created a vacuum to be be filled by the superpowers. Japan's surrender in 1945 left Korea divided into two occupation zones. By 1950 the peninsula was aflame in war, with the United States and China directly involved and the USSR supporting the Chinese and North Korea. Similarly, the French departure from Indochina eventually led to a division of Vietnam, with the Soviet Union supporting the North and the United States allied with the South.

Newly independent countries face problems associated with state building—the creation of viable and sovereign political entities where none had existed before. The political conflict such endeavors engender often erupts into fighting, either among indigenous factions seeking to control the new state or by external actors attempting to extend their spheres of influence. Conflict has been and continues to be a part of the development process. For example, Africa was the scene of several rebellions and civil wars as fledgling states attempted to establish and consolidate their power in the wake of the departure of British and French rule. In the Middle East, the creation of the Jewish state of Israel in 1948 led to war between the Arab states and Israel over the latter's right to exist. Other wars were fought in 1956, 1967, and 1973, as Arab states reacted to Israel's attempt to secure its position in the region and Israel responded to Arab efforts to undermine its sovereignty.

The relocation of fighting from the industrialized North to the developing South seems to be holding in the decade of the 1980s. Presently, wars are being fought in Central America, Southeast Asia, Afghanistan, and the deserts of the Middle East and North Africa. The application of force by the large powers has also been focused on the developing world: the U.S. air raid on Libya, the French intervention in Chad, Western peace-keeping efforts in Lebanon, and the Falklands/Malvinas War, which involved Great Britain and Argentina.

For a variety of reasons, too numerous to explore in this chapter, conventional military forces are frequently involved in conflicts over political, economic, and sociocultural resources in newly emerging states. At the same time, the ability to project power and intervene in conflicts (largely a function of technology and the economic base to support a large, modern military) rests with the advanced industrial states. For reasons of politics, ideology, economics, or bipolar competition, these states have had occasion to exercise their capabilities in the developing world, and are likely to continue this type of policy intervention in the future. This is certainly a reflection of the persistence of problems such as inequality and the enduring image of a competitive and anarchic international system to which most world leaders ascribe.

The Nature and Measure of Power
Another change in the postwar world has been a shift in the measure of power. Traditional methods of assessment have concentrated primarily on military power, and only secondarily on those national attributes that have contributed to military prowess. Increasingly, other issues, especially economic issues, have come to dominate the relations between states. This in turn has led to a new emphasis on economic strength and vitality as an indicator of national power. As the agenda of issues between states expands and the hierarchy of issues adjusts, new capabilities and strengths become important. The ability to wage, sustain, and prevail in conflict is not the sole determinant of major power status. Japan, for example, is a major power in the modern world, but this status rests on its powerful economy. Japan is an economic giant, and its importance on the world stage is indisputable; however, Japan is at the same time a military

midget, with a small self-defense force and little ability to affect world events through military power. Similarly, the newly industrialized states of Asia, such as Taiwan, Singapore, and Hong Kong, have the capacity to influence the international system beyond what could be attributed to their minimal military power.

Economic, social, and political relations between states, especially those of the advanced, industrialized countries, have become so complex and pervasive that some theorists have used the term "complex interdependence" to describe the relationship. (Keohane and Nye 1977) This is not the place to describe this phenomenon; however, it is important to note the effect complex interdependence created by multiple linkages between states has had on war in the system. Economic relations are, in many cases, as important as security relations and these exchanges of goods, services, and investments are very vulnerable to disruption by conflict. Interdependence as a condition in the system mitigates against violence and war between states that are linked in complex and multiple-issue webs of exchange and interaction. These webs of interdependence have not, however, prevented lower-level conventional conflicts from breaking out all over the globe.

Economic Cost of Weaponry and Troops
The costs of maintaining modern conventional military forces and conducting warfare are escalating in real terms. The amount of money spent on weapons and other security and defense expenditures continues to rise, and not just for the major powers. The United States spends about 25 percent of its national budget, and just over 6 percent of the gross national product (GNP) on defense. Estimates of Soviet costs are even higher, approaching 11 percent of GNP. The rising cost of arms combined with the increased technological sophistication and increasing destructive potential of weaponry raises questions about the ability of states to protect their interests by waging an offensive or defensive war. This is especially true for small and medium powers, but equally valid for the major powers. The United States learned in Vietnam and the Soviets in Afghanistan about the costs associated with conducting intense warfare over a period of years. Rapid technological development makes it increasingly costly for states to stay abreast of modern weaponry. The major powers and some of the regional powers in the developing world (e.g., Brazil, Libya and Saudi Arabia) seem to be able to keep up in the arms race. The poor states are likely to lag behind in the arms race, yet the leaders of these states will continue to spend valuable resources trying to keep up with potential enemies.

Developing states often spend scarce resources and foreign exchange credits (since they rely so heavily on arms imports) on their military rather than on badly needed economic development and other basic human-needs programs. In some cases, the military-spending programs are aimed at responding to security challenges. In a signficant number of developing states, the military's prime function is to maintain internal stability or act as a palace guard to protect the political, economic, and sociocultural interests of the current regime. However, external threats cannot be discounted and are very real for many of these countries. Regional power imbalances often lead to expansionist actions by a state seeking to establish itself as a regional hegemon. This requires that poor states act unilaterally or multilaterally to counter the expansionist state. Thus, scarce economic resources are spent in pursuit of that most elusive of commodities—national security.

War in the modern system retains its purposiveness. As the situation stands currently, systemic war (that is to say, almost automatically, nuclear war) would not benefit any state, but conventional conflict retains its efficacy for changing the status quo in less drastic ways. Iran and Iraq struggle for the position of predominant power in the Persian Gulf region. The outcome, while certainly not without import for the world as a whole, will not change the system. Nor will the insurrections in Central America alter the system unless, of course, the Soviet Union and the United States were to be drawn into direct confrontation with one another. However, for each of the participants in these conventional conflicts, war is the means for attaining some political goal, be it preeminence in the Persian Gulf, the overthrow of a government, or the preservation of a political system.

PERSPECTIVES ON CONVENTIONAL WAR

War and the prospect of war have always been an issue in international politics. Exactly why the issue persists and what to do about it, however, are matters of contention between different worldviews or images of the international system.

The System-Maintainer Worldview

The system-maintainer worldview on conventional war is rooted in a traditional, realist perspective. Those leaders and policy observers who identify with the core values of this worldview see power at the center of international relations and states' competition for power as natural. The most extreme form of competition is war. While those who hold this perspective pay respect to the idea that war can disrupt order, most accept the fact that international disagreement and the war that sometimes comes from that disagreement are inevitable features of international politics. War has been and will be a persistent feature of the relations of states and those leaders who wish to succeed had better face that reality.

In the system-maintainer view, the protection and furtherance of national interests are the central tasks of the state. When states come into conflict over issues considered to be of vital interest, war may result. *Raison d'état* ("reason of state," or the purpose and function of the state) may demand war in such cases. For system maintainers, war can be a tool of policy, a rational application of force in the pursuit of national interest. The assumptions defining the system-maintainer view are predominant among policymakers in the international system. Their policy orientations represent traditional values about the place of the military within national policy and the place of war within the international polity.

Both the United States and the Soviet Union should be seen as system maintainers. Both maintain large conventional military establishments and have used these forces on a number of occasions to preserve what they saw as favorable circumstances. In 1945, the two superpowers established spheres of influence over much of the world. Many of their policies have been aimed at ordering activity within those spheres. This ordering has included aiding and propping up friendly governments, unseating unfriendly governments, and, perhaps most important, seeking to exclude the other superpower's influence from its own sphere. A number of tools of statecraft have been used by the United States and the Soviet Union in their struggle for power and influence, such as foreign aid and technological assistance; however, three policies have been of considerable importance: (1) alliances, (2) arms sales, and (3) intervention.

Alliances
The formation of alliances is a traditional method of power managing and balancing from a system maintainer's policy perspective. Both the United States and the USSR are members and leaders of alliances. It was a continuing theme of U.S. foreign policy in the 1950s to enter into alliances with other countries for the primary purpose of keeping the Communists, that is to say the Soviets or those aligned with and receiving support from the Soviet Union, from expanding their control over other countries. This reliance on formal alliances has largely withered away, but the United States still retains its position of leadership in NATO. NATO was formed in 1949 with its central purpose being to counterbalance Soviet conventional military power, and prevent a Soviet invasion of Western Europe. In response to NATO, the USSR formed the Warsaw Pact in 1955. This military alliance, which includes Eastern European satellite countries such as Poland, Czechoslovakia, and East Germany, provides a useful military counterbalance to NATO and a means for the Soviet Union to consolidate its position and influence in Eastern Europe.

For both the United States and USSR the two competing and confronting alliances represent a way to augment their military power and retain a say in the future of Europe. NATO and the Warsaw Pact are the two most important and powerful military alliances in the world. Their forces are the most modern, sophisticated, and expensive in the world. Europe may be at peace but it is definitely an armed peace.

In addition to their alliances in Europe, both the Soviet Union and the United States maintain somewhat less formal and committed relationships with countries around the world. These alignments are usually militarily one-sided, with the superpower extending military aid and protection in exchange for a

Exhibit 2.2 A Comparison of NATO and Warsaw Pact Military Strengths

	NATO	Warsaw Pact
Expenditures in U.S. $ millions	310,867	187,020
Manpower:		
Active	2,992,000	2,829,000
Mobilized	5,502,000	5,348,000
Divisions (total war mobilized)	199.3	268
Tanks	30,500	68,300
Artillery (MRL and ATK guns)	21,500	50,400
Aircraft	9,458	11,696
Naval Forces		
Submarines	238	301
Carriers	37	6
Aircraft (bombers, attack, and interceptors)	923	637

Notes: Manpower: "Active" refers to uniformed personnel already in position; "mobilized" refers to strength about thirty days after mobilization, which would occur only in the event of crisis or conflict. The numbers do not include the sizable French army (296,000, with three divisions in West Germany) or Spanish forces, since they do not fall under direct NATO command.

Divisions: The number given is for total divisions after mobilization and includes formations based in the continental United States. It is important to note that Warsaw Pact divisions are significantly smaller in terms of manpower than Western divisions: approximately 11,000 troops to 16,000.

Tanks: The total is for main battle tanks.

Aircraft: This is an aggregate total for land attack planes, interceptors, reconnaissance aircraft, and armed helicopters.

Sources: Expenditure figures: Ruth Leger Sivard, *World Military and Social Expenditures*, Washington, D.C.: World Priorities, Inc., 1985. All other figures: *The Military Balance 1987–1988*, London: International Institute for Strategic Studies, 1987. *Strategy and Tactics* 109, September–October 1986. U.S. Department of Defense figures, 1987.

client state and an extension of its sphere of influence. Such alliances are pursued because they usually result in an increase of power, influence, and prestige. The larger and more powerful state may gain access to resources, military bases, and other geostrategic advantages.

Arms Sales

The sale of arms is another way in which states seek to maintain their advantages in the international system. It is not surprising that the most advanced technological and industrial states are the major arms suppliers to the world. These states have the necessary technical expertise and industrial base to produce modern weaponry, and they also, by and large, use weapons sales and transfers to extend their power and influence. The major exporters of arms are, in descending order, the United States, the USSR, France, West Germany, and Great Britain. The major importing regions, again in descending order, are the Middle East, Africa, the NATO and Warsaw Pact states, Asia, and Latin America. (Pierre 1982) System maintainers believe that arms exports can prove to be valuable tools in controlling the international system and keeping it ordered in a favorable way. For example, arms sales to small or middle-sized powers can be used to reward a particular policy stance or geopolitical alignment, aid a country in defending itself from others (particularly if those others are opponents of the exporting nation-state), or as a way to encourage a country to defect from one alignment to another.

Andrew J. Pierre (1982, 13–27) has outlined three rationales for arms sales. First, the sale of arms can provide influence and leverage over the receiving state. Armaments serve as symbols of support and demonstrate a desire for friendly relations; when sold to allies they strengthen the alliance commitment. In cases involving large power sales to small powers, it is important to note that arms transfers provide the seller with a certain amount of control over sensitive foreign policy decisions. Thus, arms can be offered as an incentive for following a given course of action. For example, if a state is dependent on another as a source of weapons, it will find that it needs the seller's tacit approval to engage in military operations of any size or duration.

Arms sales can be made also for the purposes of stability and security. Allies and friendly states are supported and their ability to defend themselves is enhanced by weapons transfers. An imbalance in military power in a given region may present a threat to the supplier's interest; this imbalance may be rectified by transferring weapons to friendly states in that region. For example, both the United States and the Soviet Union have responded to the needs of their client states in the Middle East with arms transfers. The United States has countered the growth of Arab military power in the Middle East by the transfer of weapons to Israel. Similarly, the Soviets have balanced Israel's power with shipments to Syria and other front-line Arab states. The United States has responded to a perceived buildup of Nicaragua's military capability by granting military aid to neighboring states such as Honduras and providing armaments to the antigovernment guerillas (i.e., the Contras) in Nicaragua.

A third rationale for arms sales relates to the economic benefits associated with the actual selling of arms. Modern weaponry is high-technology weaponry, difficult to build and expensive. When one considers that a single jet fighter can cost twenty to thirty million dollars, and an antitank missile five or six thousand dollars, it is obvious that the money spent to equip and maintain even a small army can have a significant impact on economic and political climates in both rich and poor states. Arms have become important exports for some countries; they provide an avenue to favorable export-import trade balances and a means to bolster the domestic economy and provide jobs. It is interesting to note that most of the large weapons exporters (the USSR being the notable exception) are the Western industrialized states, the largest importing region is the Middle East. With the rapid rise of oil prices in 1973, arms sales to the petroleum-exporting states became a way for countries like the United States and France to correct in some way the increasingly unfavorable balance of payments with those states. Not surprisingly, such deals were actively sought.

Intervention
The most portentous aspect of conventional forces is their actual use. The system maintainer recognizes the anarchic nature of the international system, and subsequently, the necessity for conflict and war in this system. In an effort to secure their national interests, states will and do use force. The policy of the United States is a good example of the application of this viewpoint. As a beneficiary of the postwar international order, the United States sought to maintain the status quo, which basically entailed the prevention of any expansion of Soviet power and influence. The military aspect of this policy was termed "containment" and consisted of a network of alliances, arms transfers to states seen as threatened by the Soviets and/or internal Communist takeover, and the actual use of military power. Under the umbrella of containment, the United States formed alliances such as NATO, shipped hundreds of millions of dollars worth of arms to countries in Africa, Asia, Europe, and the Americas, and undertook major military operations in Korea and Vietnam as well as interventions in other areas of the world.

Other Western states have followed similar, if less extensive, policies. France fought long and bitter wars against insurgents in vain attempts to retain its pre-World War II colonies in Vietnam and Algeria. Together with Great Britain, France fought against Egyptian nationalism during the 1956 Suez Crisis. France has also been active in the affairs of her former colonies in Africa, most recently in an intervention in Chad to stabilize that country in the face of attacks from Libyan-backed rebels.

Interestingly enough, despite its doctrinal position as a proponent of change and transformation, the Soviet Union has displayed many system-maintainer tendencies in the area of conventional armaments. It has followed programs of alliance and arms sales similar to those of the United States. The

Soviets have jealously guarded their sphere of influence; military forces have been used in Eastern Europe to quell unrest and ensure the loyalty of satellites. Soviet forces intervened in Hungary in 1956 to put down a revolutionary movement, and again in Czechoslovakia in 1968. Currently, the Soviet Union is involved in its most serious military operation since World War II. In 1979, the Soviet Fortieth Army invaded neighboring Afghanistan to stabilize the pro-Soviet government. Over 100,000 Soviet troops, equipped with modern weaponry, vehicles, and aircraft conducted a sometimes vicious and brutal anti-insurgency campaign against the Mujahadeen guerilla forces. The Soviet Union has recently begun a phased withdrawal from Afghanistan, but fighting between the Soviet-backed government in Kabul and the insurgents is very likely. The strategic importance of Afghanistan, astride the Soviet Union's southern border and adjacent to both Iran and Pakistan, indicates that the USSR is unlikely to accept an indecisive out come in the conflict.

The System-Reformer Worldview

System reformers address the problem of conventional war and security from the viewpoint that war is an activity that the international system can ill afford to countenance. This worldview stresses the potential destruction resulting from modern warfare and the idea that other means of resolving conflict have evolved as the international system has moved from anarchy to some level of order. The result of the combination of these two factors is the desire to reform the international system in order to end war. Quincy Wright, in his work, *A Study of War,* (1964), attributes this reform movement to four types of change within the system:

1. The phenomenon of the "shrinking world," meaning that advances in modern communication and transportation have created cultural, economic, and political interdependence
2. The acceleration of historical and social change through "the progress of science and invention and the rapid intercommunication of ideas and techniques"
3. The rapid progress of military invention, an ongoing process that has now reached a point where "the preparation for, waging of and recovery from war has tended to dominate the political, economic and social life of peoples"
4. The rise of democracy in the modern world system, which implies both popular control over the decision to go to war and responsibility for that decision

The dramatic increase in linkages that seem to shrink the world, the speed of change and innovation and its impact on societies, and the inability to control or manage conflicts have caused leaders and citizens alike to assume more responsibility for actively pursuing peaceful means of conflict resolution. War has become a problem for a larger number of people, and an increasing number of these people have come to believe that the elimination of war from international relations is not only desirable but also possible. (Wright 1964, 4–5)

The system-reformer perspective on the issue of conventional arms comes from a theoretical position that does not accept either the proposition that the nature of the international system is fundamentally unchangeable or that conflict within the system is inevitable. System reformers feel that conscious, deliberate policies can be developed and implemented to resolve conflicts and manage runaway arms races. These policies reflect the common interests of humankind which all system reformers recognize.

A key element in the system-reformer perspective has been the denial of war, especially systemic war, as a means to change the system. Many reformist policies have been aimed at reforming and improving the system through institutions designed to promote peaceful change and preserve order and collective procedures to resolve outstanding issues. In this century, system reformers, referred to as "utopians" or "globalists" by their detractors, have tried two great experiments in international organization as an instrument to promote peace: the League of Nations (following World War I [1919–1939]) and the United Nations (following World War II [1945 to the present]).

The centerpiece of both of these international bodies is the concept of collective security. Collective security is the simple and sensible idea that war can be prevented and rendered useless as a policy if all of the other states in the international system move to oppose an aggressor. In effect, any state that resorted to war would be opposed by a coalition of other states in the system; faced with such an overwhelming force, the aggressor would be defeated or deterred from attacking in the first place.

The seminal assumption of collective security is that peace within the system is the prime value of the members of the system. Given this, it is only logical that the states of the world would act to preserve the peace through collaborative action. However, objective examination of the historical record indicates that collective security has failed. The League of Nations gave way to World War II, after failing to deal with Japanese aggression against China, Italian adventurism in Africa, and German rearmament in defiance of the Versailles Treaty during the decade of the 1930s. The United Nations (UN) was the League's successor. In 1950, the UN's collective security apparatus worked when North Korea invaded South Korea. However, the Soviets were not part of the vote to send UN forces (largely U.S. troops) to defend South Korea; thus the collective-security decision represented Western interests and not the interests of the entire international community. The Security Council must unanimously approve all collective-security actions. This requirement has made it impossible for the UN to act in the majority of conflicts since 1945.

The blame for this failure of collective security can be laid at the doorstep of national interest. The concept of collective security is based on the premise that peace within the international system is an objective for all members of the system. In actuality, it appears that nation-states have individual national interests that not only transcend this collective interest, but are best served by acting contrarily to the collective interest and going to war. The interests of individual states are more important than collective interests, and state-centric policies of self-help and self-reliance, such as going to war if necessary, are followed.[2]

While reformist efforts to limit war through collective security have been less than successful, system-reformer programs to limit the means to make war have been somewhat more rewarding. Arms control is the process of controlling weaponry, most commonly through limitations on numbers and types of armaments. The goal in this case is to reform the system by reducing the tensions that weapons create within the system. This is achieved by lowering the level of weapons in the system, as well as lessening the effects of war should it occur. For example, some reformists regard arms races as an important contributor to the outbreak of war; arms control agreements can be used to stop or limit such competition.

Initiatives to control conventional arms are not new; such proposals appeared in the eighteenth and nineteenth centuries. One of the more notable arms control achievements in the twentieth century was the Naval Agreement signed at the Washington Conference of 1921. In the treaty, the United States, Great Britain, France, Italy, and Japan agreed to limit the size and number of capital ships (battleships and the like) in their fleets. However, dissatisfaction grew on the part of several signatories regarding the treaty's provisions and attempts to stretch or get around the strictures. Eventually all parties to the treaty would be major participants in World War II.

Since 1945, initiatives to limit conventional arms have been surrendered to the focus on the higher-profile and more powerful nuclear weapons. Nuclear missiles and bombers, like battleships in 1921, are fewer in number, more destructive per individual weapon, and easier to keep track of than tanks, soldiers, and rifles.

For the most part, limitations on conventional armaments have been the result of unilateral national decisions based on considerations of strategy and finances. That is, states have chosen to place limits on conventional forces primarily because of the cost of creating and maintaining forces, and/or the relative lack of need for those forces, rather than as a result of bilateral or multilateral agreements to limit forces. National leaders examine their budgets and strategic needs, based on their interests and the forces of other states, and prepare conventional military programs accordingly, unfettered by arms control.

The most important contemporary conventional arms-control endeavor has been an ongoing series of negotiations between NATO and the Warsaw Pact, aimed at reducing their forces along the Central European front. These talks, the Mutual and Balanced Force Reduction (MBFR) negotiations, began in 1973 in Vienna; periodically representatives of NATO and the Soviet-bloc countries meet in that city to continue the process of negotiation.

The negotiations have not gone well as both sides seek to protect their national interests. Initially the NATO states sought to limit both alliances to 700,000 soldiers, while the Soviet bloc desired to cap forces at their current levels, preserving what many observers saw as a Warsaw Pact advantage. In 1982, both sides made new proposals and came closer to accepting both the 700,000 limit proposed by NATO and the phased withdrawal of U.S. and Soviet troops favored by the Warsaw Pact. However, from the NATO side the question of accurate data regarding the size of Warsaw Pact forces remains an obstacle. The Soviet and Eastern European negotiators have been reluctant to provide definitive information and the two sides have disagreed on exactly whom to count as a soldier. Another area of difficulty regards procedures for verification, where the two sides have differed on the need for and role of observers and inspectors. Recently, however, the Soviets have indicated a willingness to cooperate in this area as well as in the matter of notification of large-scale maneuvers. The negotiations continue, but no agreement is expected in the near future. It seems that rational considerations, the cost and risk of confrontation in Central Europe, and the political costs of breaking off the talks, have kept the countries talking. However, neither side appears to have the political interest necessary to overcome the entrenched political and military interests. (Dean 1983)

The lucrative and extensive trade in conventional arms has also been the target of reformist movements. A review of U.S. policy provides an informative example of reformist efforts. After World War I, American munitions manufacturers were criticized for being "merchants of death"; this sentiment was echoed in more recent times by President Jimmy Carter in 1979, when he announced that the United States would restrict arms sales and transfers. Carter's policy harkened back to the idealism of Woodrow Wilson, a perspective that viewed weapons as dangerous contributors to international tension and instability. Carter believed that much of the instability in the developing world could be attributed to an "unrestrained spread of conventional weaponry" and he wanted the United States to play a major role in controlling that arms race. (Carter 1979) Arms sales to Third World countries have been the main object of criticism and debate. Reformers have challenged the rationale held by most system maintainers that weapons transfers are an important and useful foreign policy tool.

Staunch opponents see arms sales in the Third World as serving few interests beyond greed. Staunch proponents see sales as automatic buttresses to containment or valuable sources of political leverage. The problem is a fundamental difference in assumptions about international relations, which can not be easily bridged by empiricism. Opponents of arms transfers usually identify with the idealist tradition, emphasizing "world order," "transnational" relations, and the "declining utility of force." From this view, war is seen as unnatural and unnecessary, more often provoked by artificial catalysts than by intractable conflicts of genuine interests. (Betts 1980, 88)

Other reformist positions point out the political and economic consequences of the arms trade. Those who hold this view believe that arms transfers create a special liaison between the transferring country and/or the arms dealers of the transferring country and an elite, usually a political-military group, within the receiving state. This group uses both its elite status and the weapons themselves to assume or maintain political control. Often, this means the suppression of those who might oppose the individuals in power.

System reformers also believe that the money spent to import arms is money not spent on more socially desirable developmental needs. The purchase of rifles, tanks, and bombs detracts from funds that might have been spent on roads, medical improvements, housing, education, and economic advancement and diversification in developing nation-states. The arguments over "guns or butter" continue to be waged as the spending for arms in developing countries continues to increase. World military spending reached U.S. $1 trillion in 1986 and the developing world spends about 23 percent of this total. Perhaps most disturbing is that 3 percent of the global total is spent by the poorest of the poor—those countries with per-capita incomes of less than U.S. $2,000. (Sivard 1986)

The issue of whether arms sales to Third World countries contribute to instability is worth a little more discussion. While it seems clear that increases in the introduction of arms into a region can exacerbate a tense situation, are these arms transfers the cause of that problem? A look at the historical record in the Middle East and Southeast Asia, two of the world's trouble spots since 1945, suggests that political differences stemming from decolonization, contests for regional dominance, and ancient rivalries create the perceived need for weapons, a need fulfilled by outside powers, most likely for reasons discussed above. If this is the case, weapons follow political tension rather than precede it, but arms competition and the fear of possible inferiority and regional imbalance would seem to exacerbate the situation.

A second critical issue deserving attention relates to the potential for arms transfers to promote system instability. This is not a simple problem. A better-armed state that seeks to overthrow the existing status quo is a clear threat to stability and may even seek to initiate a major war. Such a country may opt to use warfare, especially if it feels itself to be superior to its opponent, to fashion a new status quo. However, arms transfers to status quo-oriented nation-states may be stabilizing, in that they could balance increased military power on the part of anti-status quo states, or strengthen the position of the status quo power. The question defies simple answers.

The System-Transformer Worldview

The final worldview category to consider is that of the system transformer. Unlike the maintainers and reformers, who see some merit, to varying degrees to be sure, in the existing international system's structure and institutions, system transformers are interested in bringing about changes in the basic nature of the international system. Transformers are almost invariably critics of the current world system, and most often offer a radical program for transforming the system, usually informed by an ideology of some sort which provides the theoretical underpinnings for the blueprint for transformation. But ideology is at best only an imperfect lens for assessing the world and frequently must be compromised for pragmatic reasons.

Regarding conventional war and the modern world system, there are two broadly defined schools of thought: (1) that which seeks to transform the system by removing war from the system; and, (2) that which wishes to use war as a tool to effect the desired transformation of the system.

Approaches to eliminating war from the system have been varied. The Kellogg-Briand Pact of 1927 was an attempt to get the states of the world to renounce war as an option for settling disputes. Eventually, sixty-five states signed the accord, but the treaty lacked any provisions for enforcement and the increasing nationalism of the 1930s rendered the agreement meaningless.

In the decade of the 1980s, the questions of pacifism, conflict resolution, and disarmament have become important in the internal politics of many advanced industrial states. The West German "Greens" party, for example, works actively to reduce military expenditures and find alternatives to war as a means of conflict resolution. Similar movements operate throughout Western Europe, the United States, and even the Soviet Union. The objective of these groups is to transform the system by changing the policy priorities of state leaders. In some cases, these groups seek to reform political decisionmaking processes in an effort to reduce the power of those who advocate war as a foreign-policy tool.

Some transformers seek to replace the state-centric system with a single world government. The most common model for such an entity is a world federal government, similar to the federal system in the United States. Such a government would settle disputes, have control over military forces, and possess a monopoly on the legitimate use of force. National militaries would disappear, to be replaced by this world government's police force. The movement for world federalism is primarily composed of scholars, philosophers, activists, and other private citizens. However, advancing the cause of world government has not been a high priority for statesmen and others possessing political power.

Still other transformers target weapons themselves as the main problem. These transformers believe that the existence of large militaries invites the use of force to resolve conflicts. The solution then is to end war by banning the instruments of conflict. Disarmament is related to arms control in that limitation of weapons is the goal, but the main difference is the level of limitation sought. Disarmament means the elimination of the weapons in question. As in the case of arms control negotiations, the emphasis in disarmament has been on nuclear weapons, and the real progress toward nuclear disarmament has been minimal. Disarmament in the realm of conventional weapons is an even more problematic undertaking and would require the states of the world to give up their militaries, one of the most important guarantors of their national sovereignty. Powerful and reliable alternative provisions would be necessary. While conventional weapons disarmament may be the ultimate goal of some system transformers, the likelihood of attaining that status in the foreseeable future is virtually nil.

More threatening to the future of the international system are those who desire to transform the system through the use of warfare. The most salient example of this in the last forty years has been Marxist-Leninist-Maoist theory regarding the nature of the international system and the foreign policy of socialist states. This radical perspective views warfare as a viable, maybe even necessary means of transforming the capitalist, nation-state system into a stateless, socialist system.

In 1916, V. I. Lenin expanded upon the writings of Karl Marx to explain war in his pamphlet, *Imperialism, the Highest Stage of Capitalism.* (1950) In this work, he concluded that war, specifically the world war being fought at the time Lenin wrote, was a result of advanced capitalist states battling for control of overseas markets, resources, and labor. The establishment of a socialist regime in Russia in 1917 altered the picture. The Marxist concept of the dialectic (i.e., two groups opposed to one another creating a new situation, a synthesis, through their opposition) implied that military conflict between socialist and capitalist states was likely, perhaps inevitable. Prior to *Imperialism,* Lenin had contemplated the idea that a socialist revolution in one state could lead the victorious proletariat to rise up against the capitalist world's ruling elites, provoking revolution among the world's proletariat, a revolution that would likely need military support. Class war between the working and capitalist classes within states would be extended to the world at large, in a battle to transform and define the international system.

Earlier in this chapter, Soviet use of conventional military power was classified as reflecting the system-maintainer perspective. How is this so, given the Soviet Marxist-Leninist political orientation? It seems that as the USSR has matured as a state, its military policies have come to reflect the interests and concerns of the moment and thus have become more pragmatic. The Soviet Union has tended to behave more like a traditional rule-making state than a revolutionary transforming state. What is presented as Communist doctrine regarding war and peace between socialism and capitalism is largely a collection of propagandistic and programmatic statements made by Soviet leaders to serve the current needs of Soviet foreign policy. With the shifts in Soviet foreign-policy objectives or changes in the international environment came modifications in the emphasis between the prospects for war or peace with the non-Communist world. (Nogee and Donaldson 1984, 22)

Lenin's successor, Joseph Stalin, exhibited this sort of vacillation between ideology and pragmatism. Stalin's theory of the "Two Camps" divided the world into mutually antagonistic forces, the capitalist world and its holdings and the socialist world. Neither of these ideological or power blocs was strong enough to destroy the other, so each was forced to endure the other. Stalin felt that a conflict, and a socialist victory, was inevitable, though not imminent, and until then the USSR had to be cautious. Nikita Khruschev expanded on this "live-and-let-live" idea with his policy of "Peaceful Coexistence" in 1956. Khruschev, convinced of the potentially disastrous effects of general war, based his theory on two main premises: (1) war with the capitalist states was not inevitable; and (2) communism could be achieved by peaceful or parliamentry means. War was no longer a certainty or a necessity. The idea of a military showdown with the capitalist world in order to transform the system was pretty much a thing of the past. The use of Soviet military power was generally limited to maintaining the USSR's geopolitical position.

In the Third World, the Soviet Union has exhibited some inclination to use conventional military forces to challenge the system. There the revolutionary aspect of Soviet ideology could be renewed and Western capitalist interests attacked as well. The Soviet navy's ability to project power into and influence Third World areas has increased substantially over the last two decades, causing considerable concern among U.S. planners and strategists. However, Soviet actions of a military nature in the developing world have primarily been limited to arms sales, limited economic assistance, and military training. The use of actual Soviet forces has been rare. Instead, the forces of other socialist states, Soviet "proxies" as they are sometimes referred to, have been used to represent Moscow's interests. East German troops and, especially, Cuban forces, have been deployed in Latin America and Africa to further Soviet or world socialist interests.

Communist China has followed a similar development in policy, swinging between ideology and pragmatism. In the 1950s and 1960s, the Chinese were ardent supporters of revolutionary wars of liberation in the Third World. They were also critics of Soviet cautiousness. One aspect of the Sino-Soviet split was the Chinese accusation that the USSR was following its own brand of imperialism in the developing world. Yet by the 1970s, China had cordial diplomatic relations with the United States and was seeking increased economic ties to the West. China acted to stabilize Southeast Asia by confronting Vietnam in 1979. Again, as a state has acquired increased stakes in the existing system, its policy has shifted from policies of transformation toward policies of reform and maintenance.

There are those who feel that the activities of the Communist powers in the developing world, especially those of the USSR, are aimed not at transforming the international system but at strengthening their position in it. Soviet support of liberation movements is a means to demonstrate commitment to revolutionary transformation of the international system, but it also improves the Soviet Union's position within the system as a leader of the socialist world. Spheres of influence and the division of the world into socialist and capitalist camps does as much to strengthen the bipolarity of the modern system as it does to foster change and transformation.

PREDICTIONS FOR THE FUTURE

The Future of War in the Modern System

Predicting the future is always a hazardous undertaking; there is nothing so uncertain as the future and nothing so humbling as making predictions and being proved wrong. Nevertheless, it is safe to say that conventional warfare will remain a feature of the international system for the foreseeable future. The use of war to achieve political ends remains viable and one can not, unfortunately, predict its decline. States and subnational groups are likely to continue to resort to force of arms if they deem it in their best interests.

One reason this is so is that the international system has provided no mechanism to prevent war. Peaceful alternatives, such as mediation and international law, have been offered, but fail in situations where compromise seems impossible and neither side can retreat from what it feels to be vital interests. The collective-security function of the United Nations has had only sporadic success in preventing, limiting, and ending wars.

Powerful ideological forces are at work as well; Islamic fundamentalists in states such as Iran see *jihad,* or holy war, as both utilitarian and morally correct. Thousands of Iranians have died in the Gulf War, assured of their place in heaven by giving their lives in battle. Revolutionaries in a score of countries see guerilla warfare as the only way to attain the necessary political changes they desire. Not to engage in conventional war is to risk being accused of compromising with reactionary elements. The endurance of modern guerillas and their willingness to prosecute extended wars has been one of the continuing motifs of late twentieth century conventional warfare.

What is likely to change in the future is the way in which wars will be fought. Most states are unable to keep up with the changing technological nature of modern conventional warfare because it is just too expensive. Rather than opt out of the competition for power, prestige, and influence, many states may decide to change the rules of competition. Instead of playing to the conventional military strength of their enemies, states with fewer military resources may choose instead to resort to unconventional warfare, such as terrorism. Western states, such as the United States, Great Britain, and France, for example, have found their conventional forces stymied by truck bombs, kidnappings, assassinations, and other forms of what could be called unconventional warfare. In the future, the line between acts of political terrorism and conventional war may be rendered completely indistinct.

The Wars of the Future

In a 1973 article, Professor Louis J. Halle discussed the likelihood of war in the future. (1973, 20–34) His conclusion is optimistic: Warfare is on the decline in the modern world system. Halle outlined three new factors in the system that he felt mitigate against war:

1. The impact of technology that makes modern warfare too destructive and its consequences unacceptable for all parties;
2. The rise of collective egalitarianism, i.e., the extending to all nation-states of the concept that all men are created equal. The idea of sovereign equality for all the world's states gives the sort of great-power intervention in small-power affairs common in the nineteenth and early twentieth centuries a new stigma of illegitimacy. Great powers can no longer act with impunity regarding small states.
3. States are unable to isolate war. Conflicts tend to attract the attention of outside powers, especially the Soviet Union and the United States. The ability to fight geographically isolated, self-contained and self-directed wars may be lost.

Halle concluded that the the most likely wars in the future will be civil wars; that is, the breakdown of legitimate rule and civil violence in a state that creates a power vacuum to which other states are drawn.

How have Halle's predictions fared in the last thirteen years? For the most part, his analysis holds, with some important exceptions. The Soviet Union's invasion of Afghanistan indicates that egalitarianism among states lacks compelling force to prevent intervention, and the Falklands/Malvinas War shows that middle powers can engage in warfare without the undue interference of other powers or the world at large. Still, civil wars in the developing and under-developed world constitute the majority of the world's conflicts and will likely continue to do so into the next century. The continued volatility of these states, as well as the eagerness of neighbors, the United States, and the Soviet Union to take advantage of such situations, indicates that civil wars will remain the dominant form of conventional war in the system.

This is not to say that other forms of conventional wars are to be discounted in the future. The European front offers the possibility for the most destructive conventional war since World War II, a war that would involve both of the superpowers as well as all of Europe. The probability of such a conflict is small, however. The potential for destruction outweighs the advantages to either side and, since 1945, European states have shown an interest in increasing cooperation and eventually extending their integration efforts. The cooperative spirit is now beginning to spill over and influence relations between the Eastern and Western blocs.

Conventional war between states is more likely in the Middle East—the perennial powderkeg of the modern world. Some feel that a fourth Arab-Israeli war is not a question of "if" but a question of "when." Unresolved political issues and long-standing rivalries could break out into war at short notice. Unfortunately, conflicts in the region are not necessarily solely of an Arab-Israeli nature. There are differences among Arabs states that have erupted and could again erupt into hostility, especially now as lines are being drawn between Islamic fundamentalist and moderate states. The Gulf War, the region's longest sustained conventional conflict, could yet spread to other states in the region. It is possible that a decisive victory by either Iran or Iraq could sow the seeds for another war.

In Asia, the prospects for peace appear somewhat brighter. The People's Republic of China is no longer the revolutionary state it once was and has adopted policies aimed at stabilizing the region. Japan, despite a growing internal pressure for remilitarization in some sectors, is a status quo-oriented state, unlikely to embark on a new round of conquests. The greatest potential for conflict is to be found on the Korean peninsula, where both North and South Korea are heavily armed and neither has forsaken the dream of reuniting the nation. In Southeast Asia, Vietnam, one of the world's strongest military powers, has the power to threaten other states in the region, such as Thailand. India and Sri Lanka both are troubled by separatist movements that could break out into civil conflicts. Finally, the leadership of the Philippines must contend with internal conflicts initiated by extremist forces from both ends of the political spectrum.

In Africa and Central America, civil wars and border conflicts are frequent and may increase in future years. Continued opposition to white minority rule in South Africa could erupt into violent civil war, a conflict into which front-line African states would likely be drawn, as well as most of the major powers concerned about South Africa's strategic position on the Cape of Good Hope and rich mineral deposits. In Central America, continued opposition between socialist forces backed by the Soviets and Cuba and U.S.-supported governments and insurgents shows no signs of abating. Both superpowers are supporting friendly governments and insurgency against unfriendly governments. In El Salvador and Honduras the United States supports the national government, while in Nicaragua it backs the Contra insurgents fighting against the Soviet-supported Sandinista government. Many observers of the region feel that the next big conventional war might entail a U.S. invasion of Nicaragua.

Exhibit 2.3 touches on some of the more probable future conventional wars; there are other possibilities and the actual wars of the future may prove to be those that are least expected. For example, who would have predicted in 1980 that Argentina and the United Kingdom would be at war over the Falklands/Malvinas in 1982? The disturbing certainty is that conventional war, such an important and prominent feature of the world system in the past, will remain an important and prominent feature in the future as well.

Exhibit 2.3 Conventional and Possible Conventional Wars

War	Participants	Type
Europe		
NATO vs. Warsaw Pact	NATO/U.S. vs. Warsaw Pact/USSR	General conventional war
Northern Ireland	Catholics vs. Protestants/United Kingdom	Civil war with British intervention
Africa		
South Africa	Government vs. Blacks	Racial civil war with intervention from outside
Zaire	Government vs. Katangan rebels	Civil war
Angola	Government/Cubans vs. UNITA/South Africa	Civil war with intervention from outside
Namibia	South Africa vs. SWAPO/Angola	War of liberation
Americas		
Nicaragua	Sandinistas vs. Contras/U.S./Honduras	Civil war; invasion by U.S.
Honduras	Honduras/Contras vs. Nicaragua	Invasion by Nicaragua to destroy Contra bases
Falklands/Malvinas	United Kingdom vs. Argentina	Invasion to retake the Malvinas by Argentina
Peru-Ecuador	Peru vs. Ecuador	Border war
Argentina-Chile	Argentina vs. Chile	Border war
Mexico	Government vs. Leftists	Civil war with likely U.S. intervention

Asia

Amur River	Red China *vs.* USSR	Border war
Korea	South Korea vs. South Korea	War for reunification
Philippines	Government vs. Communists/Moslems	Insurgency
Indonesia	Government vs. South Moluccans	Insurgency

Middle East

Fourth Arab-Israeli War	Israel *vs.* Arab states	Border war; *jihad*
Israeli-Syrian War	Israel vs. Syria	Border war; conflict over Lebanon
Iran	Government vs. Rebels	Civil war; intervention by USSR, others likely
Persian Gulf	Iran vs. Kuwait/Saudi Arabia	Fundamentalist *jihad*

Sources: John Keegan and Andrew Wheatcroft, *Zones of Conflict: An Atlas of Future Wars.* New York: Simon and Schuster, 1986; James F. Dunnigan and Austin Bay, *A Quick and Dirty Guide to War.* New York: William Morrow, 1985.

NOTES

1. This proposition explains war only in the most general terms, and ignores both situational and contributing factors that may tell us why war breaks out at one instance in time and not another, and the impact of specific policies and personalities on the course of events.

2. More detailed description, discussion, and critique of the concept of collective security can be found in Hans J. Morgenthau, *Politics Among Nations,* 6th edition, (New York: A. A. Knopf, 1985) chapter 24, or Ines Claude, *Power and International Relations,* (New York: Random House, 1962) chapters 4 and 5.

REFERENCES

Aron, Raymond. *The Century of Total War.* New York: Doubleday, 1954.

Betts, Richard K. "The Tragicomedy of Arms Trade Control." *International Security* 5 (Summer 1980):80–100.

————. "Conventional Strategy: New Critics. Old Choices." International Security 7 (Spring 1983): 140–162.

Brodie, Bernard. *War and Politics.* New York: Macmillan, 1973.

Carter, Jimmy. Presidential Address, May 1979.

Carver, Michael. *War Since 1945.* New York: G. Putnam's Sons, 1981.

Claude, Ines. *Power and International Relations.* New York: Random House, 1962.

Clausewitz, Carl von. *On War.* Edited and translated by Michael Howard and Peter Paret. Princeton: Princeton University Press, 1976.

Dean, Robert. "MBFR: Apathy to Accord." *International Security* 7 (Spring 1983):116–139.

Dunnigan, James F. *How to Make War.* New York: William Morrow, 1982.

Dunnigan, James F., and Austin Bay. *A Quick and Dirty Guide to War.* New York: William Morrow, 1985.

Endicott, John E., and Roy Stafford, Jr. *American Defense Policy.* 4th ed. Baltimore: Johns Hopkins University Press, 1977.

Gilpin, Robert. *War and Change in World Politics.* Cambridge: Cambridge University Press, 1981.

Halle, Louis J. "Does War Have a Future?" *Foreign Affairs* 52 (October 1973):20–34.

Harkavy, Robert. *The Arms Trade and International Systems.* Cambridge, MA: Ballinger, 1975.

Herf, Jeffrey. "War, Peace and the Intellectuals: The West German Peace Movement." *International Security* 10 (Spring 1986):143–171.

Hoffmann, Erik P., and Frederic J. Fleron, eds. *The Conduct of Soviet Foreign Policy.* New York: Aldine, 1980.

International Institute for Strategic Studies. *The Military Balance, 1984–1985.* London: IISS, 1984.

Janowitz, Morris. *Military Conflict: Essays in the Institutional Analysis of War and Peace.* Beverly Hills, CA: Sage, 1975.

Johnson, Chalmers. *Autopsy on People's War.* Berkeley: University of California Press, 1973.

Keegan, John, and Andrew Wheatcroft. *Zones of Conflict: An Atlas of Future Wars.* New York: Simon and Schuster, 1986.

Keohane, Robert, and Joseph Nye. *Power and Interdependence.* New York: Little, Brown and Company, 1977.

Kidron, Michael, and Ronald Segal. *The New State of the World Atlas.* New York: Simon and Schuster, 1984.

Lenin, V. I. *Imperialism: The Highest Stage of Capitalism.* Petrograd: 1917.

Luttwak, Edward N. *The Pentagon and the Art of War.* New York: Simon and Schuster, 1984.

Macksey, Kenneth. *First Clash: Combat Close Up in World War Three.* London: Arms and Armour Press, 1985.

Nelson, Keith L., and Spencer C. Olin, Jr. *Why War?* Berkeley: University of California Press, 1980.

Nogee, Joseph L., and Robert H. Donaldson. *Soviet Foreign Policy Since World War II.* New York: Pergamon Press, 1984.

O'Neill, Robert. "Future Trends in Conventional Warfare." In *Strategy and Defence: Australian Essays,* edited by Desmond Ball. Sydney: George Allen & Unwin, 1982.

Organski, A.F.K., and Jacek Kugler. *The War Ledger.* Chicago: University of Chicago Press, 1980.

Payne, James L. *The American Threat.* College Station, TX: Lytton Publishing, 1981.

Pierre, Andrew J. *The Global Politics of Arms Sales.* Princeton: Princeton University Press, 1982.

Preston, Richard, and Sydney F. Wise. *Men in Arms.* New York: Holt, Rinehart & Winston, 1979.

Sivard, Ruth Legar. *World Military and Social Expenditures.* Washington: World Priorities, 1985.

Sokolovsky, V.D. *Soviet Military Strategy.* Edited by Harriet Fast Scott. New York: Crane, Russak, 1975.

Steel, Ronald. *Pax Americana.* New York: Viking, 1970.

Tillema, Herbert K. *Appeal to Force.* New York: Thomas Crowell, 1973.

Waltz, Kenneth. *Man, the State and War.* New York: Columbia University Press, 1959.

Weltman, John J. "War in International Politics Today." In *Strategy and Defence: Australian Essays.* Edited by Desmond Ball. Sydney: George Allen & Unwin, 1982.

Wright, Quincy. *A Study of War.* Abridged ed. Chicago: University of Chicago Press, 1964.

—————————— 3 ——————————

Nuclear Arms Proliferation
STEVE SMITH

There is a paradox about nuclear weapons: Their vast destructive potential makes ours the first generation in human history that can end history. Yet, this very fact means that these weapons are virtually unusable. In this sense, nuclear weapons are different from virtually all other weapons. Their rationale lies essentially in their utility in preventing conflict. Many think this situation is a stable one; the awesome destruction that would inevitably accompany the use of nuclear weapons induces caution in those who control them. Others think the world is poised on the edge of a disaster, with misunderstanding or miscalculation liable to lead the world into nuclear war. The task of this chapter is to look at nuclear weapons from the three perspectives discussed in Chapter 1: system maintainer, system reformer, and system transformer. The purpose is to see how those with different worldviews analyze nuclear-weapons issues. It will become apparent that each worldview results in a distinct notion of the paradox of nuclear weapons, with accompanying prescriptions for how to deal with this complex issue.

Before turning to look at the three perspectives, it is important that something be said about the nature of the nuclear weapons issue. It is worth stressing at the start that a nuclear weapon really cannot be seen as "just another weapon." The destructive power of contemporary nuclear weapons is vastly greater than the power of conventional chemical explosives. As an inevitable result of a nuclear detonation there are, in addition to the blast and thermal effects, radioactive by-products produced that have long half-lives, posing an enormous threat to human life. These by-products are not produced by chemical explosives—in short, nuclear explosions are different from chemical explosions in both quantitative and qualitative dimensions. The combination of the vastly greater blast and thermal effects of nuclear explosions with the radioactive by-products means that any large-scale use of nuclear weapons could conceivably destroy life as citizens of the world know it. There are many estimates to choose from, but a major nuclear exchange between the United States and the USSR, involving only a fraction of their nuclear arsenals, could kill approximately 100 million people on either side.

More than just human life could be affected. The "nuclear winter" theory predicts that the smoke produced by nuclear-explosion fires could plunge the earth into a winter that would last up to a year, (Schell 1982) because the smoke would be injected into the atmosphere above the level at which our weather occurs, and would prevent sunlight from reaching the surface of the earth. Temperatures would plummet and the survival of those who had escaped the immediate destructive effects of nuclear explosions would be threatened; plant and animal life would not survive such low temperatures and lack of sunlight. There is now debate over whether the effects of nuclear winter would be as severe as was originally suggested, but the crucial point is that nuclear weapons could have this effect.

In addition to the radiation and nuclear winter effects, we must consider that nuclear conflict is likely to destroy societal infrastructure, and produce immense psychological trauma. Finally, there is the possibility of war occurring by accident, either through an accidental launch or through misunderstanding.

What, then, are the main aspects of the nuclear weapons issue? At present, there are only five unambiguous nuclear-weapons powers, that is to say that there are five states who have admitted to testing and producing nuclear weapons. These are the United States (which tested its first atomic bomb in 1945), the Soviet Union (1949), the United Kingdom (1952), France (1960), and China (1964). There are also some possible nuclear powers, that is, those who have either conducted a test of a nuclear device (although not a miniaturized nuclear weapon), such as India (which tested a device in 1974), or are rumored to have a nuclear arsenal, for example, Israel. There are the powers who could "go nuclear" soon, principally Pakistan and South Africa. The "nuclear club" is a small one, one whose membership has been growing very slowly.

These members of the nuclear club have different quantities of nuclear weapons. If we look at the number of strategic warheads they possess (with strategic defined as those that can travel from the territory of one power to that of one or the other of the superpowers, or those placed on submarines), we note that the United Kingdom, China, and France currently have (about) under 150 warheads each, while the United States and the USSR have over 10,000 each. In other words, the nuclear world is essentially a bipolar one. Most of the discussion of nuclear weapons concerns the arsenals of the two superpowers, simply because the other nuclear powers have such relatively small nuclear arsenals that it is impossible to think of any of them initiating conflict with one of the superpowers. Their weapons are essentially deterrents, designed to prevent attacks. The central issue for the superpowers, however, is that of ensuring that the other side does not gain an advantage by developing types of nuclear weapons that may give it more options in a crisis or even allow it to undertake a disarming first strike. Essentially, then, the superpowers are caught up in an arms race in which each is developing new types of delivery systems and always attempting to prevent the other side from getting ahead. As the reader will see, the three worldviews employed in the analytical framework for this book imply very different views of the arms race.

To this point, two main dimensions of the nuclear issue have been discussed: first, the extension of membership in the nuclear club (horizontal proliferation); and second, the further development of nuclear weapons by those states who already possess them (vertical proliferation). Fundamentally, the dominant issues in the nuclear arena are: Who will get nuclear weapons in the future and with what consequences, and what will be the effects of the superpowers' refinement and buildup of their nuclear stockpiles? In each case, the three worldviews have rather distinct notions of the problems associated with the maintenance of stability; each worldview implies different problems arising from both the horizontal and vertical proliferation of nuclear weapons and different views over how far to change the current situation. The first section of this chapter will examine the perspective of the system maintainers; having described the status-quo view in detail, the next sections will review the other worldviews simply by referring to the questions outlined in Chapter 1.

THE SYSTEM-MAINTAINER PERSPECTIVE

Vertical Proliferation

For system maintainers such as the United States and the USSR, the current situation can be described in fairly simple terms. With regard to vertical proliferation, each seeks to prevent the other from gaining an advantage by achieving a breakthrough in nuclear-weapons technology. This is essentially the first law of the nuclear relationship for the system maintainers. For the leadership of both the United States and the USSR, the problem is, at a minimum, how to keep a position of essential equivalence in weapons capabilities, and, at a maximum, how to achieve some form of superiority. The argument is that it is the nature of a bipolar nuclear relationship that maintains peace between the superpowers. The nuclear relationship is, therefore, one in which each of the superpowers has to ensure that it is not left behind in technological developments; it is exactly the knowledge that efforts to keep ahead technologically are occurring on both sides that maintains stability. As neither side can allow the other to get far ahead in the arms race, each uses a mixture of building up weapons and controlling them via arms agreements to keep the weapons arsenals essentially in balance. In other words, both U.S. and Soviet decisions over weapons developments are justified by referring to the possibility that the other side might achieve a major advance. It is believed that stability can be ensured only through constant development of the nuclear arsenal.

To understand the complexities of the system-maintainer worldview, we need to be clear about the types of nuclear weapons and the uses each might have. Each side's nuclear arsenal comprises three types of delivery systems: intercontinental ballistic missiles (ICBMs), submarine-launched ballistic missiles (SLBMs), and aircraft (carrying gravity bombs or air-launched cruise missiles [ALCMs]). The history of the nuclear age has seen both sides build up all three types of delivery systems; however, the differences in preferences for weapons systems reflect the different histories, geographies, and strategies of the two countries. Broadly speaking, the United States has put most of its strategic warheads onto submarines, with about 75 percent of its missile warheads being on SLBMs. The Soviet Union has, mainly for reasons of geography, put most of its warheads on land-based systems. The Soviets have about 75 percent of their missile warheads on their ICBMs. However, given this difference in the way each side bases its nuclear forces, they each try to match the developments that they think the other side is about to achieve in its nuclear forces. Thus, as Soviet air defense is improved, the United States both converts some of its bombers from a penetrating role to a stand-off (ALCM) role and improves the penetration qualities of others. Similarly, as the Soviet Union develops an antiballistic missile system (ABM) around Moscow, the United States develops the technique of placing more than one separately targetable warhead (Multiple Independent Targeted Re-entry Vehicles—MIRVs) on its missiles. Currently, much of the debate is over what the Soviets will do to overcome President Reagan's Strategic Defense Initiative (SDI).

The point is that, for the system maintainers, the goal is one of keeping up with the developments of the other superpower. Why is this necessary given the fact that each side possesses so many nuclear weapons? The reason given by the system maintainers is that nuclear weapons have different capabilities and that the quantitative dimensions hide a mass of crucial strategic distinctions. To understand the logic of this argument, it is necessary to understand that nuclear weapons may have a critical political utility in structuring the perceptions of leaders in a crisis. In crisis situations involving high stakes and significant risks, system maintainers believe that it matters that there are certain differences in the types of weapons in the two sides' arsenals. To give just one telling example: in the late 1970s many strategists and politicians in the United States became concerned that the Soviets might soon be able to destroy the U.S. ICBM forces. Until the mid-1970s neither side's ICBM forces were accurate enough to be able to destroy hardened targets such as command centers or missile silos. But as the accuracy of strategic missiles improved, it became possible to think of a disarming first strike in which one side would attack without warning. Although the United States was more advanced in improving the accuracy of ICBMs, it had only about 2,150 warheads on its ICBM force. Given the need to aim two warheads on each target (in case of the failure of one missile to work effectively), the United States did not have enough warheads on its ICBMs to target the 1,398 Soviet ICBM silos and their launch and command centers. The Soviets, in contrast, had over 5,000 warheads on their 1,398 ICBMs. This situation gave them about five warheads for each U.S. silo. Thus, when the Soviets began introducing their new generation of ICBMs (the SS17, SS18, and SS19) in the mid-1970s, the improved accuracy of these ICBMs was seen as giving the Soviet Union a "window of opportunity."

According to proponents of this argument, the Soviet Union could target silos in the United States in a surprise attack. If this was successful, the United States would have only its SLBMs and bomber forces left. *Crucially,* although these two legs of the triad contain over 7,000 warheads, the worry was that their technical characteristics would prevent the United States from retaliating. The reason was that SLBMs are far less accurate than ICBMs (basically because a submarine never knows its *exact* location when firing a missile), and so they can not be used for targeting ICBM silos. SLBMs are essentially countervalue weapons for use in a second strike. ICBMs, by contrast, are counterforce weapons that can be used in a first strike. Accordingly, given the worry that bombers would not be guaranteed to get through Soviet air defense except if launched en masse at cities, a U.S. president might be unwilling to launch the surviving SLBM and bomber forces; their only targets would be Soviet cities. If these cities were hit, there would be nothing that the United States could do to stop the Soviet Union from retaliating. The pressure would be on the U.S. president to surrender; thus, the United States would be "deterred by its own deterrent." Of course, this scenario is a far-fetched one, but it indicates clearly the worldview of the system maintainers. Because the USSR might be able to put the United States in a situation of suicide or surrender, it is possible that the Soviet Union might use this capability to blackmail the United States in a crisis situation. More subtly, the leadership of the United States might realize that, in the event of this outcome, the Soviets would have more options. The United States could then be prevented from showing sufficient resolve in an international crisis.

The solution to this problem, it was argued, was for the United States to build a "survivable" ICBM force. Initially, this meant building the MX missile, first in a mobile-basing mode and then in the small ICBM ("midgetman") system. Most system maintainers believed that if this were not done, the essential equivalence of the two sides' arsenals would be threatened and the United States could be put in a situation of inferiority. The central point is that this kind of calculation runs throughout the history of the nuclear age and applies to all aspects of how each superpower tries to keep up with the other in all areas of strategic weapons. Given the long period of research and development that is involved in the production of nuclear weapons, this means assessing what the other side *might* be able to do in ten or twenty years time. Not surprisingly, this leads to a situation in which military planners have to assume the worst, so they predict the other side's capabilities as greater than they in fact are.

These forecasts lead to a mutually reinforcing process—a spiraling arms race. It does not matter that each side's capabilities may not be as extensive as might earlier have been assessed, or that their systems may not work as well as has been estimated. What is critical is that each superpower tends to make very conservative and pessimistic assessments of what the other can achieve. The result is an arms race. President Reagan's SDI, though presented as an alternative to the prevailing nuclear relationships, is a further example of this process. The Soviets are now engaged in finding ways around any defensive shield that the United States may already have; the United States is involved in assessing both how to overcome Soviet attempts to get around its SDI weapons system and how to get past a presumed Soviet SDI system.

In all of this, the view of the system maintainer is that the current balance of forces must, at the very least, be preserved. Given the fact that the other side might achieve some kind of breakthrough in, for example, defensive systems or antisubmarine warfare, each side carries out research in all areas of nuclear weapons. Each strives for superiority at best and parity at worst. These desires explain the resulting arms race and indicate why the current situation persists.

While arms control is used as a way of achieving balance, it can never guarantee that breakthroughs cannot occur. This is because the main arms-control agreements are concerned with quantitative limits on weapons deployment, not with research. No arms-control treaty can limit what happens in the laboratory; therefore, military specialists tend to be unwilling to rely upon arms control as a way of maintaining the stability of the superpower relationship; preferring to continue to conduct research on all types of weapons and delivery systems. Furthermore, each side uses arms control merely as a way of fixing the numbers and types of delivery systems deployed.

Horizontal Proliferation

With regard to *horizontal* proliferation, the system maintainers, such as the United States and the Soviet Union, share a common interest in preventing the further spread of nuclear weapons. This is because each is worried about the prospect of a domino or nuclear-chain effect, with one power crossing the nuclear threshold leading to others doing so, especially given regional rivalries in the international system. Not only would this threaten world peace, it could also drag the superpowers into confrontation, given their links with some of the potential proliferators. The nature of bipolarity draws the superpowers into regional conflicts, and neither superpower would wish to have to back up words of support in a potential nuclear conflict. Thus, each superpower has been a strong supporter of the institutions for preventing the spread of nuclear weapons —the International Atomic Energy Agency (IAEA) and the Non-Proliferation Treaty (NPT)—and has acted to persuade potential proliferators from crossing the threshold.

In summary, from the perspective of the system maintainers the basic characteristic of the nuclear problem is how to maintain stability with the other superpower while preventing the spread of nuclear weapons to other powers. In this, the dominant actors are the superpowers themselves, with international organizations and other states acting to slow the horizontal spread of nuclear weapons.

At the superpower level, system maintainers fear one side (i.e., the other side!) obtaining a lead in the arms race; this could at best have political consequences and at worst destabilize the nuclear relationship. The world that results is seen as having too many nuclear weapons in each of the superpower arsenals, but it is felt that it is probably the best of all possible nuclear worlds. The status quo might well look very dangerous, but it is that very danger that keeps the weapons from being used. Exactly this factor lies at the heart of the explanation as to why the two superpowers have not been at war directly since 1945. The resulting arms race is unavoidable, with arms control acting only as a way of managing that arms race. Arms races reflect, not cause, political mistrust.

Horizontal proliferation has been prevented by a series of measures, not least the pervasive effects of superpower conflict, that have led to conventional arms transfers and to the extension of bipolar conflicts into other geographic regions, most notably the Third World. The presence of the superpowers prevents or inhibits Third World states "going nuclear"; doing so would probably lead to the withdrawal of arms transfers and security guarantees from the superpowers and other members of the nuclear club. Clearly, there are differences between the United States and the Soviet Union in how each views horizontal and vertical nuclear proliferation. Without a doubt, many citizens in each society would disagree with the system-maintainer worldview described above. However, the structure of competing worldviews forces us to set out the essential characteristics of the positions, and so it will be useful to summarize the system maintainer's worldview according to the analytical framework employed in this book, which encourages a comparison of descriptions, explanations, predictions, and prescriptions from each worldview category.

System-Maintainer Descriptions of the Nuclear-Arms Issue

What is the Characteristic of the Issue?
The basic characteristic of the nuclear arms issue for the system maintainer is how each side keeps up with the other in research and at the same time prevents other states from getting nuclear weapons. The weapons themselves are not the cause of the problem, but are a reflection of underlying tensions. *Getting rid of nuclear weapons is not possible, so the problem is how to manage a world in which they exist.* This is to be achieved by not allowing one or the other superpower to gain a militarily or politically decisive advantage, and by trying to prevent the spread of nuclear weapons, especially to unstable regions of the world.

What Kind of World is Being Created Under Present Conditions?
The world being created is unavoidable: It is the best possible nuclear world. Maybe reductions in nuclear arms could be achieved; however, these reductions

would have to be balanced and mutual. The fear of nuclear war makes leaders conservative and unwilling to take risks since the situation is essentially one of "mutual assured destruction." No one can win a nuclear war, therefore no one will start one. Nuclear weapons have their utility only in preventing the other side from using them. With regard to horizontal proliferation, the world being created is as stable as can be imagined. The spread of nuclear weapons has slowed down and the superpowers have been remarkably successful in their policy of stopping other states from crossing the nuclear threshold. The same factors that ensure conservatism among the leaders of the superpowers would not affect small-power leaders, since arsenals would be so small that a disarming attack might hold a possibility of success. In both dimensions of the nuclear problem, then, the current world is as good as can be imagined, and system maintainers point to the lack of use of nuclear weapons since 1945 as proof of the underlying stability.

What Actors Play a Central Role?
In vertical proliferation issues, the only actors are the superpowers. Neither can allow its allies to divert it from ensuring that it keeps up with the other superpower. In horizontal proliferation, the actors are the superpowers and the states that are likely to proliferate. Other members of the international community can put pressure on states not to develop nuclear weapons, and international agencies can assist the construction of a non-proliferation regime. However, the crucial actors are the states within a region where nuclear weapons might be introduced and their respective superpower allies.

How do These Actors Participate and What are Their Priorities?
In the superpower relationship, each side participates by constantly checking on the activities of the other superpower. This involves assessing its military might and its intentions and trying to work out what research it is undertaking. Each side continues to maintain and refine its nuclear arsenal so as never to be faced with the prospect of the other side achieving a significant breakthrough. At the horizontal proliferation level, participation consists mainly of continual two-way discussions between potential proliferators and the superpowers. The superpowers attempt to dissuade potential proliferators from crossing the nuclear threshold and offer conventional weapons or security guarantees as alternatives. The potential proliferators participate by trying to obtain as much conventional assistance from the superpowers as possible, but they are also crucially concerned to observe the possibility of other states in their region going over the nuclear threshold. Each, therefore, attempts to ensure that it is not left behind by the activities of a regional rival. Thus, India and Pakistan, Iran and Iraq, and Brazil and Argentina are constantly watching their neighbor's nuclear research. The superpowers are simply concerned to maintain the status quo. What is to be feared is any prolonged period of change, since this makes prediction difficult.

What are the Structures and Processes of Decisionmaking?
In both dimensions of the nuclear issue, the structures and processes of decisionmaking are very restricted. This is, above all, an elite activity with little public involvement. Not only is the public seen to be only rarely interested in the issue, it is also said to understand very little. Secrecy is vital since the dispersal of information could assist the enemy. Despite the obvious differences between the political systems of the two superpowers, both share a tendency to make decisions over nuclear issues in very small groups. In the United States, Congress has a very important role, as its activities concerning the MX missile indicate. However, Congress has been unable to set the agenda for deciding on nuclear issues, nor does it have a strong record in preventing the development of weapons systems. For example, it is difficult for Congress to stop weapons programs (e.g., SDI) once the president has decided he wants the program. Congress can cut back on spending, but rarely do members of Congress vote to eliminate programs once they are initiated. The members of Congress, both House and Senate, must divide their time between domestic and foreign issues. Finally, Congress can not make the executive branch agree on arms control nor can it become involved in the details of discussions with potential nuclear proliferators.

Explanations from a System-Maintainer View

What are the Relevant Theoretical Explanations of Nuclear Competition?
For system maintainers, the key explanation is that states are always seeking to maximize power. Politicians will often dress this up into a good-versus-evil, us-versus-them view, but those theorists who would fall under the label of system maintainers (e.g., the realists) stress the centrality of the security dilemma for the leaders of all states. The self-help nature of the international system means that each set of leaders has to attempt to ensure the security of its own state; this can not be entrusted to international organizations, international treaties, or to other states in the system. The only sure way of achieving security is to have sufficient defensive capabilities. A precise definition of security depends on a complex balance of factors. National security interests can be affected by arms-control agreements (for superpowers) or by promises or threats (for potential proliferators); in the final analysis, each state's leaders must be judged in their own cause.

How Can One Account for the Persistence of Nuclear Competition?
The persistence of the problem of nuclear weapons simply reflects the fact that they have been invented and that the international system is anarchical. Until such time as the structure of the system is changed, states will have to take into account the kinds of weapons that potential adversaries might develop; therefore, we should expect the nuclear problem to remain as long as there are separate states.

In the system-maintainer worldview, there is no role for non-state actors. Nuclear weapons are issues for states alone (save for the worry that a terrorist group might obtain them). The behavior of state actors is explained by an anarchic international system.

The Future of Nuclear Issues

What are Possible Future Scenarios?
For system maintainers, future scenarios include the possibility of horizontal proliferation, but maintainers stress the need to prevent this as far as possible. If proliferation occurs, states must prevent a domino effect. The future scenarios of system maintainers stress the continuance of the superpowers' nuclear dominance of the international system, within which various levels of nuclear arsenals can be imagined. Arms control is not a desirable goal if by arms control is meant an alteration in the close competition in research on nuclear weapons between the superpowers. The most likely scenario is for a continuation of the current superpower relationship, one that is based on political mistrust. Because of that mistrust, it is unlikely that either side will be willing, despite the propaganda advantages of so maintaining, to give up nuclear weapons. The future policy agenda for each superpower will be dominated by a desire to keep a situation of essential equivalence with the other superpower and to limit the spread of nuclear weapons.

What is the Future Role of State and Non-State Actors?
Both superpowers will continue to act unilaterally; defense is the core national interest and nuclear weapons are the most important aspect in each superpower's defense posture. In essence, this is an issue area in which there is virtually no prospect of multilateral action; those agencies and treaties formed by multilateral action are secondary in comparison to the unilateral calculations of states. This is especially so in the case of superpower relations.

The issues that divide the superpowers are not easily resolved. Conflict being inherent in a society of separate states, all that can be achieved is the mitigation of the effects of international anarchy. System maintainers recognize the informational and educational contributions made by multilateral organizations; however, system maintainers generally feel that non-state actors will play only a minimal role in nuclear competition.

Policy Prescriptions from a System-Maintainer View

As discussed above, the primary strategies being advocated by the superpowers are, despite their superficial differences, concerned with maintaining the status quo. With regard to horizontal proliferation, the strength of the system maintainers' worldview is that their prescriptions have succeeded in the past, in that they have prevented states rushing over the nuclear threshold. The weakness concerns whether the example they set in their own superpower relationship is one good enough for other states. After all, the superpowers act as if nuclear weapons are useful, and their continual buildup of these weapons may make it difficult in the long run for other states to forgo them. In terms of their own nuclear relationship, the strength of the system maintainers' prescription is that it is clear that the destructive power of nuclear weapons is a significant restraint on their use. As long as the superpowers stay essentially equivalent, neither side has the incentive to start a war. The weakness of this position will be reviewed in more detail in the discussion of the other two worldviews. The criticism of the system-maintainer "balance-of-terror" position revolves around the arguments that the arms race is itself a cause of tension, that developments in technology may usher in an era that is not as stable, and that war could occur by accident or miscalculation.

THE SYSTEM-REFORMER PERSPECTIVE

There is one immediate problem that faces us if we wish to look at the nuclear issue from a system-reformer perspective: There are very different notions of reform, varying from an emphasis on arms control to the suggestion (held by India) that it is morally wrong for the superpowers to try to prevent states from becoming nuclear powers. There is no simple way of combining these rather contradictory viewpoints into one; therefore, the system-reformer worldview will be defined at the outset as a *European arms-control view*. This, of course, means neither that all those in Europe share this view, nor that no one in the United States and the Soviet Union accepts this position. System reform refers to concern with the current levels of nuclear weapons, the wish to see this level reduced, replacement of nuclear weapons by conventional weapons in Europe, and strengthened efforts to control nuclear proliferation through international regimes. The system-reformer worldview is further explored here through the same set of questions examined in the previous discussion of the system-maintainer worldview and introduced in Chapter 1 as part of the worldviews analytical model. For each question, the status-quo view has already been discussed, so our answers can be seen as critiques of that position.

System-Reformer Descriptions of the Nuclear Arms Issues

What is the Basic Characteristic of the Issue?
The basic characteristic of the nuclear-arms issue is different in the system-reformer worldview from the system-maintainer worldview on the question of vertical proliferation. System reformers tend to agree with system maintainers that the horizontal proliferation of nuclear weapons is to be avoided; but on the question of vertical proliferation, there are major disagreements with the system maintainers. The basic concern of system reformers is that the two superpowers

have built up vast arsenals of nuclear weapons, even the partial use of which could end human history. Such levels of nuclear weaponry are both unnecessary and economically wasteful. For system reformers, the continued refinement of arsenals is a self-perpetuating process in which each superpower acts as if the other will develop all types of weapons, and uses this as the rationale for its own buildup. The superpowers are caught up in a needless arms race.

The situation is more worrying than this for system reformers. They see the continual search for militarily significant breakthroughs as technology pulling the arms race. Technological developments are undertaken simply because the other side *could* undertake a like development; this suggests that strategy is not crucial in the buildup process. The result is that strategy has to adapt to the weapons that are produced rather than determine the weapons. A particularly good example of this is the development of the MIRV system in the United States. MIRV was developed to counter the Soviet ABM research program; yet once developed, it led to a set of targeting options that in turn led to fears of a disarming first strike. Putting many separately targetable warheads on one missile causes a situation in which one side fears that the other may fire first. Similarly, President Reagan's SDI is not so much led by strategy (although originally so presented) as by a desire to conduct research into exotic technologies. The worry is that these technologies, once developed, will lead to countermeasures and then to attempts to outwit the countermeasures—a case that illustrates the system reformer's fear that arms races soon get out of control.

At its best, this means that the superpowers pay a far higher price for security than is necessary. Both could certainly cut back their arsenals considerably and enjoy at least the same level of security. Yet, the search for technological breakthroughs also implies that the political relationship is unaffected by the arms race. System reformers argue that the arms race itself contributes to political tensions and is therefore a cause of mistrust. There is the danger that technology leads states into less stable situations; for example, it is now possible to think of targeting hardened military targets, an option unavailable twenty years ago when warheads were not very accurate. Yet is the U.S.-Soviet relationship more stable as a result? Reformers argue that it is not, and that such possibilities might tempt one side or the other to launch a preemptive attack.

Finally, the current situation involves a significant danger of war by miscalculation. That is, the arms race breeds distrust and each side ascribes bad motives to the actions of the other. With so many years of a military buildup, and such little political trust, the fear is that crises will become less manageable than before.

What Kind of World is being Created Under Present Conditions?
The world being created is needlessly dangerous because weapons are held at far-too-high levels by the superpowers. The drift toward ever more accurate systems increases each side's fear of a surprise attack, and each side therefore attempts to ensure that it can avoid being placed in a suicide or surrender situa-

tion. This attempt to find a way to survive a nuclear attack and win such a war by building mobile ICBMs, hardening silos, or building a defensive shield, merely encourages the other superpower to try to find a way around it, thereby reinforcing each side's worst fears. At worst, this could lead to a hair-trigger world in which any crisis could lead either side to consider preemptive attacks as a policy option. With reference to horizontal proliferation, the bipolar conflict merely accentuates regional rivalries, and the superpower buildup does nothing to convince potential proliferators that nuclear weapons are of limited utility.

What Actors Play a Major Role and How do They Participate?
The actors are the superpowers, but the reformers hope that other powers, for example alliance-bloc members or the neutral and non-aligned, will be able to move the superpowers toward reducing their arsenals. Most states are caught up in an arms race that no one is able to win or prevent. For each, a buildup is preferable to being overtaken by the other side. One must consider that participation in the arms race involves research into every type of system regardless of where this might lead the world. The goal of states in an anarchic system is to keep up with the other side, and if possible to win. System reformers would prefer that the actors were able to shift their priorities so as to enjoy equal security at lower levels of weaponry.

In this policy area, system reformers see the structures and processes of decisionmaking as too much in the control of elites within the superpowers. Reformers stress the need for groups within the political system to attempt to influence elites and are hopeful that this can be achieved. System reformers also support multilateral efforts at controlling the arms race. For example, UN conferences on disarmament are considered important forums for states attempting to influence the superpowers' nuclear policies. To date, such international conferences have had little impact on policymaking in the nuclear powers.

System-Reformer Explanations

What are the Relevant Theoretical Explanations of this Nuclear Competition?
The reformers argue that nuclear competition can be explained by the presence of large military-industrial complexes within each superpower. Military complexes are involved in worst-case analysis, so that they assume that the other side is doing as much as it can to develop all the relevant technologies. The buildup of nuclear weapons in the superpower arsenals is due to the power of those who are concerned with assessing the military threat posed by the other superpower. The structure of international society encourages this but does not logically require it. At the level of horizontal proliferation, reformers see the current situations being explained by the superpower buildup of nuclear weapons, which implies that these systems actually enhance security, and by the extension of superpower rivalry to all regions of the world. The problem

persists, say reformers, because too much was expected of earlier arms-control agreements; so much that it is now a dirty term, at least in the United States. The current superpower military buildup arises out of the United States feeling in the late 1970s and early 1980s that the USSR had gone ahead in the nuclear-arms race and that this had to be reversed.

Reformers see the behavior of actors as explicable by the process of the arms race in which they are caught up. The analogy of the prisoners' dilemma is a good one: Neither side would define the current situation as the best one but, given its preferences, better than the prospect of the other side getting ahead in the arms race. As far as horizontal proliferation is concerned, a state's behavior is dependent on the norms of international society and therefore the general disapproval of nuclear weapons is a significant restraint on other powers crossing the nuclear threshold.

The Future of Nuclear Issues

What are the Possible Future Scenarios?
At the superpower level, the possible scenarios of reformers tend to stress the continued waste of resources by an all-encompassing military buildup. They see the absence of arms control and the development of SDI as particularly worrying because each threatens to lead to an uninhibited arms race, in which the only constraints are financial. SDI in particular looks very destabilizing, as it will extend the arms race into space. It will also lead to the search for a whole range of technologies to overcome it and both sides will then get caught up in a defensive as well as an offensive arms race. At best, neither side will feel any more secure at the end of such a race; at worst, it will lead to greater political tensions and to the deployment of technologies that erode the stability of the nuclear relationship.

At the horizontal proliferation level, reformers see the world in a way that is essentially similar to the maintainers' view, except they are fearful that unless the superpowers show a willingness to cut down on levels of nuclear weapons, they will have little effect in attempting to prevent proliferation. This could lead to a world of many more nuclear states, in which the likelihood of war would be increased given the likely small size of any new nuclear power's arsenal. At worst, this could lead to nuclear war between two new nuclear powers, or even the involvement of the superpowers.

The future policy agenda should be concerned, above all, with the question of how to reduce nuclear arsenals, especially how to reduce certain types of weapons systems—those that invite preemption in a crisis (such as MIRVed fixed ICBMs). The core of the future policy agenda should be arms control at both the superpower and the horizontal proliferation levels. In each of these policy areas, the concern should be with how to set up arms-control agreements that both lower and inhibit nuclear arsenals.

What is the Future Role of State and Non-State Actors?

States, argue the reformers, should act multilaterally through international agencies or other arms-control forums. Unilateral action is likely only to lead to a renewed arms race between the superpowers and to nuclear proliferation among the threshold countries. Non-state actors could play an important role by putting pressure on governments. What is needed is to create a climate that challenges, across national boundaries, the assumptions of the system maintainers.

Is it Possible to Control Conflict?

Although superpower political rivalry will persist, a reduction in the level of each side's arsenal should improve relations and increase trust. Arms control can provide a forum in which the superpowers learn to trust one another. Arms races cannot achieve this goal. Reformers believe that the resolution of disagreements will not occur if governments slavishly follow the worst-case analysis of their military advisers. Secrecy and a lack of public accountability exacerbate this situation, so reformers tend to call for more public involvement in decisionmaking and for greater access to information.

Policy Prescriptions—A System-Reformer View

There are many different policy strategies offered by reformers, but they tend to converge around proposals for strengthening the non-proliferation regime and for reviving superpower arms control. They include proposals for nuclear-free zones, for international agreements to outlaw the first use of nuclear weapons in Europe, and for replacing nuclear forces with conventional ones. Reformers tend to see some nuclear weapons as worse than others and, therefore, are especially concerned to reduce those that threaten stability. Thus, many proposals include a ban on SDI-type deployments and favor deployment of offensive nuclear forces that concentrate on SLBMs or single-warhead ICBMs rather than on heavily MIRVed fixed ICBMs. At present, much of the attention of reformers is focused on preventing SDI from holding up a comprehensive arms-control agreement with the Soviets, of the type nearly reached at Reykjavic in October 1986.

The basic problem for reformers is that publics are in truth little interested in the nuclear issue, certainly not when it comes to voting in elections. Domestic politics rarely divides over defense issues, and elections do not turn on issues such as these. Furthermore, the case of the reformers is a difficult one since it argues neither for the status quo nor for a radical change. This is especially the case when it attempts to distinguish between types of nuclear weapons in terms of whether they promote stability. The strength of the reformer's position is that it is much more attainable than is the transformer's position. It is an incremental move away from the current situation and builds upon some of the assumptions of those who support the status quo. In an era of financial constraint, it may be the only alternative and, for this reason, the position of the reformers may well be the norm within the next few years.

A SYSTEM-TRANSFORMER PERSPECTIVE ON NUCLEAR ISSUES

As was discussed in Chapter 1, there are many versions of how to transform the international system or specific policy-related systems. These include those favoring complete nuclear disarmament as well as the more optimistic support of SDI as the only way to rid the earth of nuclear weapons. For the purposes of our discussion, transformers will be defined as those who want to abolish nuclear weapons completely and who would oppose SDI as just another spiral in the arms race.

System-Transformer Descriptions of the Nuclear-Arms Issue

What is the Basic Characteristic of the Issue?
According to transformers, the current situation threatens the survival of the human race. Vertical proliferation threatens a war by mistake, if not one by design. Horizontal proliferation carries with it the possibility of introducing nuclear weapons into already unstable areas of the world. The problem is the existence of nuclear weapons. Although they have not been used for over forty years, their use can be only a matter of time. Even their non-use is costly, in that the presence of the nuclear threat hangs over the human race; furthermore, the measures taken to protect nuclear weapons and the secrecy that surrounds them is essentially undemocratic.

Under Present Conditions, What Kind of World is being Created?
The world that is being created is one that will see the use of nuclear weapons, simply because the world cannot continue on the brink of nuclear war indefinitely. Some leaders may want to try to win a nuclear war. Nuclear weapons are becoming so miniaturized and so accurate that their use is becoming more and more determined by computers and automatic defensive systems. At the level of horizontal proliferation, the worry is that the world is becoming accustomed to nuclear weapons and that their prominence in superpower relations is a factor likely to lead to their introduction into other regions of the world. The world being created is fraught with danger.

What Actors Play a Major Role and How do They Participate?
Transformers see the superpowers as the main actors, but stress the need for citizens to act to try to change the current situation. Transformers see participation as reflecting the self-interest of small elites who become caught up in the logic of the situation. Leaders, being responsible for national security, treat the current situation as natural or as the best possible, and their behavior is determined by this logic. As participants, the leaders are unaware of or downplay the dangers of the logic of superpower rivalry.

What are the Priorities of System Transformers?
System transformers are concerned with attacking the root cause of the prob-

lem, which they see as nuclear weapons. These must be abolished, not merely reduced, and they must not be introduced into other areas of the world. Arms reductions are not enough, and arms control has been a cruel deception. All that arms-control agreements do is direct the arms race into certain areas rather than others.

For transformers, the system of decisionmaking is far too secretive and elitist. Decisions on nuclear issues must be brought firmly into the public domain, where leaders are unable to hide behind secrecy or justifications of national security.

System-Transformer Explanations

What are the Relevant Theoretical Explanations of This Nuclear Competition?
Nuclear competition occurs because national leaders take too nationalistic a view of events. What is needed is an internationalist perspective, not an ethnocentric one. The pressures toward a superpower arms race and toward further nuclear proliferation reflect the anarchic nature of international society. Therefore, overcoming the nuclear problem will require a change in the structure of the international system. Within societies, the nuclear issue is reflected in the elite nature of decisionmaking and in the increasingly secretive nature of debate. The problem persists because the anarchic and elitist structure of international society persists. Only when national leaders no longer have the power to place national interests above those of humanity, will the problem be overcome. The competitive behavior of states is caused by the unwillingness of leaders to accept the authority of international bodies and by their refusal to give up their right to undertake whatever they consider necessary to ensure the security of the state.

The Future of Nuclear Issues

What are Possible Future Scenarios?
Transformers worry that nuclear war will occur between the superpowers. Nuclear deterrence cannot last forever and, by miscalculation or by mistake, war will occur. With regard to horizontal proliferation, they fear that there will be many new nuclear powers by the end of the century and that this will lead to nuclear war.

System transformers' policy agenda consists of a fundamental restructuring of national defense. Nuclear weapons must be abolished, with international verification. Nuclear-free zones should be established and nuclear defense should be replaced by, at most, conventional forces.

What is the Future Role of State and Non-State Actors?
The control of nuclear competition must be a multilateral process, since no one state will be willing to lead the way. This requires a strengthening of interna-

tional agencies and a cross-national set of pressure groups. Non-state actors will be crucial; they will serve as lobby groups that the public will use to gain access to public officials. Those non-state actors dedicated to disarmament will put pressure on governments to give up nuclear weapons.

Is it Possible to Control Conflict?
System transformers believe that if the public mobilizes and puts pressure on governments to rid the world of nuclear weapons, the escalating arms race will be controlled. If the public does not do so, the survival of the human race will be threatened. Disarmament carries with it the hope of a peaceful means of resolving disputes because it both increases international trust and cooperation and removes a major threat to world peace.

Policy Prescriptions—A System-Transformer View

System transformers offer many policy prescriptions, but most are concerned with reducing the role of nuclear weapons in national arsenals or, as in the case of the British Labour Party, removing nuclear weapons from the country's soil. All prescriptions attempt to foster a period of greater international understanding and cooperation.

The strengths of the system-transformer worldview are that it is emotionally appealing and carries the promise of a better, more secure world. But it suffers from enormous weaknesses. Not only is it so utopian as to be practically unfeasible, it also involves considerable risks. It is not at all obvious that a world without nuclear weapons would be as stable as the present world. Would reducing the role of nuclear weapons make the world safe for conventional wars? This was certainly the view of many European leaders when they heard of President Reagan's plan to abolish intermediate-range ballistic missiles within ten years. Also, it requires a radical transformation of domestic political systems for it to be implemented. Even if this were possible in the United States, would it be possible in the Soviet Union or in potential proliferators? Finally, to be fully effective, the abolition of nuclear weapons requires a different kind of international system. How can this be achieved?

CONCLUSION

This chapter has looked at how the three worldviews deal with issues concerning nuclear weapons. It would be pointless to attempt some kind of conclusion that offered an opinion on the "correct" worldview. All that is necessary is to point out that each worldview attempts to make sense of the central paradox of nuclear weapons. *The crucial problem is how to move into the next century given the existence of nuclear weapons.* It is clear that most people would prefer that nuclear weapons had never been invented, that some arms-control agreement had restricted them at birth. The problem is that they do exist, that the superpowers have so many of them, and that several other countries can soon be expected to possess them. Appeals to emotion, common sense, or to arguments that start from the premise that the world should not be as it is, are unclear and misleading guides on how to accommodate the dynamism inherent in technology within structures and processes that encourage stability. Because this writer is concerned that the cost of the maintainers' position might be an unconstrained arms race that could lead into a period of gross instability, and because the transformers could usher in a period of rapid and unpredictable change, his sympathies lie with the reformers. At the end of the day the crucial factor is not the direction of change in the nuclear relationship, but its pace.

REFERENCES

Bundy, McGeorge, G. F. Kennan, R. S. McNamara, and Gerard Smith. "The President's Choice: Star Wars or Arms Control." *Foreign Affairs* 63 (Winter 1984–1985):264–278.

Calder, Nigel. *Nuclear Nightmares*. New York: Penguin, 1981.

Dyson, Freeman. *Weapons and Hope*. New York: Harper and Row, 1984.

Gray, Colin. "The Case for a Theory of Victory." *International Security* 4 (Summer 1974):63–87.

Jervis, Robert. *The Illogic of U.S. Nuclear Strategy*. Ithaca, NY: Cornell University Press, 1984.

Mandelbaum, Michael. *The Nuclear Future*. Ithaca, NY: Cornell University Press, 1983.

Russett, Bruce. *Prisoners of Insecurity*. San Francisco: W. H. Freeman, 1983.

Schell, Jonathan. *The Fate of the Earth*. New York: Alfred A. Knopf, 1983.

Tucker, Robert. "The Nuclear Debate." *Foreign Affairs* 63 (Fall 1984):1–32.

4

Trade: Politics and Markets

ROGER TOOZE

The contending-worldviews framework used by the authors of this book is particularly well suited to untangle the complex interactions of politics and markets and the subtleties of trade as an international issue. The issue of trade is undoubtedly characterized by a high degree of political contention, both within and among states, reflecting wide differences in genuinely held views on the nature of the system, the great difficulty of achieving satisfactory rates of national economic growth in the world economy of the late 1980s, and the current frustration felt by governments and peoples alike in the face of apparently intractable trade problems. As often happens in international issues, the perceived intractability of the problems leads to a hardening of views, with "our" view increasingly regarded as the *only* legitimate one (hence, the "truth" of the matter), and with national policy in turn reflecting the hardening of view.

Clearly, trade is now a major international issue in the relations among the advanced industrial countries (AICs) and between the AICs and the Third World. But the trade issue has to be understood in a much wider context than just as the political issue of the day, at least if states are to resolve longer-term problems. This chapter will look at three interrelated elements in order to provide a necessary context for understanding worldview positions presented later in the chapter. The issues reviewed include: the evolution of the international trade order (or regime), where order means "the framework of rules, regulations, conventions and norms" governing trade relations between states (Cohen 1977, 3); the development of the world economy and the changing role of trade in that economy; and the implications of the forgoing for national trade policies. Because of the complex nature of the interaction of these elements we shall first consider trade as an international issue before assessing the development of the international trade system.

TRADE AS AN INTERNATIONAL ISSUE: CONCEPTS AND ASSUMPTIONS

Markets do not exist in a political vacuum; they need a framework of order to provide a minimum of stability for their continued existence and function. A minimum of regulation for transactions usually involves a procedure for disputes within the framework of a set of broadly shared assumptions as to what constitutes an acceptable market structure and acceptable market processes. Since the emergence of the state system, this framework has been provided by the authority of the state for trade within its jurisdiction and by various extensions of the state for international trade. The international market is established and maintained either by the extension of power of a single state (directly through empire or indirectly through hegemon), or by the cooperation of a group of states (with or without a hegemon). (Krasner 1976, Krasner 1983, Keohane 1984) Whatever the structure, trade between states cannot be carried out without order and stability. Because of this, and because international trade is conceptualized as trade between *national* economies, international trade has always been political, in the narrow sense that it involves government and in the broader sense that it is part of the process of "who gets what and how."

Much contemporary conventional wisdom, often offered as "fact" by economists, claims that trade is, or should be, purely economic and that government should not interfere with economic processes. The problem is that this view and the assumptions within it have become accepted wisdom and often constitute the basis of national policy, but it does not seem adequate for conceptualization of the trade problem in the 1980s and may obstruct our understanding.

A Conventional Analysis of International Trade

In the conventional view, international trade takes place when firms and consumers in one country find it in their interest (here, defined as price and profit) to sell to and buy from firms and consumers in another country. Trade theory traditionally bases this action on the doctrine of natural comparative advantage, derived from the writings of David Ricardo in the eighteenth century. Economics now has a number of competing trade theories, none of which provides an adequate analysis of trade in today's complex world economy. Whatever the explanation, international trade, by increasing exchange relationships based on economic specialization among national economies, has the effect of changing the nature of the relationships among states by creating economic interdependence. The nature and consequences of this interdependence are much disputed. (Keohane and Nye 1977, Waltz 1979, and Jones and Willetts 1984) Yet, at a minimum, interdependence makes international trade difficult to ignore in any domestic political discussion. The salience and potential controversy associated with trade will often depend on the extent to which any one state is dependent on trade.

In the much-simplified schematic model of the system given in Exhibit 4.1, the international economy is composed of exchange relationships (e.g., goods exchanged for money) between separate national economies within the context of an international economic order that is determined by the governments of the participating national economies. In this model, governments are also considered important economic entities—major producers and consumers. Within this conventional model, trade becomes an international issue when change in the exchange relationships harms or threatens to harm the interests of members of the national economies. Those individuals who feel disadvantaged by the trade system then pressure their governments to take domestic policy action or to pressure foreign governments and/or foreign economic actors to change their behavior. Government may seek to pressure other actors directly through economic diplomacy or indirectly through reference to the "rules of the game."

Alternatively, governments and the agencies of government often initiate international trade issues in their role as mediators between the domestic economy and the international economy. The growth in importance of the international economy for most citizens in all states has forced governments to accept the need to intervene in the free market in order to modify the effects of international economic conditions. As Stanley Hoffman indicates, national leaders and citizens alike are frustrated by conditions, events, and decisions which appear beyond their control:

> The international economy, manipulated by its members, operates as a constant but unpredictable system of double distribution—of incomes, jobs, status within nations, and wealth and power among nations. But the domestic victims of this redistribution do not acknowledge the legitimacy of a haphazard or shifty mechanism that is *external* to the nation and competes or conflicts with the internal redistribution schemes that have been legitimately, authoritatively, or imperatively set up within the confines of the nation. (Hoffman 1978, cited in Anell 1981, 195, emphasis added)

This means that governments have constantly to respond to developments (or ensure that only certain developments come about) at the level of the international economy in order to maintain their own legitimacy as governments. But at the same time as citizens' expectations of their government's ability to manage the domestic economy have grown, many governments have found that interdependence undermines their ability to manage their domestic economies. Hence, providing for the economic needs of their citizens requires that national leaders develop the capacity to control the international economy. (Anell 1981 and Rosecrance 1986)

The actions taken by a government on the issue of trade can be internal to the national economy. For example, governments can change the terms of access to the national market through tariffs or quotas, or give support in the form of tax concessions or federal aid for its own national exports. Governments may also attempt to influence the economic policies of foreign governments and the

Exhibit 4.1 The International Economy

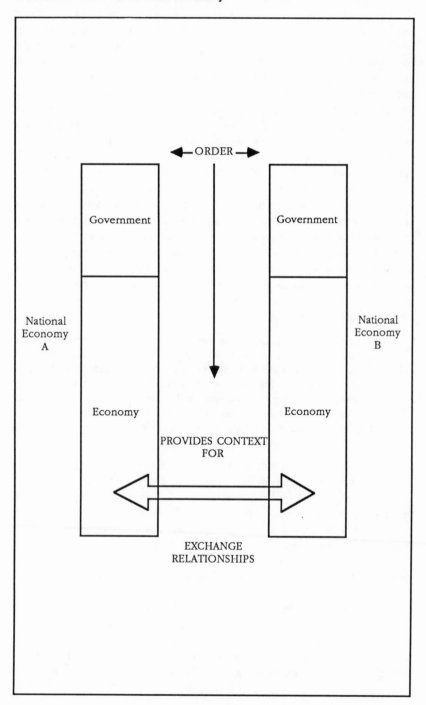

behavior of foreign economic entities by providing incentives in the form of aid or preferential treatment, or by threatening the implementation of restrictive trade sanctions. Governments may elect to resolve trade disputes at the multilateral level by referring to the "order" under which trade takes place. This involves attempting to reinforce the norms or to take advantage of any procedure or institution created to resolve disputes. If the order contains understanding about what is or is not acceptable as the basis for international trade, then each of the actions taken by government, even those purely domestic, can become an *international* issue because of their consequences for trade. One implication of this is that both at a conceptual and a policy level it is very difficult to distinguish between what is "domestic" policy and what is "foreign" or external trade policy.

With the model in Exhibit 4.1 in mind, one can see that in the case of the United States, for instance, trade was conducted principally within the international trade order set up by the United States after World War II. For leaders in the United States, trade was not generally perceived to be a major international issue so long as the majority of trading nations kept within the accepted norms of the international trade order. The political problems that did emerge were generally dealt with within the disputes procedure of the order—the General Agreement on Tariffs and Trade (GATT). However, as the U.S. economy became more integrated into the international economy with the dramatic increase of U.S. exports (5 percent of gross domestic product [GDP] in 1965 to 9 percent of GDP in 1979), other developments, such as fluctuations in exchange rates and increases in production costs, made U.S. goods less competitive. Coincidently, the international economic order became less effective as a context for trade for rich and poor states alike. These developments were reflected in the U.S. trade balance, which moved into a deficit. The U.S. economy was now much more sensitive to change in the international economy and many more people were affected by the shifts in trade preferences. Those labor and economic interest groups that were hurt economically by the loss of exports or the increase in imports used their political power to try to get the government to do something to alleviate the situation. What the U.S. government was able to do and how it was able to do it was, and still is, partly conditioned by the long-term values which constitute U.S. economic interests and define U.S. trade policy, and partly by the values which have been built in to the international trade order. These values will be considered in the second part of the chapter, because these values identify the worldviews of system maintainers, reformers, or transformers.

Measuring the Flow of Trade in Goods and Services

The model of the international economy presented earlier broadly represents the nature of trade as portrayed by most conventional analyses and, indeed, by most governments. Similarly, the model reflects the traditional means of measuring economic relations between national economies—the trade figures.

National trade figures measure, or attempt to measure, the flows of exchanges across national economic boundaries and among national economies, in two categories: visible trade (i.e., goods and commodities) and invisible trade (i.e., services such as banking, transport, insurance, etc.) Hence, the concept of a trade surplus or deficit refers to the sum of these flows over a period of time. Given the current political sensitivity of the terms "surplus" and "deficit," it is important to be aware of exactly what they signify.

Apart from the difficulty of measuring the actual flow of invisibles, there is the key question of how trade is measured—in value or in volume terms. The problem is not just academic: The impact of trade figures on political sentiment and on the foreign exchange market (and hence on the competitiveness of a country's exports and the level of a country's inflation generated by imports) is immense. In this era of rapidly moving exchange rates, trade figures expressed in, say, U.S. dollars look very different from those expressed in Japanese yen. Similarly, exports or imports measured in volume terms may tell a different story. A recent article in *The Economist* illustrates an aspect of the exchange rate dilemma: "In 1986, Japan's trade surplus with America either increased by 30.1% to $51.4 billion or fell by 7.6% to ¥8.7 trillion. While the yen value of Japan's imports fell by 30.7%, the volume of Japan's imports rose by 12.5%." (4 April 1987, 67) The problem of measurement is here a crucial one because of the political impact of the figures. Any presentation of unfavorable monthly trade figures can easily lead to a rapid increase in political tension in already tense situations.

A more fundamental criticism of trade figures, and of the model on which they are based, is that the model only measures what crosses national boundaries and does not take into account international production. What is missed includes goods and services produced by foreign affiliates of nationally owned corporations outside the national economy—the production of IBM outside of the United States, for example. International production of goods and services constitutes a second layer in the economic relationships among national economies and coexists with the exchange/trade-based relationships. (Michalet 1982) The point here is that the traditional model and the conventional trade figures derived from this model do not adequately present a comprehensive view of the nature of economic relations between AICs.

The impact of revising commonly accepted conceptualizations of economic relationships to include the effects of international production would be significant. First, it would provide the analyst with a more complex model of economic relations, with two coexisting forms—a traditional international economy based on exchange among national economies and a more contemporary world economy based on the international structure of production and services. This is a far more accurate reflection of the complexities facing governments in their attempts to manage economic growth and international trade than a more simple model which focuses almost exclusively on the economic activities between states. Second, one can draw very different conclusions about the nature and significance of trade, trade deficits and surpluses, and neo-mercantilist problems like protectionism from a more comprehensive model. For instance, if trade analysts include the production of U.S.-owned firms in Japan, the sales of which were on average four times larger than the two countries' trade balance between 1965/66 and 1983/84, the picture of a huge Japanese trade surplus with the United States is significantly altered. *(The Economist,* 11 April 1987, 70) This suggests that the whole problem of protectionism looks very different once the nature and extent of international production is taken into account. (Strange 1985)

In spite of the limitations of existing trade figures and the confusion associated with defining the various international markets, it is clear that trade has become a critical foreign-policy issue; protectionism has become an evil at the international level and a favored policy at the national level. To understand these issues one must review the development of the international trading system, particularly since the end of World War II. Additionally, the student of international political economy must also explore the structural consequences of interdependence, particularly as "interdependence only constrains national policy if leaders accept and agree to work within its limits." (Rosecrance 1986, 141) The next section of this chapter presents an overview of the trading system, identifying those values that underlay trade relationships and that initially brought about the international agreement to work within the limits of the international trade order.

THE SYSTEM OF INTERNATIONAL TRADE SINCE 1945

For the purposes of this chapter much of the interest in analyzing the nature of trade as an international issue comes from the deliberately political use of the language of international trade by governments and other authors in an effort to rationalize and legitimize judgments and values and to further their policy objectives. Labels commonly used by political elites, like "free trade," "protectionism," "fair trade," and "the liberal trading order," represent emotional appeals to an idealized image of the system of world trade rather than a clear and verifiable representation of the system itself. The political nature of trade debates is most obvious in the issue of protectionism. There is disagreement about what objectively constitutes protectionism and whether it is in fact a major threat to the continuance of the system, as liberal orthodoxy claims. (Strange 1985) The orthodox image of the trade system usually presented is the classical liberal framework of unfettered free trade, which is based on Ricardo's theory of comparative advantage. It is assumed that free trade will lead to increased wealth for everyone. However, this image of the international economy is more than a neutral viewpoint. It embodies powerful values in the symbol of "progress" and consequently determines the rights and wrongs of international trade. In the words of President Reagan: "the advance of nations [is] itself bound up with the advance of free trade." (White House Briefing, 17 July 1986) Such a powerful ideological image of free trade confers legitimacy on those who support free-trade policies and makes anything detracting from the ideal of free trade undesirable, inappropriate, and antiestablishment.

Identifying Different Worldviews

Given all the political rhetoric on free trade, it would seem logical to assume that the international trading system is therefore based on the classical liberal framework, making it very easy to identify different worldviews. However, the post-1945 trade system was *not* the same as the idealized image. Although still referred to as a liberal trade order, the liberalism embodied in the modern trade system is necessarily conditioned by the needs of states to ensure domestic stability. (Ruggie 1983 and Spero 1981) The result is what John Ruggie has called "embedded liberalism" (1983, 209–214) and differs in key respects from the image presented by the traditional free-trade ideology. Not until one makes the distinction between the image of free trade and the reality—necessary compromise between the needs of the international system and the specific political and economic needs of individual states—can one clearly identify the nature of the contemporary international trade system.

It is also clear that each worldview has its own conception of what actually constitutes *the* system of trade. This means that what is "reform" in one worldview may be "transformation" in another. For example, the reaction of the majority of AICs to the trade-system reforms incorporated and defined in the demands for a New International Economic Order (NIEO) was to define the NIEO itself as a threat of transformation. Hence, for the trade issue what actually constitutes the system is itself problematic, and any prior identification of a worldview by this author, or any other, as "maintaining," "reforming," or "transforming" the system, reflects a particular set of values.

The Core Elements of the Modern Trading System

Notwithstanding the caveats above, one can identify, within the context of historical change, the core elements of the modern trading system clearly enough for the purposes of this chapter. Historically, the integration of national economies into an international economy through trade and investment policies, and the successful working of that international economy, was achieved through the subordination of the domestic economies of the participating states to the achievement of stability and efficiency in the international economy. (Polanyi 1957 and Ruggie 1983) The mechanisms of this subordination were free trade and the international gold standard (IGS), the latter acting as an automatic payments system. Two points are important here. First, it is impossible to consider the trading system and the issue of trade without also considering the payments system (i.e., the international money system). It is the money system that facilitates trade between national economies and provides sufficient acceptable international money to allow for the growth of international trade. The United States was the provider of this liquidity through the international role of the dollar in the 1950s and early 1960s. It is also the money system that sets the eventual costs of exports and imports through the exchange rate. No matter how efficient a country's production might be, if the exchange rate for that country's currency is not appropriate, all efforts to improve exports through price competitiveness will fail. Secondly, free trade and the IGS together ensured that each national economy, given the political commitment to the common purpose of the system, automatically adjusted to the needs of its external balances. If a country was in balance-of-payments difficulties, the economy would be deflated (i.e., costs would be cut) until that country's exports were again competitive and external balances improved.

In this way, the adjustment mechanism put the needs of the international system, or the external position of the state, before the needs and interests of the domestic economy. The primacy of the international system was justified in terms of the overall benefits of increased global wealth and made possible by the internationalist elite that benefitted most from the trade system. With the growth of the modern national political economy an adjustment process that was perceived to put the interests of the system before the interest of the domestic economy became politically unacceptable. The constituencies of states became much larger and governments increasingly gained or lost their legitimacy and popularity on the success of their macroeconomic policies in achieving growth and stability. In the post-1945 system of international trade, it has become a political necessity to incorporate a critical compromise between the benefits and imperatives of international trade—to be spread through U.S.-led multilateralism—and the need for domestic stability.

The ensuing trade system was, and still is, based on this sometimes uneasy compromise. The system for free trade was a broad goal to be achieved over time, rather than a set of conditions to be imposed. Free trade was, particularly for the United States, a strategic long-term goal of the system, in that liberalism links economic well-being and economic interdependence with the limitation of war. However, for reasons of national security and domestic stability there were always exceptions to the general goal of free trade. The principal exceptions were agriculture (and those other sectors considered essential to the maintenance of national security) and regional trade organizations, such as the European Community, which encouraged free trade within their boundaries, stimulated economic development and, in the context of the 1950s, acted as an economic deterrent to communism. However, such were the imperatives of *national* economic management that the trade system, institutionalized in GATT, in effect provided many escapes and procedures for "injured parties" to win compensation. The key principles of multilateralism, tariff reduction, and, perhaps most important of all, nondiscrimination were incorporated into the trade order, as was the principle of reciprocity. This was largely a result of the extraordinary power and perseverance of the United States and not a result of a wider international commitment to free trade. (Ruggie 1983, 213) Hence, as Ruggie (1983, 214) points out, to view the postwar order as liberal, "but with lots of cheating taking place on the domestic side," not only "fails to capture the full complexity of the embedded liberalism compromise," but from the point of view of the argument developed here also constitutes an inappropriate basis for the analysis of the trade issue.

By the beginning of the 1960s economic and political considerations had changed to the extent that the needs of the majority of individual Western economies were indeed best served by a process of international trade liberalization. A flurry of activity reduced tariffs through a series of "rounds" of trade negotiations. In retrospect these negotiations clearly emphasized the importance of multilateralism and reciprocity as key elements in achieving tariff reduction. At the same time, the GATT talks highlighted the immense difficulties of negotiating on trade, stemming particularly from the problems of measuring reciprocity. (Curzon and Curzon 1976) Nevertheless, this period saw an increase in liberalization correlated with a significant increase in economic growth and, consequently, an increase in the legitimacy of the liberal order and the GATT process.

One important effect of the success of liberalization was that the liberal values, institutionalized in the GATT, that formed the basis of the postwar international trade order were reinforced. The ideology of the trade system was based on specific values or assumptions. (Aho and Aronson 1985, 17) Among these assumptions are:

1. A multilateral framework is preferable to a bilateral one.
2. Unrestricted and non-discriminatory trade will promote economic efficiency and growth in all trading countries.
3. If trade is conducted by private actors in competitive markets driven by supply and demand, efficiency and growth will be maximized.
4. Government intervention—which distorts the market, delays domestic adjustment, and hampers growth and efficiency—should be avoided.

The Rise of Protectionism

The trade liberalization achieved in the 1960s took place in a context of rapid economic growth for the world economy and during a period of relative political stability in the relations among the major trading nations. This stability was underpinned by U.S. hegemony. None of these factors was present during the 1970s when the "decline of production coincided with and intensified a number of structural problems that had long been on their way to the surface." (Anell 1981, 51) Significantly, the adjustments needed to resolve these structural problems had been made more difficult by the "long boom" of the 1960s. That long boom enabled the emergence of a more plural distribution of economic power, which heightened interdependence and made it more difficult for governments to manage economic affairs. By the time of the first oil shocks in 1973 and 1974, monetary and production problems had already subjected the international economic order to severe stress; trade reflected this stress. Protectionism became more a part of the state's response to the stresses of the system, both in the United States and the European Community. Underlying the trade problem, however, was inflation and national leaders' seeming inability to do much about it, coupled with a change in the nature of U.S. power in the international system. Perhaps more than anything else, this phase in the development of the world economy was marked by uncertainty: Without adequate levels of growth, which had averaged over 5 percent in the seven leading industrial countries from the end of the 1950s to 1973, traditional macroeconomic policies could not be successful. Uncertainty was also the product of the perceived weakening of the international trade order, through a marked revival of "neomercantilism" in trade relations. Neomercantilism is "a policy whereby a state seeks to maintain a balance-of-trade surplus by reducing imports, stimulating home production, and promoting exports." (Blake and Walters 1976, and Malmgren 1970) However, the greatest uncertainty derived from the changes in the international money system. (Strange 1986)

The multitude of changes that occurred in the trade system meant that the structure of the system was very different at the beginning of the 1980s than in 1945. The pattern of trade had grown in volume, value, and spread, and although the largest growth in trade was among the AICs themselves, other states, particularly those labelled the Newly Industrialized Countries (NICs), were now a key part of the trade system. Within this changed pattern, the economies of Japan and West Germany came to special prominence as competitors to the U.S. economy. The United States was beginning to face the consequences of a balance-of-trade deficit that had for some time been identified as a major weakness.

While the trade system had become global and more complex, the relationship of trade to money and investment had also changed as it had become increasingly difficult to separate these elements of the world economy. Less and less trade conformed to the classical model and more trade was "intrafirm" (i.e., trade that takes place within the same enterprise worldwide), with the implications that were discussed in the first section. By 1980, the international money system had greatly affected trade, principally because the volatility of exchange rates engendered uncertainty for trade relationships.

At the level of the international trade order, the core principles and their underlying values became increasingly contested. As conditions in the world economy worsened the liberal values were challenged by neomercantilist responses from states in which the adjustment process was proving very difficult. The fundamental liberal assumption that structured the international order, that through free trade mutual gains are possible, increasingly tended to be replaced by the view that trade policy "is a strategic game in which national economic gains can only be reaped at another's expense." (Aho and Aronson 1985, 23)

The agreements reached at the end of the Tokyo Round of trade talks in

1979, although heralded by the "free traders" as a continued affirmation of free-trade values over protectionism, did, in fact, only "legitimate a more differentiated international economic order." Under this order, "rules and behavior have become more fragmented. Different countries and different sectors are treated in different ways." (Krasner 1987, 360) The fragmentation of the trade order was a direct result of the dominance of particularistic interests over the general interest in the continued maintenance of a free-trade regime. In the terms we have used in this analysis, it is yet one more outcome in the process of negotiating the compromise of embedded liberalism—a compromise which leads to an increasing challenge to free-trade principles. Most notably, the principle of multilateralism was challenged, as an increasing number of governments dealt with their trade problems on a bilateral and informal (i.e., outside of the GATT) basis. For example, in automobile trade voluntary export restraints were negotiated between Japan and the United States and between Japan and members of the European Community. Whatever the economic impact of bilateralism, and its negative effects are often exaggerated (Strange 1985), one political result is to identify bilateral trading relationships and hence specific other countries as keys to short-term adjustment and as targets for political action. Political action in the multilateral framework, which is probably the only long-term way forward, is far more difficult for governments to "sell" to their constituencies. (Anell, 1981)

The focus on bilateral trade balances had led easily in political terms to the notion that for an individual country *each* bilateral trade relationship should be roughly in an actual balance where exports equal imports. So, in the case of the United States, Japan's trade surplus with the United States should be replaced by a situation in which Japan's exports to the United States should be matched by U.S. exports to Japan. However, more than this, the disaggregation of trade into bilateral relationships enables the political identification of a particular country (or countries) as the main problem, and hence facilitates the transfer of blame. It seems that the political systems of the AICs are far more willing and able to deal with specific, easily identifiable problems than to come to grips with longer-term structural needs, although the current Uruguay Round of GATT talks may achieve some change in the international trade order.

The rise of protectionism is widely regarded as a major threat to the world economy partly because of its economic effects and partly because of its assumed potential to undermine the international trade order. (Blackhurst, *et al*. 1977) The post-1945 trade system not only clearly allowed protection, but altered what was or was not acceptable according to the needs of the dominant economy—the United States. Why then is protectionism such an issue in the 1980s? Part of the answer is that protection is an easier policy choice for governments, especially when citizens are demanding action. This type of response is far less difficult than trying to tackle systemic problems. A second part of the explanation lies in the complex relationship between trade and the international financial system. However, protectionism is an issue in the 1980s primarily because governments, principally the U.S. government, say it is a major economic problem.

The World Economy in the 1980s

In addition to changes in the national patterns of trade and in the international trade order, the role of trade in the world economy has also changed. With the increased pace of internationalization of production and services, particularly banking and finance, the world economy often dominates the traditional international economy of trade among national economies. The complexity of the global economy is illustrated by the following quote:

> What happens to the economy of nations, whether in 'North' or 'South', of cities such as Birmingham or Buenos Aires, Seoul or St. Louis, Toronto or Tokyo, Melbourne or Munich is determined increasingly by their changing position in a system of production and trade which has become more and more global in extent. (Dicken 1986, 3)

International production directly integrates sectors and people into a world, as opposed to a national structure. In an important sense, these sectors partially sidestep the control of the state, although the relationship between the state and the economy of world production is extremely complex.

In the 1980s, such is the degree of integration of national economies that it is impossible to separate the many issues and problems of the world economy; for example, the link between the U.S. trade deficit, the U.S. budget deficit, external value of the dollar, and economic growth in the rest of the world seems clear. According to Lester Thurow (1985, 25), writing before the 1986 fall in the U.S. dollar, "Whenever the dollar falls and the American trade deficit unwinds, the recovery in the rest of the world stops." Moreover, the resolution of the trade issue is increasingly linked to the performance and reform of the international financial structure. (Strange 1986 and Thurow 1985) In such an integrated world economy, neither large deficits (e.g., the United States) nor large surpluses (e.g., Japan and West Germany), with their necessary money flows, can be the basis of a stable international order that produces economic growth. Unfortunately, domestic change is often difficult and unpleasant. Furthermore, domestic leaders begin to define power as the extent to which a state can put the brunt of change on others.

TRADE ISSUES: A WORLDVIEWS ANALYSIS

At all levels of change in the trade system, governments are finding it very difficult to achieve their economic and political objectives. The difficulties for policymakers can hardly be exaggerated. For example, Aho and Aronson (1985, 24–32) consider *ten* major developments that have changed the nature of the trade system and of international resolution of trade problems. The complexity of the trade issue, and the fact that it is really impossible to know enough about all these changes, is heightened by a trade system that is in a continual state of flux as states and transnational enterprises respond to new technology and new political conditions and pressures. To make a worldviews analysis possible one needs to take a very broad view of the system, based on the background assessment offered so far. One must be prepared to admit that the three categories may not be watertight and the generalizations that emerge from each worldview may not always be appropriate. However, the worldviews approach at least goes some way towards promoting an understanding of this intractable international political issue.

System-Maintainer Perspectives

Any system of international trade needs to be supported by ideological, political, and economic factors. One or two of these elements can maintain the system temporarily; however, without all three, it is unlikely that the system will survive any unexpected shocks. Hence, the present trade system may be becoming increasingly unstable as the costs of its maintenance are perceived to outweigh the benefits, and the difficulties of managing the system become greater. (Krasner 1987 and Thurow 1985) At present there is a disjunction between the ideology of liberal free trade and the economic and political conditions necessary to sustain a free-trade system. If the interests of the dominant economies are perceived as no longer served by the system, the international economic system will be changed. The ideology that legitimates the system, as well as giving it purpose and meaning, will also change. Whatever the form of the international trade system that emerges from the current crisis, it will serve the interests of the dominant economies and not the economic interests of all actors participating in the system. In this sense, the trade system has always reflected the economic, political, and strategic interests of the strong and powerful. Thus, to identify the strong economies as system maintainers is a truism because the current trade system would not exist *unless* the major economic powers maintained it. Similarly, as the trade system serves the interests of the economically strong states, one cannot expect those interests to be shared by all states, or even by individuals or groups within rich and poor states alike.

The Ideal of Liberal Free Trade

Bearing in mind all the qualifications previously discussed, the system maintainers promote an economic and political system represented by the ideal of liberal free trade and the values and assumptions inherent in this ideal. Simply stated, free trade among private actors in competitive markets within a multilateral framework, without government intervention, will promote the maximization of efficiency and growth. The actuality is the continuously fluid but necessary compromise of "embedded liberalism," with the needs of domestic stability and domestic interests countervailing the imperatives of the continuous domestic adjustment of free trade.

Clearly, although the ideal is constantly referred to in the political disputes among trading states, it is used more as an absolute standard, an ideological touchstone, to identify deviations in the progress toward the goal and to reaffirm the goal itself. No AICs have yet denied the validity of the free-trade analysis; however, they all, to a greater or lesser extent, use some form of protection or discrimination in their trade practices. Hence, what characterizes and describes the system for the maintainers is the combination of free trade values, allowable exceptions, and a commitment to some form of multilateral negotiating framework, usually in the form of the GATT rounds.

When defined in this way, the system maintainers are the AICs and those non-AICs (e.g., Hong Kong, South Korea, Taiwan, Singapore, and sometimes, Brazil, Mexico, and Argentina) who have decided to "play by the rules" of the existing trade system. The organizations of the liberal trade order, particularly the GATT, uphold the policy interests of the system-maintainer states and the financial interests of many transnational enterprises or multinational corporations. Within states, those economists who support free trade and who have influence in policy formation are important maintainers. Traditionally, and logically, multinational corporations (MNCs) have been critical system maintainers because their very existence depends on an open world economy. These actors do not always agree with interventions of government or public in the economic system. For example, MNCs do not take kindly to governments that attempt to shift the consequences of domestic economic adjustment to other countries by exporting unemployment. Thus, U.S. business leaders with a large stake in Europe would hardly encourage their government to take steps to export U.S. employment to other industrial countries, for this would only depress their own holdings abroad. (Rosecrance 1986, 149) However, given the creation of trade barriers, investment incentives, and other "distortions" to the liberal order, MNCs have rapidly responded to the changed production and trade environment. Now, the MNCs, "grandfathered in countries behind trade barriers or investment distortions benefit from them," and these firms may support a standstill on these restrictions rather than any move toward less restriction. (Aho and Aronson 1985, 30)

The system maintainers' view of the trade debates is straightforward. They believe that trade problems have arisen because of a move away from the progress toward a liberal order. If this trend continues, with protectionism being the principal indicator, trade conflicts will turn to trade wars; trade wars will inevitably change the security relationships among the AICs.

Resolution of trade conflicts will be achieved through the maximum participation of governments in the renewal of the progress toward free trade through supporting the authority of the GATT. Critical to this process will be the actions of the most significant governments, defined in terms of economic and trade power. The United States, with Japan and West Germany, is the most important actor in this policy arena. Other significant actors include Great Britain, France, Italy, and Canada. All together, these countries comprise the

Group of Seven. This group meets frequently in economic summit conferences. Other AICs (e.g., the Netherlands and Sweden) are critical actors but not rule makers. Also important are those NICs and Third World countries that have either a significant trading presence or are seen as key political actors in the trade negotiations, such as Argentina, Brazil, and India.

For the system maintainer, international trade increases overall wealth because it leads to greater efficiency. Efficiency is the core value, which is both promoted and legitimated. Efficiency leads to greater production worldwide and is thus the sole criterion of economic organization. Efficiency is only achieved through the economic processes of the market; international trade is efficient as long as it reflects and is a product of these economic processes. Thus, trade tends to be separated from international money structures and from international security. Furthermore, trade is conceptualized, in policy and intellectual terms, as a distinct and self-contained process of the international system.

This explanation says little about the distribution of the wealth produced through international trade or when this wealth will be created. A system maintainer is content to suggest that the "trickle-down" process will eventually lead to everyone sharing global wealth. Those who hold this view are not concerned with justice as such, either in the production and distribution of value or in the nature of the trade relationship. In the idealized version of free trade, these omissions are not considered of any great importance, or even as omissions because, unless and until trade is efficient other values cannot be achieved. (Ward 1979)

System-Maintainer Policy Prescriptions
Within this theoretical overview there are many divergent views and policies normally related to whom should bear the costs of adjustment; however, in general, the current policy debate assumes the fragmented trade order as a basis and is thus confined within the system-maintaining worldview. As the domestic needs of the dominant national economies are critical, the needs of the largest (e.g., the United States, Japan, and West Germany) will dominate trade issues. In terms of production, until the immediate domestic problems of these dominant economies are attended to, it is unlikely that trade issues will be resolved, although once they are, and trade attains the level of growth achieved in the 1960s, the world economy will, once more, be on track for an "explosion" of wealth. Unilateral action (i.e., protectionism) is acceptable and bilateral agreements can stabilize particular trade problems; yet, "real" progress is only possible through the multilateral framework. Thus, the renegotiation of the GATT along an agenda that meets the needs of the dominant economies—in this case the move by the United States to include free trade in agriculture and services—will enable the issue to be first contained and then resolved through multilateralization. (Woolcock, *et al.* 1985)

However, we should not assume that the general belief in the validity of the liberal model produces either coherent or similar policies. Given the fragmented nature of the trade system, policies vary greatly among states and sectors; trade-policy prescriptions reflect this fragmentation. For example, both the U.S. and Japanese administrations blame each other for the present impasse; yet, both claim allegiance to the liberal trade order. Some industries, or sectors of industries, depending on their characteristics, are more or less protective in their prescriptions than others. (Lipson 1983) Similarly, public and private organizations offer a wide variety of prescriptions aimed at getting the trading system back into some sense of order—primarily an order that will benefit them and enhance their respective interests.

Any evaluation of the suggested solutions depends on whether the evaluator accepts the broad parameters of the system-maintaining worldview. Within this worldview, progress on the issues will reflect the underlying realities of economic power in the system and the extent to which the key economies are integrated into the world economy. In this sense, multilateral negotiation represents the only way to move forward, rather than a "backward" disintegration of the world economy, as Thurow (1985) suggests. There is, however, always the potential for unilateral action by the United States if the negotiations do not bring politically acceptable results. Some analysts who support this worldview are pessimistic as to the eventual outcome, because as it is now structured, the international trading system is not working. It seems clear that structural changes will be required to make the world trading system work and this requires management. Unless there is a manager actively concerned about the future of the international trade system, the system will simply disappear in a sea of protection. Most experts suggest that only the United States is capable of fulfilling this managerial role and it appears that the United States has abdicated this responsibility. (Thurow 1985, 26) Still other analysts see a free-trade order within the context of a broad liberal international economic order as structurally impossible in the conditions of the 1980s as, "unless its effects are cushioned by deliberate policy, the success of liberalism, even embedded liberalism, tends to destroy the conditions for its existence." (Keohane 1984, 35)

System-Reformer Perspectives

Those who wish either to reform or transform the trade system do so partly because of their view of the international trading system itself, in terms of its values, operation, and material consequences. However, a primary reason for advocating change is that the trading system is viewed as an integral part of a dominant international economic order and, therefore, reflects and reproduces the values and conditions of that order. Hence both reformers and transformers define the trade issues in much broader terms than do system maintainers, who view trade in a narrow, almost technical manner, defining it as AIC trade. The AIC definition reflects the largest percentage of actual world trade, but incorporates the characteristic notion that any attempt to change the rules is a device to cover for a lack of efficiency or economic organization. However, both reformers and transformers start with a different set of core values, and focus on inequality and justice as well as efficiency. To avoid any potential overlap with Chapter 5 in this book, this section will consider more narrowly the trade aspects of these worldviews, bearing in mind the essential ideological differences in the view of trade as an integral part of a dominant economic system.

Two Indicative System-Reform Views
The reformers come from: groups within the AICs who advocate change on the basis of a global view of the current world economic crisis; or from those states on the periphery of the world economy who consider themselves unjustly treated by the trade system, who are unable or unwilling to take advantage of the existing trade system, and who do not want to or cannot take the risk of system-transforming policies. The first view is represented by the work of the Independent Commission on International Development Issues (i.e., the Brandt Commission) in *North-South: A Programme for Survival* (1980) and *Common Crisis: North-South Cooperation for World Recovery* (1983); the second view is seen in the policy strategies followed by the United Nations Conference on Trade and Development (UNCTAD) created in 1964. (Nye 1973 and MacBean and Snowden 1981) This section considers the reform worldview using the Brandt Commission and UNCTAD purely as indicative reformers, as many other groups contribute to the debate.

The essence of the trade-reform view is twofold: First, that the international trade system is not, but should be, concerned with the effects of distribution—that is with justice and equality; second, that the international trade system is now truly global and should therefore reflect the needs of all peoples, not just the rich and powerful. The reform worldview defines the trade issue in global terms as opposed to AIC terms. Trade is seen by reformers as a political problem and as an issue of values. The global economy is characterized by enormous disparities of wealth; the trade system tends to reinforce these disparities. The trade system is therefore seen as an integral part of an unjust economic relationship. This occurs because the rules of international trade are made by, and for the benefit of, the AICs. In this sense, changing the institutions of the trade system, particularly the GATT, was seen as the key to reform of the trade system. By the early 1960s, the less developed countries (LDCs) had concluded that "a major source of their problems lay in the design and conduct of the western-dominated international economic institutions." (Jones 1983, 27)

The reformist analysis of UNCTAD was taken up and modified by the Brandt Commission to produce an analysis of world economic problems predicated on the two previously mentioned assumptions: that the trade system is a global system and that as presently organized, it is an inequitable system. The Brandt Commission reform strategy differs from the UNCTAD strategy in terms of the nature and direction of reform. In both reports, an emphasis is placed on the level of interdependence in the world economy, which means that further economic progress can only be achieved through viewing the world economy as a *whole*. The solution to current trade issues will not be achieved merely through inter-AIC negotiations, but should be sought through the involvement of the LDCs and should include providing them with additional real purchasing power, rather than saddling them with debt. This strategy is not seen as altruistic, but as a matter of common survival in the long term.

Both sets of reformers predict increasing marginalization of poor states unless reform takes place; the Brandt Commission reports link this more directly to the self-interest of the AICs. Reform will involve changing the rules of international trade in order to favor the disadvantaged, such changes to be negotiated in a multilateral context. The UNCTAD scheme for a "generalized system of preferences," whereby manufactured goods exported from LDCs receive nonreciprocal preferences in developed countries' markets, is one example. However, more than this, reform involves a different view of the nature of international trade itself. The essential point of the reforming worldview is the assertion of different core values for the trading system than those assumed in the system-maintaining view. The differences are highlighted in the response to the question, "What is the *purpose* of the system of international trade?" The empirical evidence on the desirability, possibility, and effects of reform can be used to come to many different conclusions; but once the ideological legitimacy of the present trade system is questioned, one must confront its purpose and effects in a critical, as opposed to a problem-solving, manner. (Cox 1981) This means acknowledging the possibility that the maintenance of the present trade system may be undesirable for *all* those engaged in trade. In this prescription, reform is unavoidable if the world is not to enter into a trade depression and all that such a major problem entails.

System-Transformer Perspectives

Trade-system transformers reject the present system of international trade essentially because they reject the system of political economy that established and now maintains the trade system. Either from the perspective of a broad ecological-based view of economic organization that rejects the structures of present capitalist political economy, or from the international perspective that rejects a capitalist trade order as an instrument of exploitation, the transformers argue that the trade issue, as defined by the maintainers, merely reproduces the existing system whereby trade is a key mechanism in the process of economic dominance. In terms of the trade issue, this section shall consider the transformer worldview encapsulated in the political movements that culminated in the demand for a New International Economic Order (NIEO).

System Transformers' Definition of the Trade Issue
The transforming worldview underlying the NIEO shares the two basic assumptions of the reformers; however, transformers see the problem as a *structural*

one that cannot be "tinkered" with and made more equitable. (Bhagwati 1977 and Hart 1983) The only way forward is to transform the system by changing the locus of power to include the LDCs. This would, indeed, be a historical transformation. The transformers' worldview is predicated on a historical analysis of the integration of national economies into the existing system, which rejects the liberal view of economic development. It incorporates, as a result of the historical analysis, key assumptions that differ radically from the maintainer view. Income inequality and political self-determination are core concerns. Moreover, these are seen as incompatible with the existing trade order because the existing system produces an asymmetrical distribution of benefits in favor of the core economies (i.e., AICs). Transformers hold that the major obstacle to the achievement of the national aspirations of poor states is the nature of the international economic system itself, rather than the failure of domestic policies in the poor states. (Blake and Walters 1976)

The Outlook for the Future
The continuance of the existing system will lead to increasing impoverishment for the poor countries as their resources are used up and their bargaining strength diminishes. Unilateral responses are possible and involve minimizing the linkages between the national economy and the world economy (i.e., self-reliance), but multilateral responses are preferable. Initially, the example of the Organization of Petroleum Exporting Countries (OPEC) provided the potential for a changed distribution of power and the political spur for actual policy strategies. (Bhagwati and Ruggie 1984) Yet, the assimilation of OPEC into the system and the unique nature of oil as a commodity soon removed the actuality of the power base. At present the transformer worldview seems stalemated in the problems among the AICs and has failed to present a viable agenda for the LDCs. (Bhagwati and Ruggie 1984) However, the strength of the transforming worldview lies in its political appeal to leaders in poor states who are struggling with numerous problems associated with economic inequality and uneven development. The transformer view presents a critical standpoint that focuses on the weaknesses of the present trade system. It is important to note that a transformer is concerned with changing the distribution of both economic and political benefits within the international system.

CONCLUSIONS

Even though the previous discussion of reformers and transformers has been truncated it is hoped that it has demonstrated the strengths and weaknesses of each worldview. The trade system-maintaining worldview is always difficult to argue against, as is any status quo view, because the assumptions that support the system become part of its structure and individuals are socialized into accepting them. To the extent that the present trade system reflects and supports the existing distribution of power in the world economy it is difficult to see many changes in the future. Most analysts suggest that the core values will remain in place unless there is a major economic catastrophe. Perhaps the most important result of considering the strength of the system-maintaining view is to understand why it is so strong a worldview. It is not a question of "right" or "wrong" in an absolute sense, but a question of core values; only when confronted by alternative values can one critically assess the attributes of the present trade system. The ability of the strong economies to define the nature of the trade system and the routes to any solution of trade issues is an aspect of power. One of the most useful definitions of power in international politics is that power is the ability to get someone else to accept your definition of the situation. The question is, whose definition?

REFERENCES

Aho, C. Michael, and Jonathan David Aronson. *Trade Talks: America Better Listen!* New York: Council on Foreign Relations, 1985.

Anell, Lars. *Recession, the Western Economies and the Changing World Order.* London: Pinter, 1981.

Bhagwati, Jagdish. *The New International Economic Order.* Cambridge, MA: MIT Press, 1977.

Bhagwati, J. N., and J. G. Ruggie, editors. *Power, Passions and Purpose: Prospects for North-South Negotiations.* Cambridge, MA: MIT Press, 1984.

Blackhurst, Richard, Marian Nicholas, and Jan Tumlir. *Trade Liberalisation, Protectionism and Interdependence.* GATT Studies in International Trade. Geneva: GATT, 1977.

Blake, David H., and Robert S. Walters. *The Politics of Global Economic Relations.* Englewood Cliffs, N.J.: Prentice-Hall, 1976.

Cohen, Benjamin J. *Organising the World's Economy.* London: Macmillan, 1977.

Cox, Robert W. "Social Forces, States and World Orders: Beyond International Relations Theory," *Journal of International Studies; Millennium* 10 (Summer 1981):126–155.

Curzon, Gerard, and Victoria Curzon. "The Management of Trade Relations in the GATT." In *International Economic Relations of the Western World, 1959-1971.* Edited by A. Shonfield. London: Oxford University Press, 1976.

Dicken, P. *Global Shift: Industrial Change in a Turbulent World.* London: Harper and Row, 1986.

The *Economist*, vol. 303, no. 7492. London: 4 April 1987, 67.

The *Economist*, vol. 303, no. 7493. London: 11 April 1987, 70.

Hart, Jeffrey A. *The New International Economic Order.* London: Macmillan, 1983.

Helleiner, Gerald K. "Transnational Enterprises and the New Political Economy of US Trade Policy." In *International Political Economy.* Edited by J. A. Frieden and D. A. Lake. New York: St. Martins, 1987.

Hoffman, Stanley *et al. From Marshall Plan to Global Interdependence.* Paris: OECD, 1978.

Independent Commission on International Development Issues (Brandt Commission) *North-South: A Program for Survival*. London: Pan Books, 1980.

————. *North-South Cooperation for World Recovery*. London: Pan Books, 1983.

Jones, Charles A. *The North-South Dialogue: A Brief History*. London: Pinter, 1983.

Jones, R. J. Barry, and Peter Willetts, editors. *Interdependence on Trial: Studies in the Theory and Reality of Contemporary Interdependence*. London: Pinter, 1984.

Keohane, Robert O. "The World Political Economy and the Crisis of Embedded Liberalism." In *Order and Conflict in Contemporary Capitalism*. Edited by J. H. Goldthorpe. Oxford: Clarendon, 1984.

Keohane, Robert O., and Joseph S. Nye. *Power and Interdependence*. Boston: Little, Brown, 1977.

Krasner, Stephen D. "State Power and the Structure of International Trade," *World Politics* 28 (April 1976):317–343.

————. "The Tokyo Round: Particularistic Interests and Prospects for Stability in the Global Trading System." In *International Political Economy*. Edited by J. A. Freiden and D. A. Lake. New York: St. Martins, 1987.

————. ed. *International Regimes*. Ithaca, NY: Cornell University Press, 1983.

Lipson, Charles. "The Transformation of Trade: The Sources and Effects of Regime Change." In *International Regimes*. Edited by S. Krasner. London: Cornell University Press, 1983.

MacBean, A. I., and P. N. Snowden. *International Institutions in Trade and Finance*. London: Allen & Unwin, 1981.

Malmgren, Harald. "Coming Trade Wars," *Foreign Policy* Winter (1970–1971).

Michalet, Charles-Albert. "From International Trade to World Economy: A New Paradigm?" In *The New International Economy*. Edited by H. Makler, A. Martinelli, and N. Smelsner. London: Sage, 1982.

Nye, Joseph S. "UNCTAD: Poor Nations' Pressure Group." In *The Anatomy of Influence*. Edited by R. W. Cox and H.K. Jacobson. London: Yale University Press, 1973.

Polanyi, Karl. *The Great Transformation*. Boston: Beacon, 1957.

Reagan, Ronald. "The Benefits of Free Trade," Washington, D.C.: White House Briefing, 17 July 1986.

Rosecrance, Richard. *The Rise of the Trading State*. New York: Basic Books, 1986.

Ruggie, John Gerard. "International Regimes, Transactions and Change: Embedded Liberalism in the Postwar Economic Order." In *International Regimes*. Edited by S. Krasner. London: Cornell University Press, 1983.

Spero, Joan Edelman. *The Politics of International Economic Relations*. London: Allen & Unwin, 1981.

Stewart, Michael. *Controlling the Economic Future*. Brighton, England: Wheatsheaf, 1983.

Strange, Susan. "Protectionism—Why not?" *World Today* 4 (August/September 1985):148–150.

————. *Casino Capitalism*. Oxford: Blackwell, 1986.

Thurow, Lester. "America, Europe and Japan: A Time to Dismantle the World Economy," *Economist* (November 1985):21–26.

Waltz, Kenneth. *Theory of International Politics*. Reading, MA: Addison-Wesley, 1979.

Ward, Benjamin. *The Ideal Worlds of Economics*. New York: Basic Books, 1979.

Woolcock, Stephen, Jeffrey Hart, and Hans Van der Ven. *Interdependence in the Post-Multilateral Era*. London: University Press of America, 1985.

5

Maldevelopment: Explanations and Prescriptions

STEVEN L. LAMY

And while we would not impose our ideas, our policies, on anyone, we felt obliged to point out that no nation can have prosperity and successful development without economic freedom. Nor can it preserve personal and political freedoms without economic freedom. Only when the human spirit can dream, create, and build, only when individuals are given a personal stake in deciding economic policies and benefiting from their own success—only then do societies become dynamic, prosperous, progressive, and free.

—Ronald Reagan
Address to the International Monetary Fund [IMF] and World
Bank, September 25, 1984

Ten years ago, the developing countries argued that the international economic system did not function in such a way as to further their interests. Today it is evident that the same system is not functioning so as to serve the industrialized countries' interests either. In the longer run, the global economy requires a significant strengthening of its central economic institutions—the IMF, the World Bank, the GATT and many of the UN's specialized agencies. The process of strengthening will require some fundamental rethinking of these institutions' appropriate roles in a global economy quite different from that they were built to serve.

—Gerald K. Helleiner
professor of economics, University of Toronto
"North-South Relations, Then and
Now," in *Review '86/Outlook '87.*
The North-South Institute,
Ottawa, January 1987

I wish I could advocate some optimistic view of what is going to happen in the next decade, but I don't have an optimistic view of what is going to happen under the existing international system. That is why I am coming to the conclusion that more and more progress is going to have to depend upon the capacity of the Third World to explore its own internal possibilities of cooperation, to increase its own presence in the world through its own efforts, and its own cooperation. How far we can achieve this will depend on the Third World increasing its own internal strength and consequently its presence. It is out of that change that other changes will flow.

—Michael Manley
former prime minister of Jamaica,
interviewed in *Talking About Development.*
Gauhar 1983, 117–138.

These three statements represent three images of the North-South conflict, which divides the international system between rich states and poor states and rich and poor citizens within each state. This chapter examines the patterns of inequality alluded to in each of the quotations. In terms of basic human needs and access to political and economic resources and opportunities, these patterns of inequality have created and maintained two worlds within the international system. One world, the North, is economically affluent, enjoys political control of international and regional institutions, and has the military resources necessary to protect its interests. The North can circumvent attempts to transform the existing political and economic institutions used to manage the international system and maintain advantages for those in control. The other world, the South, suffers from the disadvantages of maldevelopment. These approximately 141 nation-states, which make up the developing world, suffer from the cumulative effects of continuing and reinforcing crisis situations. Johann Galtung (1980) suggests that beyond the most visible crises of misery and poverty, the North-South division is also defined by violence (e.g., the tendency for the United States and the Soviet Union to fight their battles in developing countries), repression (e.g., the denial of basic human rights), and a series of environmental crisis conditions that threaten the world's ecosystem (e.g., the depletion of non-renewable resources).

The conditions which contribute to inequality in the international system are not easily explained and there is significant disagreement over how best to respond to them. Generally, as the three introductory statements suggest, one's worldview on this issue depends upon where one is sitting in the system. Those in power and those who enjoy significant advantages seek to maintain the present system. Others advocate reforms that will give those who are disadvantaged more access to decisionmaking structures. Those who are most disadvantaged often see reforms as merely adjustments aimed at perpetuating a highly stratified and hierarchical system. Many citizens who suffer under the rules of the present system advocate transformation in order to create a more just distribution of the rewards and opportunities in the international community.

This chapter will first briefly describe the principal participants or actors in the North-South conflict. It is critically important to understand the diversity of interpretations within rich and poor states, and how each state chooses to participate in this policy arena.

The second part of the chapter explores competing descriptions of the problem of maldevelopment. *Maldevelopment refers specifically to the problems associated with the failure of some societies to develop political and economic systems capable of providing citizens with the most essential human needs and a stable and peaceful political environment.* The descriptions of this issue conform to the three worldview categories, system maintainer, reformer, and transformer, of the analytical framework employed in this book. Each description tends to reflect the "image of reality" closely related to the values and assumptions that define an individual's worldview. Just as film critics often present such contrasting views that one wonders if they actually saw the same movie, policymakers and students of international affairs often see issues and problems differently.

The third section of the chapter explores contending explanations of the persistence of inequality within the international system. In keeping with the analytical framework, explanations from the three worldview categories are presented:

- *System maintainers* tend to explain poverty by pointing to the failure of the poor states to work within the international free market system. The inequalities within these societies are generally attributed to internal problems such as ethnic group competition, political corruption, and excessive governmental interference.
- *System reformers* focus on both domestic and international factors. The failure of a development-assistance program might, for example, be connected to the lack of technical expertise in a particular country and the inappropriateness of the aid program for local needs.
- *System transformers* focus on the distribution of power and influence in the international system when explaining the persistence of inequality.

The fourth part of this chapter discusses future scenarios of conditions in the poor regions of the world, presented by political leaders and specialists in each worldview category. These prognostications also discuss the future of rich- and poor-state relations.

The final section of the chapter reviews policy options aimed at improving basic quality-of-life conditions in poor states. The specific problems presented by the economic crisis in sub-Saharan Africa provide an interesting case for reviewing competing policy prescriptions suggested by theorists and policymakers from each of the worldview perspectives.

THE RICH AND POOR—WHO'S WHO

The problem of maldevelopment cannot be understood without an understanding of the relationship between the North and the South and the specific role states, international trade/monetary institutions, and non-state actors play in this complex issue. It would be a gross oversimplification to suggest that all affluent nation-states have the same worldview or that all poor nation-states seek a radical transformation of the international system.

The North comprises the developed nation-states of the world, those generally considered the rule-makers in the international economic system. This group includes all of the principal powers in Western Europe, and Japan, Australia, New Zealand, Canada, and the United States. These countries represent the aid-giving group, called the Development Assistance Committee (DAC), within the Organization of Economic Cooperation and Development. Other Western societies, such as Greece, Spain, and Portugal, are somewhere between rich and poor and are not usually considered to be advanced industrial societies.

International Economic Institutions

The affluent states generally support an international economic system based on capitalistic or market-oriented principles. They are committed to the maintenance of the international economic system that was originally established by the participating states at the 1944 Bretton Woods Conference. Forty-four nation-states attended this meeting; however, the U.S. view of international trade and monetary order, patterned after the British free-trade system, clearly prevailed. Although initially aimed at rebuilding Europe and providing a sense of stability in the postwar era, the institutions of the Bretton Woods system were established to provide a free-trade environment, maintain a system favorable to the West, and avoid the trade and financial anarchy which had preceded the war.

One of the primary institutions of the Bretton Woods system, The International Monetary Fund (IMF), was established to contribute to international economic growth and stability in three essential ways:

- The IMF promotes international monetary cooperation by providing a permanent institution for dealing with international monetary issues.
- The IMF works to maintain stability in exchange rates between national currencies.
- The IMF makes available some resources (e.g., short-term loans) that countries can use to correct balance-of-payment problems (e.g., overvalued currency).

The IMF does not provide any long-term grants or loans for development purposes. Its general purpose is to correct short-term deficits. The IMF encourages countries to balance their books and remain as debt-free as possible. For example, if a country has a long-standing balance-of-trade problem, which means it is importing more than it is exporting, IMF resources would be used to initiate and cushion a currency devaluation. This would bring the cost of exports down and increase the cost of imports, which imposes difficulties on newly developing countries, which may have to import more in an effort to increase their production or diversify their economy.

Borrowing and voting power in the IMF are determined by quotas theoretically based on a country's strength in the international economic system. The United States is the most powerful member; its approximately 20 percent of the vote gives the United States veto power over all IMF decisions. Other important members of the executive board include Japan, France, Great Britain, West Germany, and Saudi Arabia. The rich countries of the North control approximately two-thirds of the votes, and thus exercise certain control over development processes. The 120 members of the IMF from the Third World have one-third of the power. The role of the dollar as an international currency, and the ability of the United States to deficit-spend because of its role as a world banker, certainly facilitated the implementation of U.S. foreign-policy goals in both security and economic development areas.

A second institution created by the Bretton Woods agreement is the International Bank for Reconstruction and Development (IBRD), otherwise known as the World Bank. The IBRD began primarily as a lending agency for infrastructure reconstruction in Western Europe. Although a few loans went to developing countries, most of the funds were spent on transportation and communication systems, highways, port facilities, and industrial development projects in Western Europe. The early directors of the World Bank did not support loans for social programs (e.g., health care) because it was felt that the benefits of economic growth would eventually provide resources for those social-welfare concerns.

Today, the World Bank includes three interrelated agencies, the IBRD, the International Development Association (IDA), and the Inter-Finance Corporate (IFC). The IBRD makes loans to middle-income or creditworthy states. The loans from IBRD are not considered soft loans (i.e., low-interest and long-term) and the IBRD officials do not allow for a rescheduling of payments (i.e., extension of payment schedule or renegotiations of interest charges). IDA loans are given to the poorest states (per capita GNP of less than U.S. $790) in the international system. These are long-term and interest-free loans. In 1985, IDA loans amounted to $3,028 million compared with $11,358 million for IBRD loans. (World Bank 1986) The IFC works with private commercial interests. The major goal of this agency is to stimulate the growth of the free-market system in developing countries.

As is true of the IMF, the World Bank decisionmaking process is weighted according to a member's contributions to the loan fund. The United States is the major veto power in the World Bank. Thus, World Bank loans generally support U.S. and Western interests. For example, in the early years, World Bank loans were not given to publicly owned industries. All funds were used to encourage private enterprise.

In 1968, Robert McNamara became president of the World Bank and focused the resources of this institution on a drive against poverty. The World Bank's efforts were not aimed just at economic growth and the potential increase of income. Instead they were based on providing essential basic human needs and services. McNamara supported a variety of social programs aimed at responding to dreadful conditions in the developing world. He suggested that citizens in affluent societies need to remind themselves of conditions in poor states:

> In short, compared to those fortunate enough to live in the developed nations, individuals in the poorest countries have an infant mortality rate eight times higher; a life expectancy one third lower; an adult literacy rate 60% less; a nutritional level, for one out of every two in the population, below minimal acceptable standards; and for millions of infants, less protein than is sufficient to permit optimum development of the brain. (1980, 21)

When McNamara left the World Bank in 1981, the new leadership moved to a general strategy of supporting loans which help middle-income developing states become more integrated into the Western international economy. The World Bank, through IBRD and IFC loans, is currently using its resources to help developing states become trading partners in the international system. World Bank loans assist agricultural development, transportation, communication, industrial development, education, and other infrastructure projects. Recently, it has also begun to focus its resources on efforts to respond to critical debt problems.

The third Bretton Woods institution, the General Agreement on Tariffs and Trade (GATT) is the principal multilateral instrument the affluent states use to maintain trade relations by working to overcome tariffs and other trade barriers. Ninety-six countries participate in its forums, known as rounds. These states account for over 80 percent of world trade. GATT agreements have resulted in rules of trade based on liberal or free-trade policies. Under this system, trade is motivated by conditions of *comparative advantage,* i.e., a country produces and exports products resulting in maximum profits and imports products it cannot produce at low costs. Protectionist policies are limited to tariff duties; preferential trade blocs or restrictions are not allowed in the GATT system.

The GATT system has worked well for the affluent states by removing some of the obstructions that prevent the free flow of goods and services. It is less effective today, however, because inflation, stagnated growth, and trade imbalances have increased demands for protectionist policies in most industrial societies. Although most supporters of GATT would disagree, the less-advantaged states cannot possibly benefit as much from a free-trade system with only minimal tariffs allowed. While it is true that the nation-states of the South may use this system to sell their resources and commodities, any attempt to diversify their economies by building up local industries would require controlling imports and subsidizing exports.

Transnational Enterprises
Apart from these Bretton Woods institutions, there is another important group of non-state actors. Transnational enterprises (TNEs), also called multinational corporations, or MNCs, play a significant role in international economic affairs. Most TNEs originate in the affluent North; however, these multinational corporations have become the principal instrument of economic development in many poor states. Many of the corporations, banks, and manufacturing firms make decisions that determine the amount, type, and location of international investment. Their presence in developing states is seen by some experts as an important way of integrating poor states into the international economy by providing employment, technology, and other resources. Critics of TNEs suggest that their investment policies tend to reinforce existing inequities within societies. Rather than contributing to economic growth throughout developing societies, TNE activities usually benefit a small group of elites and result in the exploitation of workers, with related cultural and political distortions.

The state and non-state actors described above are important participants in the international economic system. Since most benefit from the structure and organization of this system, these actors are generally supportive of the status quo. Although some actors in the affluent North support reforms aimed at addressing potentially destabilizing inequities, most try to work within the existing institutions, seeking reforms only when their interests are at stake.

The Eastern Bloc

The Soviet Union and its Eastern European allies—the Eastern bloc—has played a significant role in international political and military affairs; however, these states have played only a minimal role in international economic-development policy. This group of command or centrally planned economies is designated as a distinct group by the World Bank and other Western public and private economic institutions for two reasons: its decision not to join the Western system and the general Western apprehension about the Soviet model, which professes an economic and political philosophy antithetical to the Western liberal democratic system. Likewise, the Soviets have remained concerned about the controlling interests of the United States in the institutions that coordinate trade and development policies in the international economic system.

With political interests as their primary concern, the Soviets opted not to become part of the postwar economic system. Instead, their leaders sought to establish their own economic system based on the principles of Marxist-Leninist economic strategies. With the Marshall Plan in the West and Soviet resources in the East, most of the development activities after World War II were focused on rebuilding Europe. However, with the coming of the Truman Doctrine and the dismantling of colonial empires, the geopolitical interests of both the United States and the USSR necessitated the establishment of development-assistance strategies. In 1949, Truman announced the creation of a technical assistance program to help citizens in the poor regions of the world deal with hunger, poverty, and potential oppressors (e.g., Communists). Although the program was primarily designed to support U.S. private investment in Latin America, the establishment of this program indicated a new interest for the United States in managing the processes of change in the newly emerging nation-states of the South. Soviet activities in these same states were generally limited to countering U.S. gains.

Recently the Eastern bloc has begun to move from its postwar independent economic-development strategy to trade and development policies that link it to the West. Trade with the capitalist countries of the West represents about 30 percent of Soviet trade. The USSR is the United States' fourth largest agricultural market; exports to the Soviets will increase as the West seeks to provide them with agricultural products, technology, and other manufactured goods.

The Soviet Union is presently actively attempting to change its image in the developing world. The Soviet leadership is pursuing policies aimed at strengthening economic ties with non-Marxist nation-states by exploiting anti-U.S. feelings related to the debt problem, U.S. military actions in Central America, and U.S. support for South Africa. Unfortunately, the Soviet Union has little to offer the developing world. Its income has declined as oil prices have dropped and its manufactured goods are not of the highest quality. Currently, the Soviets export agricultural products and military equipment to the developing world.

Soviet support for the developing world is primarily rhetorical. The Soviets blame the capitalist system for most of the problems in the developing world and see attempts to reform the international system, like the Brandt Commission proposals, as new attempts to extend the Western imperialistic system. As the self-proclaimed leader of socialism, the Soviets see themselves as natural allies of the poor; however, the Soviets have never given substantial aid to the South. (Desai 1984) On a yearly basis the Soviets only give about 5 percent of the world's total official development assistance. (Stevens 1982)

The Eastern-bloc countries are not major players in the North-South conflict, but their political and emerging economic interests suggest that the Soviets may be playing a more prominent role in efforts aimed at responding to conditions of maldevelopment.

The Developing States
The final group of actors in the international system are the "rule-takers" or the developing states which make up the South. The World Bank classifies the developing states into four distinct groups. These categories are based primarily on GNP figures and other economic and social indicators.

- The richest group of nation-states in the South includes the high-income oil-exporting states such as Kuwait and Saudi Arabia.
- The newly industrialized countries (NICs), such as Brazil, Argentina, South Korea, and Yugoslavia, are considered to be upper-middle-income countries.
- The lower-middle-income countries are those who are dependent upon the export of primary products or are suffering from political and social upheavals. Egypt, the Philippines, Nigeria, Thailand, and Peru all fall into this category.
- The poorest nation-states of the South, the low-income or least less-developed countries include thirty-one states with low incomes, minimal manufacturing or industrial capacities, and little or no public services such as education and sanitation facilities. Botswana, Chad, Ethiopia, Haiti, and Bangladesh are considered "least less-developed" states. These states are the favorite clients of some affluent states, most notably the "like-minded" member states of the DAC, and private organizations interested in assisting the poorest of the poor and thereby enhancing their humanitarian image. The Scandinavian countries, the Netherlands, and Canada are currently focusing their aid on these poor states, whereas the United States tends to give its assistance to states like Israel and Egypt for strategic reasons.

The "South" in this chapter will refer to the diverse group of nation-states which make up the Group of Seventy-Seven (G77). This lobby group, which now numbers 125 countries, emerged at the end of the first United Nations Conference on Trade and Development (UNCTAD) in 1964. Calling itself a "trade union of the poor," this group is pledged to cooperate in efforts to establish more favorable trade and development programs. It uses the United Nations General Assembly and particularly UNCTAD sessions to push for its plan for a New International Economic Order (NIEO). The mandate to promote global trade in an effort to accelerate economic development has been the major theme of most UNCTAD conferences. The first meeting launched the development debate, especially in the areas of trade in commodities and preferential tariffs for exports from developing societies. The United States voted against the conference's first four policy principles, including the first, which called for "noninterference in the affairs of other countries," and the fourth, which called for the recognition that economic development and progress should be the common concern of the international community. The United States was the only country which voted against this latter principle. (Stevens 1982) Other UNCTAD conferences have dealt with monetary regulations, economic imperialism, commodity trade, and debt.

Today, the unity of the developing world in UNCTAD and other organizations is being challenged by recession, debt, and domestic unrest. Many poor states are seeking bilateral rather than multilateral solutions to their problems, but these bilateral solutions simply increase the South's dependency on the North. In an effort to remain relevant, some UNCTAD leaders have argued for an agenda focusing on services, the debt crisis, domestic economic conditions, and strategies for economic cooperation.

The South, by no means a homogeneous group of nation-states, represents different political orientations, levels of economic development, and cultures. Within this group of states there is significant disagreement on how best to address the problem of inequality. Some advocate working within the system; others suggest the need for a new economic order. However, all of these states are disadvantaged relative to the states in the North. They suffer from dependencies which limit their foreign policy options and adversely influence the state's ability to meet basic human needs. These states are united by their common experiences and their desire to respond to conditions that threaten order and stability within their societies.

CONTENDING DESCRIPTIONS OF MALDEVELOPMENT

When examining the problems associated with international inequality there are certain indicators of reality which are difficult to deny regardless of one's worldview. Maldevelopment in the international system is generally described by looking at the following categories.

Income Factors

The developed countries of the world (about 20 percent of the world's population) enjoy a per-capita income of $11,100, whereas the poorest of the developing states (about 50 percent of the world's population) have a per-capita income of only $275. (World Bank 1984 and Sivard 1985) The 1983 GNP per capita in North America ($13,310) is fifty times larger than in the poorest states. Figures related to the absolute growth of income are more revealing. A study measuring twenty-four years of income patterns suggests that in South Asia per-capita income has increased $3.60 a year. In Africa the increase has amounted to $8.00 a year and in North America the increase in the last twenty-four years amounts to $206 a year. (Sivard 1985) These figures suggest that in both absolute and relative terms, the income gap between rich and poor states has widened.

Employment-Unemployment

Most of the individuals who make up the global underclass live in rural areas. Over 600 million people are landless laborers who own no property or lack access to productive farmlands. Many of these landless are moving to cities, increasing pressure on governments to provide employment and basic social services. In 1985, the unemployed in the rich states numbered 31 million compared to 500 million in the poor states. (Eckholm 1982) As unemployment increases, problems associated with rapid urbanization, uncontrolled migration, and challenges to traditional family and authority patterns also increase.

Food and Water

World Bank studies suggest that over a billion people are chronically undernourished. Some 50,000 people die every day from malnutrition. The children of the world are most affected by the patterns of food distribution and production. In 1984, during the recent famine, approximately 5 million children died in Africa due to chronic undernutrition. The problem is not food production; studies indicate that there is enough grain produced to feed all people two loaves of bread each day. (Sivard 1985) This may suggest that food is produced for those who can pay and not necessarily for those in need.

The availability of safe drinking water is a major problem. The United Nations identified safe water and sanitation as major health issues. Its studies indicate that approximately 50 percent of the population in developing countries has no clean water. This number increases dramatically when rural areas are considered. (WHO and UNDP 1981)

Health and Medical Services

The global underclass is generally denied access to basic health-care facilities and services. Public spending in health-care services amounts to only $2.00 per capita in the poorest countries. This compares with a per-capita figure of $327 in the most wealthy states. There are approximately twenty physicians per 10,000 people in the richest fifth of the world and only two physicians for a similar population group in the developing world. There are problems associated with the distribution of critical medical supplies, hospital facilities, and research in many basic health-care areas. Although infant mortality is increasing in the rich countries, its incidence is seven times greater in the poorest 20 percent of the world's population. The infant-death figures are one of the most illustrative indicators of poor health facilities, malnutrition, and inadequate shelter.

Education

Government expenditure on education of the wealthiest 20 percent of the world's population averages $430 per capita; the adult literacy rate is approximately 97 percent in those same states. The poorest areas of the world spend only $4 per capita on education and only 5 percent of the world's expenditures in research and development. The literacy rate in the poor states reflects the low spending priority. Only 37 percent of the adults in the poorest 20 percent of the world's population are considered literate. (Sivard 1985; Brandt 1982; Crow and Thomas 1983; and Murdoch 1980)

Investment and Production Patterns

Other indicators of maldevelopment reflect the historical evolution of the international economic system. Third World states are often considered to be

suppliers of raw materials, cheap labor, and markets for the sale of surplus industrial goods. At times, these states also provide opportunities for investors
and lending institutions looking to put excess dollars back into circulation. For
example, approximately thirty-eight nation-states in the South have economies
based upon the export sale of one or two commodities. Unfortunately for these
states, the price of commodity goods has decreased while the price of manufactured goods has increased dramatically. Partially to offset this loss of income,
many of these states have increased their borrowing in the international system.

In 1986, total debt for African states was estimated to be as high as U.S.
$200 billion. The economic gains from policy reforms, initiated by individual
African states, after the UN Program of Action for African Economic Recovery
and Development was adopted by the 1986 UN General Assembly, have been
diminished by a growth in debt burden, continuing internal armed conflicts,
drought and insect infestations, and a substantial reduction in commodity
prices. African states now contribute over 50 percent of their earnings to the
costs of their debt. (African News, 1987)

Cultural Factors
All of the factors discussed above contribute to what Oscar Lewis described as
the "culture of poverty." Lewis suggests that the culture of poverty is a condition
of malaise that influences how the poor think, feel, and interact with the world
around them. (Lewis 1959) Lewis's work suggests that other less objective
characteristics—such as value systems, habits, kinship ties, customs, and religious practices—must be considered along with the measurable indicators of
maldevelopment. Some critics of the international economic system have
suggested that development is a historical process reflecting the values and
traditions of the Western World. Many of the goals of development, as expressed by Western institutions, reflect their interests and their view of achievement and accomplishment. Hence, an understanding of maldevelopment must
include an awareness of how cultural insensitivity and inappropriate development strategies contribute to the inability of many states to begin the development process. Many donors ignore both cultural issues and the fact that many
countries, because of their level of economic, political, and social development, are not able or willing to absorb new technologies, investments, and
other aspects of Western modernization schemes. (Galbraith 1983)

Civil and International Violence
World military spending is now over a trillion dollars a year, 25 percent of which
is spent by the poor states of the world, including China. Since 1945, over 20
million people have been killed in wars that have occurred, primarily, in the
developing world. One study suggests that 99.9 percent of the deaths from civil
violence and 91 percent of the deaths from international violence have occurred
in the poor states of the South. (Kohler 1982) Internal conflicts fueled by ethnic
or ideological divisions, and the geopolitical competition for control of
strategic regions that is exacerbated by U.S. and Soviet rivalries, contribute to

much of this violence. It is an understatement to suggest that societies wracked by violence and with excessive military budgets might find it difficult to maintain a stable and prosperous economy.

These various indicators of maldevelopment suggest that many of the growth-oriented economic policies prescribed by economic and political leaders in the post-World War II era have simply not resulted in uniform stability or efficient and equitable societies throughout the developing world. The order of importance one assigns to these indicators depends upon how one sees the world.

A System-Maintainer View

The system-maintainer perspective of world affairs is generally defined by the assumptions and beliefs of the realist or geopolitical perspective. Those who see the world through this lens see an anarchic international system in which nation-states act to enhance their own power and resources in an effort to secure their national interests. In this competitive international system, states cannot rely on the goodwill of other actors. Self-help is a ruling axiom for political and economic leaders.

On this issue, the system maintainers represent the leadership in the Western World (the North). From their perspective the basic characteristics of the maldevelopment issue fall into economic, political, and sociocultural categories. Most system maintainers emphasize that poor countries have failed to work within the international system. Thus, system maintainers' descriptions of the problem will highlight areas that they feel can be rectified if countries become active participants in the international marketplace. In an address to the Southern Center for International Studies, Secretary of State George Shultz (1983) presented an illustrative system-maintainer description of problems in the developing world.

Secretary Shultz explained why developing countries are important to U.S. national interests. He suggested that U.S. economic prosperity depended upon economic growth in the developing world and that global stability depended upon peace in this region. The secretary's speech emphasized the following characteristics of the problem (1983, 2):

- Developing countries are important customers and suppliers for the advanced industrial world. These countries purchase 40 percent of U.S. exports and supply the United States with 40–45 percent of resources critical for the U.S. economy.
- The debt crisis in the developing world has been fueled by a prolonged international recession and exacerbated by excessive government spending and inefficient uses of these funds.
- Political instability in the Third World societies is exploited by the Soviet Union and its allies.

The goals of U.S. system maintainers are to promote economic and political stability and economic growth in the developing world; Thus, from the U.S. system-maintainer position the problem of maldevelopment has the following major characteristics:

1. Internal factors (e.g., ethnic conflict, and inexperienced and corrupt leaders) that result in both economic and political instability
2. Excessive interference in the free market system
3. Soviet political and military interference
4. Inadequate economic institutions for monitoring and managing investment, production, and other financial policy decisions

The system maintainers strongly support efforts by individual nation-states and multilateral institutions to use their development-assistance funds to address basic human-needs issues. U.S. aid programs, for example, emphasize health, education, food production, and technology transfer. By providing resources to respond to these problems, the system maintainer aims to create a more stable and productive society, and thus dissuade those advocating more substantial changes in the international economic system.

A System-Reformer View

The system-reformer worldview is generally described as a perspective that recognizes the linkages binding both state and non-state actors in situations of interdependence and dependence. Furthermore, these interconnections result in a common agenda of problems and opportunities. Maldevelopment is one of the "common crisis" situations which require cooperative and multilateral policy responses. The work of the Independent Commission on International Development Issues (the Brandt Commission) best represents this reformist viewpoint. In two studies, *North-South: A Programme for Survival* (1980) and *Common Crisis North-South: Cooperation for World Recovery* (1983), the members of this multinational commission paint a picture of development emphasizing areas of mutual interest, including problems in all eight of the areas mentioned at the beginning of this section. A major emphasis is placed on conditions of poverty that prevent effective and productive participation in public and private affairs, such as unemployment, poor sanitation facilities, inadequate health care, expensive and unreliable public service systems, and insufficient educational systems. These conditions are best summarized by the following statement from the Brandt Commission:

> Permanent insecurity is the condition of the poor. There are no public systems of social security in the event of unemployment, sickness or death of a wage-earner in the family. Flood, drought or disease affecting people or livestock can destroy livelihoods without hope of compensation. In the North, ordinary men and women face genuine economic problems—uncertainty, inflation, the fear if not the reality of unemployment. But they rarely face anything resembling the total deprivation found in the South. (1980, 49)

System reformers emphasize the importance of seeing the linkages between domestic or internal factors and international or external conditions. Generally, a system reformer's description of the basic characteristics of this problem is related to the ideals of social-democratic societies. Whereas the U.S. system maintainer emphasizes characteristics of maldevelopment that indicate the failure of societies to work within a market-oriented economic system (which may or may not be supported by an open democratic political system), the reformer presents a description of conditions which show the inability of societies and the international system to provide for participation, freedom, equity, cultural diversity, democracy, and a minimum standard of meeting basic human needs.

It is important to note that a system reformer sees inequality as a global problem that must involve all state and non-state actors. The Brandt Commission reports call for the participation of all states, including the Soviet Union and other planned economies, in any efforts aimed at responding to problems associated with maldevelopment. Consequently, major emphasis is placed on regional or international institutions as the fora for policy development and implementation. The "mutuality-of-interests" theme suggests a bias toward multilateral rather than unilateral responses. The 1986 Special Session of the United Nations General Assembly on the critical economic situation in Africa aptly illustrates the system-reformer approach to development problems. The assembled delegates all agreed that African states must recognize the need to face their own problems. Yet, non-African delegates accepted the responsibility to use their resources to assist the African states. (United Nations 1986b)

A System-Transformer View

Transformation of the international system is most difficult to describe because, in terms of the analytical model, it is divided among three distinct worldviews: alternative-left, radical or *dependencia,* and alternative-right perspectives. In this chapter, the focus is on the alternative-left and the *dependencia* views.

The Alternative-Left View
The alternative-left worldview is best represented by the work in alternative-world futures presented by the World Order Models Project (WOMP). This worldview is based on the assumption that the present international system, with its emphasis on unilateralism, national interest, self-help, and power politics, needs to be restructured and transformed. State-centrism must be replaced by an emphasis on human-centric values. Some who hold this worldview advocate opting out of the present hierarchial international system and creating more decentralized and representative decisionmaking structures. Concerned citizens will thereby be able to design and implement development strategies appropriate to their needs and interests and not to the interests of distant power brokers.

The alternative-left worldview sees the development problem as resulting from the structure and organization of the system. Thus, the basic characteristics of maldevelopment are defined by the failure of the system to provide economic well-being for all citizens, guarantee peace and stability, protect ecological resources, promote social justice and participatory democracy, and create a social environment that encourages an appreciation of cultural diversity. In this worldview a system that fails to provide these necessities must be transformed. Advocates of the alternative-left perspective believe that the indicators of maldevelopment correspond to the failure of the international system to provide a political, economic, and social environment in which these basic human goals can be realized.

The Dependencia *View*
A second system-transformer view suggests that the most salient characteristic of the international system is the exploitation of the poor South by the rich North. This *dependencia* view originated in the developing world and is often labeled by analysts as a Marxist or Neomarxist perspective. Essentially this viewpoint advocates the transformation of the present international structure and the creation of a new structure in which the transformers will enhance their position of power to their economic advantage. It is suggested that these transformations should be aimed at establishing an ideal society where societal goods and services are distributed by public leaders who are guided by mandates aimed at guaranteeing that no individual is denied access to basic dignity and human needs.

An illustrative example of a transformation strategy that includes proponents of both the alternative left and *dependencia* positions can be found in a review of the evolution of the Non-Aligned Movement (NAM). The Non-Aligned Movement was developed by newly independent African and Asian states as an alternative to being subsumed under either U.S. or Soviet hegemony. These countries had a shared experience of colonialism and most of the states were at a low level of economic and political development. Non-alignment provided a potential strategy for reducing external dependencies and overcoming domestic opposition groups that might emerge if one superpower were to be chosen over the other as an ally.

The economic philosophy of the Non-Aligned Movement began to emerge at the 1970 meeting in Lusaka, Zambia, where a disassociational (i.e., departing from the status quo) strategy of self-reliance was discussed. The self-reliant economic program urged cooperation among non-aligned states in policy areas such as trade, industrial development, agricultural production, and trade in commodities.

The description of maldevelopment presented at the 1973 Algiers Summit meeting went beyond a focus on deficiencies in categories of basic human needs. The Algiers Economic Declaration described the problem as one of colonialism, neocolonialism, and imperialism by the affluent states and economic actors within those societies. The structure of the international system and the distribution of political power and influence were considered to be central factors in the maldevelopment of the Third World. The realization of political freedom, and the restoration of sovereignty and control within their societies, was seen by Third World leaders to be an essential part of resolving their economic problems. (Carty and Smith 1981, Clarke and Swift 1982, Clapham 1985, and Harries 1979)

The political and economic strategies developed at Algiers and refined at later meetings provided the basis for the formulation of a comprehensive program for restructuring the international economic system. Fueled by the producer-power strategy used by OPEC and the spirit of change expressed by the Non-Aligned Movement, the NIEO Program was presented to the world at a 1974 UN General Assembly session. Although the provisions for restructuring the international system presented in the program do not go far enough for some transformation advocates, they do represent a desire to create a more equitable system by changing the distribution of power in economic-policy areas.

In summary, the basic characteristics of the maldevelopment problem from a system-transformer viewpoint relate to severe shortages in basic human needs, particularly in the areas of food production, access to technology, energy resources, and health care. The system transformer's description is primarily focused on power issues related to the control of decisionmaking institutions. Most transformers seek access to international power structures. Most would emphasize the failure to designate and respect global common regions like the oceans and space (which could be used to benefit all humankind), and the manipulation of poor states to further the political and economic interests of rich states, as indicators of maldevelopment. These issues and others suggest a lack of trust and failure to recognize the need for power-sharing in a pluralistic international system.

CONTENDING EXPLANATIONS OF MALDEVELOPMENT

One of the major goals of the social scientist is to develop and then confirm or disconfirm theories that explain the behavior of states and account for the persistence of societal problems or the emergence of crisis situations. An individual's choice of explanations is often closely related to the core beliefs which define his or her worldview. In such a complex area as international inequality, it is extremely important for the student of international affairs to examine the contending explanations from each worldview category.

Explanations from System Maintainers

System-maintainer explanations generally focus on the failure of Third World states to integrate into the world market. How then do system maintainers account for the failure of the market system to create even modestly prosperous conditions in many areas of the developing world? How do system maintainers explain the great disparities and the related conflicts throughout the Third World? The answers to these questions should provide the student of international affairs with some ideas about how system maintainers see the world around them.

Most system maintainers recognize some flaws in the international system; however, the failure of the system to work properly for the poor states is attributed almost entirely to factors internal to those states, which serve to negate any possibility for creating prosperous societies. The first and most-cited culprits are arbitrary, centralized, and excessively interventionist governments in the developing world. As suggested by the British economist, P.T. Bauer, economically static societies are created when public authorities use economic controls to preempt private initiative. (1981) Bauer further suggests that Third World governments actually use development assistance to extend their power over their citizenry. Consequently, he advocates controlling aid programs in order to avoid the politicization of economic life.

A significant number of internal factors affect the level of development in most societies. System maintainers generally believe that the resources and expertise necessary to respond to these conditions can be found within the existing system. For example, political inexperience, mismanagement, or corruption could be dealt with through training programs or by the establishment of a more open political process. Other conditions which contribute to poverty—such as population growth, uncontrolled migration, misuse of natural resources, excessive military spending, and inadequate education and technological training programs—can all be dealt with through existing public and private authorities.

Most system maintainers will admit that some political, economic, and social conditions were adversely affected by colonial rule. However, they tend to point out the positive effects of colonialism, such as the introduction of educational systems and, in some cases, the development of commercial infrastructures. Furthermore, maintainers believe the international system presents extensive opportunities for economic growth. Development assistance from individual countries and multilateral institutions has been generous. System maintainers point to the success of NICs such as South Korea, Singapore, and Malaysia. These countries are singled out by system maintainers as societies that have used the Bretton Woods system and other multilateral and bilateral programs to build prosperous economies.

The system maintainer hails free enterprise. U.S. Secretary of State George Shultz traveled to Africa in 1987 to congratulate several countries for reforming their economies by reducing or ending price controls, import restrictions, food subsidies, and other market interventions. As his comments suggest, system maintainers strongly believe in a global trickle-down theory that the benefits of trade will reach the poor. In describing the U.S. position as a partnership in helping the poor help themselves, Shultz articulated the motivations behind U.S. activity in the developing world:

There is nothing wrong with wanting to help people and see them do better. I am not knocking generosity. But I think it is more important to be more hardheaded than that. So I think it is in our interest to see countries become market-oriented in their economic system. (*New York Times*, January 18, 1987)

Explanations from System Reformers

System reformers emphasize the need to develop policy programs reflecting a more pluralistic international system, in which the well-being of all citizens is affected by the persistence of poverty and misery in the developing world. Poverty and misery are seen as the root cause of conflicts that are accentuated by the overemphasis on military spending in most developed and developing states. All states, rich and poor, have a common interest in closing the gap between rich and poor. How then do system reformers account for the persistence of inequality?

A cursory review of reports from the 1986 UN Special Session on the critical economic situation in Africa provides a useful list of explanations of global poverty from a system-reformer perspective. The system reformer's emphasis on looking at a combination of domestic and international factors is reinforced by several studies prepared for this conference, which warn that critical food shortages should be expected in twenty-four African countries because of natural phenomena, e.g., drought accompanied by internal strife or civil war, cutbacks in development assistance, a global recession (that has caused a drop in commodity prices), and misuse of public funds by inexperienced or corrupt officials. (Africa Emergency Report 1986) A more detailed list of explanations is discussed below.

Internal Economic Factors in Maldevelopment
A large number of developing countries are dependent upon the export of a narrow range of primary commodities. Honduras, for example, is dependent on the sale of bananas and coffee. Indonesia bases its economy on the sale of rubber and oil. Diversification of the economy is the solution; however, investment policies, land ownership, and the politics of trade often work against a major restructuring of the economy. In Africa, only two countries are considered highly diversified—South Africa and Kenya. Thirteen African states depend upon the sale of a single commodity for export earnings. (Crow and Thomas 1983) All of these states are highly dependent on and sensitive to external market conditions. A drop in demand will cause lower earnings and will adversely influence quality of life in these societies.

Dualistic economies also impede growth in the developing world. Many societies have reasonably successful commodity industries, such as mining or agriculture, existing alongside subsistence-level industries that produce virtually no surplus for trade outside a very local environment. These industries provide enough profit or production for local subsistence but not enough product for gowth and diversification. A change in attitude and the infusion of new ideas and technology is required to resolve this situation.

The inability of many states to provide for basic food needs is a major internal problem. Land distribution, the availability of seed, water, fertilizer, and other technologies, as well as storage and distribution capabilities, all contribute to food-production problems. The goal has to be self-sufficiency. However, even in developing states with successful agricultural programs, food may not be readily available for domestic consumption. For example, when a farmer in India realizes he can make more from growing and then exporting wheat than from selling it domestically, food must be imported or people go hungry. Thus, the role of domestic and international economic policies in encouraging production for domestic consumption or export must also be examined. When one considers that one out of five Africans depend upon food imports and 25 percent of what they receive comes from food-aid programs, the goal of self-sufficiency seems even more formidable.

A fourth internal factor contributing to inequality relates to the inability of many Third World countries to shift resources or production priorities to reflect shifts in the world economy. Some of these deficiencies reflect a lack of resources; however, a major problem is the lack of public and private institutions having the resources and authority to manage and direct the economy. For example, if prices for a particular import increase tenfold, a sophisticated economy would shift domestic production toward that area. This is not easily done, but the result of failing to shift production is doing without a critical product or borrowing to pay for it.

Other internal factors that system reformers consider as contributing to inequality include population growth and distribution patterns, ineffective or authoritarian political systems, the lack of economic opportunity and social mobility induced by a rigid elite system, and the failure to provide adequate educational and training programs.

External Factors Contributing to Maldevelopment
The Brandt Commission reports and previous studies such as the Pearson Report presented in 1969, all focus on the need to develop a new rationale for international interactions. This rationale would emphasize international responsibility for economic and social development. A major cause of persistent problems is the continued emphasis on national interest and unilateral policy action in a world where long-term problems such as poverty and the arms race threaten the existence of the world as we know it.

The failure of the world's leading powers to reform the Bretton Woods institutions to reflect new power arrangements and the maturation of developing states is part of the problem. Most system reformers see the need to create functionally specific global institutions (e.g., a world energy commission), wherein every nation-state has one vote and an emphasis is placed on finding multilateral solutions that reduce rather than increase external dependencies. System reformers do not go as far as to suggest that the principle of one state, one vote should extend to all policy areas. However, they do advocate the creation of more possibilities for cooperative behavior and the sharing of resources and opportunities. From this position, the failure of the system to encourage and reward cooperative behavior is a major factor in the persistence of system-wide problems.

A major contributor to maldevelopment, according to a system reformer, is the global arms culture. Leaders in the Third World states spend approximately 20 percent of the world's $940 billion military budget. (U.S. Arms Control and Disarmament Agency 1986) In some fifty-two countries in the South, governments are controlled by the military or the military acts as a major political force. (Sivard 1985) The concept of security must include social justice and economic well-being. Unfortunately, expenditures in military areas take directly from public funds that could be used to provide for basic human needs in disadvantaged countries.

Similarly, the emphasis on self-help in the international system and the failure of regional or international peace-keeping efforts prompt many Third World leaders to opt for an increase in military spending or the entanglements of an alliance, with either a regional power or one of the superpowers. The result is a further commitment to military spending, and the potential for involvement in regional conflicts prompted by superpower competition or by asymmetrical power distributions triggering defensive or offensive moves. Any resolution of this arms race will require the efforts of East and West and North and South. Systems reformers regard this as an area of mutuality of interests.

Other external factors affecting distributional patterns in developing states include the decline of development assistance, protectionist policies, no stability in commodity pricing, and the burdens of debt. These are all problems that system reformers believe demand the collective attentions of the world community. The reformers believe that the interventions of key public and private actors could result in the elimination of many obstacles to equitable growth in the South.

Explanations from System Transformers

Alternative-left and *dependencia*-transformer perspectives identify the inequality problem as structural. Simply stated, the international system is structured to favor the rich and exploit the poor. The international system is seen as divided between core states (i.e., the North and the Soviet bloc) and the periphery (i.e., poor states of the South). Under the present system structure, the periphery serves the economic and political interests of the core by (1) acting as primary suppliers of raw materials and agricultural products; (2) providing areas for capital investment; and (3) serving as a market for "first world" manufactured goods. In the political-security area, Third World states are pawns in the geopolitical conflict between the Soviet Union and the United States.

From this view, the world capitalistic system has worked well for the core states but not for the periphery. In fact, the *dependencia* system transformers suggest that foreign investments actually increase dependencies and accentuate inequalities within the developing society. Foreign investment brings with it political and cultural interests and these cause trade, economic, and sociopolitical distortions in the periphery. All of these distortions create a structurally dependent state; the goals, needs, and priorities of these states can only be realized through the willing cooperation of the affluent states. This complex relationship between rich and poor states is presented in Exhibit 5.1.

System transformers seek to change the present system, which provides only opportunities for dependent development. Maldevelopment in the South is the result of an imperfect capitalistic world economy because those with power in the international system have designed international decision structures which give them an advantage in the system. States are not equal in the marketplace and do not have equal access to resources and opportunities to enable them to compete. The system transformer advocates a restructuring of this system as the antidote to global inequality.

The alternative-left system transformer accepts most of the explanations offered by the *dependencia* perspective. However, alternative-left transformers are not sanguine about the chances for real change if the structure of the system, with its emphasis on state-centrism, is not addressed. Inequalities will persist unless the system is changed to allow for more participation by groups and individuals with human-centric policy interests. For example, leaders in a state-centric system will support policies that keep them in power and not policies that might result in structural reform aimed at addressing power and resource inequities in international systems. Thus for alternative-left transformers, the system maintainers' ethos and the resulting international system of power and decisionmaking is the root cause of the global economic crisis. A system based upon a minimum standard of living and participation for all societies in decisions about the use of global resources is the goal of these system transformers. A competitive international system in which state policies are based on self-help, national interests over global interests, and Cold War internationalism (East-West competition) is seen as perpetuating the unequal distribution of global resources.

PREDICTIONS ABOUT THE FUTURE OF NORTH-SOUTH RELATIONS

Problems associated with conditions of maldevelopment in the international community will most likely persist. Inequities are inevitable and there will always be struggles over real or perceived differentials in the distribution of goods, services, and opportunities within and among societies. However, each worldview has its ideal future scenario based upon the assumptions defining its particular image.

Exhibit 5.1 A System-Transformer View of Foreign Investment

Foreign Economic Penetration

Presence of transnational enterprises

Loans for economic development

Trade-Sector Distortions

New patterns of trade

Production for export and the import of goods and services

Internal Economic Distortions

Local elite gain financially

Local industries put out of business by external investors

Local industries abandoned for more lucrative export production

Sociopolitical Distortions

Elites use the political system to maintain their advantages,
maintain stability and order, and prevent change

Elites in the poor states owe their position of affluence
and power to elites in the core states

Elites have little support in their own societies

Conflict and Repression of Basic Human Rights

Public authorities must use their coercive power
to maintain control and order in an inequitable society

A System Maintainer's View of the Future

System maintainers see a bright future if states agree to maintain a free-market system with only minimal intervention by public authorities. System maintainers identify two challenges to global prosperity: neomercantilist policies and excessive public interventions. The free market will work if interference is minimal. Neomercantilist policies, which include protectionist trade policies and public subsidies for industrial and agricultural products, are more likely to emerge from affluent states no longer capable of competing in a free-trade system. Excessive public interventions, such as laws aimed at guaranteeing a minimum wage or requiring that a percentage of TNEs' profits stay in the host country, are more likely to be promulgated by developing countries. According to system maintainers, these interferences in the world trade system will cause the same damage that accompanied the "beggar-thy-neighbor" policies preceding the two world wars. The maintainers believe that the path to peace and prosperity is free trade.

System maintainers recognize the need for international institutions and multilateral efforts to manage the global economy. Their goal is to strengthen the Bretton Woods institutions and, when appropriate, convene special conferences to deal with problems that threaten global economic stability. The state should maintain its sovereignty in economic-policy areas. International organizations and TNEs should work with the state to maintain an open and free-market system. In future years, political leaders are more likely to use economic policies to further their national interests. Economic statecraft will become an important foreign-policy tool; those benefiting from a free-trade system will work to keep it open and those disadvantaged by the economic system will work to adjust rules in their favor. This tension will define the system in future years.

The system maintainers believe the gap between rich and poor will never close completely. Excessive differentials will shrink as the benefits of growth begin to trickle down to the poorest sections of the international community.

A System Reformer's View of the Future

System reformers are generally more pessimistic about the chances of addressing the problems of maldevelopment. This pessimism leads them to support reforms in the international system. System reformers reject the system maintainer's emphasis on liberal or market economics. Reformers believe that without interventions in the market aimed at redistribution, differentials within and among societies will increase. In political terms, rich and poor states will be further polarized.

Reformers believe that state and non-state actors will have to work together to overcome trends toward nationalism and unilateralism. The most serious problems that threaten global stability include an uncontrolled arms race (fueled by U.S.-Soviet competition), continuing misery in the poorest of the poor states, an international economic system favoring the affluent, and an increase in authoritarianism within old and new states, which threatens a global strategy based on negotiations and the politics of accommodation. An accommodationist approach is not synonymous with appeasement. Instead, it is a political orientation which encourages finding policy solutions that do not unfairly advantage or disadvantage any one actor or group of actors in the system.

The ideal world for the system reformer is one that resembles a democratic social-welfare state. In this community of states, public and private actors work together to provide a global welfare "safety net" that will prevent any citizen from falling below a minimum standard of living. In this global "caring society," nation-states would recognize their mutual interests and establish issue regimes to manage and regulate international affairs. Reformers suggest that this ideal world will emerge if decisionmakers agree to support gradual and incremental reforms in the international system. If national leaders develop an attitude that recognizes that cooperative behavior can be as rewarding as unilateral action, the system will move closer to providing an environment for equitable economic growth in all societies.

A System Transformer's View of the Future

Transformers seek a major overhaul of the international system. Most believe the spread of capitalism throughout the poor states will result in greater inequality. Three future scenarios emerge from this prediction:

- First, the present system of inequality and exploitation will continue. This system can only be maintained by increased authoritarianism and an extensive repression of basic human needs and aspirations. The citizens of the Third World will provide cheap labor and products for the affluent societies while living at subsistence levels. Elites within the South will be co-opted to serve the interests of the North and will use their power and influence to continue to repress efforts aimed at changing the status quo.
- Second, as the absolute poor become more aware of their deprivation and more concerned about progress, pressure for change will increase. Reform of the system is possible but unlikely. Many transformers ardently believe that change is not possible without an armed struggle—a revolution transforming the society into a more interventionist social-welfare state. (Weisskopf 1972)
- Third, Third World states will disassociate from the present international economic system through self-reliance. Advocates of this strategy seek to create a world that rejects capitalist models of growth and the Soviet alternatives emphasizing state control over production processes. These transformers seek to create an economic system that considers their country's historical experiences, national values, and other national attributes. The goal of these self-reliant systems will be to reduce dependencies on external actors by efficiently utilizing the two principal resources of poor states—land and people.

Self-reliance has been a goal of many leaders in the developing world. The policy strategies of Gandhi, Mao, and the former leader of Tanzania, Julius Nyerere, reflect values and policy goals similar to those supported by the alternative-left system transformers. Their preferred future would be an economic and political system which is decentralized to encourage participation by all legitimate actors. Those participating in this localized system would plan and implement all economic policies. This system would not rely on the "impartiality" of a market system. Instead production would be motivated by local needs. This system of self-reliance could not survive without the support of other actors in the international system. Thus, this transformation model depends upon a new tolerance for alternatives to the capitalist model or a major transformation in the international economic system.

STRATEGIES FOR RESPONDING TO THE PROBLEM OF MALDEVELOPMENT

This section reviews contending policy proposals aimed at closing the gap between rich and poor states. More specifically, it examines how system maintainers, reformers, and transformers propose to respond to the conditions of poverty and misery that threaten global stability.

A System-Maintainer Policy Agenda

The system maintainer's primary goal is to strengthen the international free-market economy. This means strengthening international institutions charged with managing the economy, and allocating or transferring resources to countries in an effort to integrate them into this economy. Although President Reagan has suggested he prefers trade and investment as solutions to global inequality, development-assistance programs remain an important tool for responding to maldevelopment. These aid programs are seen as an effective method of furthering U.S. interests and maintaining a supportive environment for international trade and investment. System maintainers, however, do not believe that the development gap can be closed by development assistance alone. The multilateral institutions created to manage and control the world economy must also be strengthened. U.S. Agency for International Development documents clearly state the four principles that guide the United States' development strategy:

- Encouraging a policy dialogue among rich and poor states and when appropriate initiating reforms of international and domestic institutions
- Transfering technology to assist in the development process
- Building institutions that will encourage foreign investors and motivate trade
- Supporting private-sector actors and market forces as engines of economic growth (USAID 1986)

U.S. policies and the policies of the World Bank, the IMF, and GATT are aimed at creating strong free-market economies. Most loan and aid programs are based on conditionalities that require the recipients to adopt free-market strategies. In 1985, the World Bank initiated a three-year plan for coordinating bilateral and multilateral aid programs tied to policy reforms aimed at opening Third World economies to foreign investors.

U.S. development assistance is linked to U.S. national interests. The major purpose of the U.S. aid program, U.S. Security and Development Cooperation Program, is to "create conditions of growth, security and freedom in developing countries." (Schultz 1983) The basics of this program have been in operation since the Truman administration; however, the Reagan administration has focused most of its attention on bilateral aid programs. Most of this aid is focused on five policy areas: the Middle East, the Caribbean Basin Initiative, population-control programs, food assistance, and security and economic assistance to strategically important Turkey. These targets of U.S. assistance reflect U.S. national interests and provide an important confirmation of the relationship between assistance and the economic and political interests of the donor.

Although the system maintainer prefers the leverage which bilateral assistance provides, international economic institutions do furnish a veneer of political neutrality and can be used to strengthen the free-market system. With promises of more grants or loans, poor states can be directed toward import liberalization policies and other such reforms, linking the country to the world market. The goal of the system maintainer is to implement a global strategy for economic growth. The policy programs of system maintainers are aimed at realizing conditions of order and stability in the poor states. If an area is free of conflict and war, it is easier to encourage foreign investment. Foreign investment will lead to trade and ultimately, suggests the system maintainer, *trade, not aid, offers a way out of abject poverty.*

A System-Reformer Policy Agenda

The Brandt Commission reports outline a bold policy agenda illustrating the goals of the system reformer. Other system-reformer plans of action have been prescribed by the Organization of African Unity (OAU) in its Lagos Plan and the follow-up to that plan, the New Priority Programme. These plans have had some impact on actual development policies; however, for the most part, a system-reformer approach to development assistance has been implemented by only a few nation-states. The most progressive reform policies have been implemented by non-state actors, private aid organizations from the United States, and Western Europe.

The Brandt Commission Recommendations
The Brandt Commission report reflects the combined interests of reformist leaders in the South and "like-minded" or reformist interest groups in the North.

Unfortunately for those who favor reforms, few of the reformist advocates in the North are in positions of great influence and power. The reformers support the free market; however, reformers favor an expansion of the role of governments in an effort to respond to persistent inequities. System reformers are international Keynesians supporting public interventions aimed at economic redistribution, land reform, and the provision of basic human needs.

The Brandt Commission has advocated significant reforms in development-assistance programs, debt-relief efforts, food production and distribution, energy consumption, and in the processes of international economic policymaking. The commission has proposed changes in the constitutions of the IMF and the World Bank in an effort to give poor states more power in these institutions. The Brandt Commission report also recommends the establishment of a new institution, the World Development Fund. (1982, 291) The developing states would play a greater role in the management and policymaking of this organization. The report also advocates changes in trading rules and regulations, including a stabilization of commodity prices and support programs that give poor states more access to commodity production and distribution processes. The general goal of the reforms outlined in the report is to provide the necessary resources and the essential decisionmaking authority to developing states that will enable them to be productive participants in the international system.

The Lagos Plan Recommendations
A second system-reformer plan of action, the Lagos Plan, emerged from the frustrations associated with the failure of the affluent states to embrace the plans for the NIEO, presented in 1974. Increased inflation and a global recession had seriously damaged the developing economies of Africa. In response to this crisis, the OAU, in 1980, proposed a reformist strategy for development by advocating multilateral action in six policy areas.

First, the OAU sought to encourage African self-reliance by urging members to accept aid for supplemental purposes only. Secondly, the plan supported the establishment of an integrated common market. This would help the OAU reach its third goal, the reduction of dependency on external sources of technology and other goods and services. This reformist strategy also called for a food-production plan to reach self-sufficiency. The members also agreed to pool their resources and expertise to develop a more effective African transportation and communication system. Finally, the Lagos Plan urged member-states to implement policies to protect and preserve the natural environment.

The Lagos Plan was not successful for several reasons. At the time African leaders were attempting to implement these programs, most of their economies were hurt by a global economic recession. Many of these same states were devastated by drought and other adverse weather conditions. Many other states were involved in civil wars fueled by U.S., Soviet, or South African geopolitical interests. A significant number of African leaders believed the plan failed because of an unjust and inequitable international economic system. (UN Special Session 1986)

In a 1985 OAU meeting in Ethiopia, African leaders reviewed the Lagos Plan and accepted a new plan, the New Priority Programme. (UN Special Session, 1986) The new program called for more political and economic support for the implementation of the Lagos Plan. It also called for a new multilateral effort aimed at improving food and agricultural production and a renewed cooperative effort to alleviate the African debt burden. This program also urged leaders to make a commitment to developing a policy program that would respond to future crisis situations. Finally, the program advocated the implementation of a collective response to the South African strategy of destabilization in front-line states.

The African famine crisis, which came to the world's attention in 1986, continues today. This situation has prompted the African nation-states to work for reforms in the international system that will enable them to survive and eventually prosper. Although these plans may never be fully implemented, they represent a reformist strategy of sharing resources and expertise, and actually transferring sovereignty to regional and international institutions in an effort to respond more effectively to crisis conditions.

The African famine prompted many states to examine their development-assistance efforts. Indeed, at the 1986 Special Session of the UN General Assembly, the affluent states were asked to increase both their emergency aid and their annual allocations. For the system reformer, the ideal assistance program would have five characteristics.

- It would focus on economic development and humanitarian purposes.
- It would give aid through multilateral organizations in order to minimize political controls.
- Aid would be in the form of grants, not loans. If loans must be given, these loans should be low-interest and long-term.
- A reformist aid program would not tie aid to purchases in the donor country. Those loans with fewer requirements to purchase goods in the donor country are more useful to recipients and usually allow them to buy more cheaply what they want and need.
- A reformist aid program would give a very high percentage of its funds to the least less developed countries.

The system reformers believe that by giving to the poorest of the poor a state shows its true humanitarian colors. Usually, assistance to these states has few security and economic implications. System reformers use development-assistance programs to help Third World states become productive trade partners. Donor states want to sell their goods and want access to primary products in Third World states. Aid is seen as an effective way of encouraging trade cooperation among rich and poor states. Development assistance can also be used to encourage and promote cultural exchanges, policy conferences, technological and scientific research, and cooperative education programs. The policy strategies promoted within the Commonwealth and the conferences of

French-speaking states provide illustrative examples of the potential for community-building from the reformist perspective. The reformist states'-assistance policies tend *not* to focus directly on geopolitical and military-security objectives. Thus, correctly or incorrectly, aid recipients find aid packages from many of these reformists states to be less objectionable than aid from some of the major powers.

System reformers generally believe that the answers to inequality will not result from any attempt radically to transform the present international system. However, they also recognize that if inequities persist, the disadvantaged are more likely to support violence as a means of changing their status. The system reformer prescribes policies that will result in gradual and purposive reforms in national, regional, and international institutions charged with determining the distribution of goods, services, and opportunities within the international community. The purpose of these reforms would be to create a more equitable international system.

A System-Transformer Policy Agenda

There are three different transformer policy strategies to be explored here: (1) the policy recommendations identified with the NIEO; (2) several self-reliance plans; and (3) an alternative-left or WOMP development-assistance program.

The majority of the nation-states in the South have supported all or some of the NIEO proposals, which they see as a way to avoid major economic crises and close the gap between rich and poor states. The NIEO program suggests significant transformations in the international system, aimed at breaking the dependency conditions that limit the flexibility and independence of poor states in the international system. This set of policy recommendations is more than just a set of economic regulations. It is an attempt to change the power game in the international system. The nation-states of the South seek greater access to decisionmaking in all international economic institutions. First proposed in 1974, the NIEO recommendations have not been implemented; however, they still remain as a basis for discussion and a model for those leaders concerned with inequities within and between societies. (Meagher 1979)

The NIEO platform calls for significant reforms in trade, foreign investment, technology transfer, and development policy. In addition, the document includes calls for structural reforms in international economic institutions, which would give developing states more decisionmaking power.

Trade is an important source of finance for continued development within the poor states. Intending to increase prices and volume of exports to the wealthy states of the North, the South seeks to expand access to markets in wealthier states by establishing preferential tariffs and by initiating a program of buffer stocks to stabilize and eventually increase commodity prices. Those states supporting the NIEO also want to link the prices of commodities to the costs of manufactured items they now must import. The leaders of the Group of

77 (i.e., states which support the NIEO proposals in the UN) also hope to increase production of manufactured goods (i.e., import substitution) in their countries and, thereby, diversify their economies.

The states supporting NIEO reforms believe that their societies have been exploited by foreign investors, particularly TNEs. To rectify these injustices, the South seeks the capacity to increase surveillance and control over foreign corporations. If necessary, these states want to be able to nationalize foreign-owned property or to receive financial compensation for property or resources used by foreign-owned TNEs.

The NIEO document also calls for an increase in benefits to the developing world. This includes an increase in technology transfers from rich to poor states and greater access to international financial resources. NIEO proponents want assurances of a consistent flow of development assistance from more affluent countries. This would include long-term aid agreements without conditions and more funds for emergency programs such as the UN's World Food Programme.

The NIEO is a political document. NIEO proponents are seeking greater access to decisionmaking processes in the IMF, World Bank, and in the GATT. These states also seek to improve the chances of developing states by urging negotiations regarding the postponement or forgiveness of the South's debts and the establishment of a system that would allow poor states to borrow a new form of international currency based on their development-finance needs rather than on their international credit rating.

The NIEO document advocates an expanded definition of security to include the provision of basic economic opportunities and needs for all citizens. To this end, the advocates of the NIEO program urge a comprehensive international education program aimed at increasing awareness of the conditions within poor states and the complexity of these issues. (Meagher 1979)

Proposals for disassociating from the international system and establishing either an autarkic economy or a collective self-reliance system have been advocated by many leaders in the developing world. Generally, advocates of these strategies reject pressures to select either a free-market or a state-planning model, seeking instead an economic-development strategy that is most appropriate to their country's cultural setting and considers other national attributes. Self-reliance means focusing on local resources and needs and building an economy based on internal trade and not external linkages that usually create dependencies.

The Indian political and spiritual leader Gandhi felt that self-reliance meant freedom for the people of India. His salt- and cloth-production campaigns were aimed at providing employment, reducing the control of outside forces on the economy, and giving people some control over consumption and production policies. In addition, workers developed skills, competencies, and dignity, which would enable them to contribute politically in an independent India. In China, Mao Zedong advocated policies that placed people at the center of the development process. The past president of Tanzania, Julius K. Nyerere, suggested that poor states must build their economies around their two primary resources—people and land. All three of these transformation strategies advocate policies that encourage poor states to depend on local resources and work to reduce dependent development strategies. These strategies also advocate decentralization of economic decisionmaking in an effort to increase local participation and to encourage the development of an economic system reflecting local interests and needs and effectively and appropriately utilizing local resources. The imperatives of the international economy are not naively dismissed by these transformers. Instead, they suggest that trade should be used to build solidarity with nation-states with similar historical experiences, values, and needs.

Self-reliance strategies have not been very effective because it is so difficult for states to provide for their citizens' welfare without external trade. Self-reliance is an expensive strategy and few Third World states can afford that independence.

The alternative-left transformer perspective is best represented by the work of scholars in the World Order Models Project (WOMP). In his seminal work, *The National Interest and the Human Interest,* Robert Johansen compares U.S. development-assistance objectives in India with a strategy based on the WOMP goals of economic well-being, social justice, peace, and ecological balance. The policy objectives he presents provide an excellent example of a system-transformer strategy. (1980, 194–95) They include a commitment to a minimum standard of living, a concern for the environment, and development programs that involve local citizens in all decisions about how to use assistance funds. They also propose programs aimed at decreasing overconsumption in affluent states and the establishment of international institutions in which states have equal access to power and resources. A WOMP strategy would include aid programs based on human needs and not on national-security goals or the economic interests of the donor. Furthermore, a WOMP strategy recognizes the importance of non-state actors in the development process and supports the involvement of these organizations to insure that aid reaches the very poor. The WOMP transformers also support a commitment to a level of aid that reflects a recognition of the importance of burden-sharing in the redistribution of global resources and opportunities.

The three transformation strategies presented in this section are based on a common assumption—the desire to change a decisionmaking or power structure perceived to perpetuate violence and poverty throughout the international system. Not all transformers are as interested in the poor as their rhetoric might suggest. Although many transformers advocate change, once successful in their quest for power and resources, many leaders readily become system maintainers. This, however, is not reason enough to dismiss this worldview as either irrelevant or utopian. The transformations advocated by individuals who identify with this worldview are as much an effort to change the international power structure as they are policies aimed at alleviating human suffering. This may be why many leaders in the affluent world have so much trouble embracing these ideas.

CONCLUDING REMARKS

The purpose of this chapter was to introduce the student of international relations to a complex global problem thought by many to be the most critical problem that leaders of the world must consider. The inequities associated with maldevelopment certainly affect all societies. The reader was presented with three different worldview perspectives on this very controversial issue. The worldviews approach encourages the student to examine his or her assumptions about how the world works and particularly how different individuals see and respond to inequalities within the international community. The various indicators of maldevelopment presented in this chapter suggest that growth-oriented measures have not worked satisfactorily in all countries. Perhaps more traditional strategies of development must be combined with more equity-oriented reforms and measures. These might include programs that encourage local decisionmaking and self-sufficiency, and policies aimed at decreasing dependencies on external markets or investors. These reforms might also include a commensurate transfer of political power to local groups and adequate resources to provide basic human needs and maintain cultural integrity. As Margaret Mead (1962) once suggested, the technical skills and resources exist to provide for the basic human needs of citizens in all countries. It is hoped this chapter will encourage students to look for additional information that presents a contending-perspectives analysis of international affairs. After carefully assessing this information, students might consider a personal plan of action in this policy arena. Whatever form this participation takes it should be an informed response. Policy programs aimed at alleviating poverty must consider the interests and priorities of the absolute poor and the most affluent. For these policies to be effective, they cannot be biased disproportionately toward the interests of one actor or a small group of actors in the international system. Issues of equity and economic well-being must be considered with issues of efficiency and economic growth. It does not seem that any one political orientation or economic philosophy has a monopoly on solutions when one unravels the inequalities that divide the international system.

REFERENCES

Africa Emergency Report, No. 6, April-May 1986.
Africa News. "Following the Cash Flow." November 2, 1987:11.

Ambrose, Stephen. *Rise to Globalism*. New York: Penguin Books, 1980.

Australia. Department of Foreign Affairs. *Australia and the Third World*. Report of the Committee on Australia's Relations with the Third World, Harries; 1979.

Bauer, P. T. *Equality, the Third World, and Economic Delusion*. Cambridge, MA: Harvard University Press, 1981.

Brandt Commission. *North-South: A Program for Survival*. Cambridge, MA: The MIT Press, 1982.

―――. *Common Crisis North-South: Cooperation for World Recovery*. Cambridge, MA: The MIT Press, 1983.

Carty, Roberta, and Virginia Smith. *Perpetuating Poverty: The Political Economy of Canadian Foreign Aid*. Toronto: Between the Lines, 1981.

Clapham, Christopher. *Third World Politics*. Madison: The University of Wisconsin Press, 1985.

Clarke, Robert, and Richard Swift. *Ties That Bind: Canada and the Third World*. Toronto: Between the Lines, 1982.

Crow, Ben, and Alan Thomas. *Third World Atlas*. Story Stratford, England: Open University Press, 1983.

Desai, Padma. "The Soviet Union and the Third World: A Faltering Partnership." In *Power, Passions and Purpose*. Edited by J. N. Bhagwati and J. G. Ruggie. Cambridge, MA: The MIT Press, 1984.

Eckholm, Erik. *Down to Earth: Environment and Human Needs*. New York: W. W. Norton, 1982.

Galbraith, John K. *The Voice of the Poor*. Cambridge, MA: Harvard University Press, 1983.

Galtung, Johan. *The True Worlds: A Transnational Perspective*. New York: The Free Press, 1980.

Gauhar, Altaf. *Talking About Development*. London: Third World Foundation for Social and Economic Studies, 1983.

Harboe, Jorgen, editor. *The European Ten and the Third World*. Brussels: The International Coalition for Development of Action, 1983.

Johansen, Robert. *The National Interest and the Human Interest: An Analysis of U.S. Foreign Policy*. Princeton, NJ: Princeton University Press, 1980.

Kohler, Gernot. "Global Apartheid." In *Toward A Just World Order*. Edited by R. Falk, S. Kim, and S. Mendolvitz. Boulder, CO: Westview Press, 1982.

Lewis, Oscar. *Five Families*. New York: Basic Books, 1959.

McNamara, Robert. *Address to the Board of Governors*. Washington, DC: World Bank, 1980.

Mead, Margaret. "The Underdeveloped and the Overdeveloped," *Foreign Affairs* 41 (1962):78–89.

Meagher, Robert F. *An International Redistribution of Wealth and Power*. New York: Pergamon Press, 1979.

Mortimer, Robert. *The Third World Coalition*. Boulder, CO: Westview Press, 1984.

Murdoch, William. *The Poverty of Nations*. Baltimore: Johns Hopkins University Press, 1980.

Pearson, Lester B., *et al.*, *Partners in Development: Report of the Commission on International Development*. New York: Praeger Publishers, 1969.

Sivard, Ruth. *World Military and Social Expenditures 1985*. Washington, DC: World Priorities, 1985.

Shipler, David K. "Schultz Visits Africa With Gifts and Exhortation," *New York Times* (January 18, 1987): Section IV p. 3.

Stevens, Ross. *A Matter of Right—The Rich, The Poor and the UN*. New York: Global Negotiation Information Project, 1982.

UN General Assembly. Special Session on the Critical Economic Situation in Africa. *The Background*. Prepared by the Division for Economic and Social Information, 1986a.

UN General Assembly. Special Session on the Critical Economic Situation in Africa. *The Major Issues*. Prepared by the Division for Economic and Social Information, 1986b.

U.S. Agency for International Development. "Privatization and the Private Sector: Keys to Third World Development." *AID Highlights* 3 (Summer 1986).

U.S. Arms Control and Disarmament Agency. *World Military Expenditures and Arms Transfers 1986*. Washington, DC: ACDA Publications, 1987.

U.S. Department of State. *Foreign Aid and National Interests*. Address by George Schultz to the Southern Center for International Studies, Atlanta, Georgia. February 24, 1983.

U.S. Department of State. *Foreign Assistance Request for FY 1986*. Statement by George Schultz before the House Foreign Affairs Committee. Washington, DC, February 19, 1985.

U.S. Department of State. *Sub-Saharan Africa and the United States*. Discussion Paper. December 1985.

U.S. Department of State. *FY 1987 Assistance Request for Sub-Saharan Africa*. Statement by Chester A. Crocker before the subcommittee on International Operations of the House Foreign Affairs Committee. Washington, DC, March 18, 1986.

U.S. Department of State. *Warsaw Pact Economic Aid to Non-Communist LDCs, 1984*. Bureau of Intelligence and Research, May 1986.

U.S. Department of State. *The Challenge of African Economic Reform*. Address by George Schultz to the Senegalese Business Council, Dakar, Senegal. January 8, 1987.

Weisskopf, Thomas. "Capitalism, Underdevelopment and the Future of the Poor Countries." In *Economics and World Order*. Edited by J. N. Bhagwati. New York: The Free Press, 1972.

World Bank. *The Development Data Handbook*. Washington, DC, 1984.

World Bank. *The World Bank and International Finance Corporation*. Washington, DC, 1986.

World Development Report 1985. New York: Oxford University Press, 1985.

6

Human Rights and Sovereignty
SUSAN WALTZ
FARROKH JHABVALA

Many prisoners of conscience indefinitely confined to psychiatric hospitals [in the Soviet Union] are reported to have been given forcible treatment with disorienting and pain-causing drugs by doctors. . . . In one known case a prisoner's health deteriorated so dramatically that in 1982 doctors offered to grant him invalid status.

—Amnesty International, *Torture in the 80's*

Extensive prison archives kept in one Cambodian death camp—a former secondary school in Phnom Penh—document the torture and eventual execution of 15,000 Cambodians under the four years of Khmer Rouge rule (1975–79).

—Stover and Nightingale, *The Breaking of Bodies and Minds*

In August 1984, a 23-year-old man was held for interrogation in Belfast, Northern Ireland. He was allowed access to his solicitor only after 72 hours had passed, during which time he was allegedly punched, slapped, kicked and spat on, and after black plastic bags had been repeatedly pulled over his head and molded to his face so that he could not breathe.

—Amnesty International, *1985 Report*

During the summer of 1985 the Ethiopian government began emptying aid centers. . . . The International Red Cross distributed seed, tools, and food to everyone and was authorized to continue its distribution of food on a monthly basis. But in October, the Red Cross was forbidden to distribute any more food to the peasants.

—"Doctors Without Frontiers," *Ethiopia Report, 1985*

At the entrance to the torture chamber [in an Iraqi prison] there is a doormat with "Welcome" written on it in English.

—Amnesty International, *1985 Report*

Between 1975 and April 1980, 233 cases of "disappeared prisoners" were documented by the Task Force Detainees of the Philippines. Some of these prisoners were eventually found dead and mutilated in isolated areas . . . , while others reappeared . . . with tales of torture at the hands of their military interrogators.

—Amnesty International, *"Disappearances" : A Workbook*

The Guatemalan government has admitted that its military has destroyed 440 Indian villages and, as a result, created 200,000 orphan children since 1978. Today Guatemala has more refugees than any other Latin American country.

—*Maryknoll Justice and Peace Office Newsletter*

THINKING ABOUT HUMAN RIGHTS

Torture and murder of political opponents is a widespread and daily occurrence in the world today. To punish and destroy their opponents, many governments appear to have combined the most barbarous instincts in human beings with the sophisticated tools placed in their hands by science, technology, and psychology. Governments resort to many other devices to silence opposition: They declare national emergencies to justify their arrogation of absolute power; suspend constitutions and individual rights; muzzle the media; and declare martial law, with all of its derogations from due process, to replace the civil law of the state. Human rights, citizen rights, are disregarded, even flagrantly violated.

We introduce this issue by focusing on a dynamic tension between rulers and ruled because to be understood properly, today's human-rights problem must be seen as part of the relationship between a people and its government. Generically, human-rights problems are born of that relationship and the treatment that a government metes out to its people. Controversy in the whole area of human rights is inevitable, because any improvement of the human condition entails placing limitations upon a government that has been harassing or oppressing its people.

Individuals in poor societies seek to attain minimum standards of living, including food, shelter, health care, education, and employment. Individuals in the more advanced societies seek to improve their existing standards, including, in addition to the items listed above, leisure and leisure activities. Everywhere, individuals seek some freedom, privacy, dignity, and the opportunity to run their own lives. Dignity may be defined as the inviolability of the individual's person. Slavery, bonded labor, and other similar practices are, therefore, antithetical to human dignity.

Individuals live in societies with other individuals, deriving economic, political, cultural, social, and many other advantages through association. Clearly, modern societies could not operate at an optimum level in any of the numerous functions they perform were they no more than an aggregation of individuals. Thus, a balance needs to be struck between the interests of the individual on the one hand, and those of the society on the other. The exact nature of the balance will vary from society to society; and within societies, from time to time. The balance is often struck through political bargaining between the various and overlapping groups, associations, and sectors of a society, and then is cast into a constitution, into laws, and into practices and conventions particular to the society concerned. As a society evolves and the needs and interests of its citizens change, the basic balances struck and encoded in the constitution, laws, and conventions must change apace.

The basic and most important needs and interests of people are often called "rights" or "human rights," and are most typically so declared in state constitutions. They may be viewed as claims upon the society or its government, or as limitations on society and its government. Thus, the right to free speech may be viewed as a limitation upon society and the government—one's right to free speech will be interfered with only under certain specified conditions. The right may also be viewed as a claim of the individual upon society and its government—society and the government have the duty to ensure the opportunity for free speech. But this right of the individual has to be balanced against the interests of society at large; thence comes the necessity of limits to the right to free speech, and to other rights.

The critical importance of rights to the daily lives of individuals stems from the unalterable fact that rights are indispensable in pursuing and attaining one's needs and interests. The opportunity to earn one's livelihood depends upon a host of rights, including, but not limited to, the right to employment, to a fair wage, to job security, and to freedom from racial or other discrimination in employment. Similarly, if one chooses to form a family, one needs to have the right to marry the person of one's choice, to have children, to raise one's children in the value system of one's choice, and so on. The indispensable connection between other human rights and human needs and interests can be similarly demonstrated. One may go further and assert that human rights are important not only because they are the vehicles through which human beings attain their goals and needs, but also because rights have an intrinsic value in themselves, enriching human life and elevating it far above the level of mere existence.

Categories of Human Rights

Human rights may be grouped into several categories for analytical or other purposes, always keeping in mind, however, that rights in the several categories are interdependent and that the person, who is an integral unit, needs all rights and not just some. One category of rights, called "personal" rights, includes those rights concerned with the integrity and dignity of the person, such as the right to life, the right to be free from slavery and other forms of bondage, the right to be free from torture and cruel punishment, the right to be recognized as a person under law, the right to a fair trial and due process of law, to be presumed innocent until proven guilty, and so forth.

Another category of rights, called "political" rights, includes the rights of full participation in the political processes of the state and the government. Political rights include the right to choose one's leaders and one's government at stated intervals of time, the right to stand for political office, and the right to hold one's leaders and government accountable for their decisions and policies. Other categories of rights are "economic" rights, "social" rights, and "cultural" rights.

That these various categories of rights are interdependent and that all are essential for human fulfillment may be easily demonstrated. To survive physically, one needs to have employment, which is immediately determined by economic rights. However, economic rights may be arbitrarily abridged by the government or by powerful segments of society. Therefore, to protect one's economic rights, one needs to have political rights—to place a check on arbitrary government action—and personal rights—to ward off encroachment by others in society. Employment is also related to, and dependent upon, education, health care, and the like, which comprise, with others, the category "social" rights. To fulfill some of one's emotional, intellectual, and spiritual needs one must be able to associate and communicate freely with others having the same interests, be they linguistic or ethnic; these constitute "cultural" rights.

Thus, human-rights problems may be seen as occurring when the societal balance between the individual and the government is struck too far in favor of government. The individual gives up, or is forced to give up, a disproportionate degree of freedoms, needs, and interests, and the government commensurately gains the extra degree of control over the individual's life. Power tends to corrupt, and absolute power corrupts absolutely: Lord Acton's words have never rung truer than in regard to modern late-twentieth-century states and governments. The enormous power wielded by states and governments in recent years has also been accompanied by unprecedented levels of corruption in many forms, including the political and moral corruption that produces massive human rights violations.

Human Rights in the International System

For nearly four centuries, world politics has been premised on the notion of the sovereignty of states, and the world political system—if that be the correct term—may properly be described as the Westphalian system. The modern system of sovereign states is said to have been ushered in by the Treaties of Westphalia, which concluded the Thirty Years War (1618–1648) in Europe. Sovereignty is a complex concept and one not easy to define. It has always included the element of absolute independence in internal or domestic matters, i.e., a sovereign state had the right to be absolutely free from external interference in its internal affairs. Practical matters did not always run according to precept, but even when external interference occurred in a state's internal affairs, the interfering party usually felt constrained to explain its interference while it upheld the principle in rhetoric.

The enormous and threatening corollary to the notion of absolute internal sovereignty of a state was that the relations between a government and its people were regarded as no one else's business. Sovereignty meant, in part, that no matter how badly or cruelly a government treated its own people, it was a domestic or internal matter and not one about which other states or their peoples could have anything to say. Thus, large-scale and barbarous violations of human rights could be perpetrated by a government upon its own people without any other government or people having the right to step in and stop it. The most extreme of such violations occurred during the Holocaust wreaked by Nazi Germany on Jews, Slavs, and others during World War II.

Largely in reaction to the Holocaust, but also building upon other trends and developments during the hundred years prior to 1945, the framers of the United Nations (UN) Charter made the promotion and protection of human rights everywhere the business of the world body. Given that virtually every country in the world is today a member of the UN, the human-rights principles enshrined in the UN Charter, the world organization's constitution, have been accepted globally, at least on paper. An evaluation of the UN's work on human rights would be too lengthy to be undertaken here. At the risk of distortion and oversimplification, however, it may be said that despite the UN's efforts and despite its charter and other human-rights documents, many countries have yet to arrive at the stage where they will cease to insist that human rights are domestic matters and abide by the human-rights standards that have been set.

Basic Human Rights Instruments

The past generation's efforts to promote and protect human rights have proceeded along several paths. Sustained efforts have been made by concerned individuals and groups at the global level through the UN and its associated organizations, such as the United Nations Educational, Scientific, and Cultural Organization (UNESCO). Parallel efforts have been made at the regional level in Western Europe and the Americas. More recently, international activity seeking to promote and protect human rights has commenced in Africa and Asia.

Progress at the global level has been impressive insofar as the setting of standards is concerned; on the other hand, progress in the actual protection of individuals from governmental oppression has been slight and largely disappointing. Because progress at the global level often can occur only when a sufficiently large consensus has emerged on a given matter, it is remarkable that relatively rapid progress has been made in the setting of human-rights standards. However, when it comes to an investigation of a government's oppression of its people, or to publicizing and criticizing such oppression, member-states of global international organizations shrink back. It ought to be mentioned that in a Westphalian system, publicity is often the only means available, other than private protests, to international human-rights bodies.

The issue of human rights is often politicized in international organizations by overlaying it with other broader global conflicts such as the East-West, the North-South, and the Arab-Israeli conflicts. Other than South Africa, whose system of apartheid has been consistently opposed by a large majority of states, UN bodies have until recently found themselves unable to name governments violating human rights and to criticize them publicly. In recent years, a few states, such as Chile, have been specifically cited by name as being violators of human rights.

The progress made by the UN and other global bodies in setting standards must be evaluated in light of the fact that until the end of World War II there were no standards that could be said to have been accepted by all or most states. There were, of course, national standards. In a Westphalian world, however, international standards for state behavior are generally set by the states themselves. It is, therefore, remarkable that within three years after the establishment of the UN, its General Assembly had adopted the Universal Declaration of Human Rights as the minimum standard to be achieved by states through their individual and collective efforts.

Since then, numerous multilateral treaties on human rights have been negotiated and accepted by states. The idea behind this effort has been that states can legitimately be expected to live up to the treaty obligations they have voluntarily accepted. The most important global human-rights treaties are the International Covenant on Civil and Political Rights (CCPR) and the International Covenant on Economic, Social and Cultural Rights (CESCR), both adopted by the UN General Assembly in 1966. These treaties received the necessary state ratifications by early 1976 and entered into force that year. They provide for periodic reports on their implementation by the states that have accepted them. These reports are studied by an expert body called the Human Rights Committee in the case of the CCPR, and by a subsidiary body of the UN's Economic and Social Council in the case of the CESCR. Whether individual states not fulfilling their treaty obligations are to be named in the public reports of these bodies is a question that has yet to be resolved.

Perhaps the best way to protect the rights of individuals is by conferring upon them the capacity to bring petitions or complaints against their governments before impartial international bodies in cases where the domestic legal system has been unable to protect them. Provision for such a development is made in the Optional Protocol to the CCPR. However, the Westphalian order calls for states to consent to the conferral of such a capacity upon their citizens, and only a handful of states have been so willing.

The greatest progress has been made in Western Europe, where the European Convention on Human Rights has been in force since 1953. The convention has created two bodies, the European Commission of Human Rights and the European Court of Human Rights. Any state that becomes a party to the convention may bring a complaint to the commission alleging a violation by any other member-state of the rights protected by the convention. In addition, member-states may voluntarily confer authority upon the commission to hear petitions by individuals alleging a violation of their rights, after the individuals have sought and failed to obtain redress from the domestic legal order of the state concerned. Eighteen of the twenty-one members of this treaty system have conferred such authority upon the commission. The states that have not yet done so are Cyprus, Malta, and Turkey. These three states are nevertheless subject to complaints by other member-states.

The commission investigates the complaint and seeks an explanation from the government concerned. If the government's explanation is found to be reasonable the matter ends there. If not, the commission attempts to resolve the issue amicably in a manner that will protect the individual's violated right. Often this attempt proves successful. However, the commission has the authority in cases where it finds that a right may have been violated and the government is not accommodating, to publish its findings against the government. The commission may, further, take the matter to the European Court of Human Rights if the state being accused has conferred jurisdiction upon the court. All the member-states except Malta and Turkey have recognized the jurisdiction of the court. In the court, the government has to defend its position as a matter of law, and it may lose. Often West European governments modify their practices before an adverse decision is handed down by the court.

A similar system has been established in the past several years for the Americas. The Inter-American Court of Human Rights in San José, Costa Rica, has been functioning since 1978. Conditions peculiar to the American hemisphere, however, have retarded the effectiveness of this system. First, several large and important states have not yet become parties to the Inter-American Convention on Human Rights: the United States, Brazil, and Mexico are the most prominent holdouts. Second, socioeconomic and political conditions in much of Central and South America continue to be in a state of considerable flux and uncertainty, and the necessary socioeconomic and political bases for the success of a human-rights system do not appear to be in place. While a system to protect the individual from governmental oppression may contribute to the establishment of the essential socioeconomic and political bases, it is doubtful whether it can do so single-handedly and against powerful and entrenched domestic vested interests.

POSITIONS ON HUMAN RIGHTS

There is no credible actor in the international system today declaring itself "against" human rights. Even the most abusive of governments pays some lip service to the notion of human dignity and human rights. No government officially endorses a policy of torture: Most, in fact, deny that they even practice torture, despite well-documented evidence. Human rights are an area of debate today, but the issue is *not*—at least in theory—about the merits of such rights. Virtually every country in the world gives tacit assent to basic standards of rights, which, if implemented, would put many human-rights groups happily out of business.

Human rights receive loyal lip service; the idea is easy to endorse. The critical problems arise only with implementation, and thus it should not be surprising that the major human-rights debate concerns respect for human rights and, more precisely, the *guarantee* of those rights. How, ultimately, should the individual be safeguarded against abuses? Human rights can be effectively guaranteed only by domestic law. The international system does not now possess, and is unlikely to possess in the foreseeable future, anything that approaches the capacity that would be needed to resolved all the individual claims of human-rights violations. Only national governments possess such a capacity today and they will, in all likelihood, retain this capacity for themselves. Real relief for the individual often entails some domestic action or limitation of authority. Only national governments are able to give such relief.

International actors—whether states, national subgroups seeking to influence foreign policies, or international non-governmental organizations—react differently to an international system that acknowledges, implicitly or explicitly, the state's preeminent role in the protection of human rights. Some, including many human-rights offenders, are quite content with the situation as it stands. Others seek change in varying degrees. How can the range of positions be sorted out?

Many analyses of international human-rights questions consider arguments about the relative importance of different sets of rights (civil/political versus social/economic) or the role of human rights in economic development. As we have pointed out, however, the different categories of rights do not thrive in mutually exclusive conditions; economic rights frequently depend on political and personal rights, and vice versa. It is our view that arguments promoting one set of rights over another obscure rather than illuminate the issue. The role ascribed to national sovereignty is the paramount issue as far as the international perspective on human rights is concerned, and it is the dimension along which we would array different positions about human rights. (See Exhibit 8.1.) The arguments of international actors should be evaluated in terms of whether they consider human-rights issues subordinate to or superior to the issue of national sovereignty.

Exhibit 6.1 Contending Perspectives on Human Rights

	Statement of Position	Prescriptions for the Future
System maintainer	Abuses may be regretted and denounced, but ultimately human rights are a domestic issue.	Encourage domestic reforms; undertake limited foreign-policy initiatives.
System reformer	Human rights are established and guaranteed by international law, agreed to and accepted by sovereign states. International law, like all duly enacted law, must be respected by governments.	Extend and enforce international law.
System transformer	Human rights are universal, a "collective" good. The historical artifact of national sovereignty must not be allowed to abrogate human rights.	Support the work of non-governmental organizations and international advocacy groups in calling attention to problems. Where domestic institutions fail to protect rights, supranational institutions should provide opportunities for redress.

System Maintainers

Some actors in the international system, though they may deplore abuses perpetrated by their foes, have no basic quarrel with the system. They accept without qualms the principle that a sovereign state has the right to be free from external interference in its domestic affairs. From this perspective, there can be no appeal on human rights beyond the state. It is considered acceptable for outside governments to draw on normal foreign-policy instruments to apply limited pressure—as in recent U.S. Congressional hearings on Romania's trade status, which took into consideration its human-rights offenses. The emphasis, however, is on pressure being *limited,* and the acceptability of pressure depends at least as much on the nature of the human-rights offender as on the human-rights offense. In any case, open interference is frowned upon because, ultimately, human rights are seen as a domestic issue. Those who hold such views, be they states or individuals, endorse the status quo: They are system maintainers.

In the contemporary system, most states effectively espouse this position (though sometimes official statements designed for public consumption may seem to belie it). Certainly, major human-rights offenders among the poorer states hail this principle, but so do both the United States and the Soviet Union—both of whom claim to embrace a certain mutually conflicting view of human rights. The Soviet Union, representing socialist states, has frequently defended the notion of socioeconomic rights, castigating the Western powers for their failure to meet such claims as the right to work, the right to decent housing, or the right to medical care—all enshrined in the Universal Declaration of Human Rights. From the Soviet perspective, equality is the most important human right and the *sine qua non* of other rights. For its part, the United States draws on its tradition of Western liberalism and in its rhetoric holds liberty—political, civil, and economic—as the paramount right. Social and economic rights are regarded as social values not within the government's duties to promote. The Soviets are condemned for their disregard of civil and political liberties, such as freedoms of speech and assembly and due process protections for persons on trial.

Scholars entering these battles of rhetoric discern the dichotomy, and much has been written about the relative importance of socioeconomic versus civil and political rights. Some arguments dismiss one and elevate the other; other arguments pose the familiar chicken-and-egg question: Which comes first? David P. Forsythe argues that both sets of rights are integrally related. If the socialist systems have failed to create liberty along with their pursuit of equality, it must also be noted that Western societies like the United States have found it necessary to implement egalitarian, economically redistributional measures, such as minimum wage and social security, in order to soften and make socially acceptable the brutality of "pure" economic liberty. The point we wish to make here, however, is that in one very important way, each of these principal actors —however different they may appear—endorses the same basic approach to human rights. That approach is quite simple: Each state determines for itself how it will promote the international human-rights standards it has accepted. The sovereignty principle is upheld intact. As one author notes: "If the United States and the Soviet Union are locked in competitive imperial geopolitics, they are united in their conservative attempts to check the historical tide of anti-hegemonism. The common ideological denominator of their global human rights politics is the defense of what may be called superstatism. (Kim 1984, 239)

The United States has demonstrated its attachment to the sovereignty principle, or "superstatism," in its reluctance to ratify most of the international human-rights treaties, even those in basic harmony with its own Bill of Rights. President Carter signed the two UN covenants, but for ten years both have languished in the Senate awaiting ratification. It took almost forty years for the Senate to ratify the Genocide Convention outlawing atrocities against groups, such as those perpetrated in Nazi Germany or, more recently, in Pol Pot's Cambodia.

The Soviet Union, for its part, has readily affixed its seal to many of the human-rights treaties, but then has blatantly disregarded them. This situation is likely to endure so long as jurisdiction for human-rights abuses lies exclusively within the area of state sovereignty. The USSR has argued vigorously within the UN against any changes that might allow UN officials to circumvent the state in their surveillance of human rights. Such arguments themselves are based on an absolutist notion of sovereignty.

System maintainers see human-rights questions as essentially domestic issues and do their best to keep them off the global agenda. Tellingly, one proposal in 1986 to trim the UN budget involved eliminating a summer meeting to be held by a subcommission of the UN's Commission on Human Rights. That subcommission, unusually, has developed rules to allow members to sit as individuals rather than state representatives, and thus the group has been operating with considerably greater aplomb than most committees can. In its relatively independent probes into torture, mass disappearances, and slavery, the subcommission has succeeded in offending human-rights violators on both ends of the political spectrum, and many UN members would happily see it shut down.

When human-rights issues are admitted, however reluctantly, to the foreign-policy arena, system maintainers relate them and hold them subservient to questions of national interest. Condemnation of human rights is added to the foreign-policy arsenal for use against unfriendly governments; the abuses of friendlier governments are more readily overlooked. In one recent report, three U.S. human-rights watchdog groups took the Reagan administration to task for just such behavior. They denounced the administration's apologies for the abuses of U.S. allies, citing, *inter alia,* attempts by Elliot Abrams (a former assistant secretary of state for human rights) to explain away widespread use of political imprisonment and torture in Turkey by pointing to Turkey's geographic juxtaposition to the Soviet Union. The administration was not so charitable to its foes. The Soviet Union was criticized relentlessly. At official commemorations of Human Rights Day in 1984, the groups argued, the administration stacked the deck by inviting twelve former human-rights victims blatantly unrepresentative of the overall pattern of violations around the world. The "special foreign guests" came from the Soviet Union, Poland, Iran, Cuba, Nicaragua, Afghanistan, and Kampuchea. (Americas Watch, *et al*. 1985) The selective application of human-rights standards often brings charges of hypocrisy from government critics, though system maintainers are not likely to find such charges troublesome. From their view, universality in the application of international standards is much less important than the immediate concerns of the individual state. Policy inconsistencies are inevitable and, except for the difficulties in explaining them to the public, are not a source of embarrassment to the system maintainer.

System Reformers

Without challenging the legitimacy of the international system, a second group of actors actively encourages respect for existing human-rights treaties and the ratification of new ones. Reformers take the position that, for better or worse, the Westphalian system is here to stay. A practical course thus dictates a solution to human-rights issues that focuses on changing the behavior of states within the basic system established four centuries ago. Rather than initiate radical change, these actors advocate reform of existing norms and practices as well as some limited changes in the international system itself. Whether as nongovernmental organizations, individual states, or international bodies, these actors uphold the notion of universality that underlies the Universal Declaration of Human Rights. They find legitimacy for their reformist cause in the international covenants. At the bottom of their arguments is not so much a moral position as a legal one: Both the UN Charter and the Universal Declaration of Human Rights set internationally recognized standards; international human rights covenants have treaty status and must be respected as such.

Several states from various geographic regions have been exceptionally active in the furtherance of international human-rights law. Many nongovernmental organizations, domestic and international, monitor human-rights abuses with an eye to the law. In the United States, the American Civil Liberties Union is well-known for its role in upholding the Bill of Rights. In other countries—including some Third World countries, such as Tunisia and Chile—a domestic league of human rights or a human-rights commission fulfills a similar function, though sometimes restricted in practice. To monitor adherence to specific international agreements pertaining to human rights, a specific, though restricted, group may be established, such as the Helsinki Watch group formed after Western and Soviet-bloc powers signed the Helsinki Accord, promising respect for and promotion of personal rights. Professional legal groups, such as the International Commission of Jurists, or the Lawyers' Committee for International Human Rights, have more universal interest in assuring that international human-rights law is respected.

System reformers find hope for human rights in international law, and their overall goals are essentially twofold. First, they seek compliance with the law, and they view international law, the solemn agreements between and among sovereign states, as both morally and legally binding. International human-rights laws take on the quality of "general principles" or "moral truths" that have historically been used in the international legal system to rid the world of evils such as slavery and the slave trade. Reformers have problems in pursuing their aim because the international legal system itself is established and maintained by states who, most commonly, act to protect their narrowly defined national interests. International law is a part of the same Westphalian order that has created other obstacles to the international protection of human rights. Because the human-rights covenants are essentially treaties, states are free to subscribe to them as they please. The Westphalian order places no penalty on a state that does not ratify or accede to a human-rights covenant.

The second goal of human-rights reformers is the furtherance of law. The view is that the protection of human rights can be best achieved as a matter of daily practice across the world only through the establishment of international legal standards that come, over time, to be incorporated into domestic legal systems and are then routinely implemented domestically. The international legal system is, therefore, expanded by the introduction of new treaties, such as the Convention on Torture, introduced for ratification by UN members in December 1984. Similarly, the African Charter on Human and Peoples' Rights, which entered into force in October 1986, was welcomed warmly by reformers, however sceptical they may have been about the Organization of African Unity's ability to carry out its mandate.

The legal regime is also extended when innovative elements are introduced into otherwise conventional instruments, such as the Optional Protocol to the CCPR. With some originality, the Optional Protocol shifts attention from states who sign the treaty to the individuals who may be actual victims of human-rights violations. Drafted alongside the CCPR, the Optional Protocol has a single purpose—to allow the Human Rights Committee established by the CCPR to receive and consider communications from individuals claiming to be victims of violations of rights set forth in the the CCPR. A similar innovation, undercutting state resistance to testimonies presented by individuals, was introduced by the UN's Economic and Social Council in 1970, wherein a complex and highly confidential procedure was elaborated to allow individual complaints to be heard by its own subsidiary Human Rights Commission.

Cumbersome procedures and restrictions on formal responses limit the effectiveness of such reforms, but advocates argue that progress in a system of loosely bound autoncmous states is necessarily slow, while a major overhaul of the system itself is only a utopian dream. Reformers focus on progress made in the international system, where only forty years ago not even lip service was paid the notion of international human rights, and where none of today's international human-rights standards were on the books. Today, at the very least, sovereignty-sensitive human-rights offenders do have to acknowledge the human-rights principles now anchored in the international system. Following the well-documented kidnapping and murder-by-torture of Joelito Filartiga in 1976, one of the Paraguayan policemen involved took up clandestine residence in New York. The Filartiga family was able to pursue justice in U.S. courts under a little-used 1789 Alien Tort statute. That statute allows foreign nationals to present cases before U.S. courts involving personal wrongs committed in violation of international law or a U.S. treaty. A U.S. appellate judge ultimately gave a judgement—uncollected—of $10.4 million in favor of the Filartigas, noting that torture was now widely and consistently condemned in international law and that a UN declaration called for redress and compensation for torture victims. The availability of U.S. courts to foreign victims of torture or other gross human-rights abuses has become a controversial issue and one on which U.S. courts are divided. Thus, after a complicated legal procedure, the federal district court in Los Angeles ruled in the case of *Siderman v. Republic of Argentina,* F. Supp. (C.D.Cal 1985), that the 1789 Alien Tort Claims Act recognized the absolute sovereign immunity from suit of foreign sovereigns and that alien plaintiffs could not, therefore, get relief from U.S. courts on claims of torture against a foreign sovereign.

Rulings about the limited applicability of the Alien Tort Claims Act notwithstanding, reformists take heart from developments such as that of the Filartiga decision and find in them hope for a world universally respectful of rational legal principles, including those of human rights.

System Transformers

Most states either endorse the sovereignty status quo or seek some reform of the international system to improve the human-rights climate. Initiatives are coming from a variety of quarters today that, intentionally or not, challenge the sovereignty principle as applied to human rights.

Among the attempts at innovative reforms, we noted the Optional Protocol, which in principle enables the Human Rights Committee to receive and examine communications from victims of human-rights violations. The scope of application of this protocol is limited, however, by the fact that adherence is voluntary and very few states have agreed to accept its provisions. Of the five permanent members of the UN Security Council, only France has acceded to this international agreement.

Transformation of the system, as opposed to reform, requires movement beyond voluntarism. Fortunately, one important example exists to indicate how progressive human-rights commitments can be successfully instituted beyond the domestic boundaries of individual nation-states. In 1953, the European Convention on Human Rights, and its institutions, the Commission and the Court of Human Rights, came into existence under the auspices of the Council of Europe. As mentioned earlier in our treatment of basic human rights instruments, all the members of this treaty have recognized the right of the commission to receive complaints by one member-state against another. Eighteen of the twenty-one member-states have recognized the right of the commission to receive complaints by individuals. The suprasovereign novelty of these institutions is their ability to hear cases brought by individuals, groups, or corporations against their own states or any other member-states that may have infringed any of the rights covered by the European Convention. Thus, in the well-known *Lawless* case, the court examined the special measures abridging civil liberties taken by the British government in Northern Ireland. Because such institutions move beyond the sovereignty principle, they are truly system-transforming. As also noted earlier, in the same section, the Inter-American Convention of Human Rights has established a similar system that is gradually consolidating its position within the Americas.

Supranational human-rights institutions with the teeth of compulsory jurisdiction are rare animals in today's world. But creating new institutions is not the only means of beating the international sovereignty system. Since World War II, several private, international non-governmental organizations have relied on the moral force of their armies of volunteers to make an impact on the international system. Some groups, such as Oxfam or Doctors Without Frontiers, are principally relief agencies and address only sporadically the broader questions of international human rights. Other organizations, including church groups and professional associations, have committees or working groups that direct policy and plan membership actions in the area of human rights. Still others, frequently called "solidarity groups," work on human-rights issues in a particular country or region and sometimes link themselves to a particular cause and/or ideology. Often these groups are composed of expatriates who lend an international dimension to the efforts at home of indigenous human-rights groups seeking to correct patterns of abuse.

One volunteer organization in particular has come to be associated with international human rights and, in fact, received the Nobel Peace Prize in 1977 for its efforts. Amnesty International (AI) was born in 1961 out of the reaction of one private British citizen to a newspaper report of two Portuguese students' imprisonment for raising glasses in a toast to freedom. Peter Benenson was appalled at the story and invited his friends to join him in a concerted effort to stop such abuses wherever they occurred. Today, the organization counts almost 700,000 members and subscribers in over 150 countries and territories. In twenty-five years, AI's mandate has expanded beyond the wrongful incarceration of individuals it calls "prisoners of conscience" to include work to abolish torture and the death penalty and to assure fair trials for all political prisoners. In addition, it has campaigned in recent years to stop such practices as disappearances and political killings.

AI has made a success of its work largely through careful research and documentation and a commitment to political impartiality. The organization's spokespersons frequently cite attacks by both the political right and political left, Arabs and Israelis, Africans and South Africans, as evidence that it has no political soft spots.

In some ways, AI can be considered a system reformer rather than a system transformer. In much of its work, the organization tacitly accepts the basic premises of the international system: law and the sovereignty of states. Like other human-rights groups, AI places great emphasis on the furtherance of international covenants governing human rights. Appeals launched by the organization always refer at least to the Universal Declaration of Human Rights and usually to domestic law and/or one or more of the human-rights treaties. Furthermore, in recent years there has been some indication that AI is energetically seeking to sensitize major Western powers to human-rights issues and to encourage them to use their political influence to ameliorate human-rights problems abroad, an essentially reformist approach.

On one very important dimension, however, AI, like the other voluntary association mentioned above, moves beyond the Westphalian system. In its essence, AI is an organization of individuals working internationally on behalf of individual victims of human-rights abuses. In important ways, organizations like AI ignore the strictures of sovereignty. Individuals, in their view, can be significant actors in the international system. Members regard themselves as belonging first to a global community of human beings and do not leave it to their own governments to denounce abuses by other governments. (Indeed, many members of AI around the world live under notably repressive regimes.) Human-rights violators are held accountable not to the world assembly of states, but to the perhaps more influential court of world opinion. European members of AI, like their American counterparts, do ask their elected representatives to intercede with an offending government, but they neither start nor stop there. The backbone of their work, letters from private citizens in one country to the repressive government of another, is system-transforming. It says, in effect, that however well, through geopolitical ties or legal sleight of hand, a government manages to escape scrutiny by the formal international system, there must still be accountability for human-rights violations to the world's people. Although organizations like AI rarely take on the international system directly (and other more functionally diffuse organizations almost never do so), the message implicit in the operating norms is system-transforming: Collective human interests override the more narrow interests of individual states.

EXTENT OF HUMAN-RIGHTS PROBLEMS AND FUTURE IMPLICATIONS

Important violations of human rights take place in many states of the world today. AI's 1987 report, for example, lists entries for 128 countries. Those who believe in progress frequently ascribe abuses to development problems, or an ideology, or somehow not being like us . . . yet. There is implicit in such a view the notion that, given enough time, the situation will improve. The record does not bear out such optimism.

Although the extermination of more than twelve million persons by Nazi Germany shocked the world and inspired the Genocide Convention, the same world a few decades later sat through Idi Amin's massacre of from 100,000 to 500,000 people in Uganda and the Khmer Rouge's eradication of over 300,000 Cambodians, many of them identified as enemies of the revolution simply by the glasses they wore. Death squads and disappearances are a fairly new historical development, and modern technology—electric shock, for example—has added one more cruel dimension to the ancient practice of torture.

Gross violations of human rights do not occur in social or political vacuums. Readers will recall that we have argued that various categories of human rights—social and political, economic and cultural—are all intertwined. Governments that fail to extend political rights to organizers of a peasant union or who turn a blind eye to systematic harassment of sharecroppers by large landowners also, in essence, violate economic rights. Similarly, governments that fail to provide equal access to education may severely curtail civil and political rights when the disgruntled unemployed express their discontent. Opposition to governments arises in almost all cases from one or more of the following causes:

1. Economic deprivation
2. Denial of cultural or ethnic identities
3. Disenfranchisement from meaningful participation in political processes through which societal decisions are made and policies carried out

Frequently, a government responds by portraying opposition as an assault upon the integrity of the state and by repressing it with the familiar tools of governmental power. In other words, popular opposition to the denial of economic or cultural or political rights often reaps a response from the government that further denies rights, whether they be personal, political, economic, social, or cultural. A vicious downward-spiraling cycle of repression and opposition, marked by increasing violence at every turn, is thereby established. In some cases, the situation descends into an unspeakably barbaric nightmare. Three specific practices today make common assault on the most basic personal right, that to life itself: disappearances; political, extrajudicial killings; and torture.

Disappearances

Disappearances occur frequently in many a modern society. Children are kidnapped, adults are murdered, and bodies turn up in swamps and forests. These are horrible, often gruesome deeds, perpetrated by individuals considered evil or sick. We abhor the deeds, but we consider them common crimes rather than human-rights violations.

Disappearance as a human-rights violation is qualitatively different from an ordinary abduction. In the first place, there are generally witnesses to the disappearance. In the midst of a wedding feast, for example, a black limousine may arrive. State security guards ask to see the brother of the groom, who is escorted to the waiting car. He is never seen again. Second, the perpetrators can frequently be identified—by their dress or their vehicle—as agents of the state. Family and friends know who must be held accountable. But the state, though it has participated in the abduction, denies responsibility, and frequently covers its tracks well enough that claims are difficult or impossible to substantiate. There are no records of the "disappeared." In Argentina, where from 1976 to 1983 more than 10,000 individuals disappeared, members of the ruling junta angrily rejected charges by the Organization of American States that special units in each branch of the Argentine armed forces had been heavily involved in disappearances and that the decision to form such units had been made at the highest levels of the armed forces. They countered that the disappearances were due to terrorist groups and unrecorded deaths in armed clashes, or, alternatively, they argued that the numbers were inflated and that many of the disappeared were themselves terrorists gone underground. (Amnesty International 1981, 12–13) Although the junta vigorously denied its role in the disappearances, it did pass a statute conveniently allowing the state to declare any missing person dead. Since 1983, with the return of civilian rule to Argentina, a government-appointed National Commission on Disappeared People has identified 340 clandestine detention centers used in Argentina at the height of the repression and has catalogued almost 9,000 still unresolved disappearances.

Disappearance as part of a pattern of human-rights violations frequently arises in countries where there is nominally a notion of governmental accountability but where effective legal and constitutional guarantees have been abrogated. Whereas a government's openly repressive policies may engender political violence, a clandestine policy of secret abductions that cannot be traced, with proof positive, to the state avoids all the messiness and embarrassment of legal process and allows the state to act at will without even the charade of accountability. Over the past two decades, disappearances have formed a pattern of human-rights violations in Afghanistan (1978–1979), Argentina, Chile, El Salvador, Ethiopia, Equatorial Guinea, Guatemala, Guinea (1970–1977), Morocco, the Philippines, and Uganda.

Those distantly acquainted with disappearances often assume that the disappeared have died. Some have, but others may be maintained in secret detention for many years. Others reappear just as mysteriously as they disappeared. From this fact, disappearances as a human-rights violation takes on a particularly cruel dimension. The abuse is not simply perpetrated against an individual; an entire family, perhaps an entire community, suffers grievously. Lives are held in limbo and grief is thwarted. Moreover, the belief that the loved one may yet live—a belief heightened by judicious reappearances—creates new leverage over a family or community of dissidents.

Political Killings

Political killings are sometimes referred to as "extrajudicial executions," a term meriting some consideration. The prefix *extra*, beyond, implies that there are some killings that take place within the law. All states sanction killing of soldiers by soldiers in time of war, and some states impose the death penalty for certain crimes. However one may feel about death under either of those circumstances, political killings as a human-rights concern is something else. Political killings constitute a clear and unequivocal violation of international legal provisions forbidding the arbitrary deprivation of life. Political killings take place outside the judicial process; victims are denied protection of law. Many victims are abducted, illegally detained, and/or tortured before they are killed.

Most importantly, the state must be held accountable for the deaths. Sometimes, the killings are ordered at the highest level of government, as in 1979 in the Central African Empire when, on the orders of ruler Jean Bokassa, some one hundred schoolchildren were summarily executed for not wearing the appropriate smocks to school. After a successful coup, the government of the Central African Empire prosecuted the case. Bokassa returned voluntarily to his country in 1985, and in early 1987 a trial to determine his responsibility in this and other heinous human-rights crimes was under way. He was convicted and sentenced to death in June 1987.

At other times, the government deliberately fails to investigate killings or, alternatively, fails to take measures to prevent deaths. Thus, for example, the present El Salvadoran government admits to 40,000 killings perpetrated by death squads from 1979 to 1984 under a military regime. The government denies any connection with the death squads, but though the killings continue and charges are made by victims' families, the state, according to President Napoleon Duarte, sees itself as "incapable of prosecuting the criminals." (Amnesty International 1985, 144)

Political killings are one effective way for a government to rid itself of individuals who are troublesome. But it is both more and less than that. The victims are not always individually targeted; frequently, children as well as adults are murdered. The purpose is just as much intimidation as extermination. In Guatemala, where political killings have been endemic under successive governments since 1966, corpses left in public places, far from the scene of abduction, have been so mutilated as to render identification impossible.

Like other major offenses, political killings are not limited to one geographic area. Latin America—and most notably Argentina, Chile, El Salvador, and Guatemala—has achieved some notoriety in the United States, but in terms of sheer scale, Indonesia has been (1965–1966) responsible for the most massive extermination policy since that of Nazi Germany. During a single nine-month period, more than 500,000 individuals directly or indirectly connected to the Indonesian Communist Party were brutally murdered at the order of two Indonesian generals. In several places the killers held feasts in the company of their victims, after which each guest was invited to decapitate one of the prisoners. (Amnesty International 1983, 37) A decade later, the revolutionary government of Pol Pot and the Khmer Rouge in Cambodia (now Kampuchea) launched a campaign to purge the country of supporters of the overthrown Lon Nol and other "worthless ones." The latter included teachers and, often, pupils beyond the seventh grade. Illicit sexual relationships, resistance to mandatory communal eating, and even "laziness" were punishable by death. (Amnesty International 1983, 41) In India, political suspects have been killed in encounters with the police that many Indians believe are staged; the press, in fact, frequently refers to "encounter killings." In 1980, Libya's Colonel Muammar Qaddafy launched a "physical liquidation" campaign to rid the revolution of its Libyan enemies at home and abroad; Iran has eliminated over 6,000 individuals in minimally judicial executions since 1979.

The crime of genocide—defined as a number of acts, including killings, "committed with intent to destroy, in whole or in part, a national, ethnic, racial or religious group" (UN General Assembly, Genocide Convention, 1948) whether in peacetime or in war—is a special genre of political killing, in that it is directed at an identifiable cultural community. Although the Genocide Convention entered into force in 1951, there have been at least six instances of post-World War II genocide, including assaults on the Hutu of Burundi, the Bengalis in East Pakistan, various indigenous groups in Brazil, and East Timorese in Indonesia.

Torture

The 1984 Torture Convention defines torture as: Any act by which severe pain or suffering, whether physical or mental, is intentionally inflicted on a person for such purposes as obtaining from him or a third person information or a confession, punishing him for an act he or a third person has committed or is suspected of having committed, or intimidating or coercing him or a third person, or for any reason based on discrimination of any kind, when such pain or suffering is inflicted by or at the instigation of or with the consent or acquiescence of a public official or other person acting in an official capacity. (UN General Assembly, Torture Convention, 1984)

In 1984, AI issued a report accusing a third of the world's states with routine practice of torture. That report includes entries on many countries notorious for human-rights abuses, but it also documents the practice in such moderate countries as Italy, Spain, Yugoslavia, Mexico, and Tunisia. (Amnesty International 1984) Charges of ill-treatment are frequently levied against the British in Northern Ireland; even before the 1987 escalation of conflict in Israel's occupied territories, detainees there were often hooded, beaten, and subjected to electric shock. Torture, whether used to obtain confessions or create fear, reflects the state's efforts to achieve its ends by claiming physical, and sometimes psychological, control over its opponents. The torturer's job is to destroy the humanity of the victim—without, or sometimes only before, actually killing him or her. As Stover and Nightingale put it, "Nothing negates one's sense of what it means to be human more than the deliberate infliction of unnecessary pain and humiliation on a helpless victim." (1985, 4)

Physical torture takes advantage of pain centers in the human anatomy and includes prolonged beatings, lengthy periods of standing, near-suffocation by submersion in water or urine, burning with lighted cigarettes, intense light or light deprivation, or electric shock to the genitals. In Syria, some prisoners have suffered the Black Slave—a heated skewer inserted into the anus; in Chile, others have told of *la parrilla*, the metal grill, consisting of electric shocks on the most sensitive parts of the victim's body while he or she is secured to a metal bed frame. Psychological torture includes not only threats, mock executions, or witnessed rapes of wife or children, but also the non-therapeutic use of drugs, or the injection of toxic substances that cause pain or disorientation. In the Soviet Union, many political dissidents have been compulsorily confined to psychiatric hospitals, where they have been forcibly administered disorienting drugs such as haloperidol, chlorpromazine, and trifluoperazine. In the mid-1970s, two Western scholars were able to document nearly 500 dissenters forcibly hospitalized over the previous two decades, usually as schizophrenics with grandiose ideas to transform the world by "fighting for truth and to exclude injustice." (Bloch and Reddaway 1985, 132–141)

Certain governmental institutions and legal provisions facilitate the state's practice of torture around the world: emergency legislation allowing preventive detention and suspending any provisions of habeas corpus, secret detention centers, and incommunicado detention provide government torturers the cloak of secrecy they need to carry out their dark deeds. Although no government publicly affirms torture, and many governments even specifically outlaw it, legal provisions allowing an individual to be held for long periods of time without access to family, lawyers, or physicians frequently allow interrogators great latitude for torture and ill-treatment without fear of prosecution. In South Africa, which prides itself on an independent judiciary, detainees held in the past under the Internal Security Act and today under emergency legislation are frequently subjected to torture in the form of beating, hooding and partial suffocation, electric shock, cold exposure, and suspension from an iron bar with hands and legs shackled.

As the testimonies of former Greek torturers indicate, torturers today are frequently trained as such and learn to be insensitive. During the years of the Greek junta, young recruits at the security police training camp were continuously abused themselves and, physically denied the opportunity to question those in charge, learned to accept and internalize brutal authority and use it against others. Former U.S. Ambassador Robert White's words about Paraguay unfortunately are readily applicable to many countries where torture is institutionalized: "Perfectly normal people get up and go to work, and their work is torture." (Stover and Nightingale 1985, 93) Milgram's well-known experiments requiring a subject under the direction of a "scientist" to administer increasingly strong "electric shocks" to a "victim" separated from him by a glass pane demonstrate the willingness of ordinary people to submit to authority even when it means inflicting intense pain on others. (1965) Milgram's findings reveal just how fragile is the respect for human life and dignity.

THE COSTS OF HUMAN RIGHTS ABUSE

The most obvious cost of systematic human-rights abuses is human suffering. The pain of the victims of torture or other serious abuses does not cease with their release from their ordeal; long-term physical and psychological damage is a very frequent consequence. Treatment and rehabilitation of such individuals, and their and their families' shattered lives, is a cost immediately borne by the victim and his support group, but at some point a part of this cost is ultimately shared by the society.

The society pays far greater costs, too. A situation in which a government systematically oppresses its people can properly be described as one in which a government is at war with its people. Such a government can only be described as illegitimate because it fails the most elementary test of promoting the interests of the people. The attendant social and political turmoil, which may at times be subterranean rather than on the surface, is a cause of enormous social, economic, and political loss.

Socially, fear is omnipresent; traditional social associations such as the family, labor unions, and other groups are infected with suspicion of one member for another; normal human intercourse becomes dangerous and is therefore often avoided. Systematic human-rights abuses are often possible only with the cooperation of the agencies of government charged with the maintenance of law and order—the judicial system, the police, and other paramilitary and military organizations. Thus, systematic human-rights violations weaken respect for and bring into disrepute those very elements within the society upon whose integrity normal human activity depends. Any future effort to restore normal social conditions has the enormous task of counteracting the cynicism and distrust that has been built up with regard to some of the most fundamental institutions on which society rests. In addition, the society is confronted ultimately with a Hobson's choice between laboriously pursuing and punishing past wrongdoers (at the risk of dragging out the wrenching experience and postponing other urgent actions), and allowing torturers and other abusers of the people to go unpunished (with the enormously dangerous example that may set).

Human-rights violations also exact an enormous, though intangible, price from society in lost political development and skills. Experience with open debate, open political campaigns, open legal proceedings, holding governments accountable through the ballot, the open petitioning of one's government, the rendering of peaceful changes in society, all of these and the other experiences necessary for the peaceful working of the political order are unavailable and have to be learned anew. Meanwhile, time and resources may have been wasted either through misguided or self-interested governmental decisions. Populations may have grown in the years of oppressive rule and problems facing the successor governments may be that much more difficult to resolve. In short, oppressive rule inevitably retards the political development of the people and the society.

Society also pays enormous economic costs. In many cases the targets of governmental oppression and liquidation are persons of some skills and leadership qualities—school teachers and university professors, journalists, labor leaders, priests, physicians, lawyers, and politicians. The forcible exile of such persons, their being forced underground, or their physical destruction removes vital human resources from the society.

Perhaps even more significant, although again intangible, the channels of communication between the government and the people are interrupted or severed so that the government is unable to receive vital economic, political, and other signals from the people. In terms of the direction and pace of economic development and investment activity, such a lack of popular participation in decisionmaking can, and often does, have a greatly deleterious effect upon economic activity. Finally, human-rights violations and social oppression are frequently undertaken to protect narrow vested interests and to prevent a broad-based and more egalitarian economic development. When this is the case, society obviously pays through the forced continuation of outdated economic forms and relationships.

Domestic society and the victims themselves pay the highest price for human-rights abuses, but effects are felt internationally, too. Where individuals fear persecution for their political beliefs, religion, or creed, or where governmental policies fail to protect individuals in their right to even basic economic necessities, refugees are created. From 1940 to 1960, most refugees seeking asylum in the United States were fleeing from totalitarian regimes. Today, countless refugees slip over the United States' southern borders with a somewhat different story to tell. U.S. immigration officials call them economic refugees because they are usually unskilled and they come hoping to find work and an income they could not obtain at home. That label, however, is only partially descriptive. These are not the economically deprived victims of natural disasters—earthquakes, droughts, or floods—seeking temporary relief. They are the victims of politically imposed public policies, policies that alternatively may limit their access to income-producing activity or may restrict their ability to protect themselves against economic encroachments by more powerful citizens. In either case, they may be considered human-rights victims, and their impact on the country to which they flee—whether Mexico, Canada, or the United States in this hemisphere—is the same. Host countries may receive benefit from labor produced by refugees, but most countries today view unskilled immigrant labor as a liability rather than an asset. Willingness to work may be easily offset by all the problems attendant to large refugee populations: political divisions resulting from poor cultural and linguistic integration; health and education expenses; and burdens on housing and public infrastructure. Ironically, countries which themselves have the best domestic human-rights records may be seen most favorably by the victims of abuses in other countries; thus they may be made to bear the lion's share of the international cost of human-rights violations.

PRESCRIPTIONS FOR CHANGE

To redress the grievous situation in which human rights are violated with impunity across the world, widespread changes are imperative at the domestic level and, arguably (depending on which of the three views above is adopted), important changes are necessary in the international system as well. Because, as argued above, only domestic governments now and in the forseeable future have the capacity to guarantee human rights, primary attention must be directed to the domestic front.

Within a given country, improvements in human rights may require hard-to-find political will to stop abuses that have become endemic. The most elemental prescription is for governments to adopt laws protecting human rights where such laws do not exist, and take action to enforce them where they exist but are ignored. In 1984, AI introduced a "Twelve-Point Program for the Prevention of Torture," advocating such domestic measures as limits on incommunicado detention, independent investigation of reports of torture, exclusion in court of evidence extracted under torture, and instructing police in training procedures to refuse to obey any order to torture. Domestic human-rights groups around the world are calling for similar measures.

Such prescriptions come easily, but rare is the government with the courage to take the medicine. A change of government, as in Argentina in 1983, is often required before genuine ameliorations of human-rights abuses can occur. But frequently, even a change in government is no guarantee of improvement. In Uganda, the grossest sorts of torture and killings continued even after Milton Obote replaced Idi Amin (just as widespread abuses continue under the military regime that toppled Obote himself in 1985). Similarly, though charges of human-rights violations helped bring down Iran's shah in 1979, the Khomeini government has continued to torture and execute prisoners in the shah's prisons.

What can be done about domestic abuses at the international level? Human-rights observers all agree that the primary difficulty is a domestic one, but at the international level, positions diverge. System maintainers regret the human-rights abuses of their friends and denounce those of their foes, but they essentially adopt a position that human rights is not appropriately placed on the international agenda.

System reformers criticize the politicization of human-rights policies. Arguing that human-rights principles extend to all peoples and that abuses are heinous wherever they occur, they vigorously advocate the rule of law. They seek extension and expansion of the international legal system and cry shame on Western countries who, by their refusal to ratify human-rights treaties, weaken the regime of law. As lobbyists, reformers in the United States helped secure the U.S. Senate's ratification of the Genocide Convention in 1986.

System reformers and transformers alike approve and support the work of various domestic and international non-governmental organizations concerned with human rights. Ultimately, the most important lobbyists for human rights are domestic groups calling for change in their own countries, but because members are often placed in personal jeopardy for their stance, these groups need international support. Private voluntary organizations such as the International Red Cross and Red Crescent also play a valuable role in gathering and disseminating information about delicate, sometimes treacherous situations, and in such matters have a capacity that surpasses that of both outside governments and UN bodies. In addition, international advocacy groups comprised of private individuals—whether professional groups or human-rights organizations like Amnesty International—may by their impartiality be able to apply the most effective pressure on repressive governments. Letters from private citizens to prison wardens in countries far away have sometimes worked small miracles, stopping torture, restoring clothing to naked prisoners, improving food and sanitary conditions, and sometimes even securing release.

Finally, system transformers—those who remain skeptical about the will or ability of some repressive governments ever to reform their abusive human-rights practices—prescribe changes in the system itself to overcome obstacles arising out of the Westphalian system. For them, the question of guaranteeing human rights must not be left, ultimately, to the state and its narrow interests. Basic human rights are a collective good that transcends state interests and cannot be abandoned to the whims of an individual state that may or may not be interested in protecting them. That is not to say that states should have no role in guaranteeing human rights. To the contrary, states alone have the capacity to process any large volume of complaints. But when a state fails in its duties to protect human rights, system transformers argue, there needs to be an institution to which victims may appeal for redress. For efficiency alone, national governments should have priority in resolving human-rights disputes, but frequently national channels cannot be used with any guarantee of safety or, when used, do not prove satisfactory. In such cases there is a need for individuals to have the capacity to bring petitions and complaints against their government to some impartial supranational body, itself capable of rendering judgments against an offending government. Only when such capacity is conferred on individuals, system transformers argue, will systematic violators of human rights have the necessary incentive to change their practices. Although such developments on a worldwide scale seem far away, the Western European experience with the supranational Court of Human Rights indicates at least that such goals are not idle dreams.

REFERENCES

Americas Watch Committee, Helsinki Watch Committee, and Lawyers' Committee for International Human Rights. *In the Face of Cruelty: The Reagan Administration's Human Rights Record in 1984* (January 1985).

Amnesty International. *1985 Report*. New York: AIUSA, 1985.

————. *"Disappearances": A Workbook*. New York: AIUSA, 1981.

————. *Political Killings by Governments*. New York: AIUSA, 1983.

————. *Torture in the 80's*. New York: AIUSA, 1984.

Bloch, Sidney, and Peter Reddaway. "Psychiatrists and Dissenters in the Soviet Union." In *The Breaking of Bodies and Minds*. Edited by Eric Stover and Elena O. Nightingale. New York: W. H. Freeman, 1985.

Convention Against Torture and Other Cruel, Inhuman or Degrading Treatment or Punishment, adopted by the UN General Assembly, 1984.

Ethiopia Report. "Doctors Without Frontiers." 1985.

Forsythe, David P. "Socioeconomic Human Rights: The United Nations, the United States, and Beyond." *Human Rights Quarterly* (1982):433–449.

Kim, Samuel S. *The Quest for a Just World Order*. Boulder, CO: Westview Press, 1984.

Milgram, Stanley. "Some Conditions of Obedience and Disobedience to Authority." *Human Relations* 18 (January 1965):57–75.

Stover, Eric, and Elena O. Nightingale, editors. *The Breaking of Bodies and Minds*. New York: W. H. Freeman, 1985.

United Nations General Assembly. *Convention Against Torture and Other Cruel, Inhuman, or Degrading Treatments or Punishments*. 1984.

United Nations General Assembly. *Convention on the Prevention and Punishment of the Crime of Genocide*. 1948.

7

Global Resources and Growth

ROBERT B. WOYACH

In 1973, the Club of Rome published *The Limits to Growth,* the public version of its computer forecast of world economic growth into the next century. *The Limits to Growth* predicted a bleak future. It portrayed a world in which natural ecological systems were about to reach their physical limits. In some computer runs, investment capital proved to be insufficient to allow economic growth to keep pace with a growing population. In other runs, industrial pollution grew so severe that food production declined radically. In all models, given current rates of growth for population and consumption, the computer predicted that world population would "crash" within a hundred years.

The Limits to Growth proved highly controversial. It had a radical and lasting impact on the debate over resources and growth. The approach taken by the Club of Rome made policymakers, scholars, and ordinary people look at the question of resource scarcity in global rather than national terms. Its findings shifted the fundamental debate away from age-old questions about how to feed a growing population and how to secure access to industrial raw materials. The critical issue now appeared to be whether the earth's ecological system *could* feed billions of new people, and whether industrial civilization itself could survive the ever higher material standards of living that were the *raison d'être* of economic growth.

This chapter looks at: (1) global-resource issues and the worldviews that dominate debate and policy with respect to these issues, (2) the emergence of those worldviews historically, (3) the values, images of the future, and key policy prescriptions of system maintainers, system reformers, and system transformers.

It will be immediately apparent in this discussion that a subtle but critical difference exists between the worldviews that influence thinking about resource issues and the worldviews related to most other issues in this book. With respect to most issues dealt with here, the contending worldviews disagree about how to organize the international political and economic system. With respect to resource issues, people who hold diametricly different views of the best international system—Marxists and capitalists, for example—often agree on basic values. The contending worldviews disagree about a more basic question: Can modern industrial civilization with its emphasis on material consumption continue to be viable? Further, individuals who hold contending worldviews with respect to resources and growth tend to see each other not as misguided nuisances, but as the primary obstacles to achieving their own version of a preferred and viable future.

HISTORICAL PERSPECTIVES ON RESOURCE ISSUES

While *The Limits to Growth* changed and popularized the debate over resource issues, it did not invent those issues. Indeed, concern over resource scarcity and especially the limits to population growth have a long history.

Resource Issues in the Pre-Industrial World

Making generalizations about the attitudes, concerns, and structures of all preindustrial societies is obviously a risky business. Yet, there are some common threads within the preindustrial world's experience with resource issues that separate it from the present in important ways. These differences help place the current debate over resource issues into some perspective.

The Limits on Material Consumption
In general, societies within the preindustrial world assumed that their resource base and production possibilities placed distinct limits on material consumption. The very stratification of preindustrial civilizations reflected limited consumption possibilities. From the earliest civilizations of Mesopotamia to early-modern Europe, material consumption was the prerogative of a relatively small elite—a priestly or warrior class, an aristocracy, or a merchant class. Even in the wealthiest societies, the vast majority of people—peasants, serfs, or slaves—lived very near subsistence levels, with little chance for significantly improving their material lot in life. In short, there was no expectation that the entire society could enjoy a high material standard of living or even that the elite could consume resources at an ever-increasing rate.

The preindustrial world assumed and accepted the *absolute* scarcity of resources as a fact of life. The world, at least the world that was available to individual communities and nations, had limited potential for growth of any kind. In the thirteenth century the Italian political philosopher Machiavelli argued that:

> When countries become overpopulated and there is no longer any room for all the
> inhabitants to live, nor any place for them to go, these being likewise fully

occupied . . . then of necessity the world must relieve itself of this excess population . . . so that mankind, having been chastised and reduced in numbers, may
become better and live with more convenience. (1940, 298)

Machiavelli clearly perceived that his world had limits and that there was a
distinct and unavoidable trade-off between population growth and living
standards.

The Production Process
The limits on consumption in the preindustrial world were intrinsic to the very
process of production.

For the agricultural peasantry, who constituted the majority of the population, material consumption was for the most part limited to those goods that
could be produced at home. For such people, the opportunities for amassing
great material wealth or consuming large quantities of goods were distinctly
limited even in places with plentiful raw materials.

Even for the elite, or those with access to trade goods, dependence on craft-
based production limited consumption possibilities. The rudimentary nature of
the tools available to craftsmen meant that even full-time workers required a
significant amount of time to produce a few goods. In the ancient world, for
example, an army's supply of weapons and armor stayed relatively constant
from one year to the next. Large changes came about primarily through the redistribution of existing arms, as the weapons of enemies were captured in battle. (McNeill 1982, 2)

It was not possible simply to add more craftsmen and thus expand consumption possibilities. In the short run, the long apprenticeship required to train
skilled craftsmen made it difficult to increase production quickly. But even in
the long run, larger numbers of craftsmen may have had little impact on consumption. The cost of producing goods, as opposed to their market value, was
dependent on the productivity of individual craftsmen and apprentices, not on
the number of craftsmen. Increasing the number of craftsmen without increasing their productivity was more likely to lead to impoverished workers than to
large quantities of affordable goods.

Similarly, the development of long-distance trading networks, which appear to date back to the earliest civilizations, contributed only to the living standards of the elite. The warriors of Bronze Age Greece depended on the tin ores
of Britain. Roman magistrates clothed themselves in Chinese silks and their
women in Indian damask. But the production process itself remained expensive, even if trade increased market opportunities and thus the number of
craftsmen that could be supported. Long-distance trade, rather than decreasing
costs by opening new markets, tended to increase costs. Merchants faced innumerable natural and human obstacles en route. Trade could be disrupted for
long periods by war, plague, or even the collapse of empires. Prices reflected
both the risks of trade and the scarcity those risks ensured. Thus, luxury goods
dominated trade between centers of civilization (for example, between Ghana

and Rome and between Rome and China). Where basic commodities for mass consumption moved in long-distance trade (e.g., grain within the Roman Empire) their cost was subsidized by the military might of the government (i.e., the commodities represented tribute to the empire).

This is not to say that elites within the preindustrial world assumed that their material standards of living could not be raised. They did. However, it was equally assumed that the process of increasing wealth involved the redistribution of existing wealth, not the creation of new wealth. The nearly universal trend toward large-scale empires reflects in part a drive to improve material living standards. Even democracies like Athens easily turned to empire to expand the consumption possibilities of Athenian citizens. But it was only by charging tributes and by dominating trading relationships (i.e., only by taking wealth from others) that the Athenians could achieve sufficiently large and rapid increases in wealth to significantly raise living standards.

Food and Environmental Decay
Growth within the preindustrial world, especially population growth, was even more limited by food-production possibilities. While peasants, serfs, and slaves did not expect to consume significant amounts of craft goods, they did need to eat. Despite the relative gains brought about by the neolithic revolution, the moldboard plow, and new types of foods that became available at various points in history, most preindustrial societies remained very close to their agricultural limits to growth. (Roberts 1980, 667)

Periodic famines in the preindustrial world are evidence that these societies lived close to their agricultural limits to growth. Even a society as rich as the Chinese suffered famines so regularly that they were a barometer of dynastic decline and revival. Famines tend to be local affairs. In large empires like China, local shortfalls in any one year could easily be alleviated by bringing in foodstuffs from non-famine areas. But when dynastic governments grew weak and corrupt, they generally failed to get surplus food to the areas where it was needed. Thus the Chinese saw an increasing number and severity of famines as evidence of the declining virtue of the dynasty.

Food-production possibilities and population growth in some preindustrial societies were also limited by environmental degradation. Ecological problems, and a resulting decline in soil fertility and food production, probably played a significant role in the decline of civilizations in both Mesopotamia and Mesoamerica. (Deevey 1979) In both places, population growth led to highly intensive land-use patterns. Over time, erosion, overgrazing, the increased use of marginal lands, and prolonged irrigation caused soil fertility to decline. As a result, food production declined. Even when food could be imported, as in Mesopotamia, small-scale societies with insufficient local food supplies could not compete effectively with those that had larger or more secure food supplies.

Thus the preindustrial world generally was acutely aware of the limits to population growth. Indeed, in 1798 when Thomas Malthus wrote his famous

Essay on Population predicting the collapse of British industrialism because of a growing food shortage, he was voicing an old, not a new concern. His perspective on the problem of resource scarcity was a decidedly traditional one. That, in a nutshell, was Malthus's now equally famous mistake. While his analysis of Britain's situation was founded on traditional assumptions, the very processes that had led to British industrialism and population growth were transforming the world.

Malthus failed to predict the importance of a new international market in food. He could not see how technological changes would allow people to transport foodstuffs over long distances, and still offer them for sale at affordable prices. This revolution in transportation technology would open up vast new agricultural areas in the Americas and Australia, allowing populations in Europe and Asia to expand far beyond their food-producing potential. Similarly, Malthus failed to see that the new scientific ways of looking at the world would lead to new ways of growing food. The agricultural revolution preceded the industrial revolution just as the neolithic revolution had preceded the urban revolution. Expanded productivity per unit of land allowed population to grow far beyond what had been possible before.

Industrialization: Changed Attitudes
Toward Wealth and Consumption

The scientific, industrial, and democratic revolutions of the West brought with them a whole new way of looking at the material possibilities of life. Just as the agricultural revolution resulted in an increase in the productivity of farmers and land, the industrial revolution (i.e., the advent of machine-made goods) significantly increased the productivity of the makers of goods. Indeed, the industrial revolution transformed the very nature of the worker. Machines not only expanded the productive capacity of skilled craftsmen, they allowed even unskilled workers to become productive.

Creating the Consumer Society
Regardless of one's position on the political spectrum, the new industrial age appeared to change the very nature of wealth. No longer was progress primarily dependent on redistributing the existing stock of wealth. Now it was clearly possible to think of progress in terms of creating new wealth. As Adam Smith wrote: "The abundance or scantiness of [wealth and goods] . . . seems to depend more upon . . . skill, dexterity, and judgment . . . than upon . . . the soil, climate, or extent of territory of any particular nation." (1937, 13) Radicals like Karl Marx (1959, 44) agreed, arguing that "the productive forces developing in the womb of bourgeois society create the material conditions for the solution of that antagonism" between social classes brought on by economic scarcity.

These changes in looking at the world did not occur suddenly or without opposition, of course. The ideal that the industrial worker was also a consumer—and thus should be paid more than a subsistence wage—only came after Henry Ford launched his assembly-line process and began paying auto workers the unheard-of wage of $5.00 a day. High wages and the seemingly unlimited production made possible by the assembly line laid the foundation for a new consumer society.

The Global Spread of Industrial Civilization

The industrial, scientific, and democratic revolutions were all part of the Western experience. But beginning with the nineteenth century's imperial age, the values associated with industrial civilization began to take root throughout the rest of the world as well.

Imperialism helped spread industrial civilization in several ways. The obvious technical superiority of Europeans demonstrated the power of their scientific ways of looking at the world. While few Asian societies immediately accepted the democratic impulses implicit in the Western model of mass consumption, elites throughout the world gradually did see that their own power depended on matching the West in the areas of science, technology, and industry. In most cases that meant adopting Western models of how to imbed science and technology into society simply because they were the only models available. Although many societies, like the Japanese, hoped to adopt Western technology while retaining Eastern values, they usually found that Western values were intimately tied to Western science and industry.

The colonial powers themselves contributed to the spread of Western industrial ideas by making Western education available to the elite groups within their empires. As a result, even in places in which industrial values did not penetrate deeply into a society, they permeated the thinking of this Western-educated elite. National policies and priorities eventually came to be guided by Western industrial values even when the majority of a new state's population retained more traditional worldviews.

As the new nation-states of Africa and Asia were created following World War II, two new forces further increased the hold of Western industrial civilization throughout the Third World. Multinational corporations (MNCs) had operated within the colonial world and in penetrated societies since the 1800s. But new MNCs, interested in establishing manufacturing facilities to take advantage of relatively cheap labor, increased popular contact with industrial ways of living and thinking. Their importance within the new national economies further reinforced the hold Western economic models had on national policy.

Similarly, within newly independent Asian, African, and Latin American societies, entrepreneurs and new socialist governments began creating an indigenous industrial sector. Their efforts were encouraged by international development policies. Western experts generally emphasized the importance of industrialization in the process of economic development. Development assistance from both multinational and bilateral sources was typically targeted at projects that would facilitate industrial growth in one way or another. Thus, international interests reinforced the power of those elites in the new states who shared the basic values and orientations of industrial civilization.

Access to Raw Materials

The scientific revolution deferred concern about the availability of food supplies, at least in the Western world. Scientific agriculture had eliminated the spector of starvation and famine. However, industrial society still required secure access to various raw materials. In fact, as industrial society's list of needed raw materials lengthened, and as high-grade domestic supplies of some key raw materials declined in many of the first nations to industrialize, access to cheap sources of industrial raw materials became a question closely linked to national security.

Without secure access, states could not sustain modern industrial output. Unable to sustain output, they could not ensure the rising standards of living that had become important to domestic stability. More importantly, as military forces came to rely more and more on industrial products (e.g., tanks, airplanes, and ships rather than horses, wagons, and human footpower) the security of supplies translated immediately into the state's ability to protect itself in time of war or to project its power abroad. Relatively few states had domestic supplies of every relevant mineral—especially as new technologies added more and more esoteric minerals to the list. Essential raw materials had to be obtained abroad, through less-than-secure long-distance trade.

In the uncertain world of the 1930s, a rush of studies was published looking ahead to a growing shortage of raw materials that would threaten national security. The forecasters were not concerned about an absolute or global shortage. But it was projected that even resource-rich countries like the United States would increasingly depend on foreign countries for cheap raw materials.

Japan's response to this concern for secure access to raw materials was the Greater East Asian Co-Prosperity Sphere. This neomercantilist arrangement would give Japanese industrialists preference over competitors from countries like the United States for the raw materials of East and Southeast Asia. The perception that the United States could not prosper, or even survive, as an industrial giant in a world dominated by neomercantilist spheres of influence helped commit the Roosevelt administration to opposing the Japanese as well as the Nazis.

After World War II, the Truman administration proceeded to create a new economic world order designed to ensure access to needed raw materials. U.S. policymakers assumed that the world's supply of raw materials, even nonrenewable ones, was sufficient to provide a high standard of living for everyone. If so, then the way to protect individual nations against resource shortages was to create a regime of perfectly free trade. A truly free market would ensure that the earth's resources would be fully developed. It would also eliminate local shortages due to the unequal distribution of resources. Resource-poor Japan would have equal access to Malaysian resources as the

United States. Humankind would finally and forever put the problem of resource shortages behind it.

The Emergence of an Ecological Worldview

The industrial age not only brought a new way of looking at consumption, it also brought a new way of looking at nature. Thanks to science and technology, humanity could for the first time in history begin to think about "conquering nature" and "managing natural forces."

The very idea that society could manage nature, coupled with concern over industrial society's impact on it, led to a historically novel concern for protecting the environment. In the United States, President Teddy Roosevelt popularized this new environmental concern. But the environmentalists of the nineteenth and early twentieth centuries did not challenge the worldview of the industrialist; they epitomized it. Humankind was nature's master. An enlightened master would preserve the natural heritage, would put some natural areas aside to serve the recreational needs of the present and to remind future generations of what the world had once been like. In short, industrial society had a responsibility to use its science to manage and preserve natural areas as well as to exploit them.

By the late 1960s, a new type of environmental movement had begun to challenge this image of humans' relationship to nature. It also challenged industrial civilization's assumption that there was unlimited potential for human consumption. Born out of a new science of ecology, the new environmentalism saw the world as a system. Humanity was a part of this system—if not necessarily equal to every other part then at least a part that was equally dependent in the long run on the effective working of the system.

As they looked at the world's resource system, ecologists saw several problems with the image of unlimited expanding consumption. The first and most evident problem concerned non-renewable resources. Could a rapidly expanding world population also expect to enjoy an increasing material standard of living and could consumption grow generation after generation? From where, on a finite planet with finite resources, were the oil and gas, the uranium and manganese, the copper and cobalt for future generations to come?

The question was radically different than any that had ever been asked before. The ecologists were questioning whether there were actual physical limits, applicable to the entire planet. This was not the structural scarcity of the preindustrial or prewar world. The new ecologists saw the earth as finite and the possibility of absolute resource limits as very real.

The new ecologists raised even more novel and troubling questions about the planet's ability to produce unlimited renewable resources. Unlike coal or tantalum ore, the quantities of which were presumably fixed for all intents and purposes, resources like food crops, fish, timber, and the like were renewable.

New crops could be planted year after year. New fish could be hatched and new trees grown to replace those used.

However, ecologists questioned whether it was possible for human consumption to go beyond the carrying capacity of the renewable-resource system. Statistics on declining fish yields in the world's oceans raised fears that the world's fishing fleets were so depleting important fish stocks that the actual number of fish were decreasing year after year. At some point, the number of fish might fall below levels necessary for successful reproduction.

Similarly, industrial wastes were clearly raising the levels of various toxins in the planet's atmosphere and water system. How high could the levels of these toxins go before producing serious direct health hazards? How high could they go before threatening other renewable-resource systems—like the food-production system—thus threatening living standards or life itself?

In essence, the ecological movement was asking whether the industrial world might not prove to be too successful. It suggested that too much success in expanding living standards and allowing for increased human population might well bring industrial civilization face to face with new, global limits. If so, then society would need to reassess its attitude toward scarcity—and toward the good life.

THE WORLDVIEW PERSPECTIVES

The dominant perspectives on resource issues in today's world have grown directly out of the industrial revolution and the ecological movement. Exhibit 9.1 outlines the key values and assumptions that distinguish system maintainers, system reformers, and system transformers.

System maintainers and system reformers, with respect to resource issues, share a materialistic worldview conditioned by the Enlightenment, the industrial and scientific revolutions, and the democratic revolution. Both worldview categories have been characterized as having a modernist perspective (Hughes 1985, 33–37), distinguishing them from the traditionalist perspective of pre-industrial societies. The hallmark of the modernist perspective is its image of a future characterized by universally high levels of material consumption. What chiefly distinguishes system maintainers from system reformers is the maintainers' confidence that this high-consumption future can be achieved simply by attaining high levels of economic growth.

The ecologists or neotraditionalists as they have been called (Hughes 1985, 33–37) represent system transformers with respect to resource issues. They see modern consumption and growth-oriented societies as illogical in the face of the physical limits to growth implied by a finite planet. The arguments of these system transformers have actually set the agenda for the debate over resource issues.

Exhibit 7.1 Key Dimensions of the Dominant Resource-System Worldviews

	System Maintainer	System Reformer	System Transformer
Worldview perspective	Modernist	Modernist	Neotraditionalist
Core value	Rising material consumption	Rising material consumption	Sustainability in the face of finite resources
Image of future	Steady-state; high consumption	Steady-state; high consumption	Steady-state; low low population and low consumption of material goods
Perception of resource problems	Individual, short-run challenges that can be handled with wise policies	Individual, short-run challenges that can be handled with wise policies	Short-run problems as manifestations of long-run threats to industrial civilization
Definition of the real problem	Neotraditionalist images of the future	Short-run problems if left unattended	Materialism of industrial society
Policy to achieve preferred future	Fast economic growth	Intervene as necessary to limit pressure on resource base	Change core values of industrial society to avoid catastrophe
Image of technological change	Will solve short-run problems and create a sustainable high-consumption future	Given time and investment, will solve all problems	Part of the problem, not the solution

Materialism and Economic Growth: The Modernist Perspective

The core of the modernist perspective, and what most distinguishes this worldview from others, is the value modernists place on material consumption. This is also an element of the modernist perspective that is so basic and widespread that we often fail to recognize its profound impact on our thinking about resource issues.

Among U.S. writers, Herman Kahn (1976, 1981) epitomized the modernist (system-maintainer) view of material consumption. To Kahn, it was axiomatic that having more to consume, in a material sense, is better than having less to consume. While the more qualitative aspects of life (e.g., enjoyment of the arts, leisure activity, self-improvement, and social recognition) have relevance, these values seem obviously less basic than material consumption. Nonmaterial values become truly important only as material needs and wants are met. To modernists like Kahn, the history of industrial civilization provides ample evidence that this hierarchy of values is deeply rooted in human nature. It seems equally evident that human nature is not easily, if ever, altered.

It is equally axiomatic to modernists that the only way to satisfy the material needs and wants of the world's billions is through economic growth. Only by expanding the world's output of goods and services can consumers satisfy their material wants. Only by expanding production can more and more people find the income opportunities they need to take their place in the consuming society. The importance placed on growth by modernists can be seen in the economic policies of governments, businesses, labor unions, and virtually every other institution in the industrialized world. Even individuals who may not benefit from additional economic growth rarely question the wisdom of or need for an ever-expanding economy.

These basic modernist attitudes toward material consumption and economic growth are at the core of industrial civilization. They cannot be associated with a single economic or political philosophy. For example, despite their radically different values and their different assumptions about the best *organization* of economic and political life, such philosophers as Adam Smith and Karl Marx shared these core modernist assumptions. Both saw human progress, at least in part, in terms of increasing satisfaction of material needs and wants. Marx, even more than liberal philosophers, denounced Malthus's predictions of the collapse of industrial civilization. By arguing against the materialism of the new capitalists, Malthus was, in Marx's eyes, acting as a "shameless sycophant of the ruling classes." Malthus's policies could forever condemn the working class to abject poverty despite the abundance they and their machines were creating. (Meek 1953, 123) In short, both Adam Smith and Karl Marx, despite their obvious differences, can be considered system maintainers with respect to industrial civilization.

The Modernist Image of the Future

Regardless of their politicoeconomic philosophy, modernists (both system maintainers and system reformers) have come to share an image of the future characterized by high universal standards of living. According to the modernist, all people can and should try to achieve the level of consumption seen today in the West, especially in the United States. In the future, two-car families, convenience foods, disposable packaging, and a kitchen full of exotic appliances will be taken for granted everywhere.

Depending on their political and economic philosophy, modernists do differ significantly about the importance of equality in achieving this future world. Advocates of free market capitalism, like Herman Kahn (1976, 49), argue that equality is irrelevant as long as everyone's level of consumption is rising. Neomarxists, on the other hand, would argue that grossly unequal levels of consumption are a source of instability and thus impede progress toward the modernist utopia. Both capitalists and Neomarxists, however, believe that the ultimate destiny of industrial civilization is to raise living standards all around the world to the point that material needs and wants are being fully satisfied.

A steady-state economy. When material wants have been satisfied, modernists argue, the world will see the natural emergence of a steady-state economy. The concept of a steady-state economy is at least as old as industrial civilization. In essence, an economy has achieved a steady state when population and the aggregate consumption of material resources become roughly constant over time. Modernists believe this steady-state economy will emerge inevitably as the world moves toward postindustrial civilization.

As the world economy grows and the absolute living standards of people rise, all societies will presumably also undergo a demographic transition. The value of having more children will be replaced by the value of ensuring higher living standards for those already born. As this change in values occurs, birth rates will fall just as death rates have fallen in the last 200 years. Population growth will slow and eventually stop.

Similarly, when industrial civilization has become fully diffused throughout the world, it will finally be possible to fulfill all the material needs and wants of people. At that time, industrial civilization will naturally give way to a postindustrial set of values. People will take material consumption for granted. It will appear less important relative to the satisfaction of other wants and needs. Thus, greater priority will be placed on the non-material values. As this happens, consumption of resources will level off, albeit at a very high level of overall resource use.

Solving short-run problems. Modernists do not necessarily believe that the process of achieving this future world will be an easy one. Bottlenecks in the supply of critical resources and shortages of resources will inevitably occur. The equally inevitable result of economic scarcity will be conflict among individuals, social classes, and political communities.

While resource shortages and related challenges must be taken seriously, to the modernist they simply represent individual, short-run problems. Wise political and economic policies, along with the continued development of new scientific and engineering knowledge can overcome these challenges as they emerge. Industrial society is better equipped to deal with these challenges than was any past civilization. The scientific approach to the world and the wealth of technological knowledge already held by the international community represent a formidable base upon which to respond to future challenges.

Again, modernists of different political stripes prefer different strategies for identifying and responding to resource problems. Neomarxists, for example, may argue that many alleged resource problems are caused by the inequities of capitalist economies. They stress the rationality possible with central government planning. According to them, government control can ensure effective responses to resource problems and greater equity in the sacrifices that resource shortages inevitably involve. Modernists like Herman Kahn are heirs to the tradition of the classical liberal philosophers like Adam Smith and John Stuart Mill. They believe that impersonal markets and entrepreneurial self-interest can best guide efforts to solve resource problems. By allowing each person to follow his or her self-interest, based on the price signals of free markets, the most efficient solutions to resource problems will emerge.

Despite these and other considerable differences, however, all modernists see resource problems in essentially the same light: as individual, short-run obstacles. Although challenging, they can be solved one by one through science and ingenuity. Problems do not reflect the progressive emergence of some ultimate limits to growth. Nor should they be seen as cumulative, creating some kind of systemic threat to industrial civilization.

The Neotraditionalist Challenge

Traditionalists are system transformers who have always objected to the materialism of the modernist perspective for spiritual reasons. However, the challenge to the modernist worldview took on a new shape with the emergence of the neotraditionalist perspective. Most neotraditionalists reject the materialism of the contemporary world because of the perceived long-run vulnerability of a society that seeks to satisfy all the material wants of all people.

To the neotraditionalist, the critical flaw in the modernist image of the future is the essentially finite nature of planet Earth. Lindsey Grant (1983) highlights the basic dilemma: "Even if the entire mass of the earth were petroleum, it would have been exhausted in 342 years if pre-1973 rates of increase in consumption had been maintained." The message is simple: Because the earth is not infinite, at some point in the future, industrial society will run into physical limits to growth. There are three key dimensions to these limits:

1. The limits imposed by non-renewable resources
2. The limited ability of the planet to produce renewable resources
3. The limited ability of the planet's ecosystem to compensate for the pollutants produced by human activity

Non-Renewable Resources
Industrial society depends on certain non-renewable resources such as metals and fossil fuels. By definition, non-renewable resources have a fixed quantity. Any use of these resources will lead to their exhaustion at some point in the future. Ever-increasing rates of use, as a result of economic and population growth, only hasten their exhaustion. At some point industrial civilization may fail because we have come so near to the physical limits of many non-renewable resources that several key resources will become uneconomical to produce. At that point, neotraditionalists argue, industrial civilization will cease to be sustainable. Value changes will not only be forced upon society, but the absolute material standard of living will decline far below what might have been possible had we adopted no-growth policies earlier.

Renewable Resources
Similarly, industrial civilization may reach the limits of the carrying capacity of the renewable-resource system. There is only so much land on the planet that can be farmed. There are only so many fisheries. There are only so many forests. Resources (food, fish, lumber) taken from these lands and fisheries can reproduce themselves. They are renewable resources. However, if we take those resources faster than they can be renewed, we ultimately draw down the resource and impair the ability of the ecosystem to produce it. Thus, as certain fisheries have been overfished, some fish species have virtually disappeared. As more and more food is grown on marginal farmland, the soil has become exhausted or has become susceptible to encroaching deserts. At some point this renewable-resource system may fail to provide the food or other resources needed by the world's population. At that point, not just living standards but population itself will decline.

Environmental Decay
Finally, industrial civilization inevitably produces toxic waste and the undesirable or unhealthy by-products that we call pollution. The planet's ecological system can filter out these pollutants, but only up to a point. As industrial civilization spreads, pollution may grow to the point at which the ecological basis of life is destroyed. Throughout the global community, we may see the problem in rising rates of certain diseases or in declining food production. At some point, death rates from disease or hunger will rise enough so that world population will again be brought within the carrying capacity of the planet.

Whichever of these three physical limits to growth proves to be the most imminent is virtually irrelevant. The neotraditionalist or system transformer would argue that the international system is headed toward disaster if the present course of industrial society is maintained. Future generations can be saved from such a disaster only if leaders and their citizens come to terms with resource limits now rather than when those outer limits to growth have been reached or exceeded.

The Proximity of the Physical Limits to Growth

Neotraditionalists tend to portray the various physical limits to growth as just over the horizon. *The Limits to Growth*, for example, predicted a global population collapse within a hundred years. (Meadows, *et al*. 1972) In *The Population Bomb*, Paul Ehrlich (1971) predicted mass starvation within two decades if population growth were not brought under control.

To some extent, the neotraditionalists' sense of urgency serves a rhetorical purpose. By portraying the physical limits to growth as just over the horizon, neotraditionalists have been better able to raise popular support for their agenda. The rhetoric of future disaster may also serve to draw attention away from less widely shared definitions of the problem. Paul Ehrlich, for example, explicitly argues that overpopulation, by his definition, is not a problem for the future but a problem of the present. Population has already, according to Ehrlich, grown to the point where it compromises key quality-of-life values. While many people shared Ehrlich's concern about mass starvation, most probably did not agree that the United States was overpopulated in 1968.

Neotraditionalists' portrayal of the limits to growth also stems from their view of the growth process and the time lag between growth-related problems and our ability to respond. Growth in population and economic production, the system transformers argue, tends to be geometric, not merely arithmetic. As a result, the limits to growth are not likely to emerge gradually, allowing time for human adjustments. Rather, they are likely to emerge suddenly. The point is summed up in the riddle of the lily pond:

If the lilies growing in a pond double in number every day, and the pond will be completely filled with lilies in 30 days, on which day will the pond be half full?

The answer—on the 29th day—reveals how dangerous it may be to wait for resource problems to become obvious before responding to them.

It is in this light that neotraditionalists interpret current challenges. To the modernist, world hunger represents a straightforward if challenging problem. Modernists who are system-maintainers would solve world hunger by increasing food production or the economic efficiency of food distribution. They would support investments in genetic engineering, opening new farm land, or building roads in the Third World to improve the efficiency of distribution. Modernists who are system-reformers would support these policies but would also support subsidies to the poor—a policy that responds to the problem but may decrease overall economic investment and efficiency. To the neotraditionalist, however, none of these resposes recognizes the real problem. Neotraditionalists see world hunger as one piece of evidence pointing to a larger systemic problem with long-range implications. Data on global hunger, coupled with data on soil depletion and desertification, coupled with rising population and urban sprawl, coupled with data on water pollution from increased fertilizer use and the salinization of irrigated soil cumulatively suggest that the problem of feeding the world's people has reached such a proportion and complexity that easy solutions are no longer available. More importantly, the solution of any one problem has implications that often are negative for other problems. Thus, to the neotraditionalist, nothing less than a transformation of the basic values of industrial society can adequately respond to the problem.

Neotraditionalist Images of the Future

While neotraditionalists have devoted considerable attention to describing future scenarios of doom, it would be biased to characterize them as pessimists. The neotraditionalist image of the future, while it contrasts starkly with the modernist, is pessimistic only if judged on modernist terms.

Neotraditionalists, like modernists, believe that the world must achieve a steady-state economy. However, they do not accept the modernist notion that a steady-state economy can be achieved through the satiation of material wants. More importantly, while modernists believe that the material needs and wants of people around the world can be fully, even abundantly satisfied, neotraditionalists argue that such a world could not be sustained on a finite planet.

The neotraditionalist image of the future is neither crude nor rustic. It recognizes the need to satisfy basic material needs and the natural desire for a "comfortable life." It does not promise the satisfaction of *rising* material desires. Rather, neotraditionalists argue that citizens throughout the world, especially those who consume freely and at times excessively, need to accept a simpler lifestyle premised on expectations of lower levels of material consumption.

Leftan Stavrianos (1976) sees a civilization based on neotraditionalist values as one characterized by human-centered technology, participatory democracy, and readily available opportunities for personal self-actualization. Similarly, the neotraditionalist steady-state economy may continue to grow. But as in the ultimate modernist image of the future, growth would be based on the increased consumption of services, not on the growth of population or the increased consumption of goods. (Daly 1977)

This new lifestyle will require us to change the value base of society. The goal of consuming goods cannot occupy a central place in our value hierarchy. It must be replaced by less materialistic goals (e.g., increasing one's knowledge or engaging in recreation). Social status must be determined by social contribution rather than by material wealth. The ideal of growth and economic efficiency must be replaced by such things as an emphasis on smaller-scale institutions, participation, a clean environment, and the preservation of natural wilderness for its own sake.

In short, neotraditionalists call for a radically different approach to material consumption. Modernists accept and even value resource-intensive consumption (e.g., the rapid turnover of durable goods like automobiles) and disposable goods (e.g., throwaway bottles and diapers). Such resource-intensive consumption and goods make life easier and, as importantly, encourage economic growth and income, making it possible for more people to consume more goods. In contrast, neotraditionalists value patterns of consumption that limit resource use (e.g., use of durable goods meant to last a lifetime and consumer goods that can be used over and over). Likewise, where a renewable resource can replace a non-renewable one (e.g., the use of solar power rather than fossil fuels), the neotraditionalist favors immediate use of the renewable resource even if it is less efficient economically.

The Debate Over Technology

In general, modernists reject the idea that the only sustainable future given the earth's finite resource base is one in which material consumption must be limited. Their rejection of any physical limits to growth highlights the importance of technology and technological change to the modernist worldview.

Technology's Promise
Modernists look at the history of the past 200 years and see the steady increase in humanity's mastery over nature. This progressively greater ability to manipulate and exploit the environment, the modernist argues, is the natural order of things. It has led to profound improvements in the quality of life. This process of technological change is likely to continue, given sufficient faith in the future and investment in technological research and development.

The idea that technology can solve virtually any resource problem has become part of the common culture of the industrial world. Most U.S. citizens, for example, would agree that technology provides an immediate response to the problems of feeding a growing population. If farmland in the traditional breadbaskets is declining in fertility, technology will allow us to open new lands in tropical areas, to grow food in depleted soils, or even to grow food in air and water without soil. As easily accessible deposits of oil, coal, gas, or other minerals are depleted, technology will allow us to find more resources, to extract remaining resources more efficiently, and to develop synthetic substitutes.

For most modernists, technology also holds the key to creating a high-consumption society that is indefinitely sustainable. For example, modernists accept the idea that fossil fuels must inevitably become so depleted that they cease to be a source of cheap energy. But as fossil fuels run out in some distant future, new technologies will be developed that can harness the virtually unlimited energies of the sun and the atom. Cheap energy is itself an answer to the depletion of other non-renewable resources. With appropriate technology and cheap energy, many necessary raw materials can be extracted from seawater— greatly increasing the available reserves. New space technologies may make the essentially unlimited resources of the cosmos available to the global community. But even in the absence of space exploration, as mineral or other resources are progressively depleted, new technologies will allow experts to find substitutes, or to recycle these resources more efficiently. In short, given the will and adequate investment in developing new technologies, humankind can push back the physical limits to growth indefinitely.

The Limits of Technology

Neotraditionalists question the efficacy, and more importantly the wisdom, of trying to use technology to push back the physical limits to growth. In the near term, some resource problems may evade technological solutions as humankind nears the limits of existing technologies. It may, for example, be technically impossible to increase substantially the amount of heat energy people can extract from fossil fuels. If so, as older energy plants (e.g., electric plants and home furnaces) are fully converted to state-of-the-art technologies, any future savings must be achieved through conservation (i.e., by limiting consumption). Even if greater energy efficiencies are theoretically possible, people cannot count on the breakthroughs needed to achieve them.

Many neotraditionalists also reject technological solutions to resource problems on more fundamental grounds. Technological solutions, or "technological fixes," to resource problems inevitably have an impact on the entire ecological web. Most of those impacts tend to be undesirable as well as unforeseen. For example, the need to grow more food has been met through the development and application of irrigation, increased fertilizer use, and opening new lands. But irrigation has also increased the salt levels of soils, threatening to make them virtually unusable in the future. Fertilizer use contributes to water pollution and soil erosion. Land in arid regions or tropical rain forests is often unable to support agriculture without huge capital investments. Further, farming such land has led to erosion and even desertification.

Faced with these problems, modernists again look to science and technology for answers. Many neotraditionalists, however, see this as a dangerous cycle in which new, more powerful technologies create new and more dangerous problems. At some point, the scope or nature of the problems may evade human solutions, resulting in disaster. In the short run, they argue, the very process of technological change only creates new problems that distract us from truly long-term solutions to the serious problems of environmental decay and resource shortages.

Maintaining the System: The Need for High Growth

The debate over the ability of technology to solve short-run and long-run resource problems hinges in part on assumptions about the pace and timing of innovation. It also hinges on a fundamental assumption that the investment capital needed to produce this technology will be available. Acceptance of these assumptions is what most clearly separates system maintainers from system reformers with respect to resource issues. It also helps to explain why economic growth is so critical to the modernist image of the future.

The Need for Investment Capital
A high-consumption future is only achievable, and more importantly only sustainable, if radically new technologies are developed. A society based on fossil fuels is not sustainable in the long run. But the technologies for effectively harnessing solar power on a large scale or for harnessing the virtually unlimited power of fusion have yet to be developed. Five billion people may not exceed the carrying capacity of the renewable-resource system. But ten billion may, unless genetic engineers greatly enhance the productivity of plant and animal species.

But developing new technologies that not only push back the limits to growth, but actually create long-term sustainability at high levels of consumption, will require equally high levels of capital investment. Indeed, as the limits of old technologies are reached and as the sophistication of new technologies grows, the level of investment required to achieve technological breakthroughs will actually increase. (Brown 1978, 250–253) Thus, past levels of investment in new technology may not be sufficient.

At the same time, investment in technological innovation is only one of four demands being placed on the pool of capital the global economy generates. If the modernist image of a high-consumption future is to be achieved, capital must also be invested in new social and economic infrastructure. As the world's population grows, societies will need more schools, more highways, more communications facilities, and more factories. This type of new infrastructure must be built just to satisfy the needs of today's population. In addition, old capital stock must be replaced as it is used up. Old schools must be replaced, old highways and bridges repaired, old machines and factories replaced. Finally, if the modernist image of the future is to have any meaning, capital must also be used to increase consumption itself. Both within the more industrialized world and within the less developed world, new wealth must be devoted simply to satisfying the material needs and wants of people.

While trade-offs can clearly be made among the four demands on new capital, none of these demands can be put off indefinitely. If consumption is allowed to lag, it may be impossible to motivate people to achieve high levels of productivity. Population growth rates may not decline as modernists assume. This would only increase the need for investment in new social and economic infrastructure. Conversely, if consumption is too high, there may be insufficient capital to invest in developing new technology. Then the breakthroughs needed to sustain high levels of consumption may never materialize.

The Availability of Capital
Whether sufficient investment capital can be generated is problematic. A British team of world modelers (Gribbin 1979) saw the scarcity of investment capital as the most serious potential limit to growth. Neotraditionalists generally doubt that the future pool of capital will be enough to satisfy all four investment demands, especially when one considers the deficient infrastructure and

high population growth in much of the Third World. The hallmark of the system maintainer, however, is the belief that the necessary capital will be available. For example, in his world-development model, Wassily Leontief (1977) simply assumes levels of economic growth and investment capital necessary to meet investment needs. Even cautious system maintainers, like Herman Kahn (1976, 4–8), assert that the capital can be available as long as (1) sufficiently high levels of economic growth are maintained, particularly in the more developed countries, and (2) the pool of capital that is available at any one point in time is invested wisely.

Policies to Promote High Growth

The needs to maintain high rates of economic growth and to invest available capital "wisely" guide many of the policy preferences of system maintainers. This can be most clearly seen in the area of environmental policy, in which there are often clear trade-offs between a cleaner environment and economic growth.

The resistance of many U.S. citizens, including government and corporate leaders, to Canadian demands for cleaning up acid-rain should be seen in this light. System maintainers strongly resisted most alternatives to the acid-rain problem. They demanded clear linkages to alleged sources of sulfur-dioxide pollutants. They questioned why people in one place (e.g., Ohio) should pay the cost of environmental policies that would primarily benefit people in other places (eastern Canada, New York, and New England). Most importantly, they questioned whether the economic benefit of "cleaning up a few lakes for sportsmen" justified the economic cost of installing new coal scrubbers or using low-sulfur coal, thus undermining the economies of many Appalachian states. This last concern highlights the root concern of system maintainers. Cleaning up acid rain, or other forms of pollution, is really only acceptable when it comes at little or no economic cost (i.e., when it does not significantly reduce consumption or growth rates), when the clean-up actually creates new growth opportunities (e.g., new industries and employment), or when the economic cost of the pollution (e.g., lost timber resources, depleted fisheries, and lost recreation revenues) add up to more than the economic cost of installing new technologies or using more expensive resources.

Many Third World nations have adopted a system-maintainer perspective on environmental problems generally. Despite obvious environmental problems in most Third World cities, pollution has been characterized as a "rich-country" problem. Investments in pollution-control devices or environmental clean-up efforts appear less important when capital is so limited and the need for investment in new infrastructure so great. Until and unless air and water pollution cause serious health hazards, or more precisely until the economic costs of pollution threaten economic growth, most Third World countries are likely to ignore environmental problems.

The need to promote high levels of economic growth and thus generate an ever-larger pool of investment capital also explains the vehemence with which system maintainers reject the policies of neotraditionalists. According to system maintainers like Herman Kahn (1981), a premature concern for physical limits can be a self-fulfilling prophecy. Kahn argues that the neotraditionalist vision of the future threatens to sap the morale of industrial society. Without the impetus to grow and to search for new resources and new products, the neotraditionalist image of a limited future cannot help but come true. Kahn echoes earlier criticism of Malthus when he notes that the neotraditionalist image threatens to condemn the poor of the world to lives of poverty and misery by forgoing the global economic growth needed to raise their levels of consumption.

Buying Time for Industrial Civilization: System Reformers

Not all modernists agree with Herman Kahn and other system maintainers that high economic growth in and of itself can ensure that enough capital will be generated or that new technologies will emerge in a timely fashion. These modernists, while not rejecting the ultimate goal of a high-consumption future, accept the need for policies that buy time for industrial civilization even at the cost of lower economic growth in the short run. Many of these same modernists also accept the need to invest scarce capital in preserving or cleaning up the environment. As a group, these modernists can be labeled system reformers, though that label may suggest a greater philosophical integrity than really exists.

In this area, system-reformer policy positions are not significantly different than those of system maintainers. They are characterized by a belief that industrial civilization will achieve a steady-state economy characterized by universally high material standards of living. They have faith in the ultimate ability of technology to push back the physical limits to growth and make the post-industrial order sustainable indefinitely. They also tend to view emerging resource-related problems as short-run individual challenges and not as indicators of long-run or systemic vulnerability of industrial civilization.

However, system reformers have less faith that all the pieces of the puzzle will fall into place automatically. Those system reformers who hold capitalist politicoeconomic views may doubt that price incentives will ensure timely responses to severe resource problems. Marxists may not accept the idea that population growth is actually good as long as economic growth continues at high rates. Both may question whether new technologies will be developed in a timely fashion or that pollution becomes relevant only when its economic or social costs make it impossible to ignore.

Many debates over resource issues in past decades have been shaped by system-reformer perspectives. Most policies dealing with resource limits have been introduced or supported by system reformers. In particular, system reformers have in large part controlled the policy agenda with respect to two types of policy: (1) efforts to reduce population growth, and (2) efforts to reduce consumption of scarce resources.

Reducing Population Growth
Like system transformers, system reformers have paid a great deal of attention to the question of population growth. Yet, system reformers have not viewed the problem of population growth in the same way neotraditionalists do.

Lester Brown (1974) and other system transformers speak of a population explosion that may herald the doom of industrial civilization. Population growth in the developed world, where living standards are already high, is seen as just as serious a problem as growth in the Third World. Because per capita use of resources is higher in the developed world, each new U.S. citizen places far greater stress on the ecosystem than does each new African. System reformers, on the other hand, see population growth as an instrumental problem. To many, the negative effects of population growth in the Third World had become apparent by the mid-1970s. In many parts of Africa, Asia, and even Latin America, per-capita income had apparently changed little or even decreased despite a decade of high economic growth. Population growth was outstripping economic growth. As a result, investment in infrastructure often lagged behind what was needed. For the majority of people, consumption did not rise as expected. It seemed that dramatic gains in living standards could only be achieved if population growth rates were reduced.

The perspective of system reformers was clearly dominant in official U.S. thinking about the population issue during the first World Population Conference in 1974. (Harf and Trout 1986, 192–199) U.S. delegates advocated family-planning programs, the dissemination of birth-control technologies, and educational campaigns designed to show people they could have a better life if they had fewer children. System reformers and system transformers cooperated in supporting these programs. Neotraditionalists saw them as a partial step toward the no-growth values that they saw as necessary for creating a sustainable future.

At the first World Population Conference, the arguments of many Third World representatives reflected a system-maintainer viewpoint. They argued that population growth was not the problem. People—with their skills, knowledge, and ability to work—represent a productive resource, not primarily a source of demand. Therefore, given the goal of higher and higher economic growth, more people were seen as good. What was needed was even higher levels of economic growth. This would require greater economic aid from the developed countries, or a restructuring of the world economy to distribute the benefits of world trade more equitably. Rather than contributing to the solution of the problem, family-planning programs would simply reduce economic growth by redirecting resources that could be better invested in development projects.

By the second World Population Conference in 1984, a dramatic shift had taken place in perspectives on population growth. The Reagan administration in the United States had for a variety of reasons fashioned a new U.S. policy around the perspective of system maintainers. Emphasis, they argued, should be placed on increasing economic growth rates, although this was to be done through investment and trade rather than aid. Third World delegates argued that family-planning programs had greatly contributed to declines in birth rates during the years between the two conferences. Those gains would be lost if support for family-planning programs were reduced.

No country better exemplified the shift in Third World thinking, or the system reformer's attitude toward population growth, than the People's Republic of China. With about one-quarter the world's population in 1974, the Chinese were at the forefront of the argument that population growth was not the problem. Western efforts to reduce population growth in the Third World, the focus of system reformers' concerns, were seen as a defensive and racist reaction to the emerging power of non-Western peoples.

By the 1980s, however, the Maoist line in China had given way to the pragmatism of Deng Xiaoping. The new Chinese policies were essentially system reformist, if draconian. A policy calling for one child per family carried severe penalties for exceeding that limit. But the policy was not spurred by a neo-traditionalist concern that the world could not support two billion Chinese. The rationale for the policy was that material living standards for the Chinese could be raised more easily and more quickly if population were reduced. The Chinese saw population reduction as a path to a modernist future of high material living standards, not as a path to a neotraditionalist future of limited consumption and population.

Reducing Resource Use

System reformers have paid far less attention to policies that directly reduce pressure on resources. Recycling efforts, for example, can push back the physical limits to growth by increasing the use of the stock of physical resources. Even when market signals or other signals of scarcity (e.g., actual shortages) do not warrant conservation and recycling, system reformers might be expected to support such policies simply because they buy time. They keep serious resource problems from occurring before technological responses can be found.

With one significant exception, however, there has been little reason for system reformers to focus on the direct reduction of resource use. The relative prices of most raw materials on the world market have actually declined over the past three decades. While there have been periodic shortages of certain commodities, these have clearly been transitory phenomena or the result of political conflicts. They have been mere blips in the long-term trend toward lower resource prices. Thus there has been little incentive to limit resource use.

The one resource that clearly does not fit this general pattern of abundance has been petroleum. The ability of the Organization of Petroleum Exporting Countries (OPEC) to quadruple oil prices in the 1970s encouraged system reformers to look at oil and energy in general in a new light. Many system reformers believed that OPEC's ability to raise oil prices constituted a signal that industrial society was approaching the economic limits of oil production. No great new oil discoveries were likely to be made. Global resources would become more and more concentrated in a few areas of the world. As a result, industrial civilization was on the threshold of an energy transition—a change in the dominant source of energy.

This perspective was not shared by most system maintainers. System maintainers argued that oil prices would soon decline because of natural responses to resource scarcity and high current prices. Higher prices would, for example, spur short-run conservation. Changes in lifestyle, exemplified by smaller, more fuel-efficient cars, would weaken demand. New oil discoveries, spurred by the promise of higher prices, would increase supply. Together, these responses would undercut the artificially high OPEC prices.

For their part, neotraditionalists (system transformers) saw the oil price increases not merely as the onset of a new energy transition but as the beginning of the end of industrial civilization. Cheap energy had enabled the industrial world to grow economically. The kind of high growth rates called for by the modernists would simply not be possible in an era of expensive energy.

Despite their differences, neotraditionalist system transformers and system reformers within the developed world joined forces to create a wide array of policy responses to the energy crisis. They passed a 55-miles-per-hour speed limit in the United States, despite the economic inefficiency of longer travel times. They encouraged a broad array of conservation measures, including investments in solar-energy systems that were largely unproven and not always economical. They even created costly new programs to develop alternative energy sources, not only in the United States but even in countries like Brazil, even though only the most gloomy forecasts of future energy prices made those new sources cost effective.

Despite their apparent alliance in response to the energy crisis, there were clear differences in the types of policy and technology favored by system reformers and transformers. Neotraditionalists (system transformers) favored the development of small-scale solar technologies which would decentralize energy production and distribution. System reformers, with the support of some system maintainers, argued that research needed to focus on technologies that, while more sustainable, were also amenable to large-scale production and distribution systems. As modernists, system reformers were looking for new ways to produce the cheap energy needed by the world's large cities and complex industrial plant. The system transformers, reflecting neotraditionalist images of the future, were looking for technologies consistent with a low-technology, high-independence lifestyle.

Many of the policies enacted in response to the energy crisis were seen as benign from the point of view of system maintainers. Others were not. In particular, efforts to develop new technologies and to subsidize solar energy in effect served to invest scarce capital in ways that were not economically justified. They diminished the growth that might have occurred and thus only worsened the situation created by OPEC's artificially high prices.

When oil prices fell in the 1980s, system reformers saw the change as vindication for their policies. At the same time, the short-run challenge had now been met. Reformers saw little or no need to continue costly support for research into alternative energy technologies, or for lower speed limits, or for subsidies to solar energy.

Neotraditionalists and system maintainers viewed the declining oil prices somewhat differently. System maintainers saw the fall in prices as the natural result of price-induced conservation and increased exploration. Many actually regretted the drastic fall in oil prices because it undercut the incentive to explore for new oil sources. However, they predicted even further cuts in oil prices and the emergence of a new era of cheap energy. On the other hand, neotraditionalists saw the price declines of the early 1980s as an illusory gain. They believed that consumption would again rise, and as it did, industrial civilization would again rush headlong and unprepared toward the next oil crisis.

CONCLUSION

The debate over global resources and growth is at one level characterized by starkly contrasting positions. System maintainers accept the values and imperatives of industrial civilization. They see economic growth as a necessary and sufficient condition for attaining a world characterized by material abundance. System transformers regard such a world as unattainable, or certainly unsustainable. They call for the modern world to turn away from its obsession with material consumption. System reformers, believing both in the promise of industrial civilization and the severity of some ecological threats to it, accept the need to intervene in the system, at least in order to reduce population growth and conserve critical resources.

Despite these stark contrasts, however, the politics of everyday life are often less clear-cut, at least on the surface. Responding to resource problems rarely takes the form of "transformational policies." Food for future generations is in part ensured by saving farmland from erosion. This may require education, the application of alternative farming technologies, and government policies designed to create new incentives for farmers. Values may change in the process, but only as a result of practical, incremental changes in the way things are done.

Incremental changes are unlikely to be posed or justified in stark, value-based terms. System reformers and transformers may support particular programs designed to reduce teenage pregnancy or to clean up toxic wastes basically because these goals are consistent with a more sustainable future. But they may oppose other programs with similar goals because they see those programs as technically inadequate. On the other hand, system maintainers may also support efforts to reduce teenage pregnancies or clean up toxic wastes. But their support is likely to be based on economic considerations. Do the programs appear to compromise growth (i.e., how much do they cost)? Is the problem so severe that the economic cost of doing nothing outweighs the cost of acting? In order to build winning political coalitions, system transformers are likely to justify preferred programs primarily in economic and technical terms, not because they are consistent with a sustainable future.

In short, in the world of practical politics, values and assumptions are typically revealed in decision rules and rationalizations for one's own position, not in sweeping proclamations or even in fixed positions on an issue. The challenge faced by anyone who would understand the debate over global resources and growth is to read between the lines. Values and assumptions are revealed in the questions and concerns of decisionmakers, and in the criteria they use to guide their decisions in particular situations.

REFERENCES

Brown, Lester. *In the Human Interest*. New York: W. W. Norton, 1974.

―――. *The Twenty Ninth Day*. New York: W. W. Norton, 1978.

Daly, Herman E. *Steady State Economics*. San Francisco: W. H. Freeman, 1977.

Deevey, E.S., *et al*. "Mayan Urbanism: Impact on a Tropical Karst Environment." *Science* (October 19, 1979)

Ehrlich, Paul R. *The Population Bomb*. New York: Ballantine Books, 1971.

Grant, Lindsey. "The Cornucopian Fallacies: The Myth of Perpetual Growth." *The Futurist* (August 1983): 16–22.

Gribbin, John. *Future Worlds*. New York: Plenum Press, 1979.

Harf, James E., and B. Thomas Trout. *The Politics of Global Resources*. Durham, NC: Duke University Press, 1986.

Hughes, Barry B. *World Futures: A Critical Analysis of Alternatives*. Baltimore: Johns Hopkins University Press, 1985.

Kahn, Herman, *et al. The Next 200 Years: A Scenario for America and the World*. New York: William Morrow, 1976.

Kahn, Herman, and Ernest Schneider. "Globaloney 2000." *Policy Review* (Spring 1981): 129–147.

Leontief, Wassily, *et al. The Future of the World Economy*. New York: Oxford University Press, 1977.

Machiavelli, Niccolo. *The Prince and the Discourses*. New York: Modern Library, 1940.

Malthus, Thomas R. *An Essay on the Principle of Population*. Philip Appleman, ed., New York: W. W. Norton, 1976.

Marx, Karl. "Excerpt from 'A Contribution to the Critique of Political Economy.'" In *Marx and Engels*. Edited by Lewis S. Feuer. Berkeley: Ramparts, 1959.

McNeill, William H. *The Pursuit of Power*. Chicago: University of Chicago Press, 1982.

Meadows, Donnella H., *et al. The Limits to Growth*. New York: Signet, 1972.

Meek, Ronald M., editor and translator. *Marx and Engels on Malthus*. London: Lawrence and Wishart, 1953.

Roberts, J.M. *The Pelican History of the World*. Harmondsworth, England: Penguin Books, 1980.

Smith, Adam. *An Inquiry Into the Nature and Causes of the Wealth of Nations*. New York: Modern Library, 1937.

Stavrianos, Leftan. *The Promise of the Coming Dark Age*. San Francisco: W. H. Freeman, 1976.

8

U.S. Perspectives
on the Soviet Union
DEBORAH ANNE PALMIERI

In the United States, references to the Soviet Union evoke strong feelings. Reactions may range from total condemnation to high praise for the accomplishments of the world's first socialist country and worker's state. For many people, a mention of the USSR conjures up images of an "evil empire" driving for world domination and posing an imminent threat to the values of the Western world. There are those who are sympathetic to the accomplishments of socialism in raising the Soviet standard of living despite the effect of two devastating world wars and other formidable obstacles, including Western blockades. Still, a good number of individuals have mixed feelings about the Soviet government and its people. The different images held by leaders and citizens must be carefully considered as one attempts to understand the very complex and critical relationship between the United States and the USSR. The worldviews analytical approach presented in this book encourages the student of international affairs to consider carefully all relevant images of significantly controversial issues. This chapter identifies three differing interpretations of issues defining relations between the Soviet Union and the United States. Contending images of the superpowers are built upon the scholarly contributions of historians and political scientists, and the evaluations of experienced policymakers. Each perspective or worldview discussed in this chapter is based on a set of assumptions that serves to define an analytical orientation. Scholars and policymakers continue to use such analyses to describe and evaluate the interactions between these two competing powers.

The U.S.-Soviet relationship is particularly important as an area of study because this relationship and the worldviews associated with it tend to structure other international relationships and worldviews. For example, in a tense bipolar Cold War environment, the relations between the United States and its allies are significantly different than during an era characterized by detente or cordial relations between the United States and the USSR. In times of tension and uncertainty in U.S.-Soviet relations, other states must respond to this tension, often with little hope or means of influencing the actions of either state. The superpower relationship and the perception of the relationship by leaders in the United States and the Soviet Union become part of the environment of international politics for other states and bring about certain policies and policy responses. Ultimately, it is the U.S.-Soviet relationship that determines whether the global community as we know it continues to exist. This fact underlies the importance of the U.S. views of the Soviet Union and the Soviet perspectives of the United States.

The analysis of Soviet foreign policy is a complex undertaking which involves, as do all political questions, opposing points of view. (Horelick, et al., 1975) The controversial nature of U.S.-Soviet relations necessitates a careful assessment of different interpretations of U.S. views of Soviet foreign policy. In its portrayal of the Soviet Union, it has not been uncommon for the U.S. media to draw a Cold War or confrontational image of the Soviets. The Cold War image is reinforced by those policymakers who consider the Soviets as the major competitor of the United States. But this is only one of several ways to see the Soviets. It would be safe to say that this "us-them" or "evil empire" view of the Soviet Union is held by many citizens in the United States. (Welch, 1970) And conversely, the dominant Soviet perspective is best described as a mirror image of the U.S. view of the Soviet Union. (Lenczowski, 1982) (Schwartz, 1978) (Gilbert, 1977)

Three main worldviews affecting the U.S. study of Soviet foreign policy and U.S.-Soviet relations have been identified. These views reflect a range of perceptions about the nature of the superpower relationship and the international role of the Soviets. They also reflect a U.S. view of the international system: Hence the system maintainer regards the Soviet Union as an enemy, an irreconcilable antagonist that should be dominated or controlled by the United States. The system reformer sees the Soviet Union more as an equal and legitimate competitor. In this worldview, the United States must cooperate closely with the Soviet Union to avoid systemic war. The United States and the Soviet Union, as rule makers, continue to control a significant proportion of the spoils in the international system. The third perspective, that of the global cooperationist, is akin to that of the system transformer. In general, it is critical of U.S. foreign policy toward the Soviet Union. U.S. foreign policy, according to this perspective, engenders conflict and confrontation rather than encouraging peace. While these worldview categories are broad and subject to exceptions and caveats, they provide a useful analytical framework to better organize and understand the official and unofficial U.S. perceptions about Soviet foreign-policy behavior.

THE SYSTEM-MAINTAINER WORLDVIEW: "THE ENEMY"

The system-maintainer perspective is often associated with a conservative political orientation in the United States. The Soviet Union is regarded as an implacable enemy. The intellectual origins of this perspective date back to the post-1945 Cold War era. The underlying key assumption in this stridently anti-Communist mode of thinking is that the Soviet Union is an aggressive, hostile, and inflexible totalitarian dictatorship incapable of change. Those who hold this worldview suggest that the motive behind Soviet policy is one of unbridled expansionism, driven by Moscow's desire to spread revolution and communism worldwide at the expense of the capitalist-democratic states of the Western world and their spheres of influence. (Pipes, 1981) (Conquest, 1979) (Tucker, 1981) (Brezezinski, 1977)

From the system-maintainer point of view, the Soviet Union's foreign-policy goals are hostile to U.S. interests. The goal of Soviet actions in the international system is to gain advantages over the United States and the West. Thus, any possibility of long-term peaceful coexistence between the East and West is considered unlikely. The United States is seen as a representative of all that is good and virtuous in the world. System maintainers recognize the responsibility of the United States to uphold the interests of the free world, contain, and even attempt to bring the Soviet system to an end. The conflict between the United States and the Soviet Union is seen as a total war. It involves competition in all regions of the world in economic, political-diplomatic, and sociocultural policy areas.

The Role of the Military and Diplomacy

One of the basic assumptions of the system-maintainer worldview is that military strength is the key to success in the international system. The anarchy of the international system requires that states maintain enough power to guarantee that other states do not challenge their national interests. The distribution of power in the international system since 1945 has resulted in a bipolar East-West world, which system maintainers see as the major division in international politics. This East-West analysis of world affairs influences all policy actions. At the heart of competition for control of the international system is an expensive and potentially dangerous arms race. Military competition drives and defines the relationship between the world's two superpowers.

The "enemy" motif is central to the system-maintainer perspective. (Finlay, Holsti, Fagen, 1967) It sees the USSR as an inherent adversary of the United States. The enemy is evil, ominous—a force that should be eliminated. President Reagan, for example, earlier in his presidency, denounced the Soviet Union as the "focus of evil" in modern civilization. It follows that if a country is perceived as an enemy, there is little chance to live side-by-side with it peacefully. Enemies are to be defeated, tormented, and humiliated. Everything the enemy does is suspect, motivated by self-serving or deceitful causes. This is the nature of the logic characteristic of a system-maintainer view, which champions the cause of a virtuous U.S. society against an evil Soviet totalitarian dictatorship. (Berman, 1958) It is noteworthy that Mr. Reagan repudiated the "evil empire" characterization of the Soviet Union following the May 1988 summit with Mr. Gorbachev.

When translated into foreign policy, the system-maintainer worldview emphasizes cautious and incremental bargaining with the enemy, supported by a strong military position aimed at containing any expansionary moves by the other side. The containment policy stresses a posture of aggressive and hostile confrontation of the Soviet Union. Since Moscow is regarded as a political adversary, this view stresses the need for a strong military buildup, limited economic or diplomatic interaction, and a tough, untrusting, and cynical style of diplomacy. Historically, this policy orientation has resulted in an atmosphere of Cold War tensions, confrontational politics, East-West competition in the Third World, minimal economic relations, and unregulated military competition. The danger of the Soviet threat is stressed, and U.S. policymakers are generally pessimistic about the future viability of the relationship.

Deterioration of U.S.-Soviet Relations in the 1980s

The Reagan administration through late 1987, despite showing some willingness to talk with the Soviets about controlling the continuing arms race, best typifies this perspective in recent history. (Nye, 1982) In national-security policy areas, President Reagan has promoted unregulated military competition as exemplified by Star Wars or the Strategic Defense Initiative (SDI). This has resulted in a sharp escalation of the arms race between the United States and the Soviet Union and has encouraged the deployment of new weapons systems. On the economic side, the Reagan administration in the early 1980s was responsible for initiating a wave of sanctions, restrictions, and barriers designed to minimize or severely limit trading relations with the East. Economic sanctions against Moscow in the early 1980s included a grain embargo to halt the shipment of 17 million tons of U.S. grain to the USSR; trade sanctions to block the sale of equipment to build the Yamal Pipeline Project, which would transport gas from Western Siberia to Western Europe; and expanded restrictions on exchange and cooperation agreements on energy, technology, and joint research.

Social and cultural links were curtailed, despite a few efforts to revive them. By the mid-1980s there began some movement toward warming relations between the superpowers; however, these efforts are still subject to the barriers accompanying the traditional perception of the USSR as the enemy of the United States.

Nonetheless, the success of Soviet and American summitry in 1987 and 1988 has been a major factor in breaking the stalemate between both countries. As a result of the good will generated at these summits, political, economic, and cultural relations markedly improved by the late 1980s, engendering a new wave of business activities, and cultural, artistic, and student exchanges. It remains to be seen whether this budding detente is cosmetic and short-term or will result in a longer-term stability.

U.S.-Soviet relations until recently, experienced, under the Reagan administration, the greatest deterioration since the post-war tensions of the late 1940s and the early 1950s or the Cuban missile crisis of 1961. Many factors have contributed to U.S.-Soviet distrust and competition:

1. Escalation of the arms race by both superpowers
2. Growth of a conservative domestic political trend in the United States
3. On-going conflict in the Middle East
4. Soviet invasion and occupation of Afghanistan
5. Soviet military activity in the Pacific
6. Continued differences over U.S. and Soviet activities in Third World regions such as southern Africa and Central America

The Effects of U.S.-Soviet Competition on the World

During most of the Reagan years, a persistent political and diplomatic stalemate punctuated by ups and downs left the United States and the USSR deeply suspicious of and hostile to each other. Each blames the other side for causing the deterioration of the relationship. In public discussions, both sides claim to have made sincere peace proposals and attempts to reach an accommodation at the negotiating table. Some U.S. and Soviet specialists suggest that military interests and political leaders need the other side to enhance their power and influence. Leaders in both countries are continually reacting to the actions of their enemies and blaming the other side for most of the world's problems. The implications of this image of the world for the superpowers and other states are serious and far-reaching. When the superpowers are experiencing tense relations the rest of the world cringes. An increase in arms productions in the Soviet Union or the United States usually means more arms transfers to client states and an increase in uncertainty and tensions in unstable regions of the world.

What has resulted is increased military competition with new and less stable, less verifiable conventional- and nuclear-weapons systems. The nuclear-arms race between the two superpowers threatens the continuation of civilization. Citizens throughout the world are fearful of an escalating level of tension between the superpowers. This tension is played out in Third World areas where the Soviet Union and the United States (or their surrogates) are involved in armed conflict (e.g., Nicaragua and Afghanistan). An increasing number of people believe that these conflicts could escalate beyond a regional and conventional exchange with superpower involvement. U.S. citizens are frequently warned by their government that the Soviet Union is an expansionary power out to take over the world. Such an assessment creates not only fear and distrust, but an often irrational evaluation of Soviet motives and intentions. In a similar style, Soviet citizens are told by their government that aggressive and militaristic U.S. foreign policy has imperialistic goals. Furthermore, official Soviet foreign policy suggests that U.S. military strategy is to seek global domination and that, unless the United States is checked, the result will be war against the Soviet homeland. This has contributed to a periodic siege mentality among Soviet citizens and, likewise, fear in the United States that Soviets will do anything to prevent this. Many people in both societies strongly believe that hostilities between the superpowers are inevitable. Thus, for system maintainers in the United States, the nature of the U.S.-Soviet relationship is best described as a confrontational one in which the security of each state is based on having military strength enough to deter the other side from hostile attack.

Reagan's maintainer position, however, was softened by the rise to power of Mikhail S. Gorbachev, and his attempts to democratize the Soviet Union through policies of *glasnost* and *perestroika*. Gorbachev's personal charm, combined with his extraordinary diplomatic skills and flair for promoting friendly relations with Western nations has managed to neutralize even the harshest U.S. critics of the Soviet Union, and the bitter acrimony characterizing U.S.-Soviet relations for most of the decade of the 1980s is subsiding.

THE U.S. SYSTEM-REFORMER PERSPECTIVE: "MANAGE THE COMPETITION"

The working assumptions underlying a reformer position are perhaps more utopian than those of the traditional realist or system-maintainer position. Core assumptions are the belief in the viability of U.S.-Soviet cooperation and the recognition that both superpowers have shared interests. Policymakers tend to be more optimistic about the use of conferences, treaty sessions, and summit meetings as forums for resolving conflicts and thereby easing tensions. The Soviet Union is recognized as a responsive and flexible partner, open to U.S. overtures and willing to discuss points of contention. Reformers see the Soviet Union as sincere about becoming a more reliable custodian in the international system. It is thought that the strident and militant Marxist-Leninist ideological orientation has been modified in favor of a more pragmatic position that in many policy areas upholds the status quo.

In the system-reformer worldview, the Soviet Union is identified as a great-power competitor of the United States. In contrast to the system-maintainer view, reformers emphasize the necessity to manage carefully the dynamics of superpower competition through open diplomacy. This worldview is often associated with a more moderate foreign-policy position in the United States.

The Uses of Diplomacy

Foreign-policy decisionmakers who hold a system-reformer view have often focused their efforts on the use of diplomacy as an instrument of projecting U.S.

power and prestige in the international political system. These same leaders tend to emphasize "carrots" rather than "sticks" in their attempts to move the Soviet leaders in a desired political direction. From this perspective, both the United States and the Soviet Union are seen to be competing in a global chess game with each trying to outmaneuver the other. The stakes are high—the hearts and minds of the citizens of the world. U.S. policymakers have acknowledged that Soviet expansionism poses a tough challenge; nonetheless, they have expressed confidence and optimism that the challenge can be controlled through managed competition, negotiation, and tough bargaining within the context of a responsible and regulated bilateral relationship.

Thus, system reformers see the Kremlin leaders as pragmatic actors who have abandoned the former zeal for constant disruption and upheaval of the international political system. U.S. reformers emphasize that the Soviet Union and the West have many common interests, such as the prevention of systemic war, the regulation of Third World conflicts, and the promotion of trade and economic development. The reformers are not so naive as to assume that cooperation between the United States and the Soviet Union will eventually result in a world free of conflict and war. Instead, they support the maintenance of a cautious and incremental bargaining posture vis-à-vis the Soviets. The key is to move away from the inordinate fear of the Soviet system that has driven U.S. foreign policy in the past. The reformers among U.S. policymakers and interest groups believe that a mixture of cooperation and competition, with a heavier emphasis on cooperation, will lead to a more successful and stable U.S.-Soviet relationship. (Kennan, 1982), (Legvold, 1980), (Shulman, 1984) Furthermore, their image of the Soviet Union is that of a society that can be won over to a way of doing things more consistent with U.S. values. The liberalization policies currently being suggested by Soviet leaders represent affirmations of this position.

From this viewpoint, the Soviet Union is regarded as a limited adversary. A natural outcome of this is policymaking that advocates a two-track approach featuring more "carrots" but some "sticks." This means that the United States will assume a firm and strong posture (sticks) on some issues, and encourage cooperation (carrots) in other policy areas. Through an adroit combination of constraints and incentives in dealing with Moscow, reformers believe that it is possible to improve U.S.-Soviet relations without sacrificing U.S. security. A calculated use of concessions and other confidence-building measures (such as recognizing Soviet security interests in Eastern Europe and East Asia) and positive inducements (such as trade) are used to influence Soviet behavior. These concessions and inducements can be used to shape Soviet foreign policy or to deter some Soviet activities. The continuation of this policy position is linked to Soviet behavior. As long as the Soviets act in a pragmatic fashion and do not attempt to challenge U.S. interests, cooperation will continue. Not unlike the earlier efforts at community-building in Europe, the U.S. and Soviet cooperation will spill over into other policy areas. Cooperation will eventually create a political environment based on managed and regulated connections or linkages between the superpowers and their allies. Thus, as long as the rules of the game are followed and no encroachments are made by either side, both states can and will coexist. Incentives to bargain must be kept high and disincentives for any attempt to change the system must also be high. However, if the relationship is carefully managed and cultivated, detente can be achieved and tensions minimized. This will obviously depend upon a willingness by both parties to share power and collaborate for mutual gain. (George, 1983) This represents a move away from the zero-sum attitude of the maintainers (i.e., Soviet gains mean U.S. losses) to a positive-sum attitude (i.e., the United States and the Soviet Union can both win).

The Breakdown of Détente

In the defense-policy area, the system reformer is likely to want to maintain limits on offensive weapons set in the Strategic Arms Limitation Treaty (SALT) I and SALT II negotiations, and strengthen treaties such as the Anti-Ballistic Missile (ABM) Treaty. Reformers stress the need for arms-control negotiations in an effort to manage the arms race. On economic issues, the system reformer hopes to increase trade between the East and West by eliminating the most restrictive of the tariff and non-tariff barriers. Trade and economic development policies are seen as primary tools that the United States and the West can use to effect change in Soviet behavior. With the goal of increasing understanding of each system by the other, social and cultural contacts are encouraged by reformers. This might include an increased number of high-level diplomatic consultations, along with more citizen, sports, cultural, entertainment, and student exchanges.

The Carter administration policies toward the Soviets through late 1978 comes the closest to this worldview. However, it should be pointed out that the Nixon-Kissinger era of détente (early 1970s) did represent a break in the hardcore maintainer position and a move toward a system-reformer position. The Nixon-Brezhnev Summit in 1972, opened the gates for the expansion of trading, economic, and more meaningful diplomatic activity. Both Nixon and Kissinger promoted a foreign policy that represented the ideals of the system maintainer; however, they recognized that the transformations defining the contemporary system required a more non-traditional strategy, one which utilized trade, alliances, personal diplomacy, and other non-military tools of statecraft. Similarly, in the late years of his administration, Reagan gravitated towards a similar position.

The Carter administration hoped to moderate the U.S.-Soviet relationship further by moving U.S. foreign policy away from its emphasis on containment and its almost exclusive concentration on the Soviet Union as the source of all of the world's problems. Carter encouraged a shift away from a peace-through-strength view to one of arms control. He also urged the U.S. citizenry to consider North-South as well as East-West issues. Carter's emphasis on human rights and his concern about the indigenous causes of conflict in the Third World were indicative of his efforts. Carter was considered by many to be too soft on the Soviets, allowing them to build more weapons, move ahead of the United States, and increase their power base. However, supporters claim the foreign policy of the early Carter administration represented an attempt to replace a balance of terror with a more pluralistic vision of world order.

While the first half of the Carter administration reflected the system-reformer point of view, in the later years a shift occurred that essentially redefined foreign-policy goals in terms of a maintainer worldview. The Soviet invasion of Afghanistan seemed to destroy the arguments put forth by those who disputed the old warning that the Soviets only reacted to a show of force. This invasion sparked a new wave of embargoes on grain and technology, restrictions on Soviet fishing off U.S. shores, the Olympic boycott, and the renewal of draft registration. It also inspired the Carter Doctrine, which pledged to respond to Soviet incursions in the Persian Gulf region with military force, if necessary. The goals of this doctrine were twofold: first, it acted as a symbolic expression of U.S. outrage and disapproval at the Soviet intervention, and second, it hoped to discourage future aggressive Soviet activities in the Third World. (Garthoff, 1985) In other words, a changing set of conditions had brought about a deterioration of détente and the relatively stable U.S.-Soviet relationship that had accompanied it.

Soviet aggression and the perception that U.S. power had declined contributed to a shift in public attitudes. The people's wish for a strong United States removed most of the incentives for U.S. leaders to embrace the reformer position. Many believe that Carter's attempts to shift U.S. foreign-policy priorities to the reformist position contributed to his electoral defeat. The Reagan administration for the most part has taken a system-maintainer position and only recently has shown signs of increasing U.S.-Soviet cooperation.

A U.S. SYSTEM-TRANSFORMER VIEW OF U.S.-SOVIET RELATIONS

As the introduction of this book suggests, there are several different perspectives within the system-transformer category. The most appropriate characterization of the transformer position within the context of U.S. foreign policy toward the Soviet Union is best described as an "idealist" or "alternative" perspective. Proponents of this position tend to blame unilateralism and the emphasis on power politics for tensions between the United States and the Soviet Union. Although seeing both sides as contributing to this climate of fear and tension, transformers in the United States tend to focus their criticisms on their own society because this is where they have the potential to change policy. Generally, those who hold this position feel that the traditional views of state-centrism, anarchy, and self-help must be replaced by multilateralism, the recognition that common rules of behavior must exist, and that non-force policy options must be used to resolve conflicts.

The Rise of a New Perspective

Alternative perspectives on U.S.-Soviet relations gained attention in the early 1960s when many scholars realized the need to revaluate the Cold War literature on Soviet foreign policy written by more traditional scholars. (Williams, 1962, Alperovitz, 1965, Kolko, 1968) Since then, various alternative positions have challenged the conservatism and realist orientation of mainstream U.S. academic writings on the Soviet Union and international politics in general. These alternative perspectives include writings from the disarmament and anti-nuclear movement, the peace movement, and literature on anti-imperialism and dependency. In general, writers within these schools of thought trace belligerent Soviet foreign policy behavior to what they see as militant and imperialistic U.S. policies. These policies are seen as attempts to expand the power and influence of the United States far beyond its own borders. While system maintainers emphasize Soviet rigidity and totalitarianism, proponents of these alternative views stress the reactive and adaptive nature of Soviet policy. Western diplomatic practice, accordingly, is held responsible for exacerbating tensions between the United States and the Soviet Union. These transformers often oppose mainstream U.S. government policies and blame the unbridled pursuit of U.S. political and economic interests as the major cause of international tension.

This system-transformer perspective gained a significant number of adherents during the 1960s. This was in part the result of the reflection on and evaluation of U.S. foreign policy caused by the Vietnam War and a climate of turmoil and unrest in U.S. society. During that period, the intellectual foundations of this view of U.S.-Soviet relations were further developed and became a major part of the policy debates in Washington, and caused many U.S. citizens to reassess the direction of U.S. foreign policy since 1945. Events in the 1970s (e.g., the "eagle-defiant" attitude of the Reagan administration) moved the alternative view to the periphery of intellectual and policy debates. However, in recent years many activist groups interested in peace, social justice, and ecological issues have brought this viewpoint back into discussions about the future path of U.S.-Soviet relations. These groups are generally supportive of policies that challenge status-quo or system-maintainer viewpoints.

The policy positions that evolve from this worldview are very diverse. Nonetheless, a few consistent common beliefs are apparent, among them advocating a halt to an expansionary and aggressive U.S. foreign policy, cutting military spending, and fostering a cooperative rather than confrontational posture toward Moscow. The alternative view stresses in no uncertain terms the need for U.S. leadership in ending or minimizing East-West tensions. However, most who ascribe to the assumptions of this view are opposed to both U.S. and Soviet foreign-policy orientations, regarding both states as superpower aggressors engaged in the calculated pursuit of their respective national interests and the extension of their own spheres of influence, especially in the Third World— often endangering world peace in the process. Proponents of this view stress policies designed to contain the incursions of both superpowers in Third World nations, and to protect the integrity of neutral or non-aligned nations that might otherwise become caught in the middle of superpower conflicts.

Identifying System Transformers

It is difficult to identify one type of organization or a country that has built a policy position around the goals of this worldview. System transformers in this policy area include some members of the Non-Aligned Movement in the Third World, political movements such as the Green Party in West Germany, and disarmament-advocacy groups in the United States. These transformers are not always condemnatory of U.S. policy nor can many of them be considered as political radicals attempting to impose an ideal system. In the United States, most of the members of the peace and social-justice community of advocacy organizations embrace the transformer's views. (Reardon, 1982, Caldicott, 1981, Griffiths and Polyani, 1978) Many of the organizations in this movement represent religious groups opposed to war and concerned about social justice, economic rights, and the militarism and violence that seem to rule U.S. society. These transformers believe one solution is to return power to the people, eliminate domestic power structures favoring the elite, and change an international structure dominated by the United States and the USSR. "Equality for all nations" and a "world without war and injustice" are the opinions uniting advocates of this position. Many have a desire to transform the world's present "state of anarchy" into a system of "states in cooperation" mutually working together to solve common problems without resorting to force. Finally, the perspective of anti-imperialism, popular in the early 1970s, condemns the expansionist and aggressive policies of either one or both superpower nations. (Fann and Hodges, 1971) (Mack et al., 1979) (Greene, 1971) Dependencias, or those who adhere to a dependency perspective of international politics, focus mainly on the effects and causes of U.S. imperialism in the Third World. (Cardoso and Faletto, 1979) (Moran, 1974) (Evans, 1979)

One significant outgrowth of dissatisfaction with traditional or "establishment" approaches to conflict, arms control, and peace has been the rise of a broad-based citizen's diplomacy movement in the United States. (Warner and Shuman, 1987) Numerous U.S. organizations, ranging from church to anti-nuclear activist groups, are initiating people-to-people-exchange delegations to hold political discussions, share ideas about important issues, and foster international good will. "Global town meetings" have linked Soviet with U.S. citizens through radio link-ups, featuring well-known moderators such as Cable News Network-owner Ted Turner. The "Donahue" show has featured a television link-up allowing U.S. and Soviet people to communicate with each other via satellite. The discussion often became lively and heated as both audiences shared common social experiences and queried each other about foreign-policy issues. Other efforts, in addition to the traditional peace marches, have included a "Peace Cruise" down the Mississippi River. A group of U.S. and Soviet citizens from all walks of life held seminars on the arms race and spoke to people about peace as the ship stopped at several ports. Upon completion of the journey, they drafted "A People's Appeal for Peace," which was later presented to President Reagan and General Secretary Gorbachev.

This transformer view is still a minority position in U.S. policy debates. However, the number of people urging cooperation and an end to the arms race is growing. The "peace and cooperation" alternative is gaining momentum as more and repeated attempts by the superpowers fail to sufficiently limit or halt the arms race. Advocates of this perspective have rejected several ideas common to today's international politics, including the basic assumption that one or two states should control the international system and that leaders of states should instinctively regard each other as enemies in pursuit of divergent goals. Instead, system transformers hope to alter fundamentally relationships of exploitation and domination in favor of working together for the common good. In other words, in this specific policy area the focus is on the need for the United States and the USSR to work with other states through regional and international organizations to achieve peace. This multilateralism must replace unilateralism if peace is to be achieved.

CONCLUDING REMARKS

Each of the three worldviews discussed in this chapter is based on an image of the world built upon differing assumptions about the nature of Soviet foreign policy, the character of the U.S.-Soviet relationship, and how each country should respond to the other. No one worldview has a monopoly on the truth. Each has its own biases in what it does and does not consider important and relevant data.

First, it is most important to recognize that alternative interpretations of Soviet foreign policy do exist. It is up to students of international affairs thoroughly to critique and assess each one, before dismissing any view as illegitimate or accepting one as legitimate. Second, it is essential to realize that when applied to actual foreign-policy processes or when put into practice, the assumptions of each worldview may lead to vastly different conclusions, policy outcomes, or consequences. How U.S. leaders look at and evaluate the Soviet Union ultimately has important consequences for a variety of issues and actors in international politics—especially considering the different policy outcomes characteristic of each worldview. Political awareness is necessary to encourage thoughtful and informed decisionmaking, and to aid citizens in their efforts to develop their own views on the foreign-policy process. The application of an analytical framework that encourages a review of contending positions encourages critical and evaluative thinking, and a deeper appreciation of the complexities and choices involved in the policy process.

There are three primary goals to keep in mind when learning about different U.S. perspectives of Soviet foreign-policy behavior. The first is to be a critical, comparative thinker when analyzing the issues defining this complex relationship. The second relates to the controversial nature of the issue. It is important that students develop a sophisticated research design which encourages an in-depth exploration of each perspective. The third is to recognize that there are available a variety of sources of information reflecting contending perspectives. These varied sources must be considered in order to reach a thorough understanding of the issues that define U.S.-Soviet affairs and to develop informed responses to these issues.

REFERENCES

Alperovitz, Gar. *Atomic Diplomacy.* New York: Vintage, 1965.

Berman, Harold J. "The Devil and Soviet Russia." *The American Scholar* 27 (1958):147–152.

Brzezinski, Zbigniew K. *The Soviet Bloc: Unity and Conflict.* Revised. Cambridge, MA: Harvard University Press, 1977.

Caldicott, Helen. *Nuclear Madness.* New York: Bantam, 1981.

Cardoso, Fernando and Enzo Faletto. *Dependency and Development in Latin America.* Berkeley and Los Angeles: University of California Press, 1979.

Conquest, Robert. *Present Danger: Towards a Foreign Policy.* Stanford: Hoover Institution Press, 1979.

Etzold, Thomas, and John Gaddis, editors. *Containment: Documents on American Policy and Strategy 1945-50.* New York: Oxford University Press, 1982.

Evans, Peter. *Dependent Development.* Princeton: Princeton University Press, 1979.

Fann, K. T. and Donald C. Hodges, eds. *Readings in U.S. Imperialism.* Boston: Porter Sargent Publisher, 1971.

Finlay, David, Ole R. Holsti and Richard Fagen. *Enemies in Politics.* Chicago: Rand McNally, 1967.

Gaddis, John. *Strategies of Containment: A Critical Appraisal of Postwar American National Security Policy.* New York: Oxford University Press, 1982.

Garthoff, Raymond L. *Detente and Confrontation: American-Soviet Relations From Nixon to Reagan.* Washington, D.C.: Brookings Institution, 1985.

George, Alexander. *Managing U.S.-Soviet Rivalry: Problems of Crisis Prevention.* Boulder, CO: Westview, 1983.

Gilbert, Stephen. *Soviet Images of America.* New York: Crane, Russak & Co., 1977.

Greene, Felix. *The Enemy: What Every American Should Know About Imperialism.* New York: Vintage Books, 1971.

Griffiths, Franklin and John C. Polyani, eds. *The Dangers of Nuclear War.* Toronto: University of Toronto Press, 1978.

Horelick, Arnold, A. Ross Johnson, and John D. Steinbruner. *The Study of Soviet Foreign Policy*. Beverly Hills, CA: Sage, 1975.

Kennan, George. *The Nuclear Delusion: Soviet-American Relations in the Atomic Age*. New York: Pantheon, 1982.

Kolko, Gabriel. *The Politics of War: The World and U.S. Foreign Policy 1943-1945*. New York: Random House, 1968.

Legvold, Robert. "Containment Without Confrontation," *Foreign Policy,* Vol. 40, Fall 1980.

Lenczowski, John. *Soviet Perceptions of U.S. Foreign Policy*. Ithaca: Cornell University Press, 1982.

Mack, Andrew, David Plant and Ursula Doyle. *Imperialism, Intervention and Development*. London: Croom Helm, 1979.

Moran, Theodore H. *Multinational Corporations and the Politics of Dependence*. Princeton: Princeton University Press, 1974.

Nye, Joseph S., Jr. "U.S. Power and Reagan's Policy." *Orbis* (Summer 1982):391–412.

Pipes, Richard. *U.S.-Soviet Relations in the Era of Detente: A Tragedy of Errors*. Boulder, CO: Westview Press, 1981.

Pipes, Richard. *U.S.-Soviet Relations in the Era of Detente: A Tragedy of Errors*.Boulder, CO: Westview Press, 1981.

Reardon, Betty. *Militarization, Security and Peace Education*. Valley Forge, PA: United Ministries in Education, 1982.

Schwartz, Morton. *Soviet Perceptions of the United States*. Berkeley: University of California Press, 1978.

Schulman, Marshall D. "What the Russians Really Want," *Harper's Magazine,* April 1984.

Tucker, Robert W. *The Purposes of American Power: An Essay on National Security*. New York: Praeger, 1981.

Warner, Gale and Michael Shuman. *Citizen Diplomats*. New York: Continuum, 1987.

Welch, William. *American Images of Soviet Foreign Policy*. New Haven, CT: Yale University Press, 1970.

Williams, William Appleman. *The Tragedy of American Diplomacy*. New York: Dell, 1962.

Zimmerman, William. "What Do Scholars Know About Soviet Foreign Policy?" *International Journal* 37 (1982):198–219.

2

REGIONAL ISSUES AND AREAS OF TENSION

9

The Politics of Information
LAURIEN ALEXANDRE

Communications—the very process that brings people together—has become a major point of contention dividing the nation-states of the world. Despite the promises heralded by the information age, ours is a culturally united *and* divided world, technologically wired *and* severed, information-interdependent and -dependent. We live in a global community of nation-states that have or have-not control of media, characterized by an unequal exchange of information technology and an unbalanced flow of media programming. With each passing year, the communications chasm between these groups of nations grows. It comes as no surprise, therefore, that the Western dominance of communications, the transnational ownership of information and technology, the role of media in national sovereignty, and the debate between "free flow of information" versus "justice in communication," have all become explosive issues in contemporary international relations. The worldwide system of communications and information exchange has, indeed, been brought into fundamental question.

For more than a decade, these and other global-communications topics have formed the basis of critical debate contouring national media policies, regional communication efforts, and international polarizations. The fabric through which these issues have been woven is the New World Information and Communication Order (NWICO). If taken to their conclusion, the goals of the NWICO—restructuring global communications and democratizing foreign- and domestic-information channels—would indeed be a transformational program. If achieved and implemented, the NWICO agenda would rectify and transform the current system of global communications, a system under which most of the world's countries have remained media-poor, informationally disadvantaged, and culturally dependent.

Primarily, the industrialized media-rich and technologically expansive countries, led by the United States, have stood firm in their opposition to such global-communications proposals. As maintainers of the current communications-exchange system, the advanced industrial states including the United States, Japan, and several Western European states and powerful transnational enterprises (TNEs), see unrestricted cultural and informational access to Third World countries as essential to their own international status and power. At the same time, they assert that such exchange relationships benefit recipient states in their own development as well. These system-maintainer actors, while utilizing the philosophical doctrine of the free flow of information, hope to ensure their hegemony over the world's information production and dissemination. In short, the goal of the system maintainers is to use the current communications flow and new information technologies to shape an international system that will allow for continued political, cultural, and economic domination by the West.

Proponents of the NWICO, being the majority of the world's developing, non-aligned, and socialist states, have, in the last decade, argued that the current system is inequitable, that the Western model of cultural development is not universally applicable, and that the unrestricted access to the developing world's hearts, minds, and radio sets is unacceptable. While the original conceptualization of these criticisms came from the Third World, socialist states (e.g., Eastern European countries and progressive states of Western Europe) have allied with developing countries in their call for creating a new, more balanced, and interactive information order, and support restrictions on trade, communication flow, and even journalists' movements as necessary conditions for establishing a new order. The stated goal of NWICO is to change the economic, political, and cultural rules governing the conditions of life and the international divisions of communication or information wealth. Among proponents, one finds a variety of forms of resistance to the current global-communication system, from movements for restructuring to degrees of cultural dissociation from the transnational communications industry. (Hamelink, 1983) There are, therefore, myriad strategies within the transformer category.

Some nation-states of the First and Third Worlds are disposed to accept the current communication system with some adaptations. They are willing to negotiate communications exchanges in such a way as to provide markets for the West and transnational media corporations as well as reform it to satisfy certain demands for cultural sovereignty and communications equality. In essence, many of these "reformer" countries are working toward a polycentric global-communications system, wherein the United States and Western TNEs are forced into a more equitable sharing of the world's market. In this sense, nations such as Canada (under the leadership of Pierre Trudeau), Brazil, the like-minded nations of Northern Europe, and certain Western European countries, have recognized the need for changes, have supported efforts to build up their own communications production and distribution centers, and have often organized regional cooperation and exchange activities. Their efforts, though, are not directed toward a systemic transformation, a break-up of the exploitation of Third World markets, or the democratization of hierarchical domestic-communications structures. Nor do they necessarily reflect politically progressive positions. Still, because of their desire to modify the current order into one of multiple communication centers, they are placed within the reformer category.

These, then, are the general parameters of the debate over the New World Information and Communication Order. This chapter explores the international context for this communications controversy. It will examine the current system of communication exchange and media flow, and the development of the NWICO and its key principles, and provide an overview of the perspectives and policies of state and non-state actors.

WHY MEDIA? WHY NOW?

Much of the recent concern over the communications order is rooted in fundamental changes in the international political and economic system. The proliferation of newly independent nation-states, resulting from the decolonization movements of the 1960s, established a new context for national and international communications agreements. Structures established for colonial rulers no longer matched the priorities of independent states. By the early 1970s, more than a hundred newly independent countries comprised a majority of the United Nations' member states. Their concerns changed the previously superpower-dominated agenda. Their collective stance could voice stronger criticisms of informational systems established before they even existed. For many of these states, experiencing political independence for the first time in centuries, another liberation drive was necessary to gain cultural sovereignty as well as economic self-reliance. Cultural and informational dominance by foreign powers came to be seen as an unacceptable arm of neocolonialism. The spirit of that sentiment was captured eloquently in the 1980 Yaounde Declaration on African communication policies:

> In Africa, in the communications field perhaps more than any other, the prevailing situation is the direct result of the heritage of colonialism. Political independence has not always been followed by a decolonization of cultural life. Communication structures often still conform to the old colonial patterns and not to the needs and aspirations of the African peoples. We resolve to decolonize them in their turn. (Nordenstrang 1986, 177)

Yet, at the very time that Third World countries began to flex their united muscles for change in the international communications environment, transnational corporations increased in size, scope, and influence. Coupled with augmentation in intrastate and interstate transactions as a result of economic interdependence or dependence, the role and power of media corporations has taken on a transnational character that challenges the very sovereignty of traditional nation-states. The various TNEs involved in the communications and media industry have contributed dramatically to the vast increase in the volume of international information flow: They are both users and producers of most of the communications traffic. As such, they are eager to maintain their unrestricted freedom to expand into foreign markets and to utilize data and information at will. That these TNEs originate in the wealthiest countries and that they virtually control communications production, collection, and distribution throughout the globe further deepens antagonisms based on existing North-South imbalances.

North-South imbalances continue to widen the gulf between the developing and the developed world. The current concern over the international communication order must, therefore, be placed within the context of a very few media-rich countries prospering while the majority of states remain poor and their people illiterate. Some startling facts might help illustrate the communications inequities that today scar the world. Developing countries represent over 75 percent of the world's people, but only 5 percent of its population has access to computers. (Rada and Pipe 1984, 73) The industrialized West, with only 10 percent of the world's population, has control of 90 percent of the broadcast spectrum. The developing world accounts for only 10.2 percent of cultural products exported in the 1980s; however, 85 percent of that comes from just three countries: Hong Kong, Singapore, and South Korea. (Shea and Jarret 1984, 12) While there are 500 million television sets in the world, almost half of the globe's TV audience resides in just two countries, the United States and the Soviet Union. (Varis 1986, 57) As of 1980, in seventeen countries over 90 percent of all female citizens were illiterate. (Seager and Olsen 1986, 24) Third World women's lack of access to media is, in fact, startling: For example, 70 percent of rural Indian women have never seen a film. (Gallagher, n.d.) In the midst of media plenty, there is communications poverty and information scarcity.

The phenomenal technological innovations that today wire the globe must be added to this list of relevant changes in the international political and economic system. This proliferation of new technologies has expanded the potential for increased understanding just as it has heightened fears of unwanted data collection and storage, unsolicited broadcasting across borders, and the expansion of a homogenized Western-value system transmitted via mass media to the detriment of indigenous cultures. Likewise, the growing use of telematics, computers, and satellites for international trade and diplomacy means that those states without the technology lack not only access to the stored data, but are also denied information parity in international diplomacy. Purchasing computer-age equipment is prohibitively expensive for developing countries with limited financial and material resources unless, and even if, other social services and development programs are sacrificed. Thus, the flow of primarily Western-produced and Western-owned communication and information technologies has caused concern, suspicion, and despair among the majority of developing states. Along with the cultural benefits and educational services, the new technologies can and do facilitate and extend the power of the Western world and its TNEs.

Another factor must be added to this brief list of international factors propelling forward a re-examination of communication exchange between countries: Communications brings with it the potential of understanding. Many believe that dialogue is the most effective deterrent to conflict. At a time when the world is on the brink of innumerable crises, when the potential for humankind's annihilation lurks behind the machinations of governmental disinformation and media diplomacy, communication among nations and peoples seems ever more important. Significantly, it is at this very moment that we are less likely to communicate face-to-face and more likely to base our opinions and judgments about international affairs on the representations and/or misrepresentations of media messages produced by a communication order that, according to many, is imbalanced in its flow and biased in its content. The issues of the NWICO are, therefore, critical to us all.

NWICO—THE ROOTS

Calls for a new world communication order exploded on the international scene in the 1970s, coming close on the heels of demands for a new world economic order. Both of the "new" orders—informational and economic—were expressions of the developing world's quest to create new terms of international relations and new definitions of national sovereignty. While disparities in the global-communication system had been recognized by the late 1960s, the NWICO was born at the 1973 summit of the Non-Aligned Movement (NAM) when, in its program for action on economic cooperation, NAM called on developing countries to take concerted action in the field of mass communications to promote greater exchange between themselves, thereby reducing dependency on their former colonizers and other rich and powerful states. Such a proposal was consistent with the organization's declared fundamental principles of sovereignty, non-interference, mutual benefit, and opposition to all forms of foreign domination. These principles were to be the essential underpinnings of the cultural declaration rising out of that body.

Under the auspices of the United Nations Educational, Scientific, and Cultural Organization (UNESCO), this NAM proposal was researched, examined, debated, and promoted throughout the decade. By 1973, a plan of action in the field of mass communications was released, identifying several key elements of the burgeoning NWICO movement: the need for reorganization of colonially inherited communication channels; the need to promote collective ownership of communication satellites; and, the need to increase contact between the developing states independent of information channels promoted by or transmitted through the industrialized countries.

The MacBride Commission

It was at the UNESCO General Conference in Nairobi that the formation of an international commission to "undertake a review of the totality of the problems of communication in modern society" was authorized. The sixteen-member MacBride Commission, so known for its chairman, former Irish foreign minister, Nobel and Lenin Peace Prize winner, Sean MacBride, began its work in 1977 and presented its report at the 1980 21st session of UNESCO's General Conference in Belgrade. The report is an essential document of the NWICO debate because it provided the foundations of a NWICO program. In its conclusion the MacBride Commission document notes:

> Communication can be an instrument of power, a revolutionary weapon, a commercial product, or a means of education; it can serve the ends of either liberation or of oppression, of either growth of the individual personality or of drilling human beings into uniformity. Each society must choose the best way to approach the task facing all of us and to find the means to overcome the material, social and political constraints that impede progress.
>
> The basic considerations which are developed in the body of our Report are intended to provide a framework for the development of a new information and communication order. We see its implementation as an ongoing process of change in the nature of relations between and within nations in the field of communications. (*Many Voices* 1980, 191–193)

In terms of strategies for the future, the MacBride Commission report called for strengthening independence and communications self-reliance, promoting and protecting cultural identity, selecting appropriate technologies and integrating them into development planning, reducing the commercialization of communication, improving international reporting and the considerable responsibility of journalism to the general social welfare. Underlying such proposals was the belief that, if implemented, they would rectify past inequities and balance a system of information exchange that was unfair, unacceptable, and unsustainable. In a conciliatory posture, the commission's report neither called for the "free flow" promoted by the United States nor the "balanced flow" postulated by the Third World, but instead, proclaimed the need for a "new and more just and more efficient world information and communication order."

It is important to note that the MacBride Commission report did not choose to close off exchange or suggest that nations dissociate from one another; nor did it propose to license journalists. Perhaps the primary objective underlying many of the recommendations was the *democratization* of communication, including providing for a plurality of sources and easier accessibility to multiple communication channels. As the report says it:

> Communication, with its immense possibilities for influencing the minds and behaviour of people, can be a powerful means of promoting democratization of society and of widening public participation in the decision-making process. This depends on the structures and practices of the media and their management and to

what extent they facilitate broader access and open the communication process to a free interchange of ideas, information and experience among equals, without dominance or discrimination. (*Many Voices* 1980, 216)

UNESCO Action on the MacBride Commission Report

Intense debate took place upon the MacBride Commission's presentation of its findings at the 1980 UNESCO conference, concluding with the adoption of two significant resolutions, one outlining the new world information and communication order (See Appendix I), and the other recommending a program to assist in the establishment of national and regional communications infrastructures necessary for the desired parity in international communications exchange. The first resolution outlined the precepts of the new order (many of which repeated the MacBride Commission report), calling for the elimination of imbalances and the negative effects of monopolies, the removal of domestic and foreign obstacles to a true free flow, the establishment of developing countries' capacity to improve their situation, the expression of sincere interest on the part of industrialized countries to assist these objectives, the consideration of journalists' freedoms as well as responsibilities, and the respect for the right of all people to participate in international information exchange on an equal basis.

In its second resolution, the 1980 UNESCO conference launched an Intergovernmental Programme for the Development of Communication (IPDC). Originally, the IPDC was to establish a fund, built of contributions from wealthy states, that would finance communications projects in developing countries. But funds pledged in the first six months totalled only $2 million and requests for assistance amounted to over $50 million. Despite the fact that the United States claimed it should have greater representation on the thirty-five-member council because it would be putting in most of the finances, the United States and a few allies have not to date placed any monies into IPDC's Special Account. (Zassoursky 1986, 154) The United States, for one, has argued instead for making the IPDC a recipient of aid from private banks and has pushed for bilateral agreements, arrangements that some at the UN feel would marginalize UNESCO and other multilateral efforts to develop communications infrastructures. Those policy recommendations from the United States are consistent with its system-maintainer viewpoint. France, on the other hand, became the largest IPDC contributor, followed by Japan, India, and the Soviet Union. (Fenby 1986, 248) Other pledges came from the Netherlands, Canada, Austria, and Italy, with Benin and Bangladesh putting forth $5,000 each. Significant donations also came from various countries of the Arab Gulf.

Opposition to NWICO

Throughout the 1980s, as developing states pursued the course suggested by NWICO, an aggressive campaign against any restructuring was also under way, sponsored by those most interested in maintaining the status-quo arrangement. A pivotal moment for the counteroffensive was the May 1981 meeting in Talloires, France, where nearly seventy delegations representing leaders of "free journalism" met to discuss the recent NWICO developments. The Talloires meeting emphasized what its participants perceived to be UNESCO's tendency toward censorship and government restrictions on information, indicated that the NWICO was riddled with Soviet influence, and focused on technical, free-market remedies for any problems in the international communications system. Thus, the solution was to be found, not in political legislation but by employing the very systemic techniques that were being criticized. The Talloires Declaration stated:

> We promise to cooperate with all genuine efforts directed toward the expansion of a free flow of information throughout the world. We think the moment has come for UNESCO and other intergovernmental organizations to abandon their efforts to regulate the content of news and to draw up rules for the press. Efforts should be directed toward the search for practical solutions such as improving the technical process, increasing professional exchange and the transfer of equipment, reduction of tariffs on communication and the production of cheaper newsprint. (NACLA 1982, 26–27)

The focus on technical procedures was consistent with Western states' interests in maintaining the communications arrangement as it exists and their pragmatic belief in free-trade approaches as solutions to political problems. The U.S. government was so impressed with the Talloires Declaration that it distributed the document to all U.S. embassies. Giant communications corporations also thought highly of the declaration. Smith Kline Corporation, a large high-tech enterprise, ran a four-page supplemental advertisement in *Time* magazine entitled "Danger in the UN," in which it said, "The defenders of economic freedom, led by President Reagan, have begun to fight back." The Talloires meeting, it continued, "recognizes that the New World Information Order imperils freedom . . . [and] marks a historic turning point for world press liberties." (Nordenstreng 1984, 94)

The polarization and passions that arose as a result of calls for the NWICO, and as indicated by the above history, deserve additional exploration, for it is clear that the conflict over restructuring a communications order touches the very core of national interests, political philosophies, and global economic systems.

ACTORS IN THE DEBATE

The United States, TNEs, and Other Maintainers

While the United States has already been mentioned as a system maintainer, little has thus far been said about another *key* system maintainer, the media TNE. Because central concerns of the new communication order revolve around changes in the transnational production and distribution of information, media flow, and communications technology, the role of TNEs has come under intense scrutiny. For companies like the U.S.-based Gulf & Western, RCA, ITT, and IBM, or the British EMI, the source of power lies in their very control of technology, finance capital, and marketing, as well as in the unhampered dissemination of ideas, products, and values favorable to their operations. Be they TNEs that own or control foreign media operations, TNEs that market and advertise products and services, or TNEs that, although not directly involved in media operations, utilize transnationalized information storage and retrieval to conduct business, it is through the established exchange processes that an international environment conducive to extending their goods and services is maintained. Some observers suggest that the free-trade consumption model created by the TNEs, through sales and advertising, promotes a system that many feel deepens social inequality. Further, critics of TNE involvement in the Third World believe that far from democratizing access to cultural goods, the TNEs' imported values and new technologies reinforce segregation, economic hierarchies, and a lifestyle accessible to only a small percentage of the world's population. As mentioned earlier, the scope, power, and influence of these TNEs have increased dramatically over the last few decades, precisely at the time that developing countries have been pushing for economic, political, and cultural independence.

Because the NWICO sentiment is, in fact, to restrict and/or remove the TNEs from such a powerful and uncontrolled position, proposals for the new order have met with great resistance and opposition from the giant corporations. In defense of their unrestricted access, corporate public-relations campaigns employ the principle of free flow of their goods and services, which, in this case, is equated with a free and democratic press (media). IBM's Director of Programs said, "The free flow doctrine must be the single most important objective simply because of the immense economic and political impact of free information flow in today's society." (Schiller 1981, 20)

It is, in many ways, a predetermined conflict because the NWICO does, indeed, represent a threat to the transnational system from which the TNEs benefit. Thus, UNESCO and other UN agencies involved in scrutinizing TNE procedures have incurred the wrath of these giant enterprises in recent years. When, for example, the World Health Organization (WHO) passed a 1981 resolution condemning abuses in the transnational advertising campaign for breast-milk substitutes, the United States and Switzerland voted against all other members in condemnation of the resolution. (Switzerland is the headquarters of Nestlé Enterprises.) In 1984, only the United States voted against (West Germany and Japan abstained) a WHO resolution condemning abuses in transnational advertising of pharmaceutical products.

The U.S. government's response to such actions has been unequivocal and unflinching. Former U.S. Assistant Secretary of State Gregory Newell said, "A large number of UNESCO members have pressed for action to create a code of conduct controlling the operations of multinational corporations in UNESCO's various fields of interest. . . . We simply cannot abide by the constraints that UNESCO would likely seek to apply someday." (Szesko 1984, 101)

The Third World—Transformers

Obviously, among the 140-odd countries making up the Third (and Fourth) World, there are those who have been committed to the NWICO at various points in their recent histories, such as India, Chile (under the Allende administration), and Tanzania, and those who have, at times, been its arch-enemies, such as Paraguay, Uruguay, and South Korea. There are Third World countries who have given lip service to the democratization of global communication but have remained committed to internal censorship and a closed society. And, among the newly industrialized countries (NICs), such as Brazil and Mexico, one encounters efforts to limit the expansion of Western economic and cultural interventionism, but this is less to change the system than it is to protect their own commercially based, privately owned communications monopolies. Today one can find TNEs from the Third World engaged in South-South cooperation, efforts that perhaps better adapt products to Third World markets, but that do not challenge the transnational model of growth. Thus, it is impossible to make sweeping generalizations about a unified Third World transformational strategy: Some have employed programs to reform the system and augment their own participation, some have opposed internal democracy while condemning in a nationalistic spirit dominance by foreign powers, and still others have promoted a complete economic and cultural overhaul of the world order.

As a bloc, however, the developing world represents system transformers advocating change in the communications/information flow based on the principles of economic self-reliance, communications democracy, cultural sovereignty, and information parity in the international system. Developing states that have focused on more equality in the international flow have established cooperative training efforts and regional news agencies, and have worked within UNESCO for implementation of the NWICO agenda and for its necessary economic counterpart. Other developing states have chosen to focus on democratizing the domestic channels of communication, providing access for the widest participation of citizens, and harnessing media for the creative and productive use of national development. Mozambique, for example, has questioned the centralizing tendency inherent in a national television system and has been cautiously attempting to establish a horizontal, non-elitist, and decentralized communication system. Its efforts have been greatly hampered by lack of technical experience and serious financial shortages. Mozambique is, according to many, carrying out a unique transformational experiment, one oriented to the satisfaction of basic communication needs of the majority of the population, one where the communication system closely links rural and urban interests, and one where technologies are introduced based on social imperatives. (Mattelart, et al. 1984, 107–108)

Another example of this national dimension was captured in a recent examination of Tanzania. (Nordenstreng 1986, 177–191) As one of the world's least developed countries, 90 percent of Tanzania's population is rural with a per-capita income of U.S. $240. Since independence in 1961, literacy has increased to 70 percent of the country's residents, but an absolute majority of its population is still cut off from media because the infrastructure is unable to provide such things as newsprint, transport facilities, batteries for radio sets, and the like. As an independent country, searching for a model of socialism based on self-management, previously foreign-owned media were nationalized; today, the media are closely connected to the state's political policies. Tanzania's national media policy provides: that the means of communications should be nationally owned; that the media are instruments for public service and not for profit; that the media support a socialist ideology; that the media maintain open debate and constructive criticism of the government; and, that the media establish a two-way communication between government and people. A national news agency and a journalism-training institute were established; exchanges were initiated with news operations in other Third World countries. While there have been obstacles, including inflated rhetoric and political strains, the downward trend of the nation's economy, an unresolved imbalance between rural and urban media, a weak infrastructure, lack of resources, and poor media leadership at both the government and the ruling-party levels, the pursuit of a more democratized communications system continues. Nordenstreng commented:

> The idea of a new information order emerged in Tanzania spontaneously—without calling it by that name. It was primarily the national dimension of the new order that was pursued under the objectives of self-reliance and socialism. The international dimension with Western dominance in news flow, etc., was no longer a central issue once the foreign-owned media had been nationalized, but naturally, Tanzania joined the voices of the developing countries when they were raised to demand decolonization of information. By and large, Tanzania provides convincing proof that the new information order is deeply rooted in the social reality of developing nations, and that it is far from just a rhetorical notion of international politics. (1986, 188)

The Reformers

There are a number of nation-states, First and Third World alike, who want a more equitable share of the international communications/information market. Brazil, Spain, France, Italy, Mexico, and Portugal have been, since the early 1980s, trying to promote cooperation among themselves, aimed at establishing balance between the creation, distribution, and production of cultural products. (Mattelart, *et al.* 1984) There can be little doubt, however, that France, for example, would like nothing better than to continue the exportation of its own culture throughout the world, and Brazil hopes that its own TNEs can grab a share of the global trade in information technologies and media programming.

In Australia, one finds opposition to the Americanization of that country's media system, and broadcasting authorities have tried to encourage the production and distribution of Australian film and television. But the move toward national media production is coupled with a desire to export Australian productions. (Hamelink 1983, 35–36) Thus, the reformers are in a classic paradox: They want to protect themselves from cultural invasion and, at the same time, they want to invade others with their Westernized products and values.

Take the example of Canada, a country that has long been engaged in a struggle to protect its cultural autonomy in the face of a dominating U.S. cultural and commercial presence. Many in that country have pondered the problems inherent in an expansion of the nation's own media system, for with that growth comes a demand for more programming, and that programming is frequently filled with U.S. cultural imports. In 1975, the Canadian secretary to the minister of communication said: "Their [U.S.] penetration of our area can seriously threaten our identity and culture if that penetration undermines the very existence of healthy Canadian television." (*Cultures in Collision*, 1983, 43)

On a domestic level, Canada has taken the matter into its own hands, oftentimes to the chagrin of the United States. Canada initiated restrictions on the flow of information and programming across borders to insure that a certain percentage of broadcast hours remained purely Canadian. Other restrictions required that Canada's media be required to be Canadian-owned; that U.S. firms advertising on Canadian television employ a percentage of Canadian talent and pay a tax to the Canadian government; and that by 1977, 75 percent of TV advertising be Canadian. In terms of its domestic policies, Canada's reformist strategy, while not cutting itself off from U.S. culture and communications industries, has restricted U.S. penetration, attempted to negotiate issues in bilateral talks with the United States, made its own public monies available to support Canadian talent and indigenous culture industries, and promoted Canadian communications self-reliance. The current Mulroney government, which tends to support a free-market or laissez-faire position, has taken steps to turn these earlier regulations around and is opening up Canada's cultural and economic system to closer contact with—some might say dominance by—the United States. In a recent assessment of Canada's situation William Melody and Rohan Samarajiwa wrote: "Despite its best efforts to maintain a balanced information flow, Canada's policies have not worked well. Canada has been steadily losing control of its domestic information flows to the point where they could be completely overwhelmed by U.S. information flows within a generation." (1986, 165–166)

Whereas Canada's domestic policies have contained elements of reform, its position on similar changes among Third World countries and within the international system has been less than supportive. While domestically the country emphasizes restrictions necessary for balance, equality, and diversity, in the international arena, Canada and other reformer states are not ready to accept transforming the world communications structure. Rather, they are happy to redesign it into a more polycentric network wherein their regional and national centers will participate. As do the United States and other maintainers, Canada understands that unrestrained access is best for lucrative markets to the Third World and unrestricted distribution of programming is best for engaging people in a global Western-dominated economy.

EAST-WEST AND NORTH-SOUTH PARAMETERS OF DEBATE

East-West

Some Western leaders have chosen to see the UNESCO-based communications proposals solely in terms of superpower rivalry and anti-Western propaganda. Within this system-maintainer view, it is suggested that the Soviet Union inspired the NWICO and that Soviet-bloc countries have pushed their alliance with developing countries as a manipulative move to discredit the West. Said William Randolph Hearst, Jr., (head of the large Hearst newspaper group): "The threat hanging over the free press today is virtually worldwide, through a vast international conspiracy directed by UNESCO. The latter is one of the anti-democratic agencies commanded by Moscow, although it operates in Paris under the flag of the United Nations." (Mattelart, et al. 1984, 61–62).

Socialist nations have, indeed, been involved with, and in some instances have been instrumental in, the movement forward of the new communications order. But viewing NWICO as solely an aspect of the East-West conflict denies the autonomy of developing countries and invalidates the legitimacy of their complaints. As noted, interestingly enough by Oswald Ganley, a former U.S. assistant secretary of state: "UNESCO's Resolution (1978) was not instigated by the Soviet Union, notwithstanding its active participation. The mass media resolution was the result of the developing world's discontent and it would be a mistake not to recognize that." (Ganley and Ganley 1982, 75)

Framing NWICO simply as part of a pro- or anti-communist Cold War, with proponents being dupes of the Soviet Union and opponents being freedom-fighters, not only ignores the variety of national political dispositions supporting the NWICO resolution, but is also historically inaccurate. The Soviet Union, for example, while philosophically in support of NWICO has, at times, taken positions far more moderate than various Third World countries. In the particular case of "remote sensing," or space-borne observation of natural resources, two central issues of contention were: (1) whether the sensed nation had the right to decide whether it should be sensed at all, and (2) if it had any right over determining how or to whom the collected data would be distributed. The Soviet Union called for consent by the sensed state before information about its natural resources would be disseminated. But Brazil and Argentina called for a complete prohibition against *all* remote sensing of countries without prior consent. As a side note, the United States opposed any restrictions on distribution of data and pushed for a policy of absolutely open sensing.

Interestingly enough, while the Soviet Union has generally supported NWICO, and would therefore fall into the category of system transformer, there is at least one case in which its position much more closely resembled that of system maintainer. For more than two decades, the United States and the Soviet Union held virtual monopolies on interstate communications within their own spheres of influence. They both also maintained large segments of the frequency spectrum for military and related uses. Both had a large number of satellites already in place and, under a "first come, first served" basis, had prior rights to "parking spots" for the satellites and the frequencies used. Both countries were anxious to see a continuation of this arrangement, which had been established in 1959, when eighty-six countries divided up the radio spectrum. By the time of the 1979 World Administrative Radio Conference, the majority of states had a different agenda. While both the United States and the USSR wanted to maintain their *a priori* assignment of orbital positions and frequency services, Third World states called for a fairer and more equitable distribution, a position to which *both* superpowers expressed their opposition.

North-South

Just as it is incorrect to see NWICO myopically as an anti-Western move sponsored by the Soviets in a superpower rivalry, it is also incorrect to see NWICO debate as solely a North-South issue. While the North-South axis is the primary context framing NWICO—since developing countries are the hardest hit by inequities and have the least access to channels dominated by the more wealthy industrialized states—certain developed countries have also felt victimized by the current system. While these pressures have not compelled governments to call for system transformation, countries such as France, Australia, and Canada have become increasingly worried about their own cultural sovereignty and the establishment of a more equitable, regulated competition in the marketplace of computer- and data-based trade. In 1982, for example, the French minister of culture said, "We hope that this conference will be an occasion for peoples through their governments, to call for genuine cultural resistance, a real crusade against their domination, against—let us call a spade a spade—this financial and intellectual imperialism." (Mattelart, *et al.* 1984, 14) The speech was applauded by Denmark, Norway, Finland, and Italy, and appreciated with a more circumspect attitude by West Germany, the Netherlands, and Spain. It was greeted, as one might suspect, with total exasperation by the United States.

A brief example will illustrate the potential threats and current pressures being felt by these states of the North. In 1982, the Reagan administration imposed sanctions on Western European nations who continued to honor their contracts for supplying equipment to the Soviet Union for the Euro-Siberian gas pipeline. The U.S. government acted against the French affiliate of a U.S.-based TNE by instructing the parent firm to turn off the information supply to its affiliate. Without access to the computerized data-bank, the French engineers lacked the necessary information to build the made-to-order equipment. (Schiller 1986, 23) With this kind of unbridled power, the United States and transnational corporate giants can greatly influence the fate of states, in the North as well as the South.

Suffice it to say, therefore, that the parameters of this debate are limited neither to an East-West rivalry nor a North-South debate. It is an issue of communication for citizens throughout the world.

TWO ISSUES: NEWS AND NEW TECHNOLOGIES

It would be impossible to fully discuss all issues enumerated in debates on NWICO, both by proponents and opponents. The following section considers just two points of contention: news and new technologies.

News

News is a critical body of information—a specific rendering of life—that constructs perceptions of reality, forms public opinions, and contours social discourse. News provides many of the images that become our way of knowing distant places, diverse peoples, and divergent viewpoints. Its messages are essential components of our way of understanding the world, providing the means by which we evaluate public policy and participate in decisionmaking. Thus, while news coverage represents only one small part of the total international communications exchange, it is of no small concern.

What News is Covered?
The news web blanketing the globe conforms to established patterns of power and status in the international arena. The industrialized world, particularly the United States and Western Europe, receives the greatest coverage, and is the center of news collection and dissemination, while the Third World countries receive the least. News flows from the traditional core nation-states out to the Third World or the periphery via the Big Four Western international news agencies (Associated Press [AP], United Press International [UPI], Reuters, and Agence-France Presse). Discussing news flow compels one to talk also about dependency relationships: Due to the current structure of power and influence, the developing world remains dependent for news about itself, scarce as that might be, from primarily Western-owned, Western-operated news monopolies. The MacBride Commission report estimated that the world received 80 percent of its news through London, New York, or Paris. (*Many Voices,* 145) British scholar Anthony Smith estimated that over 55 percent of world news in Latin American papers came from AP and UPI. (Smith 1980, 71)

Not only is the scarcity of Third World news coverage an issue, but the type of coverage that is presented is also of concern. Critics say that Western news coverage focuses on the "coups and earthquakes syndrome" (Rosenbaum 1979; Gans 1979; Larsen 1984), reporting crises, violence, and disorder stories, thereby creating a negative and biased image of the developing world. Furthermore, it is argued that this sensationalistic, superficial, event-oriented coverage is insensitive to the goals and values of developing countries, and that the coverage is distorted by application of Western biases, cultural perspectives and even ideological designs. Former Venezuelan president Carlos Andres Pérez, eloquently noted: "Our people live submitted to an uncontrolled invasion of news which inculcates distant values that threaten our national identity. . . . The international press only collects information that undermines the image of our people . . . ignoring our struggles, our efforts and just claims for a system of international justice." (NACLA 1982, 71)

Many believe that the Western news monopolies' concentrated control over the definition and presentation of reality has created enormous difficulties for those countries seeking economic self-determination and political autonomy. International media scholar Herbert Schiller noted:

> By their information selection and control, the Western media, wherever they operate or penetrate, assist in providing the transnational corporate business system with diverted and disoriented publics. Information management has for years permitted the dominating centers to ignore or misrepresent the Third World, and its demands for new economic, cultural and information arrangements. (1981, 2)

The Big Four news agencies are maintainers of the current communications order. Their news-gathering and disseminating operations command great influence within the current structure, their output reflecting the cultural perspectives of the media-rich industrialized states, thereby making the First World's agenda the whole world's agenda. They are, therefore, uneager to accept change or to concede to NWICO proposals. UNESCO's calls for a new definition of news, one that de-emphasizes negativity, novelty, and elites and emphasizes the dispossessed, development, and underlying processes, are viewed by the Big Four as attempts to harness news to national policies, politicize the necessarily impartial content, license journalists, and initiate state control over output. One former Reuters manager concluded that while Third World claims to imbalanced news flow were valid, their call for news responsible to national aims and political purposes was totally unacceptable. (Fenby 1986)

Third World News Agencies
The developing world's concern with imbalanced news was articulated in the early stages of NWICO, for its very existence represented a definition of reality based on political and economic patterns of dominance no longer acceptable to independent states desiring relationships based on equality. In 1973, Non-Aligned Movement members were asked to consider "effective dissemination of information of importance to non-aligned countries and to the international

community . . . to counteract the often tendentious, incorrect, non-objective and inadequate coverage given in the international information media which are controlled by agencies of developed countries which at present practically monopolise the dissemination of world information and news." (Samarajiwa 1984, 111)

Perhaps the most successful NWICO achievement to date can be found in this arena, in the establishment of national and regional news agencies and news pools. The Non-Aligned Movement and UNESCO, especially through its IPDC, have been instrumental in backing the establishment of regional news agencies such as PANA (Africa), ASIN and ALASEI (Latin America), FANA (Middle East), OANA (Asia), and CANA (Caribbean). Since 1976, the Non-Aligned Movement has also established the Non-Aligned News Agency Pool, with the Yugoslavian agency, TANJUG, transmitting most of the daily file of, originally, twelve national news agencies and, today, seventy-six agencies, in a polycentric news web.

As one example, the Pan-African News Agency (PANA), which started operation in 1983, was established as both a political institution (to "liberate African information from imperialist domination and foreign monopolies and promote development") and a mass media organization ("to promote an effective exchange of political, economic, social and cultural information among member states"). (Ansah 1986, 61) As a news-agency pool, PANA acts primarily as a retransmission center for its member states, over thirty in number, each of which has a daily quota of 1,000 words maximum. PANA can also act as a news agency in its own right by covering, for example, Organization of African Unity conferences and other topics of special concern to its members. PANA has innumerable problems with which it must contend. To name but a few: many members cannot pay their contributions; translating materials takes time and money, both in short supply; and, because of excessive government control over the media in certain African countries, there is reasonable suspicion that national news agencies feed PANA government propaganda. Thus, establishing credibility is difficult, especially in the eyes of the system-maintainer countries and the powerful media TNEs.

A case in point: after citing a particularly nasty incident of censorship by the Tanzanian government over the movement of a foreign correspondent within the country, one American journalist commented:

> The Tanzanian News Agency may or may not have been inspired by the UNESCO model of a national news agency. But its existence as a supreme arbiter over what gets reported as news in, or from, Tanzania represents the sort of Third World nightmare that Americans fear may result from UNESCO's worldwide efforts to create national communications policies and national news agencies.(Kelly, n.d., 35)

The United States and most Western journalists have been quite critical of these regional news efforts. Unequivocal about what they believe to be unavoidable dangers of state control of the media, these critics feel that the Big Four's output—based on market-based determinations—is a far freer and more objective rendering of the day's events. The Western media establishment believes that inherent in the new communications order is an underlying drive toward state censorship, harassment of journalists, licensing, and other constraints upon the news-gathering and disseminating process. Granted, not all countries promoting NWICO are democratic. Nor are the regional news agencies unbiased or free of government propaganda. But many developing countries would argue that neither are the Big Four news services. It is incorrect to label as unworthy or antidemocratic the entire NWICO agenda because of the excesses of a few. Additionally, state ownership of the media is not necessarily an indication of lack of media freedom; after all, some of the United States' best friends in Western Europe have government-controlled media operations. That there is little media freedom in some developing countries is not in dispute. But most Third World countries cannot afford to have media systems run otherwise. Said one media scholar, "If governments did not run national news agencies, there would probably be no African country with a news agency." (Ansah 1986, 60)

New Technologies

In many ways, today's new technologies have the potential to fulfill Marshall McLuhan's vision of a "global village." Satellites instantaneously connect metropolis to town, data banks supply facts about distant relatives across the globe, cable systems offer educational and cultural programming to countrysides, and remote sensors provide information about natural resources to assist in ecological preparedness. But the vision has its downside in reality. Direct broadcast satellites can intrude into sovereign states, data banks can invade an individual's or a nation's privacy, and remote sensing can supply foreign military forces or transnational enterprises with information endangering a country's national security. Depending upon one's place in the communications order, the global village can be an electronic dream or a wired nightmare.

The impact of this technologically linked world has crept into national development, international trade, and global politics. Industrialized countries urge developing ones to consider emerging technologies and new information systems as necessary ingredients for development. Citizens, in rich and poor countries alike, desire the technological wonderland advertised on programming exported from, primarily, the United States, whether or not they or their country can afford to import, employ, or control it. The question around which this part of the NWICO debate revolves is whether these new technologies are a godsend to the developing world or whether they are simply high-cost vehicles by which the world is further molded by and for advanced capitalist countries and giant transnational enterprises.

It comes as no surprise that Western states and primarily U.S.-based TNEs (with some Japanese, West German, and others) dominate the research, production, distribution, and use of advanced communications and information technology. It is estimated that 90 percent of all data-flow via satellite systems is intracorporate, and approximately 50 percent of all transborder data-flow takes place within the communication networks of TNEs. (Traber 1986, 3) To these giant business enterprises, this situation is one to be enjoyed, supported, and expanded. Any restrictions upon this technological flow would be, to these system maintainers, unacceptable. U.S. Secretary of State George Schultz explained:

> Success in the information age depends on more than our own innovation and entrepreneurship. The new age also presents us all with a global challenge. New technologies circumvent the borders and geographical barriers that have always divided one people from another. Thus, the market for these technologies depends to a great extent on the openness of other countries to the free flow of information. . . . The United States, as a country that seeks to explore and trade in technological services, has always opposed international attempts to stifle the workings of the information revolution. In our view, every country willing to open itself to the free flow of information stands to benefit. (Schultz, n.d., 2)

Proponents of NWICO take a much different view. Many are technology-weary, suspicious—and poor. They have grown tired of technologies' "benefits," as they watched the 1960s dream of mass education via satellite remain largely unachieved. They are also technology-poor—and growing poorer. The new technologies are capital-intensive and prohibitive with or without increased indebtedness to the West's lending institutions. Finally, many Third World countries are suspicious of assistance offered. Noted one scholar of NWICO:

> A growing number of countries are beginning to fear that America's use of the free flow doctrine—to encourage television broadcasting from satellites, transborder data flows by giant private corporations and satellite photography of the earth—may be a strategy for further subjugating their interests to those of the wealthy countries controlling the development and use of the new technologies . . . for the ascendancy of information industries is the direct result of the expansion of U.S. manufacturing business abroad. (Manet 1986, 143)

Direct Broadcast Satellites and Transborder Data Flow

Two controversial new technologies under scrutiny are Direct Broadcast Satellites (DBS) and Transborder Data Flow (TBDF). The concern with DBS dates back several decades. The possibility of telecasts being received directly by individuals worried potential receiver-states, which felt that the technology posed a serious threat to national sovereignty by limiting a state's ability to regulate what crosses its borders. While much of this transmission may well be benign, there was concern expressed over external propaganda, commercial domination, and cultural intrusion.

As early as 1972, the U.S. position on DBS marked its isolation in the world. In that year, the Soviet Union introduced a proposal to establish principles by which satellite TV transmission would be regulated. The United States, firmly resolved in its belief in the unrestricted flow of information and technology, took an implacable posture opposing any such regulatory principle. By a vote of 102 to one (with the United States as the lone negative vote), the UN General Assembly called upon its Committee on the Peaceful Uses of Outer Space to elaborate DBS regulatory principles. (Pavlic and Hamelink 1984, 14)

In the case of TBDF, the tremendous increase in international trade and multinational operations has made data-flow an important on-line link for business enterprises that process, store, and retrieve scientific, financial, and operational data across national boundaries. The point of contention, in this case, is to what degree sovereign states have an interest and a right to protect, conserve, and control information originated in, generated about, or retrieved across their boundaries. The current development of TBDF has amplified the dominance of multinational systems over individual countries. Many states believe that their ability to influence the direction of their own political, economic, and sociocultural development may be severely impaired or limited by this Western-controlled data-flow. They believe that the collection and dissemination of information is an integral part of international relations, not a business commodity, and as such, it should be subject to regulations.

Underlying the controversy of DBS and TBDF is the fundamental issue of whether a state has the right to give its permission before it is broadcast to, sensed from above, or used as a vehicle by which TNEs process, store, and retrieve information that gains them profit. In other words, who has control over a state's communications space? Most argue—be they system reformers or system transformers—that it is the right of host states to decide, in advance, whether to accept DBS, permit TBDF, and allow for the unregulated informational operations of TNEs.

According to the United States and other system maintainers, however, this "prior consent" is nothing more or less than the desire of states to censor information and restrict trade. Those who control transnational enterprises agree. There should be no restrictions on the international information and communication trade as long as, it might be added, they are the ones doing the selling. Such trade restrictions and legislative constraints, would, obviously, be an obstacle to their operations. In the words of Edward Hennelly, general manager of public affairs for Mobil Oil:

> The UNESCO forum has become notorious for the introduction of international norms and standards, most often based on increased state control, as panaceas for the world's problems. The best known example of this tendency was the push for a New World Information and Communication Order. Responding to prodding from radical Third World states, often allied with the Soviet bloc, the UNESCO Secretariat had produced working papers concerning international rules and procedures which, no matter what their intention, would in fact have hobbled press freedom and the free flow of information throughout the world. (1984, 173)

Frequently, in the statements of maintainers, one finds the merging of these particular economic interests and philosophical principles. Behind the damning of NWICO proposals as undemocratic and anti-free press is the fundamental concern over open markets and unrestricted trade. Noted one observer:

> The stakes in the coming battle go far beyond editors and publishers. . . . They extend to the great computer and information hardware companies whose foreign sales of billions of dollars are at stake; to the TV networks and movie-makers, whose entertainment products range the globe; to the airlines and banks and financial institutions whose need for computer-based data literally defines their business; to the multi-billion dollar advertising industry. (Manet 1986, 148)

FREE TRADE, FREE PRESS?

Underlying much of this debate is the issue of the meaning of "free flow of information." Is a belief in a free press the same as support for corporate free trade? Should international communication be organized around the free flow doctrine or by the principles of international law based on national sovereignty? It is on these issues that the nation-states of the world split. On the one hand, system maintainers set out from the principle of completely unrestricted communication unencumbered by international legislation or a concept of freedom imbued with certain responsibilities and rules. The West, based as it is on imposing as few governmental restrictions as possible on individuals and groups, upholds this conception. On the other hand, tranformers regard restrictions as a way to ensure that communication does not remain the monopoly of a few and that information will not be exploited for the benefit of the rich. In theory, those states advocating transformation of the present system are committed to the principles of democratization of media and the NWICO resolution.

One example of this basic difference in perspective can be found in the emphasis placed on communication as an issue of freedom or as an issue of justice. The United States and its allies base their position on the philosophical precepts of a libertarian (laissez-faire) doctrine of the press, as exemplified in the U.S. Constitution's First Amendment. Reflective of this philosophical predisposition is the West's (journalists, government officials, corporate executives) frequent references to Article 19 of the United Nations Declaration of Human Rights, which states: "Everyone has the right to freedom of opinions without interference and to seek, receive and impart information and ideas through any media and regardless of frontiers." This statement is used as a basis for support of the West's unrestricted flow of information and technology. Yet, even in countries considered to have the freest presses in the world there are restrictions and abridgments made to protect the public good.

Many of the developing, non-aligned, and socialist countries, though, see the freedoms of Article 19 in conjunction with Article 29 of that same UN document. The latter article qualifies the unfettered exercise of a free flow by indicating that, "Everyone has duties to the community," that these rights and duties can be subject to regulation "for the purpose of securing due recognition and respect for the rights and freedoms of others and of meeting the just requirements of morality, public order and general welfare of democratic society," and that "these rights and freedoms may in no case be exercised contrary to the purposes and principles of the United Nations."

THE FUTURE

System Maintainers

The United States, as representative of the system-maintainer worldview, has at least two distinct options open to it: one could be called the hardline and the second the reformist option. The approach of the Reagan administration—opposition to NWICO demands, an absolutist interpretation of free flow, and a withdrawal from multilateral communications efforts—reflects the hardline option. It runs the risk of further isolating the United States from the majority consensus on the global communications order and it is unlikely that such an approach will generate an environment of dialogue and negotiation over the issues.

The reformist approach—one that acknowledges U.S. dominance of the communication order and minimally recognizes the legitimate desires of sovereign states to control their own communications—is best represented by the Carter administration (1976–1980). During that period the United States agreed to a "Marshall Plan" of communications, wherein the government agreed to allocate money, through multilateral efforts, to back proposals designed to establish communications infrastructures in the developing world. Such an approach would, perhaps, indicate on the part of system maintainers a commitment to the development of communications self-reliance and a more equitable order.

Paralleling the global focus of this option, the United States could construct a more balanced and equitable domestic communications order, one which would open up U.S. markets to imports and would reflect the ethnic, racial, and gender-based diversity of this country's citizenry. The irony of a highly concentrated, commercially based, essentially white-male media system calling for communications plurality in other countries is not lost on those receiving the message. Said one Guyanese representative in 1983: "Pluralism and free expression cannot be convincingly preached by a country in which single commercial monopoly ownership and control exist in 96% of its cities and three major commercial networks dominate television viewing." (Fenby 1986, 15)

It should be noted, however, that many transformers view the "Marshall Plan" of communications to be anything but reformistic. They believe that the transfer of technology is merely a more sophisticated trap to hook developing nations into a global system to which they will remain forever hooked and dependent." (Manet 1988)

System Reformers

It seems apparent that system reformers' most likely option is to pursue and increase regional cooperative efforts at the levels of production, distribution, and development of communications technology and programming. The cases of the Latin American countries developing a communications common market is illustrative of this option, as is the further development of South-South cooperative efforts, particularly those resulting from the growth of production/ distribution centers in the newly industrialized countries, such as Brazil and Mexico. Paralleling these joint efforts, reformer states will need to continue to establish legislative policies designed to protect national industries and restrict foreign access, be it in programming or technology. Without a continuance of these practices, system reformers may well lose, or never even gain, their cultural independence and information sovereignty—as can be seen in Canada today, as result of the current government's more "open-door" policies.

System Transformers

With the downward trend of the world's economy and the weakened condition of UNESCO, the system-transformer strategy has been somewhat paralyzed. The validity of its claims, though, remains, especially as the information gap increases between the media-rich and media-poor, and the growing power of TNEs surpasses and undermines national sovereignty. But the vocal, public international debate seemed to have subsided slightly by the mid-1980s.

The options are thus limited. While pursuing their confrontational approach of strong criticism of the global order and continued dependency relationships at international forums and regional conferences, system transformers must develop national policies to break the patterns. Despite innumerable obstacles, such as an unfavorable worldwide climate, the lack of technical training, the cost of newsprint and production, the abuses of certain governments, and the unmitigated attack against NWICO by the system maintainers, Third World countries must view the development of their communications systems in terms of social need and democracy. As with the case of Mozambique, technology should be employed with caution and forethought. In some cases, transnational advertising and the importation of transnational culture might be outlawed absolutely or in degrees, or it can be resisted with effective national planning that expands upon the quantity and quality of non-Western news sources—for example, by making use of regional news agencies, the Non-Aligned News Agency Pool, and Inter Press Service. System transformers concerned about democratization need to insure that national communications systems give a voice to those who have previously been denied access—rural dwellers, cultural and linguistic minorities, and women. In Peru in the early 1970s, for example, newspapers replaced society pages with news about unions and farmers.

It is clear that stronger economies and more stable governments are better able to resist the monopolistic impulses of the global communications system. In Mozambique, a wrecked economic infrastructure is slowing down the development of cultural autonomy, although many believe this situation only temporary. (Hamelink 1983, 53) The People's Republic of China has many of the necessary conditions for success, including economic self-reliance and very little foreign influence. In its current drive for modernization, though, China has opened its doors to more foreign communications and, at the present moment, it is unclear what path China will now take as new trends frame the Chinese media policies.

CONCLUSION

The new world information and communications order is at a crossroads. The initial energy vaulting its call into the international arena has been tempered. At the same time, the transnational communications and economic order has become further imbedded in the practices of daily life and the policies of states. The global communication system will change, but whether it will be redefined in terms of decentralization and cultural autonomy or further centralization and cultural synchronization remains to be seen.

APPENDIX

The New World Information and Communication Order (Resolution 4.19)

The General Conference considers that this New World Information and Communication Order should be based, among other considerations, on:

    i) Elimination of the imbalances and inequalities which characterize the present situation;
   ii) elimination of the negative effects of certain monopolies, public or private and excessive concentrations;
  iii) removal of the internal and external obstacles to a free flow and wider and better balanced dissemination of information and ideas;
   iv) plurality of sources and channels of information;
    v) freedom of the press and of information;
   vi) freedom of journalists and all professionals in the communications media, a freedom inseparable from responsibility;
  vii) the capacity of developing countries to achieve improvement of their own situations, notably by providing their own equipment, by training their personnel, by improving their infrastructures and making their information and communication media suitable to their needs and aspirations;

viii) the sincere will of developed countries to help them attain these objectives;

ix) respect for each people's cultural identity and for the right of each nation to inform the world about its interests, its aspirations and its social and cultural values;

x) respect for the right of all peoples to participate in international exchanges of information on the basis of equality, justice and mutual benefit;

xi) respect for right of the public, of ethnic and social groups and of individuals to have access to information sources and to participate actively in the communication process.

This New World Information and Communication order should be based on the fundamental principles of international law as laid down in the Charter of the United Nations.

REFERENCES

Ansah, Paul. "African Response to the New World Information and Communication Order." In *Communication for All*. Edited by Philip Lee. Maryknoll, NY: Orbis, 1986.

Cultures in Collision: A Canadian-US Conference on Communication Policies. New York: Praeger, 1983.

Fenby, Jonathan. *The International News Services: A Twentieth Century Fund Report*. New York: Schocken, 1986.

Gallagher, Margaret. "Women and the Media World." In *Women and the Media*. International Bulletin, no. 18. Rome: ISIS, n.d.

Ganley, Oswald, and Gladys Ganley. *To Inform or to Control? The New Communications Network*. New York: McGraw Hill, 1982.

Gans, Herbert. *Deciding What's News*. New York: Pantheon, 1979.

Hamelink, Cees. *Cultural Autonomy and Global Communication*. New York: Longman, 1983.

Hennelly, Edward. "U.S. Decision to Withdraw From UNESCO." *Journal of Communication* Vol. 34, No. 4 (Autumn 1984):172–179.

Kelly, Sean. *Access Denied: The Politics of Press Censorship*. The Center for Strategic and International Studies, Washington Paper no. 55. Beverly Hills, CA: Sage, n.d.

Larson, James. *Television's Window on the World*. Norwood, NJ: Ablex, 1984.

Manet, Enrique. "Will UNESCO Be Crippled?" In *Communication and Domination*. Edited by Jorg Becker, Goran Hedebro, and Leena Paladan. Norwood, NJ: Ablex, 1986.

———. *The Hidden War of Information*. Norwood, NJ: Ablex, 1988 (forthcoming).

Many Voices, One World. Report by the International Commissions on the Study of Communication Problems. Paris: UNESCO, 1980.

Mattelart, Armand, Xavier Delecourt, and Michelle Mattelart. *International Image Markets*. London: Comedia, 1984.

Melody, William, and Rohan Samarajiwa. "Canada's Contradictions on the New International Information Order." In *Communication and Domination*. Edited by Jorg Becker, Goran Hedebro, and Leena Paladan. Norwood, NJ: Ablex, 1986.

Nordenstreng, Kaarle. "Tanzania and the New Information Order." In *Communication and Domination*. Edited by Jorg Becker, Goran Hedebro, and Leena Paladan. Norwood, NJ: Ablex, 1986.

————. "The U.S. Decision to Withdraw From UNESCO." *Journal of Communication* (Autumn 1984):93–95.

Pavlic, Brenda, and Cees Hamelink. *The New World Economic Order: Links Between Economics and Communications*. Reports and Papers on Mass Communications, no. 98. Paris: UNESCO, 1984.

Rada, Juan, and Russell Pipe, editors. *Communication Regulation and International Business*. New York: North-Holland, 1984.

Rosenblum, Mort. *Coups and Earthquakes*. New York: Harper, 1979.

Samarajiwa, Rohan. "The History of the New Information Order." *Journal of Communication* (Autumn 1984):110–113.

Schiller, Herbert. "The Strengths and Weaknesses of the New International Information Empire." In *Communication for All*. Edited by Philip Lee. Maryknoll, NY: Orbis, 1986.

————. *Information and the Crisis Economy*. Norwood, NJ: Ablex, 1984.

————. *Who Knows: Information in the Age of the Fortune 500*. Norwood, NJ: Ablex, 1981.

Schultz, George, "The Shape, Scope and Consequences of the Age of Information." Current Policy Paper no. 811. Washington, D.C.: U.S. Department of State, Bureau of Public Affairs.

Seager, Joni, and Ann Olson. *Women in the World: An International Atlas*. New York: Simon and Schuster, 1986.

Shea, Donald, and William Jarret. *Mass Communication in the Americas: Focus on the New World Information and Communication Order*. Center for Latin American Studies. Milwaukee: University of Wisconsin Press, 1984.

Smith, Anthony. *The Geopolitics of Information*. New York: Oxford University Press, 1980.

Szesko, Tomas. "The U.S. Decision to Withdraw From UNESCO." *Journal of Communication* (Autumn 1984): 100–103.

————. "Toward a New Information Order—The Times They Are A'Changing." *NACLA Report* XVI, 4 (July-August 1982): 2–35.

Traber, Michael, ed. *The Myth of the Information Revolution: Social and Ethical Implications of Communication Technology*. Beverly Hills, CA: SAGE, 1986.

Varis, Tapio. "Patterns of Television Program Flow in International Relations." In *Communication and Domination*. Edited by Jorg Becker, Goran Hedebro, and Leena Paladan. Norwood, NJ: Ablex, 1986.

Zassoursky, Yassen. "The Future of the Debate on the New International Information Order and the Intergovernmental Programme for the Development of Communication." In *Communication and Domination*. Edited by Jorg Becker, Goran Hedebro, and Leena Paladan. Norwood, NJ: Ablex, 1986.

10

The Challenge of Ethnonationalism

JOHN F. STACK, JR.

This chapter analyzes the explosive growth of ethnicity in contemporary world politics from the perspectives of the maintenance, reform, and transformation of the global system. This is an important issue for students of world politics because many of the transformations that are currently under way in the global system can be better appreciated from the perspective of politicized ethnicity. The study of ethnicity as a global political force and as a reflection of incipient patterns of change forces the analyst to move away from a perspective emphasizing the exclusive role played by states as sovereign, independent, and equal units in contemporary world politics—the state-centric paradigm. The uncritical acceptance of the state-centric paradigm helped to determine a research agenda that failed to study those forces and processes bringing about change in world politics. The study of ethnonationalism constitutes a non-traditional way to assess changing patterns of world politics. The thesis of this chapter is that as one moves beyond an exclusive emphasis on states, incipient patterns of global change may be better appreciated. The study of ethnonationalism throws light on possible changes in the structure and process of world politics when viewed through the lenses of the system reform and transformation approaches.

This chapter is divided into five parts. The first provides an introduction to the study of ethnicity. This is important because ethnicity needs to be defined as precisely as possible. Ethnicity is a dynamic force in world politics because of its ability to provide a common identity and to mobilize individuals in pursuit of common ends. In the words of Rupert Emerson, (1960, 95–96) ethnicity is "the largest community, which when the chips are down, effectively commands men's loyalty, overriding the claims of both lesser communities within it and those that cut across it or, potentially enfold it within a still greater society."

The second part of this chapter analyzes ethnicity from the perspective of the system-maintenance approach. The influence of the state-centric paradigm is evident here. Ethnicity is conceptualized as an essentially unimportant aspect of world politics. In the advanced industrial world, ethnicity is analyzed as an essentially transient atavistic force that will disappear as quickly as it first came on the scene in the late 1960s and 1970s. In the newer states of the South, ethnicity is conceptualized as a variable that can have some impact on the actions of elites who are in the process of state-building.

The third part of this chapter analyzes ethnicity from the system-reformer worldview. Ethnicity is conceptualized as a far more powerful force in world politics, as the result of transnational relations which permit non-state actors to exert influence within states and among them. Yet the long-term staying power of ethnicity as a non-state force is questioned.

The fourth part of this chapter assesses ethnicity from the system-transformation perspective. As in both the maintenance and reform perspectives ethnicity remains a controversial force and speculation about its salience in world politics remains very mixed.

The final part of this chapter evaluates the significance of ethnicity in view of system maintenance, reform, and transformation. Does ethnicity challenge fundamental conceptions of power in world politics? How does the study of ethnicity challenge prevailing ideological conceptions of world politics? Does ethnicity suggest a vision of the future premised on conflict or equilibrium?

ETHNICITY AND WORLD POLITICS

For more than a decade, students of ethnicity have been trying to define its phenomena in such a way that comparative observations can be systematically and convincingly made. The problem becomes obvious when analysts try to compare ethnic affiliations in the United States with those in Northern Ireland, Lebanon, or India. Are the ethnic bonds of Irish-Americans as salient as those of Jewish-Americans, for example? Is ethnicity really an important political force in the United States when compared with the mass slaughter and genocide that occurs with alarming frequency elsewhere in the world when ethnic issues are politicized? Is ethnicity merely a reflection of more important forms of group affiliation such as social class and/or ideology? The limitations of space preclude a systematic analysis of many of the conceptual issues surrounding the analysis of ethnicity, though the recent literature is increasingly rich. (Horowitz 1985, Connor 1984, Smith 1981, and Stack 1981)

Several generations of American scholars concerned with the study of American domestic and international politics in the years following World War II accepted the prevailing assumptions of American culture, which saw ethnicity as a transitory stage in the creation of a national-level political culture in which abstract allegiance to the state would replace parochial identifications and associations premised on ethnic uniqueness. These major theorists studying world politics and American foreign policy, led by Hans Morgenthau (1978), Arnold Wolfers (1965), E. H. Carr (1946), Karl Deutsch (1966), and Hedley Bull (1977), saw no place in their vision of America's role in world politics or the United States' Cold War diplomacy for ethnic identity, either as a relevant factor in foreign policymaking or as an appropriate aspect of Cold War politics. It was hoped that such parochial and self-interested perspectives could be removed from America's vision of itself and its role in the global system. Such a perspective is not surprising because it was premised on the belief that ethnic distinctiveness would sooner or later disappear from the fabric of American domestic politics, hence making ethnicity irrelevant in the conduct of American foreign policy in the evolving global political system of the 1950s.

The resiliency of ethnic identity and its emergence as a relevant factor in both domestic and international affairs surprised many policymakers. In American politics, the 1960s and 1970s are a watershed in which ethnic consciousness seemingly reintensified and became explicitly embedded in the fabric of American political concerns. (Greeley 1974, Novak 1971) While the founding myths of the United States paid lip-service to the concept of cultural pluralism, the explicit assumptions concerning national participation were focused on non-ethnic factors. In this respect, the assimilationist values of the melting-pot myth illustrate a deep concern over the creation of a unified cultural and political system. Thus, cultural differences were tolerable among immigrants as long as they did not threaten fundamental values and ideals of the society. Ethnic food, humor, and voluntary organizations were acceptable. However, political mobilization by threatening foreigners, as the case of Sacco and Vanzetti tragically illustrates, were unacceptable and deemed incompatible with U.S. national identity because it threatened fundamental political values. The Red Scare in the 1920s, and the concommitant decision to restrict immigration to the United States, document the determination by elites in the United States to challenge any overt manifestations of ethnic diversity.

The American Civil Rights Movement, the Black Power Movement, and the resurgence of ethnic identity as a salient political factor in Italian, Polish, Greek, Jewish, and Irish communities in the 1970s demonstrate that, however enthusiastic U.S. state-builders were between the 1920s and the 1960s, ethnic diversity was not eradicated nor did it become a curious cultural artifact. Ethnicity remained a vibrant touchstone for people whose socioeconomic success would seemingly predict that ties to the old homeland three or four generations removed should have been irrelevant. What is remarkable about the resurgence of ethnicity in the United States is the persistence of ethnic consciousness, not only for Black Americans—whose struggle for equality was immediate—but for white ethnics as well. Ethnicity had not disappeared in American politics whether social scientists could or could not convincingly explain its reappearance. (Greeley 1977) Ironically, and perhaps not coincidentally, ethnicity was becoming a major factor in political disputes in new and old states. In Northern Ireland, Belgium, Spain, France, the Soviet Union, China, and in countries throughout Africa, the Middle East, and Asia, ethnic concerns came explicitly to dominate the most intractable political problems. Standard analyses of international politics had failed to appreciate the salience of ethnic ties; in fact, such analyses had ignored them.

Defining Ethnicity

In this context, it is useful to define ethnicity and offer some observations of its salience in the politics of states. There are many definitions of ethnicity in the literature of the social sciences. Richard A. Schermerhorn provides a broadly representative definition. Ethnicity is:

> a collectivity within a larger society having real or putative common ancestry, memories of a shared historical past, and a cultural focus on one or more symbolic elements defined as the epitome of their peoplehood. Examples of such symbolic elements are: kinship patterns, physical contiguity (as in localism or sectionalism), religious affiliation, languages or dialect forms, tribal affiliations, nationality, phenotypical features, or any combination of these. A necessary accompaniment is some consciousness of kind among members of the group. (1970, 123)

Schermerhorn emphasizes two important aspects of ethnicity. The first is the primordial quality—the expression of a sense of peoplehood. The second refers to the structural dynamics of the ethnic group and the broader political, social, and economic environment with which it interacts. The primordial aspect of ethnicity has been defined as "a basic group identity," in the sense that distinctive attributes of a common group are passed from one generation to the next. (Isaacs 1975) Language, skin color, food, culture, a sense of shared history are examples of primordial ties that may bind an individual to a larger group on the basis of shared identity. Clifford Geertz (1973, 259–260) describes primordial attachments in the following way: "But for virtually every person, in every society, at almost all times, some attachments seem to flow more from a sense of the natural—some would say spiritual—affinity than from social interaction." These "natural affinities" become the essence of a sense of ethnic identity in the form of cultural, linguistic, regional, or customary identifications. The unanticipated power of ethnic attachments flows, in part, from the power of primordial bonds to arouse human beings to act on behalf of themselves and their group.

In its most constructive moments, ethnicity attempts to answer the question, "Who am I?" In so doing, ethnicity can reassure an individual that "in the deepest and most literal sense . . . he is not *alone,* which is all but what a very few human beings most fear to be." (Isaacs 1975, 43) In sheltering an individual from loneliness, the ethnic group may provide him or her with a sense of self-esteem—reassuring the person that life has meaning and worth.

The irony is that even as ethnicity contributes to an individual's self-worth by placing a strong positive value on the "we," it may have profoundly destructive effects by emphasizing the "they." As the bloody history of ethnic conflicts in the twentieth century illustrates, a consciousness of kind is often accompanied by a recognition of the differences that divide humankind. The critical danger is that once primordial aspirations are aroused, they will not easily abate. Ethnicity is a double-edged sword. It may contribute to the enhancement of the group or it may just as easily result in the further brutalization of humanity.

The Emergence of Ethnic Identification

Ethnicity is more than dimly perceived emotions recalling a primordial past. Specific conditions account for the emergence of ethnicity throughout the world. In many advanced industrialized societies, the ethnic group is a significant basis for group cleavage because ethnic identification provides an effective basis of group mobilization. (Bell 1975) Thus, the ethnic group becomes an efficient vehicle for expressing demands for group advantage—power, status, and wealth—in the political system. In the face of increasingly technocratic, bureaucratic, and competitive societies, the ethnic group combines utilitarian interests with affective affiliation. Emphasis on both the affective (primordial) dimension and the instrumental dimension of ethnicity is crucial in alerting students of comparative politics and international relations to the manner in which ethnicity may become a highly effective force within the political systems of advanced industrial states (e.g., the United States and Western European countries) and developing societies of Africa, the Pacific, and Latin America. (Bell 1975)

The political process is a key variable for three reasons. First, elites within the political system ultimately oversee the allocation of resources among competing ethnic groups in any ethnically plural society. In these societies, "Status competition is diffuse and lacks a specific site. Economic competition is dispersed between interests and occupations." (Bell 1975, 161) The political system becomes the central arena on which ethnic conflicts and rivalries are focused. Thus, the political decisionmaking process becomes one of the most important avenues for the mobilization of ethnic-group interests in an effort to secure societal resources and opportunities.

Second, there has been a steady accretion of power in the political systems of most advanced industrial societies over the last two decades. Economic, cultural, and social systems have become subordinate to political ones. This is particularly evident in the economic sector where economic issues are ultimately governed by political needs. The political process becomes the final arbiter among conflicting values subsumed under "quality-of-life" policies. These include issues related to basic human needs, the environment, education and training, and enforcement of societal rules and regulations.

Third, in the developing world the political process is the focal point of virtually all activities within the state. The process of modernization requires the restructuring of a society from the top down. Decisions made by central elites are political in nature almost by definition. Questions involving the distribution of scarce resources in multiethnic societies frame ethnic cleavages throughout the developing world.

ETHNICITY AND THE SYSTEM-MAINTAINER APPROACH

The system-maintainer approach analyzes the actions, outlooks, and policies of states as the exclusive factors in world politics. This perspective falls within the parameters of political realism. Realism emphasizes the pursuit of power by states primarily in military-strategic terms and secondarily through the use of economic and psychological tools. Because states monopolize legitimate power based on sovereignty, the study of world politics becomes the study of the interaction of states seeking (as a general rule) to increase power, demonstrate power, or at least maintain power. Hans Morgenthau (1978) was the best-known theorist of political realism. His conceptual approach to the study of international relations has defined the field for some fifty years. The realist view of the international system has influenced the research orientations of scholars, and thus the policy priorities of national leaders who depend on the analyses and evaluations of the scholarly community.

The Realist Paradigm

Realism has been analogized to a billiard game—the table representing the boundaries of world politics and the balls representing sovereign independent states. The game of international politics is comprised of the interaction of the balls constantly colliding with one another, forming new coalitions and configurations. In order to understand the game, one must first appreciate that the only important actors are states and that some states are more powerful than others. Speculation as to what goes on within states is less relevant than how the state interacts with its allies and adversaries at a particular moment. Attention is necessarily directed to what happens on the billiard table because of the fast-paced nature of the game and because the risks of failure are so very high. System maintainers see the system as competitive, anarchic, and hierarchial.

The process by which states shape their formal relations with one another is central to the conceptual approach of a realist or system-maintainer view. This process is carried out through foreign policy. In this context, foreign policy is defined as the manner in which a state's elite formulates, implements, and evaluates external choices within a domestic political environment. Thus the pursuit of foreign policy becomes a process whereby states seek to structure decisions in the international arena through the use of power. Power is manifest, first and foremost, in a military context, but may also be demonstrated through economic policies or by adroitly working within multilateral institutions or other diplomatic channels. Politics in the global arena become state politics writ large. Explanations and predictions about world politics must of necessity focus on the goals of states, with the most powerful states defining the rules of the game. Policy alternatives of the realist paradigm, therefore, revolve around the relative power and influence of states. Central policy concerns encompass the size and effectiveness of a state's war-making capacity, the nature of its alliance structure, and the effectiveness of its leverage vis-à-vis other states in military and non-military contexts—for example, international organizations, regional organizations, and bilateral relations with individual states. The making of foreign policy is a crucial dimension of political realism because it emphasizes the importance of elite consensus as a means of achieving fundamental foreign-policy goals. Thus personnel recruitment for the national security bureaucracies—the State Department, the Department of Defense, Treasury, the Central Intelligence Agency—becomes a central concern. The size of its military-industrial complex is likewise a central concern of the foreign-policy process, because government and industry must work in tandem for the security needs of the state to be fully addressed. Public relations also becomes a key dimension of the foreign-policy process; it becomes crucial to disseminate information to legitimate the non-participation of the general public in making foreign policy and to encourage deferential or complacent acceptance of the national-security concerns of the U.S. elite. (Barnet 1972)

The Cold War period (1947–1974) and the foreign-policy priorities of the Reagan presidency, in which core Cold War concerns have been resurrected, illustrate the theoretical emphasis of a realist or system-maintainer position. In both eras, "Cold War I" and "Cold War II," the emphasis is on bilateral relations rather than multilateral institutions, interventions aimed at containing Soviet aggression, the identification of all nationalistic movements seeking change as Communist-inspired, and an elitist foreign policy that demands secrecy and abhors and rejects challenges to the dominant worldview by interests outside the system. The problem is that the assumptions, explanations, predictions, and policies of political realism fail to understand the complexity and dynamic nature of world politics.

The role played by ethnicity as a relevant variable in world politics or as a part of the foreign-policy process is irrelevant from the perspective of a system maintainer. Since ethnic groups are by definition non-state actors and in most cases, substate actors, the ability of ethnic groups to play a significant role in foreign-policy decisionmaking was discounted. The state-centric approach—with its emphasis on sovereignty, territoriality, and control of crucial economic resources—discounted ethnicity as a meaningful political variable and relegated it to the scrap heap of atavistic cultural nuisances. Realism's preoccupation with the power of state actors critically underestimated the power of ethnicity over "men's minds" and its power to affect not only state politics but regional and global politics as well.

The State-Centric Model of Development

Following directly from the assumption of the preeminence of states within the international system was the belief that even newly created states could mold the civic cultures of their societies on a Western model that emphasized the progressive expansion of secular politics. It was presumed that the development of a national identity would result from increasing state penetration of all aspects of the society—political participation, economic development, education, social welfare, and cultural secularization. It was believed that modernization would be accelerated by technology and that communications and transportations systems would speed the process of national integration. (Deutsch 1966) The process of nation-building was turned on its head. Throughout the developing world, increasing penetration of isolated regions by elites representing the newly established state became politicized on the basis of ethnicity. As elites attempted to mobilize their societies by using Western technology, an explosive burst of politicized ethnicity rocked new states to their foundations. Nigeria presents perhaps the best example of how ethnic identity divided a society and resulted in a costly civil war. What the state-centric approach failed to understand was that the term "nation-state" no longer conveyed an empirical reality in a world of multiethnic states in which ethnic pluralism was increasingly manifest in the most important aspects of the society. (Connor 1972)

The state-centric model's emphasis on the nation-state obscured the fundamental transformation of Western European states also throughout the nineteenth and twentieth centuries. The state-development process unleashed a growing awareness of ethnic affiliations. The process of economic development and the internationalization of commerce coincidentally caused migration and encouraged the movement of capital and human resources. The result was a dramatic upsurge in interactions somehow afforded by ethnicity. Public decisions were aimed at maintaining order in heterogenous societies—a task that often led to increased conflict. In many situations, rulers exacerbated problems by introducing more ethnics loyal to them into colonial or neocolonial regimes. No colonial power better utilized the principle of "divide and conquer" than the British, beginning in Ulster and perfecting the policy in the islands of the Caribbean, in the Indian subcontinent, and throughout Africa. Yet all European colonizers used the technique to some degree. The irony was that as Europeans introduced ethnically and racially different peoples in their empires, commerce, trade, and migration were changing the composition of their home countries. The multiethnic societies of Western Europe were created by the same forces that drove the colonizers outward to subdue the "uncivilized world." In any case, state boundaries in Western Europe, as in the newer states of the South, were no longer congruent with the historical and cultural peoples—the nations—that comprised them. In countries like the Soviet Union, the United States, or the People's Republic of China, the boundaries of the state had never coexisted with those of the nation. These societies were by definition multiethnic, arising from mass immigrations and/or territorial acquisition through war and empire building.

Even the ancient states of Western Europe, those presumed to be immune from the upheavals of politicized ethnicity, failed to live up to the homogenizing and unilinear development model of modernization that Western scholars blithely applied to the Third World. The late 1960s and the 1970s illustrated basic conflicts in which ethnicity was a core issue. In Belgium, Spain, France, Germany, and Italy, as well as in Great Britain and Northern Ireland, ethnic issues arose with a ferocity that was unexpected. The presumptions of the state-centric approach failed dismally to predict these renewed outbursts of ethnonationalism.

It would seem that the Western model of state-building, which suggests the progressive incorporation of smaller groups into larger groups until a fully developed national consciousness emerges, was premised on the eventual assimilation of ethnic communities. In considering the politicization of ethnicity in Western Europe, Anthony D. Smith (1981) has observed that the remote technocratic state, typical of Western European societies in the 1970s and 1980s, has created conditions conducive to ethnic revival. The frustrated attempts by educators and intellectuals to attain status and power in Western European bureaucracies have prompted intellectuals to articulate a powerful and persuasive "ethnic historicism." This move toward ethnic identity has a multiclass appeal and the movement is seen as an alternative to the alienation citizens feel when dealing with large, bureaucratic, impersonal, and seemingly uncaring authorities. The resurgence of ethnicity throughout Western Europe appears to be a legitimate development in a highly stratified state system, where affiliations with occupational groups or ethnic communities provide avenues for participation in a very competitive environment. Thus, identity with the state only is insufficient and perhaps impossible. This perspective stands in sharp contrast to the state-centric perspective's explicit presumption of the disappearance of ethnicity as a vibrant force in the old and new states of the North and the South.

ETHNICITY AND THE SYSTEM-REFORMER APPROACH

The deficiencies of the realist approach were in part alleviated by a shift to the system-reformer worldview, which emphasizes the transnational nature of the international policy agenda. Ethnic identity is considered a transnational issue. Transnational relations are defined as the "transfer of tangible or intangible items across state lines when at least one actor is not a state or intergovernmental actor." (Keohane and Nye 1971) Rather than conceptualizing world politics as interstate relations, the transnational-relations approach discards the formalistic and stilted billiards metaphor in favor of a model that emphasizes a multiplicity of different kinds of actors defining priorities and making decisions to realize these priorities in various policy areas.

From the perspective of the system reformer, the power of states is diminished each time non-state actors exert a powerful influence across state lines. The power of transnational enterprises (TNEs) dwarfs the economic influence of the vast majority of states. The competition for control of the policy arena between state and non-state actors challenges state leaders to respond to these newer centers of influence in different ways. So too with the proliferation of ideas and values across state lines despite the most determined efforts of states to exert control over the ideas and values of their peoples. If the technology of mass communications provides states with the power of attempting to create 1984-like territorial divisions, non-state actors too have the power of ideas rooted in the Western notion of "progress"—mass consumption—to counterbalance state propaganda, however sublime.

Ethnicity as a Transnational Force

Ethnicity is a transnational force; state leaders are finding it increasingly difficult to control the hearts and minds of citizens who may identify first with an ethnic community. In a transnational world, ethnic affiliations are often supported substantively and symbolically by community members in other societies. International migration, legal or illegal, is one of the great and relentless currents of the nineteenth and twentieth centuries, spinning linkages across countries and continents. Transportation and communication patterns facilitate the exchange of ideas, whether sanctioned or not by state actors. The power of technology through the mass media has an undeniable impact of creating new and unexpected sources of influence that challenge assumptions of the state centric model. The role of ethnicity in a complex and interdependent system is often underestimated. An understanding of the importance of ethnicity is directly related to one's understanding of some of the more persistent problems facing humankind:

> As emerging actors in the international system, they (the ethnic group and the emerging neoethnic group) are indications that our perceptions of international relations and the causes of war and peace lag behind the consciousness of the men and nations we study. The ethnic nation cannot yet compete with the state in nuclear warheads and warships, but it continues to exercise formidable influence over the primary authority patterns of men. It is from this exercise of power that revolutions are born. (Alger 1985, 326)

Insofar as the ethnic group directly challenges the authority of the state in the hope of replacing one elite with an ethnically different one, the change merely reflects the primacy of the state system. This process of mere replacement of one elite by a different one has been a common process in many African states and has been a potent source of conflict that complicates regional and superpower balances of power. But these changes, however important to the states or regions involved, do not challenge the state-centric international system. These ethnic struggles for power do strain the system in terms of the cost of additional violence.

Facilitating Ethnic Power

Dramatic increases in the scope and intensity of ethnic group contacts via technological advancements help to transform contemporary world politics by facilitating the creation of transnational networks among ethnic groups throughout the world. The proliferation of terrorist tactics among ethnic groups—Irish, Palestinian, Corsican, Croation, Puerto Rican—documents the influence of a worldwide mass media. The internationalization of the mass media has also provided ethnic groups with a new tool for mobilization. The irony is that the very process that makes ethnic groups seem more parochial than ever is, in fact, a process that is giving them new life. (Pierre, 1976) For ethnic groups with limited resources, terrorist tactics are a cheap, effective strategy for articulating demands and grievances before a global audience.

Quite aside from the existence of a powerful demonstration effect, the global mass media stimulates and reinforces ethnic identifications across state lines. For example, in the mid-1960s, civil-rights activists in Northern Ireland employed the techniques developed in the American Civil Rights Movement. The attention that Irish civil-rights activists received in the mass media legitimated the political bases of the conflict. The economic, moral, and political assistance that flowed into Northern Ireland also vastly complicated the struggle between Irish Catholic factions, in part helping to bring about the rebirth of the Irish Republican Army. In turn, Basque, French Canadian, and Croatian separatists were not unmindful of the ethnic struggles being waged in different countries. In addition to providing information, transnational linkages supply ethnic groups with vital resources necessary to carry on their struggles: money, weapons, and moral support.

Transnational relationships also challenge interstate politics by providing ethnic groups with political legitimacy. The United Nations (UN) and other international organizations have conferred legitimacy on the Palestinians. Yasir Arafat was triumphantly received at the UN on November 13, 1974. The Palestine Liberation Organization was granted observer status and the the UN General Assembly voted to equate Zionism with racism. The case of the Palestinians illustrates the limitations of the collective-legitimacy functions of international organizations in the face of the unwillingness of central state actors to alter the balance of power in the Middle East in favor of the Palestinians.

Ethnicity and Transnational Investments
The growth of transnational actors, such as TNEs, that are not restrained by traditional attributes of state sovereignty, territoriality, and nationalism, have far-reaching consequences for the politicization of ethnicity and interethnic distributions of power within states and regions. (Enloe 1979) For example, throughout Southeast Asia, Japanese TNEs have strengthened the economic power of the overseas Chinese. (Weinstein 1976) Japanese TNEs view the Chinese as the most competent and trustworthy businessmen with whom to deal. The Japanese-Chinese partnership has increased tensions among the overseas Chinese and indigenous ethnic groups in Thailand, Indonesia, Malaysia, and the Philippines. Leaders from different ethnic communities in these coun-

tries charge that local officials are bribed by the Chinese to give them and the Japanese corporations they represent unfair advantages. In this case and others, the competition for resources and opportunities is accentuated by interethnic divisions.

A second example of how transnational investments may accentuate ethnic identities and increase the chances for conflict is provided by a review of the South African situation. TNEs seeking greater profits afforded by the denial of basic human freedoms through an apartheid system of governance continue to support the white minority government. These investments have become the center of debate throughout the Western world. Campaigns for divestment and economic embargoes have resulted in a renewal of ethnic identity and ethnic group mobilization in many countries. In some cases this issue has caused the polarization of ethnically diverse communities. Old divisions have resurfaced over this case of institutional racism called apartheid.

Ethnic separatism
Demands by ethnic separatists challenge the foundations of the traditional state system. Demands for devolution or decentralization in Scotland, Wales, Northern Ireland, Belgium, Spain, Canada, and the Soviet Union illustrate perhaps a new period in the history of the state system. Because ethnic separatists attempt to reverse the course of Western European history by insisting that the territorial boundaries of the state coincide with the cultural, linguistic, or ethnic boundaries of the nation, the state system may be witnessing a period when fragmentation is seen as a solution to the kinds of ethnic problems that federalism and other reforms were intended to resolve. It is likely that transnational networks will further intensify this process. The system reformer will continue to invent policy programs that accommodate communities and the leaders of the state.

ETHNICITY AND THE SYSTEM-TRANSFORMER APPROACH

The system-transformer approach is probably the most difficult to frame because it challenges the fundamental values and assumptions of realism and reformist or globalist views.

Global Ethnic Communities

The alternative-left or World Order Models Project (WOMP) worldview supports a movement away from the state-centric system and the creation of a system that encourages rather than isolates ethnic community. Chadwick F. Alger insightfully suggests that there is nothing new about the way individuals directly interact in world politics:

> With the incorporation of transnational relations into the state paradigm, the impression has been created that so-called nonstate actors are entirely new, a product of modern transportation and communications. Certainly, jet engines and satellite

communications have greatly changed the nature of global interaction among peoples. But sustained contact between local peoples over long distances is not new. Widespread patterns of migration and commerce, the diffusion of religions, philosophies, science and technology, had all occurred before the Western state system was established, continued after its founding, and persist to the present. Yet, this more encompassing perspective has not been incorporated into mainstream international/global research, thus serving to wall off people from understanding the historical links of their local communities in what William McNeil has called the "ecumene." (1985, 326)

From the perspective of ethnicity, this alternative-left/system-transformer worldview emphasizes the self-reliance of ethnic groups and their ability to empower themselves as individuals and as members of a collective group. Those who hold this view offer an alternative scenario which suggests that ethnic groups might become the building blocks of a new global system in which the traditional power of states is replaced by the pervasive power and influence of corporate-like structures directing the acquisition, control, and accumulation of resources in regional or global systems. In either case, ethnicity is an example of the ways in which the global system moves beyond the parameters of both interstate and transnational relations.

Samuel Huntington (1973) has argued that "tribalism in politics" and "transnationalism in economics" are in some respects mutually reinforcing. He suggests that transnational relations may in fact provide more opportunities for citizen participation in the international system by linking the political activities of individuals in one state to those of groups in other states. Huntington (1973, 365) describes the possibility of a more decentralized political system: "The sovereignty of the government may, in a sense, be limited but the sovereignty of the people may be made more real by the fact that the 'sovereign' unit of government is smaller, closer, easier to participate in, and much easier to identify with." Vernon Van Dyke (1977) suggests a similar perspective when he argues that ethnic groups should be recognized as legitimate "right-and-duty-bearing units" alongside the rights and privileges granted to states and individuals in Western political philosophy. Van Dyke, therefore, challenges the assumptions of the state-centric model and extends the logic of the transnational-relations paradigm by arguing that ethnic groups represent a form of political organization that should be explicitly recognized. In other words, the ethnic group constitutes a legitimate basis of group organization and political participation and should be accorded a legal status commensurate with that standing.

Pervasive patterns of global interdependence provide ethnic groups with the capability for expanded political participation. Unlike the system reformer, the transformer sees ethnic groups staking a claim for inclusion within the global political system that alters traditional expectations. This possibility is documented in the progressive expansion of international law from the level of states to the smaller level of ethnic associations and perhaps individuals—a process that C. Wilfred Jenks (1958) referred to as the evolving "common law of mankind." This process is most explicitly evident in the growing body of international law devoted to human rights. These striking departures from the state-centric approach would not be possible without the combined efforts of individuals, non-state actors, intergovernmental organizations, and a global political climate conducive to numerous avenues of non-traditional participation. Herbert Kelman (1977) forsees the restructuring of the global system, insuring the protection of ethnicity as a fundamental step toward the realization of human rights worldwide. The demise of exclusive state sovereignty, the building of global consensus, the redistribution of wealth, and the achievement of world peace are essential components of this blueprint. This perspective assumes that ethnic groups will develop strategies to resolve basic conflicts threatening stability throughout the international system. The bloody history of ethnic conflict in the twentieth century limits the appeal of this approach.

Ethnicity and Global Dominance

An alternative view presents a less democratic and pluralistic future scenario. Instead of the state system or the more reform-oriented transnational system being replaced by an international community of ethnic nations, one ethnic community or a small group of dominant communities might control the system. Such a system, directed by a small elite of managers and technicians, would control the manufacture, distribution, and accumulation of goods and services throughout the international system. This futuristic scenario, perhaps resembling Aldous Huxley's *Brave New World* or George Orwell's *1984,* is premised on the integration of the global system into a unified hierarchy where all states are dependent on and dominated by a hegemonic state or group of states. This might be brought about by the concentration of resources and technological expertise generated by postindustrial society. It may not be far-fetched to see a small group of managers and technicians utilizing technology and other resources to dominate a national or even the international system. In this system of one-state rule, the democratic process that encourages participation by all ethnic groups would be preempted by efficient, powerful, and ruthless centers of control, which, more than likely, would make decisions designed to further the interests of the technocrats over all other groups. (Targ 1976)

In this environment, ethnic groups become the lowest common denominators capable of exerting influence over individuals. In the face of an increasingly homogeneous global culture, ethnicity remains one of the last remnants of distinctive communal identities. From the global dominance perspective, ethnicity will remain a viable identity only so long as it proves a useful form of group differentiation among global managers. The ethnic group would play an important intermediate role as the object of elite manipulation between the demise of the state system and the rise of a hierarchically ordered, homogeneous global dominance system.

The problem with the expectation that ethnicity will conveniently wither away in the face of global elites skillfully manipulating technology and material incentives is that it assumes that ethnicity is always "subservient to material considerations." (Connor 1984) Like the expectations of a generation of development theorists led by Karl Deutsch (1966), the global dominance/dependency approach may critically undervalue the complexity, resilience, and even irrationality of ethnic bonds. The predictions of liberal functionalism or Neomarxist *dependencia* theories fail to capture the "shadowy and elusive" quality of modern nationalism. (Connor 1978) Anthony D. Smith points to this unsettling dimension of ethnicity:

> Herein lies perhaps the true dimension of the ethnic revival; it is at one and the same time an attempt to preserve the past, and to transform it into something new, to create a new type upon ancient foundations, to create a new man and society through the revival of old identities and the preservation of the "links in the chain of generations." (1981, 25)

CONCLUSION

This chapter has suggested that ethnicity is a dynamic force in the hands of those seeking change. Whether ethnicity will prove to be one of the central vehicles of system change remains to be seen. As each of the three worldview models suggests, ethnicity can be manipulated to serve the goals of order, reform, and transformation in world politics by states, transnational actors and forces, and perhaps by individuals—in pursuit of personal gain or altruistic goals. In any attempt to conceptualize global issues, the multiplicity of actors and the variety of vehicles employed to reach desired ends should temper our willingness to offer simplistic explanations of complex phenomena. Nowhere is this more obvious than in the contemporary study of ethnicity as a significant global force. It is easy to place ethnicity within normative categories that reinforce our preferences for global models. For example, ethnicity may help to explain why nationalistic sentiments are helpful in providing national populations with a historical sense of identity. These identities may help to reinforce the state-centric paradigm in advanced postindustrial states of the West or the developing states of Africa, Asia, the Middle East, and Latin America. But ethnicity can also be seen as a powerful force that, like other transnational actors or policy processes such as the investment decisions of TNEs, challenges the state-centric paradigm. The study of the global dimensions of ethnicity should remind us that the very choice of a model through which to view the world is often an implicit political decision—no less than the multiple sets of identities that individuals and groups use to define themselves in an attempt to make sense out of the world, to survive, and perhaps even to prosper. Ethnicity remains a potent symbol of where we have come in pursuit of these difficult and illusive goals and how far individual, group, state, and global actors need to go to create a livable world. Any analysis of international issues, events, and conditions would be incomplete without a careful assessment of the more affective dimensions of identity and participation.

REFERENCES

Alger, Chadwick F. "Bridging the Micro and the Macro in International Relations Research." *Alternatives* 10 (Winter 1984–1985):319–344.

Barnet, Richard. *Roots of War: The Men and Institutions Behind U.S. Foreign Policy.* Baltimore: Penguin Books, 1972.

Bell, Daniel. "Ethnicity and Social Change." In *Ethnicity.* Edited by Nathan Glazer and Daniel P. Moynihan. Cambridge, MA: Harvard University Press, 1975.

Bull, Hedley. *The Anarchial Society: A Study of Order in World Politics.* New York: Columbia University Press, 1977.

Carr, Edward H. *The Twenty Years Crisis 1919–1939.* New York: Harper Torchbooks, 1946.

Connor, Walker. "Eco- or Ethno-Nationalism?" *Ethnic and Racial Studies* 7 (July 1984):342–359.

Connor, Walker. "Nation-Building or Nation Destroying?" *World Politics 24* (April 1972):319–355.

Deutsch, Karl W. *Nationalism and Social Communications: An Inquiry into the Foundations of Nationality.* Cambridge, MA: MIT Press, 1966.

Emerson, Rupert. *From Empire to Nation, The Rise to Self-Assertion of Asian and African Peoples.* Boston: Beacon Press, 1960.

Enloe, Cynthia. "Multinational Corporations and the Making and Unmaking of Ethnic Groups." In *Ethnonationalism, Multinational Corporations and the Modern State.* Edited by R. Grant and E. S. Wellhofer. University of Denver: Graduate School of International Studies Monograph Series in International Affairs, 1979.

Geertz, Clifford. *The Interpretation of Cultures: Selected Essays.* New York: Basic Books, 1973.

Greeley, Andrew. *Ethnicity in the United States: A Preliminary Reconnaissance.* New York: John Wiley and Sons, 1974.

Greeley, Andrew. *The American Catholic: A Social Portrait.* New York: Basic Books, 1977.

Horowitz, Donald. *Ethnic Groups in Conflict.* Berkeley: University of California Press, 1985.

Huntington, Samuel. "Transnational Organizations in World Politics." *World Politics 25* (April 1973):333–368.

Isaacs, Harold. *Idols of the Tribe: Group Identity and Political Change.* New York: Harper and Row, 1975.

Jenks, C. Wilfred. *The Common Law of Mankind.* New York: Praeger, 1958.

Kelman, Herbert C. "The Conditions, Criteria, and Dialectics of Human Dignity: A Transnational Perspective." *International Studies Quarterly* 21 (September 1977):529–552.

Keohane, Robert and Joseph Nye, editors. *Transnational Relations and World Politics*. Cambridge, MA: Harvard University Press, 1971.

Morgenthau, Hans. *Politics Among Nations*. New York: Knopf, 1978.

Novak, Michael. *The Rise of the Unmeltable Ethnics*. New York: Macmillan, 1971.

Pierre, Andrew. "The Politics of International Terrorism," *Orbis* 19 (Winter 1976):12–52.

Rothschild, Donald. *Ethnopolitics: A Conceptual Framework*. New York: Columbia University Press, 1981.

Said, Abdul and L. R. Simmons, editors. *Ethnicity in an International Context: The Politics of Disassociation*. New Brunswick, NJ: Transaction Books, 1976.

Schermerhorn, Richard A. *Comparative Ethnic Relations, A Framework for Theory and Research*. New York: Random House, 1970.

Smith, Anthony D. *The Ethnic Revival in the Modern World*. Cambridge University Press, 1981.

Stack, John, editor. *Ethnic Identities in a Transnational World*. Westport, CT: Greenwood Press, 1981.

Targ, Harry. "Global Dominance and Dependence, Post-Industrialism and International Relations Theory: A Review." *International Studies Quarterly* 20 (September 1976):470–482.

Van Dyke, Vernon. "The Individual, the States and Ethnic Communities in Political Theory." *World Politics* 29 (April 1977):343–369.

Weinstein, Franklin. "Multinational Corporations and the Third World: The Case of Southeast Asia." *International Organizations* 30 (Summer 1976):373–404.

Wolfers, Arnold. *Discord and Collaboration*. Baltimore: Johns Hopkins University Press, 1962.

11

Cooperation and Conflict: The United States and Canada

DONALD K. ALPER
DONALD C. WILSON

U.S. citizens and Canadians are both North Americans: neighbors, friends, customers, and allies. People on both sides of the border see the relationship as one of unusual harmony and cooperation. In virtually all areas of political, economic, cultural, and social life, strong transborder linkages have been forged. Indeed, the "longest undefended border" acts less as a barrier and more as a documenter of the vast web of interactions between the two countries.

A member of Congress once remarked, "We [in the United States] tend to deal with Canada not as a foreigner, but as a partner." (Alper, 1987) This comment undoubtedly expresses the typical view found in much, and perhaps most of the United States as it considers Canada in the context of foreign affairs. It is a view derived from tradition, ethnic and cultural similarity, and the thousands of family ties and social associations spanning the border. U.S. citizens see in Canadians an image of themselves, which is apparent in such familiar statements as "They are just like us," and "Thinking about Canada is like thinking about the 51st state." It is probably not an exaggeration to say that Canada is viewed not so much as a foreign country but more as an extension of U.S. society.

Although it is true that conflicts between the two countries have never been of a magnitude to warrant more than passing international attention, a wide variety of issues, often highly contentious, are part and parcel of this relationship. To quote from a subtitle of a recent book edited by Doran and Sigler (1985), Canadian-U.S. relations are characterized by both "enduring friendship and persistent stress." It would be remarkable if tension were absent from such a highly complex relationship. Some idea of the complexity may be gained by reflecting on the following:

- The value of U.S.-Canadian cross-border trade in goods and services exceeds U.S.$130 billion each year.

- The volume of trade is responsible for approximately 2 million jobs in the United States.
- Air and water pollutants spill over a more than 5,000-mile border.
- Fishery stocks in two oceans have transborder migratory habits.
- A lasting alliance compels regular diplomacy on matters of continental trade and world security.

Each nation views issues associated with bilateral relations differently. In the United States, irritants in the relationship are infrequently regarded as matters of national interest and therefore have a low profile compared to other foreign-policy problems. In Canada, there is a greater sensitivity to the relationship, because Canadians are affected by virtually everything that happens in the United States. Prime Minister Pierre Trudeau articulated this concern when he compared Canada's relations to the United States to those between an elephant and a mouse: "Living next to you is in some ways like sleeping with an elephant. No matter how friendly and even tempered the beast, one is affected by every twitch and grunt." (Mahant and Mount, 1984) Moreover, Canadians always feel the impact of the "colossus to the South," yet recognize that the United States' powerful influence on its neighbor is a matter of indifference to U.S. policymakers. That this is a source of frustration in Canada was revealed when Prime Minister Brian Mulroney told Vice President George Bush that Canadians are "tired of being put on the back burner and taken for granted." (*Los Angeles Times,* January 22, 1987, A1:22)

For analytical and teaching purposes, the bilateral relationship is characterized as being highly asymmetrical and interconnected. Asymmetry refers to the unequal distribution of power between the two nations, reflected in their respective gross national products, populations, and military capacities. Interconnectedness means there are multiple cross-border ties and links involving government officials, people in business, trade unionists, professionals, and private individuals. All these forces must be taken into account to grasp the essential dynamics of the bilateral relationship.

The purpose of this chapter is to illustrate how the U.S.-Canadian relationship can be better understood by employing the three worldview perspectives held by system maintainers, system reformers, and system transformers. Each worldview serves as a lens for describing the nature of the relationship and advancing prescriptions for policy actions—a lens colored by certain values, beliefs, and expectations, and used to describe and explain issues, events, and conditions. By using different lenses, multiple interpretations of the bilateral relationship can be brought to light. For this reason, adopting an approach that employs contending worldviews brings greater understanding about this significant bilateral relationship to both students and teachers of international affairs.

The system-maintainer view of U.S.-Canadian relations recognizes the asymetry of the bilateral power relationship, but does not view it as a source of serious problems. That the U.S. population is ten times larger than Canada's and that the United States is regarded as a superpower creates management problems but does not alter the basic character of the relationship. The countries are seen as forming a highly stable bilateral system, in which national interests are aligned and interwoven. As Doran (1984) notes, although sovereign and separate entities, the two countries have a common agenda and share a sense of purpose.

Describing the Relationship

The system-maintainer perspective highlights the notion of interdependence as the key condition of the relationship. Interdependence derives from the unprecedented exchange of goods, money, communication, people, and ideas between the two countries. The exchange creates a massive and complex web of interconnections resulting in each country being heavily influenced by the other. From the maintainer perspective, the condition of interdependence helps mitigate possible tensions arising from the asymmetry of the relationship because influence is exercised in both directions, instead of monopolized by one country.

The system-maintainer view of U.S.-Canadian relations is largely the U.S. view. Most U.S. citizens look upon Canada as a cousin, or a congenial northern neighbor living atop the weather map. Canada is sometimes viewed as an extension of the United States, a kind of fifty-first state. Accordingly, U.S. officials have the luxury of ignoring Canada. There are few serious foreign-policy issues that have the potential for disruption. As a well-known Canadian columnist and author put it, "They [Canadians] aren't exotic enough to command attention, or troublesome enough to compel it to be paid." (Gwyn 1985, 185) This indifference supports the status quo relationship and reinforces a "take-Canada-for-granted" mindset.

Over the years, U.S. policies toward Canada, and the beliefs and values that underlie them, have reflected the maintainer view. During most of the nineteenth century, the United States thought Canada to be unimportant, believing that it was neither a serious military threat nor an economic competitor. Canada was thought to be firmly a part of the British Empire. As long as relations were good with Great Britain then Canada's role in the world was understood and of little concern.

After World War I, the United States replaced Great Britain as Canada's principal trading partner. The two countries entered into a relationship of great intimacy and trust that has few parallels in the history of the world. A sense of closeness is reflected in a 1935 speech given by President Franklin Roosevelt:

"Between Canada and the United States exists a neighborliness, a genuine friendship which over a century has dispelled every parting rift." In 1964, President Lyndon Johnson reinforced this sense of closeness by stating: "Canada is such a close neighbor and such a good neighbor. . . . Our problems are kind of like problems in a home town." (Gwyn 1985, 41)

During World War II, Canada and the United States fought as allies, often under unified command. Following the war, the two countries remained close allies and generally viewed postwar developments in the same Cold War term—as a struggle between East and West. They worked together in the formation of the United Nations, the World Bank, the General Agreement on Trade and Tariffs, and other international organizations that, from the system-maintainer point of view, provided Canada, the United States, and other powers the opportunity to maintain a more ordered and cooperative international system.

For some time after World War II, the term "special relationship" was used to characterize the informality and "quiet diplomacy" of U.S.-Canadian relations. Even today, officials at all levels of government on both sides of the border interact easily with one another. It is not uncommon, for example, for state governors to meet regularly with provincial premiers; or for officials in the U.S. state, commerce, treasury, or other executive departments to pick up the phone and speak with their counterparts in Canada. The use of quiet diplomacy relies on private persuasion rather than public conflict. Issues are not escalated politically and specific problems are isolated from broader issues so that overall relations are not disrupted. Finally, the idea of a special relationship suggests that many bilateral issues are "technical" in nature and therefore are best resolved by bureaucrats and experts using scientific criteria in objective ways.

The system-maintainer perspective also views Canadian-U.S. relations as "exceptional." (Mahant and Mount 1984) Exceptionality consists in the ease with which people and goods cross the international boundary, the traditional practice of the United States' exempting Canada from certain taxes and import duties imposed on other countries, and the norm by which each government consults with the other continually on bilateral and global foreign-policy matters.

Perhaps most central to the idea of exceptionality is the belief in partnership. Partnership conveys the idea of working together for common purposes, the most important being maximizing affluence in North America and building and maintaining a strong continental defense system to deter the Soviet Union from a possible attack. Advantages of such a partnership accrue to both parties. The Canadian government seeks security under the U.S. nuclear umbrella while the U.S. military has access to the strategic area of the Canadian northland. In addition, Canadians realize the economic benefits of extensive U.S. investment in Canada while, on the other hand, U.S.-based multinational corporations reap the rewards of easy access to the plentiful and inexpensive natural resources in Canada.

System maintainers do not want to lose the close links between the two nations. The remarkable extent to which each country's domestic and foreign actions affect the other makes for prudence and restraint in bilateral dealings. Although differences are inevitable, the firm belief in interdependence and a strong sense of partnership ensures that differences can be resolved rather easily and with minimal disruption.

System-Maintainer Prescriptions for the Relationship

When prescribing solutions to problems, a system-maintainer view stresses the management aspects of U.S.-Canadian relations. Managing the relationship is aided by the compatibility of national leaders, close institutional ties, and by avoiding linking negotiations over issues in one policy area with outcomes in another. In addition, the handling of many cross-border transactions at the sub-national level broadens management activities and takes some of the political pressure off the central governments.

Institution-building is a prescription of the system-maintainer view. Bilateral institutions are seen as effective in reducing politicization of issues. A good example of this is the International Joint Commission (IJC). This 80-year-old environmental organization is composed of equal numbers of Canadian and U.S. citizens and has established a reputation for objectivity and political neutrality in resolving transborder environmental disputes. In recent years there have been calls from both sides of the border to establish an IJC-like economic commission for the purpose of resolving disputes in specific trade sectors.

A system maintainer view recognizes the inevitability of ever greater interdependence deriving from geographical, historical and, most important, economic factors in the relationship. This was recognized as early as 1927, when Hume Wrong, a Canadian diplomat and later an ambassador to the United States, listed in an official document the factors promoting continuing harmony between the two countries. Among the most important were: (1) a common continental feeling; (2) general similarity of economic conditions; (3) mutual economic interdependence; (4) a large amount of U.S. capital invested in Canada; (5) the even larger per-capita investment of Canadian capital in the United States; and (6), the enormous volume of interactions. (Wrong 1976) Later, in 1941, President Franklin Roosevelt and Prime Minister Mackenzie King codified, in what came to be known as the Hyde Park Declaration, a set of prescriptive principles, which lie at the heart of a system-maintainer perspective:

1. Increased economic interdependence with Canada is desirable and beneficial to the people of both countries
2. Increased economic interdependence is probably inevitable and may eventually lead to some form of tighter economic integration between the two countries
3. Open political conflict between the two governments is symptomatic of a poorly managed relationship and is possibly explosive
4. Greater economic interdependence, accompanied by greater bilateral

institutionalization, is likely to stem the propensity for intergovernmental conflict (Doran 1985, 13)

These principles emphasize both satisfaction with the status quo and the view that integrative tendencies in North America are generally acceptable, even desirable.

The Hyde Park principles still find general acceptance in the United States today. Canadians, on the other hand, are highly sensitive to "creeping integration" with the United States. In Canada, integration raises the spector of "continentalism"—the belief in a united North America directed from the United States for common advantage. Canadians fear continentalist schemes because the disparity in power among Canada, Mexico, and the United States would inevitably put the smaller powers in a politically and economically subordinate position to the United States. In 1979, when President Reagan called for a North American Accord that would require a tighter U.S. association with Canada and Mexico, Canadians reacted negatively fearing the plan was motivated by a U.S. desire to take control of Canadian energy and water resources.

Many of the principles of the Hyde Park Declaration are reflected today in the general approach taken to U.S.-Canadian relations by recent Canadian governments. This is especially true of the Conservative government headed by Prime Minister Brian Mulroney, whose party was elected in 1984 by the most lopsided margin in Canadian history. In a 1984 interview, Mulroney said, "Good relations, super relations, with the United States will be the cornerstone of our foreign policy." (*Wall Street Journal,* September 24, 1984, 32)

Free-trade negotiations with the United States are a major Canadian policy initiative that reflects the system maintainer-perspective. According to the Canadian Government, a free-trade agreement would improve the Canadian economy by increasing trade opportunities with Canada's primary trading partner. Free trade has been an on-again-off-again item on Canadian government agendas since the middle of the nineteenth century. In the late 1980s, free trade with the United States ranks as the most important issue on the bilateral agenda. For Canada, free trade would bring unrestricted access to the massive U.S. market. The Royal Commission on the Economic Union and Development Prospects for Canada (1985) calculated the gain in national wealth from free trade at between 3 percent and 8 percent and indicated that an agreement would give Canadian exports needed immunity from U.S. tariffs and other trade barriers. To quote Prime Minister Mulroney, "As a matter of highest priority, we want an agreement that ends the threat to Canadian industry from U.S. protectionists who harass and restrict our exports through the misuse of trade remedy laws." (*Seattle Post-Intelligencer,* March 31, 1987)

Continued close relations between Canada and the United States are the foundation of a system-maintainer perspective. Closeness means both psychological affinity and political-economic attachments. The system-maintainer orientation fosters the belief that the overall relationship is harmonious and that the major concern is careful management of the many problems arising from strong interdependence. It also presumes that in the asymmetrical relationship, Canada both desires and benefits from closer relations with the larger and more powerful United States.

A SYSTEM-REFORMER VIEW

A system-reformer view of the bilateral relationship focuses on the scope and imbalance in the flow of transactions between the two nations. Between no two countries are there more transactions than occur between the United States and Canada. And between few, if any, is the two-way flow of transactions so imbalanced.

Describing the Relationship

The system-reformer perspective highlights the degree to which Canada is dependent upon the United States. Approximately 80 percent of Canada's exports and virtually all her foreign investment goes south of the border. Much of Canada's industrial capacity is owned or controlled by U.S.-based firms. Canadians watch more U.S.- than Canadian-originated television programs. Much of Canada's foreign news comes from the U.S.-based Associated Press and United Press International wire services and syndicated newspapers. Canada's automobile industry is closely connected to the giant U.S. automobile companies and survives only because of a 1965 special U.S.-Canadian agreement called the Automotive Product Trade Agreement. The Canadian defense industry is heavily dependent on contracts from U.S. arms manufacturers and prospers because of a special agreement providing free trade in arms bidding and manufacturing. Finally, most Canadians who live within 150 miles of the border engage in relatively effortless and frequent travel to the United States. As Holsti (1980, 36) has commented, "What one observer might see as an extraordinarily rich relationship in terms of empathy, shared values and transactions, many Canadians came to see as over extensive United States penetration into Canadian society."

The imbalance in interactions generates a concern for loss of Canadian autonomy to U.S. influence. For this reason, a system-reformer worldview acknowledges dependence rather than interdependence as the most significant condition of the relationship.

The dependence perspective is well developed in the literature of international relations, comparative politics, and Canadian foreign policy. An important formulation of this perspective is advanced by DeWitt and Kirton (1983), who forward the notion of "peripheral-dependence," linking Canada's economic and cultural dependence on the United States to a diminution of Canada's political autonomy. A somewhat different formulation of the dependence argument is found in the classic work by George Grant, *Lament for a Nation*. (1965) According to Grant, the loss of Canadian autonomy was an inevitable consequence of accepting the "benefits" of U.S. cultural and economic values and techniques.

The dependency belief orients and informs a wide-ranging spectrum of opinion, mostly found in Canada but also evident in some political circles in the United States. In Canada, this perspective has been closely associated with the socialist New Democratic Party (NDP). The view is also expressed by some members of the Progressive Conservative Party and, since the mid-1960s, by policies of the Liberal Party.

The dependency perspective focuses heavily on the economic dimensions of bilateral relations. With approximately 80 percent of Canada's exports going to the United States, U.S. domestic economic actions can make or break the Canadian economy. In addition, many of Canada's largest industries are branch plants of U.S. firms. System reformers argue that Canada's branch-plant economy is an impediment to economic development in Canada because research is done elsewhere, exports are not encouraged, and Canadian firms are the first to be closed during recessions and last opened during recoveries.

The dependency perspective also views Canada as steadily drifting toward U.S. cultural domination. Television programs, movies, periodicals, and books spill over the border from the massive U.S. cultural market. A Canadian identity distinct from the United States is said to be jeopardized by the homogenizing influence of the massive flow of TV programming which pours out of the U.S. networks.

In the area of foreign policy, system reformers believe that Canada is so entangled in the North American defense complex that it is difficult, if not impossible, for Canada to carve out a foreign policy distinct from that of the United States. Its NORAD responsibilities force Canadians to adopt the U.S. concept of North American defense and security. As a member of the North Atlantic Treaty Organization (NATO), Canada is under pressure to use her troops, territory, and even air space in the cause of Western defense, a cause she may agree with but lacks leverage to influence. These constraints on international activities deprive Canada of developing an independent role in the world while they accentuate its subordinate status. These conditions make it difficult for other countries to conceive of Canada as an autonomous and distinctive actor in international affairs.

From a system reformer's view, Canada is disadvantaged by being a part of the U.S. dominated North American defense complex. The reformer perspective highlights the problem of costs without benefits. While Canadians share with U.S. citizens the danger of annihilation in the event of a nuclear attack, Canada has very little influence over U.S. policy decisions that would precede or even follow such a catastrophe.

System reformers point to specific issues to highlight Canada's lack of autonomy. In recent years these included the decision to test cruise missiles over

Canada and the problem of Canadian involvement in the Strategic Defense Initiative (SDI), better known as "Star Wars."

In the early 1980s, it was made public that the United States planned to test unarmed cruise missiles over Canadian territory because the landscape in northern Canada was said to be similar to strategic territory in the Soviet Union. Because of alliance commitments, the Canadian government agreed to allow the flights, though not without considerable protest from peace groups, opposition political parties, and many journalists. In 1984, an estimated 100,000 people attended an anti-cruise rally in Vancouver, while a November 1986 poll showed that the Canadian public was opposed to the tests by a margin of 60 percent to 34 percent. At the Liberal Party convention in 1986, resolutions were passed urging a nuclear-free Canada and opposing the testing of U.S. cruise missiles, despite the fact that it was the former Liberal prime minister, Pierre Trudeau, who signed the agreement in 1983. From a system reformer's position, the fact that political leaders felt obliged to go ahead with the tests demonstrated how Canada's hands are tied by its dependency relationship with the United States.

The extent to which Canada is a part of the U.S. military-industrial complex is said to be further illustrated by the dilemma posed by Star Wars. The Reagan administration invited Canada's participation in the SDI program in the belief that involvement of allies would enhance the project's legitimacy at home and abroad. The government of Canada eventually declined the invitation on the grounds that any economic advantages realized would be overridden by the political costs of further involvement in a U.S. nuclear system. Prime Minister Mulroney told the United States that Canada would not officially take part in Star Wars research but individual companies were free to bid for contracts. Mulroney's decision appeared to be a bold step toward enhancing Canadian sovereignty and autonomy. However, from the system-reformer perspective the Star Wars issue is further evidence of Canadian vulnerability to U.S. interests. The 1985 decision by the Canadian government to renew their NORAD agreement without a clause prohibiting Star Wars operations as part of NORAD activities made Canada susceptible to participation in SDI in spite of its earlier refusal.

System-Reformer Prescriptions for the Relationship

Policies that emphasize dependency have been a continuing theme of Canadian politics. For some time, all three national political parties, the NDP, the Liberal, and the Progressive Conservative, have prescribed various remedies to deal with U.S. dominance.

On the economic front, the NDP advocates public ownership of major energy and resource industries along with a home-grown industrial strategy for Canada. In the 1970s, a splinter group of the NDP, called the Waffle, went so far as to call for the creation of an independent socialist Canada and proclaim the major threat to Canadian survival to be . . . American control of the Canadian economy. (Christian and Campbell, 1974, 187)

Most NDP policies, however, have been more pragmatic. Among them were calls for establishment of a national oil policy—out of which came the government-owned oil company, Petro-Canada; Canadian-content rules for TV broadcasting; the development of an independent Canadian foreign policy; and opposition to free trade. These actions reflect a system-reformer perspective because the policies seek to alter a highly asymmetrical interdependent bilateral relationship. Concern for the implications of dependence resulting from an asymmetrical relationship is the underlying cause of the NDP policies and other similar proposals.

Although the NDP's policy proposals are most closely identified with a system-reformer perspective, the Liberal and Progressive Conservative parties have over the years made pronouncements and enacted policies with major dependency themes.

In the 1950s, a prominent government commission warned of the danger to Canadian independence of increasing U.S. investment in Canada. The commission recommended that U.S. multinationals sell a portion of their holdings in Canada to Canadians, include more Canadians in senior management positions, and do more to increase employment opportunities in Canada. The substance of its recommendations eventually became a major part of Liberal government policy in 1974 when the Foreign Investment Review Agency (FIRA) was established. FIRA's purpose was to screen new foreign investment to ensure it would provide significant benefit to Canadians.

In the 1970s, the Liberal government led by Prime Minister Trudeau formulated a new foreign-policy framework that expressed the view that Canada needed to reassess its relations with the United States. In a major policy paper issued in 1972, the government proposed three alternate courses of action with regard to future relations with the United States. The first alternative was to maintain a status-quo position. The second was to move toward closer integration. The third was to take steps to reduce Canada's vulnerability to the United States. Eventually, the Canadian government adopted the third alternative, later to be known as the Third Option. (Berkowitz and Logan 1978) In taking this course of action there was the expectation Canada would diversify its economic and political relations by developing new and stronger ties with other countries, primarily in Europe and Asia.

The Third Option was a prescriptive view of the bilateral relationship. It called into question the assumptions underlying the "special relationship" and signaled Canada's intention to reduce its economic and political dependence on the United States. Underlying the idea of the Third Option was the view that business and investment in Canada should be made to serve Canadian interests. In 1971, the Canadian Development Corporation (CDC) was formed as a government agency to finance new Canadian firms and purchase foreign ones. By 1979, the CDC had made a wide variety of purchases including large mining, chemical, and pharmaceutical companies. Purchase of Canadian companies was aided by FIRA's policies.

In practice, trade- and investment-flows changed little after the Third Option. FIRA approved approximately 90 percent of the applications received. Some new linkages with European countries were established but these did not represent significant "counterweights" to the United States. As for U.S. investment in Canada, the flow was reduced but not significantly.

What the Third Option did was to highlight a major issue that had been brewing for some time: whether Canada, with its great dependence on the United States, could forge a distinct society at home and an independent foreign policy abroad. Inherent in the Third Option was the view that becoming more independent required less U.S. influence on Canada and a weakening of the U.S. pull. In the view of Stephen Clarkson (1982), Canada's foreign policy could act as a counter to continental absorption by asserting that Canada has a separate role to play on the world stage.

It is against this background that Canada embarked on perhaps the most controversial policy in the history of U.S.-Canadian relations—the National Energy Program (NEP). The NEP was conceived in the 1970s to shift control of the Canadian energy industry from approximately 75 percent foreign ownership (mostly U.S.-based multinationals) to no more than 50 percent by 1990. To achieve this goal the federal government would employ Petro-Canada, the government oil company, to make direct purchases of foreign-owned companies operating in Canada. The government would also use tax incentives to improve the competitive position of domestic industries against foreign ones. The NEP had as one of its aims Canada's becoming self-reliant in producing energy in a time of world shortages and skyrocketing prices. However, from the point of view of system reformers, the NEP had a more important purpose: to increase Canada's economic autonomy and sovereignty by weakening the hold of foreign multinationals, and thereby reduce the influence of U.S. economic power.

By the early 1980s, a number of factors—recession, the new Reagan administration in Washington, and the collapse in world oil prices—put pressure on Canada to once again re-orient its economic policies. Many of the reforms of the 1970s were abandoned. For example, FIRA was transformed into Investment Canada, the NEP was thoroughly diluted, and the Third Option was officially ended in 1983.

Foreign ownership, however, remains a significant issue in Canada even after the Conservative government, elected in 1984, dismantled the NEP and set on a course of renewed economic ties and free trade with the United States. System reformers point to polls that consistently indicate that Canadian public opinion supports the principles of "Canadianization" and limited foreign ownership. The NDP (and many in the Liberal Party) took a solid stand against a comprehensive free-trade agreement with the United States on the grounds that such a pact would inevitably lead to greater economic and political integration. In short, the centerpiece of the reformer perspective is that an industrial and employment policy, rather than the traditional dependence on the U.S. economic giant, should be the mechanism for economic growth.

For system reformers, Prime Minister Mulroney's flirting with the United States over free trade and "renewal of traditional ties" is a momentary harkening back to the past. According to this view, the transparent weakness of the special relationship is seen in the fact that only Canadians can and will protect and promote Canadian national interests. Thus a system-reformer perspective sees Canada as having to continue to take strong actions to keep U.S. influence at bay.

A SYSTEM-TRANSFORMER VIEW

The system-transformer view of the world stands apart from the other two perspectives in that it values radical and immediate changes in global structures and relationships. It suggests revolutionary rather than evolutionary changes. Often, the system-transformer perspective is strongly aligned with an ideology concerned with human equality, justice, and economic transformation.

Describing the Relationship

As a worldview, the system-transformer perspective calls for major changes in the political and economic interactions between the United States and Canada. Because of the stability of the relationship and because issues in the relationship are not viewed as having a significant impact on world politics, there is limited discussion or action to "transform" existing relations between the United States and Canada. However, ideas have been advanced that are directed to major transformation in bilateral relations.

Historically, transformation has been discussed in terms of trade relations. Advocates in both countries have argued for decades that changes in trade and economic linkages could transform the relationship. As far back as the 1860s, the U.S. and Canadian governments attempted to negotiate an extension of the Reciprocity Treaty of 1854, which formalized trade relations between the two countries. The term reciprocity meant that each country would abolish all tariffs on imports from the other. This treaty was particularly important to Canada because the British government had repealed trade laws that gave preference to its colonies and was moving toward free trade in world markets. Canadian merchants wanted to establish their own free-trade arrangements to take advantage of the lucrative U.S. markets to the south. On the U.S. side, northern states and certain manufacturing groups favored reciprocity with Canada. Such an arrangement would, it was argued, inevitably lead to both economic and political transformation in North America.

In the early 1900s, interest in a comprehensive free-trade agreement increased in both countries. However, many groups were opposed to the ending of tariff barriers. Canadian opponents of reciprocity used a number of economic and (predominantly) political arguments. Many feared that reciprocity agreements would be a step toward the annexation of Canada. What triggered the fear was a 1911 statement by Champ Clark, Speaker of the House of Representatives, that he favored reciprocity and "hoped to see the day when the American flag will float over every square foot of the British North American possession clear to the North Pole." (Clark 1911, 2520) President Taft further aroused suspicions of U.S. motives in his "Parting of the Ways" speech:

> Now is the the accepted time. Canada is at the parting of the ways. Shall she be an isolated country, as much separated from us as if she were across the ocean, or shall her people and our people profit by the proximity that our geography furnishes and stimulate the trade across the border that nothing but a useless, illogical and unnecessary tariff wall created. (Mahant and Mount 1984, 96)

Many Canadians saw free trade as undermining Canadian sovereignty. According to this view, a comprehensive trade agreement would provide the mechanism for exerting U.S. influence over the entire northern part of the continent.

The Canadian fear of transformation of their society through a free-trade agreement again surfaced during negotiations in the late 1980s. Although the government of Canada and many trade-oriented groups saw free trade from a system-maintainer perspective, other Canadian groups viewed the proposals as a radical departure that would further increase Canada's economic, political, and cultural dependence on the United States. In a book written as a letter to "Sam," Pierre Berton (1987), a popular Canadian writer, provides a personal account of what is at stake for many Canadians. Berton makes clear that U.S. citizens and Canadians are two different peoples and that Canadians run their country in a way that fits the peculiar Canadian cultural, economic, and historical environment. He expresses strong reservations about a comprehensive trade agreement because it would transform the cultural ingredients of Canadian character. Berton recalls a statement by the U.S. ambassador to Canada in which he said he couldn't understand why Canadians were so steamed up about the predominance of U.S. programs on Canadian TV networks. According to the ambassador, the Public Broadcasting Service network in the United States was loaded with programs imported from Great Britain, but his countrymen were not a bit concerned that this was a threat to U.S. sovereignty. (Berton 1987, 10)

For many Canadians, the concept of wide-open trade with the United States is radical and transforming in its effect. Other Canadians and U.S. citizens view changes resulting from free-trade agreements from the system-maintainer perspective. In their view, such agreements are ways of maintaining the close trade connections between the two countries.

System-Transformer Prescriptions for the Relationship

Since most political and economic officials in the United States and Canada are concerned with maintaining a stable relationship, prescriptions for transforming the distribution of power and source of authority are not commonly suggested or discussed. In fact, no major policies have been advanced with the intent to alter radically the existing pattern of relations. Individuals and groups outside the formal political and economic structures have, over the years, advanced scenarios that, if ever borne out, would transform U.S.-Canadian relations. Some are rooted in "non-nationalistic" ideas of what North America is actually like.

In the early 1980s, a group of newspaper reporters and Joel Garreau, editor of the *Washington Post,* developed a new concept of how the United States and Canada interconnect, in an effort to better understand why things happen the way they do in North America. The result (Garreau 1981) was the redrawing of boundaries in North America to form nine nations based on social, economic, and political commonalities. According to this new mode of thinking, most North Americans, at some level of consciousness, feel a dual citizenship. While they are citizens of the United States, Canada, or Mexico, they are bound also by ties to regional "nations." These "nations" are not defined in terms of physical geography (e.g., the Midwest, Northeast, etc.), but instead by the kinds of social and economic interactions evident in the actual day-to-day activities of North Americans.

In order to understand his notion of "Nine Nations of North America," Garreau contends one has to forget the previous knowledge taught in sixth-grade geography courses about the national boundaries and capital cities of North America, senior history courses about westward expansion, and freshman college courses about local and state elections. Instead, one needs to be aware of the centers of power and their distinctive webs of influence, the peculiar economies found through the continent, and people's sense of emotional allegiance and shared cultural ethos with particular dialects and mannerisms. To Garreau, the nine nations look, feel, and sound different from each other. Some are separated by physical and environmental characteristics, while others are divided by language and ways of making a living. Each nation has a list of desires, ways of getting what it wants, and a lens for viewing the world. Garreau's "Nine Nations of North America" are illustrated in Exhibit 11.1.

The nine nations idea not only prescribes radical transformation by obliterating national boundaries but also legitimizes the multiple viewpoints found within and between the two countries. The redrawing of the map highlights the antagonistic views of the two Pacific nations of Mex-America and Ecotopia that divide California, the feeling among many west-coast Canadians of the self-centeredness of Ontario manufacturers in the Foundry, the shared feeling of domination by the few who occupy the Empty Quarter, and the fear Québeçois have of being a cultural enclave in Anglo-America. It recognizes emerging economic activities in Dixie and new trade connections with Pacific Rim countries for Ecotopia. Restructuring North America into nine nations would not only transform the existing bilateral U.S.-Canadian relationship from one based on national division, but it would also shift power westward. Finally, the division would encourage different viewpoints of the world that stress new

Exhibit 11.1 Nine Nations of North America

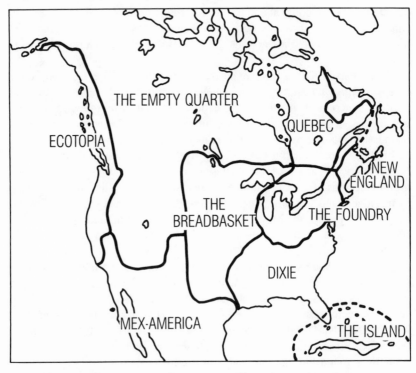

THE EMPTY QUARTER

QUEBEC

ECOTOPIA

NEW ENGLAND

THE BREADBASKET

THE FOUNDRY

DIXIE

MEX-AMERICA

THE ISLAND

Source: Garreau, Joel. *The Nine Nations of North America* (Boston, Houghton Mifflin, 1981) 204.

forms of interaction and exchange of goods, capital, and ideas. In sum, it would lead to the total restructuring of the continent and transform the individual's way of thinking about the political, economic, and cultural essence of North America.

CONCLUSION

The U.S.-Canadian relationship is frequently characterized as one of enduring friendship. Such a characterization is the consequence of the particular lens one uses to bring into focus a complex relationship shaped by unique political ties and historical events. Many individuals and groups view the extensive ties as highly beneficial to both countries and see the relationship as the world's best model of peaceful foreign relations. Others view the same state of affairs either as an unfair distribution of outcomes or as posing threats to national sovereignty and cultural values.

What is important is not which view is correct, but the recognition that a bilateral relationship can be viewed in different ways. To examine the U.S.-Canadian relationship from only one perspective takes for granted the complex nature of the relationship. Although a singular view is comfortable, it becomes unsettled and dysfunctional when tensions arise or changes in world conditions occur. Take, for example, Reich's concern for the rise of "techno-nationalism." He contends that U.S. scientists and researchers, working on new technologies, see "themselves as members of a global community of researchers, who work jointly on projects, meet periodically in international conferences, exchange papers, and publish their findings worldwide." (1987, 63) The reality of global interdependence raises questions about many of the conventional interpretations of bilateral relationships. In a changing world, new interpretations are demanded. As the United States and Canada become information-oriented societies with world-based economies, it is increasingly necessary to adopt a contending-worldviews approach as one seeks to understand the complex and potentially controversial issues linking these two societies.

REFERENCES

Alper, Donald K. "Congress, Parliament, and Public Policy in Canada-U.S. Relations," unpublished paper delivered at the Western Political Science Association meeting, March 26-28, 1987.

Berkowitz, S. D., and Robert K. Logan, editors. *Canada's Third Option*. Toronto: Macmillan, 1978.

Berton, Pierre. *Why We Act Like Canadians*. Toronto: McClelland and Stewart, 1987.

Christian, William, and Colin Campbell. *Political Parties and Ideologies in Canada*. Toronto: McGraw-Hill Ryerson, 1974.

Clark, Champ. Speech. *Congressional Record* 46 (February 14, 1911):2520.

Clarkson, Stephen. *Canada and the Reagan Challenge: Crisis in the Canadian-American Relationship*. Toronto: James Lorimer, 1982.

DeWitt, David B., and John J. Kirton. *Canada as a Principal Power: A Study in Foreign Policy and International Relations*. New York: John Wiley, 1983.

Doran, Charles F. *Forgotten Partnership: U.S.-Canada Relations Today*. Baltimore: Johns Hopkins University Press, 1984.

Doran, Charles F., and John H. Sigler, eds. *Canada and the United States: Enduring Friendship, Persistent Stress*. Englewood Cliffs, NJ: Prentice Hall, 1985.

Fox, Annette B., Alfred O. Hero, Jr., and Joseph S. Nye, Jr., editors. *Canada and the United States: Transnational and Transgovernmental Relations*. New York: Columbia University Press, 1976.

Fox, William T. R. *A Continent Apart: The United States and Canada in World Politics*. Toronto: University of Toronto Press, 1985.

Garreau, Joel. *The Nine Nations of North America*. Boston: Houghton Mifflin, 1981.

Grant, George. *Lament for a Nation: The Defeat of Canadian Nationalism.* Toronto: McClelland and Stewart, 1965.

Gwyn, Richard. *The 49th Paradox: Canada in North America.* Toronto: McClelland and Stewart, 1986.

Holsti, Kal J. "Changes in the International System: Interdependence, Integration, and Fragmentation." In *Changes in the International System.* Edited by Ole Holsti, R. Siverson, and Alexander George. Boulder, CO: Westview Press, 1980.

Mahant, Edelgard E., and Graeme S. Mount. *An Introduction to Canadian-American Relations.* Toronto: Methuen, 1984.

Reich, Robert B. "The Rise of Techno-Nationalism." *The Atlantic Monthly* (May 1987):63–69.

Wrong, Hume. "The Canadian-United States Relationship, 1927-51." *International Journal* 31 (1976):529–545.

―――――――――――― 12 ――――――――――――

The Dilemma of U.S.
Policy in Central America
ANN KELLEHER

*[The U.S. approach to Nicaragua's Sandinista government] is one of friendly
cooperation with effective and timely economic aid.*

—President Jimmy Carter, 1979.

*The problems in Central America were not indigenous but caused by Castro
and the Soviet Union.*

—President Ronald Reagan, 1980.

The two quotations above imply perspectives that are incompatible but that provide a summary of alternative U.S. approaches to the problem of social change
in Central America. These views reflect the tension between two historical
trends of U.S. policy toward the region: mutual cooperation versus direct intervention in reaction to perceived outside interference threatening U.S. interests.
Both positions would agree, however, on the importance of Central America to
the United States. (Central America as a regional conflict area includes
Guatemala, El Salvador, and Nicaragua. Because the level of internally generated violence has been minimal in Honduras, it is not referred to directly in this
chapter. Costa Rica has largely escaped flagrant inequality and brutality.)

The polarized U.S. foreign-policy debate concerning Central America
reached a critical phase in the 1970s and continues into the 1980s. Recent history has confirmed the importance of John F. Kennedy's 1962 assertion: "Those
who make peaceful revolution impossible will make violent revolution inevitable." (Schlesinger and Kinser, 1983, 255) The irony of this statement having
been made by a president of the United States is that, in general, the U.S. government has supported unpopular, right-wing local elites, often to the point of

intervention. In spite of this one-sidedness in actual decisionmaking, a real debate divides opinion both in the U.S. government and its articulate public. This debate over Central American policy reflects the region's polarized politics.

The search for a middle way, a reformist alternative, complicates the debate. Most political perspectives in the United States share the hope that moderate accommodationist political parties could emerge in Central America. In actuality, both civilian and military reformers have surfaced in Central America, but few have become strong enough or survived long enough to initiate reforms and maintain more just societies. The irony in this is that U.S. intervention has often played a role in ending reform movements. The CIA's successful plot to overthrow the Arbenz government in Guatemala (discussed in detail later in this chapter) provides the most flagrant example. U.S. suspicions and lack of support helped undermine coups by military reformists in El Salvador during 1960 and 1979. At the time, these governments and the Guatemalan Arbenz regime were believed to be influenced by leftists and, therefore, to be dedicated to opposing U.S. interests in Central America.

Such U.S. intervention in reform attempts can be explained by pointing out that political cultures in Central America and the United States are fundamentally different. Misperceptions and policy disputes are the inevitable result of applying concepts derived from U.S. middle-class politics to systems characterized by mass poverty, perpetuated by rigid structural inequality. Central American reformers have not always looked or sounded like those in North America; they often are anti-American because of the traditional U.S. support for autocratic elites.

Such reformers are exemplified by General Augusto Cesar Sandino, who successfully held out against U.S. Marines and Nicaragua's National Guard from 1928 until he was assassinated in 1934 on the order of General Anastasio Somoza García. Subsequent distortions have termed Sandino a Marxist, but his revolution was against U.S. imperialism and the local clients it supported. It was not designed to be part of a worldwide revolution. In fact, the break with the El Salvadoran Marxist Augustín Farabundo Martí (Sandino's personal secretary for a time) was later explained by Martí to have occurred because Sandino refused to become a Marxist:

> My break with Sandino was not, as is sometimes said, for divergence of moral principles or opposing norms of conduct. . . . He would not embrace my communist programme. His banner was only that of national independence . . . not social revolution. I solemnly declare that General Sandino is the greatest patriot in the world. (Dunkerley 1982, 25)

As the preceding discussion implies, only those holding extreme positions would assess the Central American question as easy to comprehend and resolve. Differentiating reformers from revolutionaries has proven as difficult as finding a local faction capable of exercising power, friendly to the United States, and yet dedicated to social change. The following discussion will analyze the problem of achieving stability with justice in Central America as a complex and controversial issue, and a historical dilemma of increasing urgency.

By using the worldviews of system maintainers, reformers, and transformers as categories for organizing information and analyzing alternative perspectives, polemical debates can be avoided. For the student of U.S. foreign policy, this analytical framework provides an effective way of evaluating contending policy choices and the values and assumptions behind them.

Describing in detail the contending views and policy positions of system maintainers, reformers, and transformers requires a definition of the system itself. Because the United States has constituted an integral part of the Central American power structure, the system functions on an international level. A full explanation of this international political system, and of its proponents and opponents follows, but a major point should be made first. Given the pivotal role of the United States and a tendency toward macroanalysis of conflict situations, few studies of U.S.-Central American relations have highlighted a fundamental change occurring at the local village level in Central America. This underlying economic change provides an essential component for explaining why the ongoing tension in the region has burst into more violent conflict during the 1970s and 1980s. The following section begins with a description of change processes which have resulted in a substantial reduction in the quality of life in many Central American villages.

THE CENTRAL AMERICAN CONTEXT

Underlying Economic Change

In the past, the *hacienda* land-tenancy system was the dominant unit of production in Central American agriculture. It embodied mutual, though very unequal, benefits. Large landowners allowed peasants to farm small plots of land in exchange for labor. Despite its being supported by values and behavior patterns that reinforced rigid class distinctions, the *hacienda* provided peasants with a recognized social role and a measure of security.

Effects of Cash-Cropping
Since the 1950s, the rapid expansion of a market-oriented cash economy has largely displaced the traditional land-tenancy system. This has caused a fundamental change in the landowner-peasant relationship, involving the peasants' loss of economic security. The majority of the rural population lost the land they farmed, moving off it with virtually nothing and no government benefits to fill the void. The result has been intensified class-based inequality and increased population pressure on the land still available to peasants, leading to a violent and continuing cycle of civil unrest and repression.

The *hacienda* system still exists, but labor is no longer provided by a per-

Exhibit 12.1 Contribution of Major Commodity Exports to
Total Value of Merchandise Exports, 1970–1972 and 1978–1980
(in percentages)

	Commodities	1970–1972	1978–1980
El Salvador	Coffee, cotton	57.7	66.3
Guatemala	Coffee, cotton	43.4	47.6
Nicaragua	Coffee, cotton, beef	53.1	63.4

Source: 1981 Annual Report of the Inter-American Development Bank,
pp. 120–121.

manent, live-in workforce. Because demand for cash-crop exports has increased, the land once reserved for tenant food-production was converted to the
more profitable four "C's"; coffee, cotton, cane, and cattle. As Exhibit 12.1 indicates, increases in cash-crop production continued through the 1970s.

It was good business to abrogate peasants' rights and remove them from
the land, thereby creating a class of seasonal wage laborers. According to a 1981
Oxfam report, in El Salvador (where the process had gone the furthest) the landless peasantry grew from 12 percent of the rural population in 1960 to 40 percent
in 1975, and to 60 percent in 1980. (McCamant 1984) During approximately
the same time period, the number of acres used for growing coffee increased
from 308,000 in 1970 to 516,615 in 1983. (Stateman's Yearbook 1973-74, 889
and 1985-86, 440)

The process of driving peasants from land they traditionally worked is super-
ficially reminiscent of the eighteenth and nineteenth century enclosures in Great
Britain, but Central America offers little promise of ever being able to absorb
the rural poor into an industrial workforce. Instead, the slow growth in non-
agricultural sectors of Central American economies bodes ill for the peasantry,
which has suffered a marked deterioration in its quality of life. The difference
has not only been one of degree but also one of kind. Substantive change is
evidenced by the fact that a sizable majority of the rural population must now
eke out a living on marginal land. Also, they must hire out during the few
months a year they can find employment as agricultural laborers for approximately U.S.$1-2 per day, the same wage that has been paid for over a decade
despite significant cost-of-living increases. Survival, not simply lower-living
standards, has become the problem.

The structural change in Central American economies exacerbated existing
disparities in wealth to the point where peasants often struggled to get enough
food. Their reactions reflected the loss of stabilizing factors that were part of the
traditional relationship. Land-tenancy meant workers were directly dependent

on the landowners; coercion could take subtle and non-violent forms. Seasonal-wage laborers, however, had few ties to their employers. They formed unions and village cooperatives, which occasionally found it necessary to seize land and confront the elite. In responding to these threats, landowning oligarchs increasingly turned to the military. Peasant leaders were jailed or sometimes killed and some peasants began organizing guerrilla bands to fight back. It may be said that peasants became radicalized in defense of traditional land rights. In this context, the ideological terms "left" and "right" distort rather than explain; the "leftist" peasantry was fighting for traditional "conservative" goals such as the right to secure basic human needs.

Effects of Development Aid
In the Central American socioeconomic context, development-aid programs increased incentives to remove peasants from the land. Foreign-aid credits provided for diversification and expansion of cash-crop production as well as the development of a transportation infrastructure needed to move more crops to port facilities. In many situations, the result of this development was more landless peasants. Thus, human misery accompanied economic growth.

The Alliance for Progress, a U.S. development-aid program in the early 1960s, made an effort at redress by organizing peasants into village cooperatives eligible for aid credits. This, of course, put them in competition with large landowners and other business interests, the usual beneficiaries of foreign funding. The goal was admirable: establishing a village-level infrastructure so peasants could share in the benefits of a market economy. Projects like these, however, challenged the power structure. Most of these cooperatives suffered the same fate as others initiated by priests or village leaders. Local elites used the police and military to repress leaders of these efforts.

In addition to structural economic change, the marked deterioration in the peasants' quality of life may be attributed to population growth. Not only did the rural poor end up living on marginal land that no one else wanted, but a constant increase in population compounded their misery.

Since government services in peasant villages range from minimal to none, the quality of life is not apt to improve in future years. The data in Exhibit 12.2 reflect what is euphemistically called the quality of life of the average citizen in Central America (i.e., the rural poor).

Central America's International Political System

A tight partnership of U.S. economic and political interests with selected local elites constitutes the Central American international political system. This system, or context for events, has existed from the earliest days of U.S. involvement. Reinforced during the twentieth century, the relationship has become closer and more pervasive with the rise of the United States as an economic superpower. The term "banana republic" reflects the dominant role of U.S. companies in underdeveloped Central American economies during the early 1900s.

Exhibit 12.2 Social Statistics

	El Salvador	Guatemala	Nicaragua
Infant mortality	75/1,000	66/1,000	88/1,000
Population with safe drinking water	53%	39%	56%
Life expectancy	63 yrs.	59 yrs.	57 yrs.
Population per physician	3,870	2,600	1,590
Literacy rate	63%	47%	58%

Source: Ruth Leger Sivard, *World Military and Social Expenditures.* Leesburg, Virginia: World Priorities, 1981, pp. 28–29.

For example, in 1914 nearly a million acres of the most fertile land in Honduras were held by U.S. companies, primarily United Fruit Company, now United Brands. So important were U.S. fruit and banking interests to the Honduran economy that in 1918 U.S. dollars became legal tender. (LaFeber 1983)

Since those early years, economic-development projects have resulted in the need for a more subtle relationship between U.S. interests and local elites. Especially since the 1950s, economic-infrastructure ventures in transportation and communication development of service and light industries, and capital investment in new export crops indicate that U.S. influence can be indirect, relying on expertise and personal contacts. The U.S. role in El Salvador's October 1979 coup provides an example. As James Dunkerley pointed out in *The Long War* (1982), three army factions took part in the removal of President Romero from power: a right-wing group, younger field officers with a "reformist cast of mind," and a group closely tied to U.S. interests. Leading the last faction were two colonels, Jaime Abdul Gutierrez and José Guillermo García, who had substantial financial investments in the state telecommunications agency, ANTEL. García was ANTEL's president and Gutierrez its manager. The agency had close ties with the U.S. multinational AT&T and U.S. officials. According to one of the reformist offices, representatives of the United States successfully lobbied for including these two colonels in the ruling junta.

In assessing what this example implies about the nature of U.S. influence, one point to keep in mind is the small number of people involved in decision-making. Not only are Central American countries governed by elites, their societies are small in scale. The population of the largest, Guatemala, is only 6.5 million. Thus, U.S. influence does not necessarily reflect an insidious attempt to manipulate these political systems, but flows naturally from economic and political contacts with the few people in the power structure, all of whom know each other. Using the 1979 coup example again, the state telecommunications agency could not have existed without the capital, communications technology, and expertise provided by AT&T. Personal contacts accompany such a relationship.

This interaction constitutes a recent variation of an old dependency. Economic development in the nineteenth century was mainly in the form of investments in coffee and bananas for export. In this century, cotton, sugar, and (more recently) beef have been added, but the pattern remains essentially unchanged. Even when locally owned, cash-crop businesses need the technology and the export markets U.S. multinational corporations (MNCs) alone can provide. Add to this the fact that U.S. government officials often can swing the balance in disputes among local-elite factions, and the picture of U.S. power in Central America begins to emerge.

A SYSTEM-MAINTAINER PERSPECTIVE ON CENTRAL AMERICA

Three groups of people comprised what seemed an unshakable elite in Central America until the Nicaraguan Sandinistas successfully overthrew Somoza in 1979. The first group of maintainers consists of U.S. system maintainers with Central American business investments, many of whom have direct connections with policy-makers in the United States. Representatives of the U.S. government, which wields much of the influence of an imperial power but without overt control, constitute the second group. Membership in the third group, a local elite with significant political and economic power, has changed since the 1950s.

In the past, Central American oligarchies derived their economic strength from land ownership. While this pattern continues to exist in these primarily agricultural societies, another elite has emerged—the military. Ironically—from a U.S. perspective—the military's rise to power indirectly resulted from economic-development projects. Investments in new cash crop production forced thousands of peasants off the land. Fear of peasant unrest led to a growing reliance on the military to keep order. Coups placing high-ranking military officers in power became commonplace in Guatemala, El Salvador, and Honduras. Nicaragua already had a military-based regime. Instead of personal or oligarchic dictatorships with large landowners as a power base, military rule became institutionalized. It should be pointed out, however, that making too clear a distinction between the old and new elites is to miss their tendency to merge. Economic wealth can be derived from political power and vice versa. Most military officers formed a *nouveau riche* class by using their political positions to initiate and invest in development projects. Such projects received financing from U.S. MNCs, international aid programs, and the U.S. government. The military, now an economic elite, also bought land, thereby becoming part of the high-status landed class.

Order being their chief objective, the two U.S. groups in the system-maintenance coalition adapted to the new military elite, whose economic position was as dependent on trade as the old elite's had been. Yet the point must be made that the three groups in the U.S.-local-power structure did not always agree and indeed, if specific events are studied in detail, dissension characterized relations both within and among the groups. Differences arose over such issues as whether to hold elections and which development projects should be financed; however, a common interest in maintaining their position overrode other considerations. In spite of internal squabbles, the net effect was a monopoly of power, until Nicaragua's Sandinistas formed the first stable government without any participation by these three system-maintainer groups.

The three system-maintainer groups in this U.S.-Central America policy arena share a legitimizing idea that economic progress depends on political stability under the existing system. This perspective makes two assumptions. First, it adopts and depends upon a free-trade growth model of economic development. An examination of this model quickly reveals its appeal to people in control of and benefiting from existing arrangements. To achieve short-term growth, the model emphasizes investment projects that are relatively large-scale, trade-oriented, and often privately owned. This means the economy must be open to the operations of MNCs since they are the best or often the sole source of capital investment, processing technology, and overseas markets. Second, this perspective assumes that local elites cooperating with outside interests can best direct the economic-development process. Societies, presumed not yet ready for an open pluralist democracy, need a period of tutelage. Therefore perpetuation of the present system is, in the long run, supposed to result in an advanced standard of living and possibly more democratic institutions.

A variation on this perspective bases the elite's privileged position on their assumption that the masses are naturally inferior. Assuming a tutelage role justifies the basis for rule and the need for permanent leadership. At its best, such a perception results in a benign noblesse oblige; but, at its worst, a vast majority of the population is subjugated to harsh controls and limited freedoms. Both consequences reflect a class bias foreign to U.S. members of the system-maintenance coalition. To them, such an attitude is unseen, ignored, or accepted as inevitable in societies "not yet as advanced" as that of a "developed" country. These two rationales for perpetuating elite rule are congruent at the practical level. Just as "protected infant industries" seem never to become free adults, those tutored seem never to advance to the point where they "graduate."

A third rationale may be added to the mix of ideas constituting the system-maintainer perspective. Especially in the eyes of the U.S. elites, the fear of a Communist takeover reinforces the need for elite rule. Such an emphasis adds an ideological component that rationalizes military repression, not just as a temporary expedient to unrest but as an ongoing practice needed to fight any leftist movement. This rationale is fully understood by the United States. It ensures continued U.S. involvement and support for local military leaders' use of force as a tool for upholding their political interests. The specter of Communist subversion highlights the fact that the three groups in the system-maintenance coali-

tion need each other. A 1974 statement by Anastasio Somoza reflects this mutuality of interests: "Nicaragua is totally aligned with the United States and the
Western World." (LaFeber 1983, 226)

A SYSTEM-REFORMER'S VIEW OF U.S.-CENTRAL AMERICAN RELATIONS

Critics in Central America and elsewhere doubt the sincerity of the system maintainers. Most reject the idea of a future in which democratic practices will widen
the system to allow new classes to receive political and economic benefits as a
myth used to legitimize the status quo. System reformers advocate an immediate opening of the power structures and the establishment of social-welfare
states. This might mean encouraging competing political parties, developing a
free press, holding elections, initiating land reform, providing rural services
(such as basic medical care, schools, and literacy campaigns), and developing
a more pluralistic political and economic system. These changes are seen as
cosmetic, but are aimed at bringing about a real sharing of power within Central
American societies. At various times in the past, the ruling elites have organized
elections, sponsored unions, and promised social services, but decisionmaking
power was not shared and few new leaders emerged. The middle class and
peasantry remained powerless and, for the most part, outside the centers of
political and economic decisionmaking. Leading reform advocates in Central
America have usually come from the ranks of the small professional middle
class—university professors, teachers, journalists, and lawyers, many of whom
have been educated in the United States. Christian and Social Democratic parties have represented the views of the system reformers in many Central American states.

From the mid-1940s to 1954, Guatemala provides the one historical
example of an ongoing reformist regime. The story of liberalization under the
Arévalo and Arbenz presidencies, as well as the untimely end to the Arbenz
regime engineered by a U.S.-sponsored local elite, is reviewed briefly at the
end of this section. This precedent, and the less dramatic demise of shorter-lived
reformist attempts, raises questions as to the probable impact of the two current
presidents espousing reformist goals, José Napoleón Duarte of El Salvador and
Vinicio Cerezo of Guatemala. One position cites the existence of these two
elected heads of state as evidence of liberalization. Critics point out that survival alone does not prove significant change has taken place. Indeed, it may be
indicative of the opposite, of an inability or unwillingness to challenge the
dominant military elite that "still holds the trump." (Lowenthal 1986, 544) In
future analyses of the reformers in this region, the accuracy of these contending
views may be judged to be demonstrated by a decline in death-squad activity,
an increase in power sharing, and changes in the distribution of economic goods
and services.

Historically, liberal reformers have been politically weak, possibly reflecting their lack of economic resources. This conclusion may be a product of hindsight or of a generalization from net effect, which ignores specific events. There have been times when reforming elites have gained enough power to influence substantial change; then their efforts have been thwarted by the system-maintainer coalition, which may perceive a threat to its privileged position. A recent example occurred in 1979, when a reforming faction of the El Salvadoran military took power in a coup. The conspirators announced plans to enact basic changes, including free elections, land reform, the prosecution of human-rights violators, and amnesty for political prisoners. Official U.S. State Department reaction was favorable, almost enthusiastic, but closer examination of this situation reveals a contradiction in U.S. policy. The Carter administration did nothing to show opposition to continuing death-squad activity. This acceptance of repressive actions persisted as the junta's right wing maneuvered reformist and other civilian elements into marginal positions.

At best, it can be said the United States had parallel policies. The United States issued statements supporting reform and warning against a right-wing coup, while at the same time continuing business as usual with El Salvador's top military commanders who were mostly hardline system maintainers. The U.S. position became clearer when, in February 1980, Archbishop Romero sent a letter to President Carter asking him to reconsider his offer of $50 million in aid because of intensified death-squad activity. This request was refused. According to Enrique Baloyra (1982, 99), Secretary of State Cyrus Vance explained that the junta had proven itself reformist, most of the aid was economic, and the United States would make sure the military aid would not be used in abuse of human rights.

If the current leaders of El Salvador and Guatemala are ever to achieve genuine reform during their tenure in office, they will need full U.S. governmental support, something such reformers have not been granted in the past. The threat of political demise has always faced Central American reformers, yet this difficulty pales in comparison to the promise of violence and repression, a menace of particular relevance in recent years. The use of death squads by a faction of the ruling elite in El Salvador and Guatemala has occasionally elicited protests by U.S. political leaders and concerned, activist citizen groups. However, when fed information from the local elite, U.S. policymakers often confuse reformers with system transformers, labeling both leftist revolutionaries. Therefore, U.S. political leaders have, at least in the past, tacitly accepted the use of death squads to maintain order and contain Communist activities. The activist interest groups are divided on this issue. Some side with U.S. government policy, which suggests that we must accept some evil to prevent the expansion of Soviet-style systems. Others, and this number is increasing, urge the United States to support governments that intend to improve the quality of life in their societies and to reject ideological requirements (i.e., anti-communism) for U.S. support.

Central American liberal reformers reflect a version of liberalism which, in its institutional expression, closely resembles that found in the United States. Individual rights are to be expressed in a pluralist political system with independent courts as well as freely elected legislatures and executives. These institutions should have the power to limit and indeed subordinate the military. Thus, the most important elements, if a liberal system is to work, include a civilian president with the political base to exercise actual control over the military and police, and an independent, competent judicial system. Thus far these elements have proven difficult to achieve in many developing states of Central America.

This discussion makes distinctions among three related but separately defined terms: Liberalism, liberal reform, and liberal parties. Liberalism refers to a specific ideology that seeks to maximize an individual's political rights. As redefined in the mid-nineteenth century, liberalism advocates political institutions limited by and designed to protect free speech, religion, press, assembly, parties, elections, and the due process of law. This curb on governmental power and respect for the individual is reflected in John Stuart Mill's ringing justification for freedom of dissent, still one of the most articulate theoretical statements of liberalism.

Liberal reformers advocate opening the political decisionmaking process to include groups previously denied access. In the Central American context, widening political participation means allowing dissenting groups to organize and take non-violent action without fear of torture or death.

A cursory examination of Central American political history may lead to the assumption that liberals have actually exercised power. Indeed, "liberal" parties did control governments during the early decades of this century. Central American liberal parties expressed an economic liberalism, meaning private economic growth with little governmental action, especially government interference designed to bring about social reform. Although Nicaragua's Liberal Party membership once included Augusto Sandino, a political reformer in his early years, he, like others, eventually parted company with such parties whose interests inclined more to making profits than sharing power. Closer analysis reveals these liberal parties were actually a faction of the ruling oligarchy. They did not advocate popular participation in government and this, plus the fact that these parties operated in a political environment where elections (if held at all) did not matter much, meant they did not attempt to mobilize a mass following. Instead, they articulated positions for one faction of the ruling elite, positions that usually coincided with U.S. political and economic interests at a particular time.

Liberal parties, as "modernizers" in Central America, supported secularization and economic development. The latter, however, depended on U.S. capital investment. Liberal rule proved as elitist as that of the more conservative parties; in some cases, it resulted in the loss of influence by leaders of the Roman Catholic Church and the expropriation of peasant lands for agricultural production for export markets. Understandably, peasants were not enthusiastic about such "progress" and periodically fought back in the late nineteenth and early twentieth centuries. Each revolt was ruthlessly suppressed, resulting in the deaths of thousands. No subsequent attempts were made to placate the discontented majority of the population by actually reforming the political and economic systems. Instead, repression continued and long-term consequences included the implementation of policies aimed at upgrading the military and creating special police and security forces to keep order in the countryside.

Nicaragua provides an example of this type of "liberal" rule. Under the Somozas in the 1930s and 1940s, the Liberal Party eroded the Catholic Church's power and encouraged cotton and sugar production for export. Cotton and sugar have an even more negative impact than coffee because their production in Central America is more capital- than labor-intensive. Large numbers of peasants were displaced from their land and forced into the money economy to compete for depressed wages.

The foregoing discussion demonstrates the fact that equality, and by extension political participation, was not always valued in Central American political cultures. In the United States, equality, in practice, has meant expanding participation in the political system by modifying existing institutions, such as removing barriers to voting. This sort of moderate reform did not become part of the political agenda in Central America until the rise of a middle class in the late 1940s.

Guatemala in the early 1950s provides the most prominent example of a government dedicated to liberal reform. The attempt by President Arbenz to broaden the base of political participation, and his subsequent failure, was a watershed in the history of reform and the key to subsequent Central American history. With the 20/20 vision of hindsight, it is clear the U.S. government misread Arbenz as a leftist revolutionary. Such a mistake can be explained by his inclusion of Marxist union leaders in his government and the pronounced anti-U.S. bias in many of his public statements. Yet the consequences of the U.S. interventions resulting in the failure of the Arbenz regime continue to influence Central American affairs. Tragic is hardly a strong-enough word to describe the ever escalating cycles of violence which have menaced most Central American states. In many Central American countries, landed elites have lost their power to a repressive military, U.S. hopes for orderly, constructive change have proven ephemeral, and interminable suffering has been experienced by thousands in the middle class and peasantry. Arbenz' reform attempt provides a useful case study of how both system maintainers and system reformers operate in practice.

Reform in Guatemala: A Clash of Interests and Images

Central America's one sustained reform movement occurred in Guatemala from 1944 to 1954. This experiment in substantial but peaceful change ended abruptly on June 27, 1954, when, threatened by civil war, President Jacobo Arbenz Guzmán resigned and was hustled off to exile in Mexico. The opening of U.S. archives has revealed more than simple complicity by the U.S. Central

Intelligence Agency (CIA). The CIA instigated, planned, financed, and controlled the overthrow of President Arbenz. A careful analysis of such interference illustrates why and how the system-maintainer coalition has for so long dominated Central America. Such analysis also provides necessary background for understanding the present level of political polarization throughout much of Central America.

President Arbenz inherited the reformist program of his predecessor, Juan José Arévalo, the first popularly elected president of Guatemala. The Arévalo administration's accomplishments seem minimal in retrospect, but at the time these reforms were monumental—the first country-wide attempt to combat grinding economic deprivation and decades of repressive personalized rule. When Arévalo took power, Guatemala had an illiteracy rate of approximately 75 percent, agricultural workers—the vast majority of the population—earned less than U.S.$87 per year, 2 percent of the population owned 72 percent of the arable land, leaving 90 percent of the population with 15 percent of the land, and peasants owed large landowners 150 days of labor a year "in lieu of taxes." (Schlesinger and Kinzer 1983, 38, 50) In addition, coffee and bananas provided virtually all foreign-exchange earnings. This meant much of the arable land did not produce crops for local consumption.

National problems and conditions associated with maldevelopment required the broadest of measures. Arévalo's reforms included a social-security system, provision of medical facilities in rural as well as urban areas, a national education system, economic-infrastructure projects such as roads and sewers in the cities, a new constitution with thirty-four separate guarantees of individual freedom, and the establishment of a national assembly, which was given power to promulgate legislation to promote rights and freedoms. In hindsight, these measures seem innocuous and hardly revolutionary, but in the context of time and place such reforms implied a direct threat to prevailing privilege and practice. The latter interpretation became a conventional wisdom for system maintainers in Guatemala and the United States. They saw system transformers in reformist guise in spite of Arévalo's prodigious efforts to leave intact the landowners' property, economic power, and social position.

The Guatemalan-elite component of the system-maintainer coalition actively opposed the reformist government. The elite's reactions included social opposition in the Chamber of Commerce and Industry, legal demonstrations, and several coup attempts. Most of the upper class saw the reforms as Communist-inspired, too expensive, unfair, and potentially destabilizing to their notion of order. They concluded chaos and revolution would inevitably result if these reforms were allowed to continue. To forestall such degeneration into lawlessness, General Federico Ponce Vaides, the old regime's last president, roamed throughout Central America trying to raise troops for an invasion of Guatemala. (Immerman 1982)

The military engaged in especially active and clandestine opposition, participating in at least two dozen plots and attempted coups during Arévalo's six-year term. These attacks ended in a particularly bloody insurrection before the 1950 election. The constitution expressly forbade military men to run for office and all soldiers had to pledge loyalty to democracy and the principle of elections. Yet, the notion that the military should run the country retained its vitality. This aspect of the political culture forestalled development of confidence in the more pluralistic competitive-party process that Arévalo sought to create.

The Labor Code presented by Arévalo drew the specific wrath of U.S. economic and political groups in the system-maintainer coalition. Although the Labor Code included provisions taken for granted in the United States, it nevertheless was cited as evidence of Communist influence in the Arévalo administration. Based on the U.S. Wagner Act, the code established the right to organize, bargain collectively, and strike. It set minimum-pay scales, regulated child and female labor, and guaranteed workers a sympathetic hearing in newly created courts to adjudicate labor disputes. The code also provided some protection for employers by forbidding unions on all but the largest *haciendas*.

Predictably, a series of strikes erupted in the late 1940s, affecting U.S. economic interests. Since the United Fruit Company monopolized virtually all U.S. investment in Guatemala, it bore the brunt of new union assertiveness. Attention focused on this company because of its overriding importance to the Guatemalan economy. By far the largest property owner, United Fruit, known in Guatemala as "la frutera," controlled about 550,000 acres. It also owned Puerto Barrios, the country's only Atlantic port, and virtually all the railroads. According to a 1951 International Development Bank report, the United Fruit Company's monopoly railroad in Guatemala charged the highest rates in the world. United Fruit exercised an almost complete monopoly on transportation and communication systems through numerous side operations, such as the country's only telegraph service. The only economic infrastructure of some significance not owned by United Fruit was Guatemala's single electric-power plant; this was controlled by a second U.S. firm. (Schlesinger and Kinzer 1983)

United Fruit's economic stranglehold resulted from decades of collusion with the indigenous political and economic elites controlling Guatemala. Deals were made with what one ex-employee called the most pliable and corrupt government in Central America. For years, United Fruit had enjoyed exemption from taxes and import duties, and a guarantee of no unions and, therefore, of low wages. In return, the company provided better benefits than most employers, including housing, medical, and educational facilities for its workers. It seemed to some, however, that exploitation and manipulation accompanied such generosity. One company policy required "all persons of color to give the right of way to whites and remove their hats while talking to them." (Schlesinger and Kinzer 1983, 71) The workers of Guatemala supported Arévalo's reforms as a way of breaking the dependency on United Fruit and the United States. They responded unsympathetically to United Fruit's cries of unfairness and injustice. However, United Fruit's protests appealed to the upper class, whose fortunes were tied to the company. As pressure continued on

United Fruit to increase wages, its executives at one point threatened to withdraw from Guatemala. They contended that the New Labor Code seriously interfered with the company's plans for future growth. Henry Cabot Lodge, whose family owned stock in United Fruit, was one of several U.S. legislators to denounce the Guatemalan government on the floor of Congress. U.S. legislators defined the labor agitation in Guatemala as a political dispute instigated not by genuine worker grievances but by Communist unions, the government, or, most likely, both forces working together to upset U.S. interests. Acceptance of this position crossed lines and included influential Democrats and Republicans in both House and Senate. The Truman administration joined the fray by protesting Guatemala's labor code and ordering the Federal Bureau of Investigation to begin dossiers on that country's government ministers. The purpose was to compile data on suspected Communist connections and activities.

The United Fruit Company made two secret but highly significant moves to create support for their position within the United States. As documented in Chapter 6 of Schlesinger and Kinzer's *Bitter Fruit* (1983), the company hired a counsel for public relations, which began a campaign publicizing the company's troubles and attributing them to a Communist threat at the back door of the United States. At the same time, articles appeared in leading journals, news stories proliferated, and all-expense-paid fact-finding trips to Central America were organized for public and private decisionmakers. The strategy had a significant impact on U.S. political and economic leaders and on the public. When the Arévalo administration took positions favorable to the United States, such as supporting the Korean War, they went unreported in most media.

In addition, United Fruit hired a lobbyist, the ebullient and well-connected Thomas G. Corcoran. A member of Franklin Roosevelt's early brain trust, Corcoran retained close contacts with political leaders in Washington. For example, in the early 1950s one of his good friends was appointed director of the CIA. Such public-private sector connections did not end with the departure of the Truman administration. Eisenhower's assistant secretary of state for inter-American affairs, John Moors Cabot, owned stock in United Fruit, as did his brother, a former company president. Through the use of media and personal networks, United Fruit, monopolized the flow of information and created a conventional wisdom that reinforced the system-maintainer position. This stifled the voices of the few specialists in U.S. political circles who interpreted Arévalo's administration as justifiably reformist.

Amid an atmosphere of suspicion in the United States and elite hostility in Guatemala, Jacobo Arbenz Guzmán succeeded Arévalo as president with 60 percent of the votes cast. (Immerman 1982) The November 1950 election marked the first time in the country's history that executive authority was lawfully transferred. As inheritor of the reform program, Arbenz took the next step and attacked the underlying cause of poverty and political elitism. He adopted land reform as his administration's major goal. In so doing he sealed his own fate and that of Guatemala's hard-won reforms. Events from this point until the

1954 U.S.-controlled coup are characteristic of a classic tragedy. Arbenz may not have had heroic character traits, but he was caught in circumstances beyond his control. In being true to his principles, he solidified the forces against him.

Such an assessment comes only with hindsight. At the time, Guatemala's leaders hoped the U.S. government, United Fruit, and the local elite would find the reforms essential and acceptable. In June 1952, after much study and deliberation, including many attempts to placate the landowners, the National Assembly enacted an agricultural-reform bill. By March 1953, over 200,000 acres of uncultivated United Fruit land was expropriated by government decree and became part of over 900,000 acres that were distributed among some 90,000 peasants. The government collected 5 percent of the value of produce in payment for the land and provided technical assistance to the new owners.

Arévalo had aroused suspicions among system maintainers; Arbenz confirmed these fears. Enemies inside and outside Guatemala decided the government and its policies had to go. Most accounts of this era suggest that the overthrow of Arbenz was the result of a CIA-sponsored operation utilizing disgruntled Guatemalan citizens. President Eisenhower approved plans for Operation Success in the summer of 1953, making his final decision in early 1954. Carlos Castillo Armas, a former army colonel, was chosen commander and, by implication, Guatemala's next president. Armas's credentials included a military background. The fact that he looked like an Indian was seen as an additional advantage. He had no particular ideology, but as the leader of one of the earlier coup attempts, he had been condemned to death, escaping only at the last moment. Above all, he seemed reasonable; i.e., he would take orders.

The covert operation needed other components. Nicaragua and Honduras provided training and staging areas. The theater commander, John Peurifoy, arrived as U.S. ambassador to Guatemala in October 1953. An especially colorful personality who even sported a pistol occasionally, Peurifoy had worked with the CIA while ambassador to Greece. There, he had effectively used heavy-handed methods to help establish a right-wing coalition in power.

Finally, all that remained was a pretext for invasion. The Arbenz government itself obliged by receiving a shipment of Czechoslovakian weapons. The U.S. ambassador knew they were destined for the Guatemalan army, which was hardly Communist-dominated. Military demands for new arms had built up over the years because the traditional supplier, the United States, had stopped shipments in 1948 and had convinced others to join an arms embargo of Guatemala. Arbenz had no plans to arm union members or other popular groups, or to attack the Panama Canal or neighboring countries. High-ranking U.S. officials charged that Arbenz did plan such actions, filling the world's media with an intense propaganda campaign. To add fuel to the fire, President Eisenhower and Secretary of State John Foster Dulles used the weapons as proof of Soviet complicity. The real threat, they concluded, was Soviet involvement in the Americas, which would only increase if Guatemala became a Communist dictatorship.

The general public seldom gets a chance to discover the secret machinations of its government officials and private businessmen. This unique case study illustrates how the Central American power structure works. While it may obscure inherent differences among the three system-maintainer groups, Guatemala's tragedy exposes significant factors in their relationship. All three groups perceived an immediate threat demanding action. This stressful situation revealed real attitudes and power unadorned by lip service and meaningless gestures. In this particular case, patterns emerge which can help in analyzing contemporary events in Central America and elsewhere in the Third World.

With the Communist connection made as early as the late 1940s, Guatemala became part of the the U.S. global battle to contain communism. U.S. policymakers saw a small country, traditionally under U.S. tutelage, in danger of becoming international communism's next victim. This issue united prominent factions of U.S. opinion. All they held dear—values and a way of life—seemed under siege. Already, this high-stakes struggle had caused thousands of U.S. deaths in Korea. Subversion in Central America had to be stopped before it led to such dire consequences. In the rigid, bipolar world perceived by U.S. officials, it made sense to have a better-safe-than-sorry policy. A net loss in U.S. power meant a net gain for the Soviet Union. In this context, an attack on U.S. interests constituted an attack on the United States itself and a direct benefit to the enemy. U.S. policymakers felt they could not afford the luxury of fine distinctions between reformers and revolutionaries. The risk of a covert operation was worth the larger risk of potential Soviet influence so close to the United States.

This 1950s logic still guides U.S. policy, particularly in Central America. However, in today's multipolar world, alternative perspectives can be equally convincing. Clearly, one-dimensional definitions of U.S. interest no longer result in effective policy. Anti-communism must be balanced with other priorities, such as regional and local stability. Often, this means negotiating with Marxists rather than fighting with them.

Guatemala's ongoing tragedy lies in the fact that successful reform requires an accommodation process, which, in turn, depends on and reinforces a spirit of compromise. Generating constructive relationships among enemies takes a long time. If continued from the 1940s, peaceful change may have developed a track record. Now the obstacles are so much greater. They include greatly increased population pressure on physical resources and a legacy of hate from decades of systematic and violent repression.

From a system-maintainer point of view, the 1954 U.S. intervention secured a pro-U.S. government at a time of Cold War tension and with a minimum use of force. What more can be expected of a policy? Long-term conflicts are seldom completely resolved. Policies must change over time to meet new contingencies. As a practical matter, decisionmakers in the early 1950s cannot be held accountable for future contingencies. At minimum, the maintainers preserved U.S. power for twenty more years. On the other hand, from the vantage point of the 1980s, one legacy of Guatemala's suffering is the current U.S. policy dilemma. In the words of a U.S. state department official, "What we'd give to have an Arbenz now. We are going to have to invent one, but all the candidates are dead." (Immerman 1982, 157)

A SYSTEM-TRANSFORMER PERSPECTIVE ON CENTRAL AMERICA

In Guatemala, reformers pitted themselves against an entrenched and vindictive political structure and failed. Sooner or later a hard choice had to be made, a choice between continuing the risky business of challenging the established system from within or attacking it from without. The latter decision became increasingly reasonable. The cause was considered important enough and the risk to reformers of losing either life or liberty great enough. Similar battles have been fought throughout Central America. Nicaragua provides an illustrative example of how reformers, once thwarted, move to a transformation strategy. The three founders of the Sandinista National Liberation Front were first student activists working for reforms. After imprisonment, torture, and the frustrations associated with the failure of reform efforts, these leaders became Marxist revolutionaries. (Booth 1982) Once this revolutionary path was chosen, violence was met with violence in an interactive and escalating cycle. This violent and polarized political environment has led to the triumph of system transformers in Nicaragua, the current civil war in El Salvador, and the seething undercurrents of political repression and terrorism in Guatemala.

Recent system-transformation movements in Central America have grassroots origins. The peasants' lot became insufferable as the growth of market economies erased what rights they had as land tenants. Forced off their land to make room for an expansion of cash crops for export, peasants had to scratch out an existence raising food on marginal land. In reaction to worsening economic conditions, the poor organized in a variety of ways and attempted to change their conditions. Governing elites responded with violent repression, coinciding with and fueled by middle-class political activism. In the cities, the cry of injustice was taken up by the intelligensia, journalists, and teachers, as well as others in the disenfranchised professional classes.

Since the first reactions to oppression were spontaneous and idiosyncratic, a variety of groups emerged with a wide range of Christian and secular ideas. This range was reflected in the variety of economic and political ideologies espoused by the activist groups. Their unifying assumption was that the economically exploitative system needed a fundamental change. Thus, a political revolution—a redistribution of power—was essential to accomplishing a redistribution of wealth. Most of these groups felt that only after a total social transformation could justice be achieved by and for the oppressed poor. Their goal is seen as democratic in its truest sense, given that poor peasants are the overwhelming majority in Central America.

Such revolutionary ideas and actions are usually considered to be Marxist.

Many system transformers in Central America have accepted this designation without knowing much about Karl Marx's political and economic theories. Since class-based, exploitative, structural inequality exists in the region, Marxism provides an appropriate analytical framework for revolutionary leaders. It explains underlying reasons for unyielding poverty and justifies the fight against it. Pointing out the intimate relationship between economic wealth and political power, Marxism considers social classes not simply as differentiated levels of income, as the U.S. designations high, medium, and low imply. This focus on power carries over into an analysis of international structural inequality. Thus, experiences of Central American revolutionaries can be linked with those of oppressed people worldwide. All see themselves as brutalized by a system of international exploitation emanating primarily from the United States, the leading capitalist state with worldwide economic connections. For many seeking a restructuring of the international system, Marxism provides a global legitimacy for revolution in Central America.

The fact that some Central American revolutionaries use Marxist concepts to analyze conditions in their societies does not mean that they are all doctrinaire Marxist practitioners. Little evidence exists of their rigid adherence to prescribed dogma. On the contrary, they realize that Marxist thought does not address their total experience. Most Central American revolutionaries have adopted a more pragmatic view of their situation and more flexible policy strategies aimed at changing political and economic conditions. While it may not be true for all elements in Nicaragua's Sandinista government, traditional or orthodox Marxism—with its rationale for centralized power, secular philosophy, and emphasis on industrial workers—has been rejected as not completely relevant to an agrarian society with Christian values.

Liberation Theology

The systemic analysis of power relationships and the predictive value of Marxist socialism defines its appeal to Central American intellectuals intent on system transformation. However, the ideas of the educated leaders must merge with the beliefs held by ordinary people if a revolutionary movement is to prove viable. Since a spiritualistic yet traditional Catholicism characterizes the beliefs of the majority of people in Central America, revolutionary Marxism must become compatible with Christianity. To those acquainted with the hostility toward religion of European Marxism, this compatibility seems impossible; however, liberation theology provides an intellectually and emotionally satisfying merger of these two value systems. Whether this unity is a formal theology or simply the statements of local priests advocating social justice, the result has been a revolutionary movement of demonstrable political potency. It constitutes Central America's contribution to Marxism in action.

The themes of economic equality and the revolutionary role of Christians in an unjust society are prominent in the words of Father Rutilio Grande, the first priest killed in the present cycle of bloodshed in El Salvador. His words challenged all of his countrymen to seek a more just world:

> So the material world is for all without limits. It's a common table with a large tablecloth like this Eucharist. With a spot for everyone. And so everyone will come up to it, a tablecloth and food for all. Christ had a reason for making a supper the sign of his kingdom. . . . And he celebrated it the eve of his total commitment.
>
> It is practically illegal to be a true Christian . . . in our country. Because . . . the world around us is radically based on an established disorder, before which the mere proclamation of the gospel is subversive.
>
> I'm afraid that if Jesus of Nazareth came back, coming down from Galilee to Judea, that is from Chalatenango to San Salvador, I daresay he would not get as far as Apopa, with his preaching and actions. They would stop him in Guazapa and jail him there.
>
> In Christianity today you have to be ready to give up your life to serve a just order. (Berryman 1984, 120–121)

Many peasant Christian communities and village cooperatives have interpreted the issue differently, denouncing violence and choosing peaceful strategies of change. The goal is self-sufficiency, which infers a denial of the state power structure. Ignoring the larger politicoeconomic system rather than fighting it fits better with the aims of such peasant communities. Tragically, however, death squads have not differentiated between peasants who use violent or non-violent tactics. Such distinctions are lost amid the frantic turmoil in Central America's polarized and violent political environment.

THE FUTURE OF CENTRAL AMERICA

Caught in a dilemma it has long ignored and now cannot avoid, the United States continues an unworkable policy in Central America. In supporting both the Contras in Nicaragua and the reformist presidents of Guatemala and El Salvador, the United States performs an old balancing act, espousing reformist goals while actively supporting more parochial national interests and the local elites willing to cooperate with the United States to maintain power. This contradictory approach seemed to work in the decades before those attempting to transform the system became strong enough to expose its flaws. Now, the United States retains a policy that is at cross purposes with itself, given the region's violent polarized politics and the existence of Nicaragua's Sandinista government.

Sorting out a new U.S. policy will prove extremely difficult for at least two reasons. First, the U.S. government and private interests have been part of the very system requiring change. Thus, a new policy necessitates breaking with decades of precedent, vested interests, and local supporters. A second major problem is the extremely polarized environment in Central America. While there are some signs of life in current reformers, the clash between system maintainers and transformers promises to continue for the foreseeable future.

Foreign policy is not made in a vacuum. Interest groups within the United States and external actors have varying degrees of influence on the decision-making debate. The United States, as a global power, must take into account how its actions in Central America complicate relations with other states that have a greater or lesser stake in the conflict. The seamless web of interacting and conflicting interests includes European allies as well as the Soviet bloc, but the group of states with the greatest concern are those nearest the potentially widening struggle. Mexico, Panama, Colombia, Venezuela, and Costa Rica have formed a working group in an attempt to provide a viable alternative to U.S. policy. The Contadora group is named after a Panamanian island where its original members—Mexico, Panama, Colombia, and Venezuela—first met, in 1983, to draft a peace treaty to which Nicaragua agreed in 1984. The treaty stipulates the withdrawal of all forces and support from outside the region, and it commits countries in the region to mutual non-interference. It also provides for free elections in all Central American countries. Most U.S. allies have accepted this framework for peace via regional neutralization.

The Debate in the United States

Perhaps one of the more constructive recent developments has been the open debate within the United States itself. Liberal innocence no longer obscures past cozy arrangements between the United States and repressive regimes. Conjuring up the spectre of Communist infiltration does not generate the overwhelming fear and aggressive reactions that it once did. Contending positions on U.S. policy options in this region fall into categories echoing the three worldviews in Central America itself.

System Maintainers
Moderate system maintainers hold that the present local elites must be supported as long as insurgency continues. Only then will some effort to broaden their political base make sense. At present, shifting support to include groups left of center would open the power structure to Cuban and Soviet influence. Certain Social Democrats in El Salvador, for example, share a pronounced anti-U.S. bias. In the past, leftists in the region, whatever their label, have proven a conduit for international communism. The Soviet Union via Cuba remains poised to exploit any opening.

To system maintainers, the argument that past actions by the United States have caused present leftist hostility misses the point. For instance, whether the Sandinistas were open to friendly relations with the United States from 1979 to 1980 cannot change subsequent events. In addition, Marxists, whether of grassroots origin or not, whether sanctioned by Catholic priests or not, share a common perception of the United States as the mainstay of global inequality. Thus, it is futile to hope for cooperation with them once in power.

So the question remains, can reformers be trusted? An added consideration is their lack of a power base. The region's class-based and extremist politics remain volatile and unstable. Changing local clients in this situation is a risk successive U.S. administrations have been loath to take. It is better to be safe than sorry.

The reality of the U.S.-USSR global rivalry transcends other concerns, since not managing it well will have the most devastating consequences. Any perceived U.S. weakness may be exploited; therefore, political ties to local clients who support the United States must continue to be strengthened. A situation must not develop where no other recourse exists but to take on the Soviet Union directly. In this global struggle, Central America is recognized worldwide as having a special relationship to the United States. Weakness in this region bodes ill for the ability of the United States to defend its friends and allies in other parts of the world.

In the immediate future, therefore, the only reasonable policy remains continued support for the ruling elites in Guatemala and El Salvador in their battle against insurgents. The military contains unpleasant extremists but their dependence on the United States means that leverage can be applied over time. Also, the United States believes opposition to the Sandinista regime in Nicaragua must continue. Aid to the Contras is negotiable; however, if dropped, some alternative action to neutralize the influence of Nicaragua's present government must take its place.

System Reformers
System-reform advocates in the United States often envision an opening to the left as a necessary move toward long-term peace in Central America. Such an abrupt departure from past U.S. involvement in the region could finally reconcile policy with practice, thus resolving the contradiction of sounding reformist while supporting repressive regimes. In response to the objection that the reformists in Central America are weak, advocates point out the existence of viable reform movements in the past. Given their use of anti-U.S. rhetoric to build domestic support, however, U.S. officials perceived a threat and actively opposed them. For instance, the Carter administration blocked the participation of Social Democrats in El Salvador's October 1979 reformist cabinet. Perhaps the example with the severest consequences was the CIA's overthrow of Guatemala's President Arbenz in 1954. Blinded by its global quarrel with the Soviet Union, U.S. "realist" policy has failed to see or has tragically misjudged reformers struggling for power in Central America.

In addition to a preoccupation with the global balance of power, a lack of knowledge about this region has contributed to a mistaken U.S. policy. Very few people in the United States knew about or had interests in Central America until the region seemed to explode into conflict in the 1970s. Therefore, a small number of military experts, government officials, and businesspeople with financial interests in the region's cash-crop economies, controlled U.S. policy. Central American policy escaped the usual comprehensive scrutiny various interest groups, political parties, and the academic community has applied to policy in other regions of the world. Also, as a consequence of the region's power structure, U.S. decisionmakers derived virtually all their information on events in Central America from their local clients.

In this political climate, most meaningful economic- and political-reform efforts died before reaching maturity, even when initiated by public or private experts from U.S. agencies. Of course Christian and Social Democratic parties had difficulty building support, when the United States used its considerable influence to prop up the oligarchy and military elites. In one sense, the strength of right-wing military factions grew artificially, stimulated by support from outside the region. U.S. aid and training for military and police personnel provided the means to repress reformers and transformers alike.

System reformers believe this policy must stop and, at the very least, local reformers should be allowed to take on uncompromising military elites without outside interference. In their view, a responsible U.S. policy would include applying substantial and persistent pressure for land reform and the purge of those in the military involved in torture and death-squad activity. As a parallel to this shift in policy within the region, the United States should drop its unilateral approach on the international level and begin negotiations with the Contadora group. Thus local and regional interests would become the initiators in resolving their own conflict.

System Transformers

System transformers generally agree with two assumptions of the system maintainers: (1) rigid class distinctions in Central America result in a virtually unnegotiable gap between elite groups and poor peasants; (2) the United States plays a special role and consequently bears a major responsibility for events in the region. System maintainers and transformers proceed to draw completely opposite conclusions from these assumptions.

Transformers contend that in class-based societies, any possibility of top-down reform exists only in the imaginations of U.S.-administration apologists trying to support a failed policy. The fiction that orderly change can emerge only from an existing power structure ignores the fact that "order" in Central America means systematic and brutal violence. Pluralist politics cannot develop where a rigid elite will not share power with a class it considers inferior.

As envisioned in pluralist democracies, a humane social order guarantees individual rights. This definition of order has superficial allure and, in the Central American context, can be used to deceive. Confusion results when both maintainers and reformers in Central America use the same rhetorical slogans as those heard in Western Europe and the United States: for example, meaningful change can be achieved through elections when political participation is supported by economic progress and ensured by an orderly due process of law. This may sound familiar and hopeful, but transformers contend that the political flexibility needed to put such ideas into practice does not exist in Central America.

Not only is order incompatible with justice on the political level, but an analysis of the underlying economic structure leads to the inescapable conclusion that economic growth will not lead to reforms in cash-crop economies dependent on international trade. Elite strength will be eroded only by increasing local economic self-sufficiency. Although this statement does not intentionally imply an anti-U.S. bias, if it is acted upon, U.S. financial interests will be undermined and its clients will lose power. Therefore, the United States must stop interpreting its long-term national political interests in terms of the short-term economic interests of a few of its citizens.

In addition, the U.S. anti-Soviet alarm rings hollow since the United States has been an integral part of a repressive and exploitative system. Polemics, whether defending a flawed but potentially redeemable system or blaming a nasty local elite for excesses, sound false. The United States bears a responsibility to assist in overturning the system it has helped perpetuate.

There can be no peace with justice without a fundamental restructuring of the social order in Central America. If it cannot assume a constructive role, the United States should pull out, allowing leftists to contend for power in El Salvador and Guatemala and the Sandinistas to work out their own power-sharing strategy in Nicaragua. Cuba and the Soviet Union also should withdraw and leave Central America on its own to redistribute economic and political power. The United States should heed the advice of its allies and the Contadora countries. A Marxism-become-benign could be in the best interest of the region. The United States has learned to live with it in other parts of the world. Why not in Central America?

REFERENCES

Annual Report 1981. Washington, DC: Inter-American Development Bank, 1982.

Baloyra, Enrique. *El Salvador in Transition*. Chapel Hill, NC: University of Northern Carolina Press, 1982.

Berryman, Phillip. *The Religious Roots of Rebellion*. Maryknoll, NY: Orbis Books, 1984.

Booth, John. "Celebrating the Demise of Somocismo: Fifty Recent Sources on the Nicaraguan Revolution." *Latin American Research Review* 17 (1982):173–189.

Dunkerley, James. *The Long War: Dictatorship and Revolution in El Salvador*. Whitetable, England: Junction Books, 1982.

Immerman, Richard H. *The CIA in Guatemala: The Foreign Policy of Intervention*. Austin: University of Texas Press, 1982.

LaFeber, Walter. *Inevitable Revolutions: The United States in Central America*. New York: W. W. Norton, 1983.

Lowenthal, Abraham E. "Threat and Opportunity in the Americas." In *Foreign Affairs: America and the World 1985*. New York: Pergamon Press, 1986.

McCamant, John. *The Central American Mess*. Colorado Consortium on International Policy, Occasional Papers. Denver, CO: University of Denver, 1984.

Paxton, John, ed. *Statesman's Yearbook 1973-74* and *1985-86*. New York: St. Martin's Press, 1974 and 1986.

Schlesinger, Stephen, and Stephen Kinzer. *Bitter Fruit: The Untold Story of the American Coup in Guatemala*. Garden City, NY: Anchor Press, 1983.

Sivard, Ruth Leger. *World Military and Social Expenditures 1981*. Leesburg, VA: World Priorities, 1981.

──────────── 13 ────────────

Geostrategy in the
Asian-Pacific Region
WILLIAM TOW

At a time when U.S. foreign policy in the Persian Gulf, South Africa, Latin America, and even in Western Europe seems to be in disarray, the Asian-Pacific region has emerged as the one apparent success story in U.S. foreign policy directed toward Third World regions. The Asian-Pacific region is defined here as encompassing land masses and oceans stretching from the U.S. West Coast to the Ural Mountains and the Indian borders. (South Asia is not included because its political identity is substantially different from those cultures and societies constituting most states within East or Southeast Asia and the Western Pacific.) The general importance of the Pacific to long-term U.S. economic and strategic interests is well known. U.S. trade with Japan now exceeds $60 billion annually. This represents a greater trade volume than combined U.S. trade with Great Britain, France, and West Germany. Altogether, 30 percent of total U.S. trade is now conducted with Asian-Pacific countries, and shifts of U.S. investment patterns to the region are pronounced. The region also provides the United States with many of its vital strategic commodities; it intersects the most critical oil routes leading from the Middle East into the industrial centers of the Northern Hemisphere. (Long 1986) The U.S. assistant secretary for East Asian and Pacific affairs recently summarized the Asian-Pacific region's importance to the United States when he concluded that the U.S. relationship with the region "is one of broad interdependence and reciprocal influence." (Singur 1986)

GEOSTRATEGY IN THE ASIAN-PACIFIC: ACTORS AND WORLDVIEWS

The U.S. worldview for explaining and responding to events and trends in the Asian-Pacific can thus be described as being derived from the assumption that a benign Asian-Pacific environment must be sustained in the interest of overall Western security. U.S. geopolitical calculations are regarded in this context as the application of political and strategic initiatives. The United States, as an obvious system maintainer, seeks to preserve its national interests in and influence over both core and peripheral Asian-Pacific regional actors. (Cantori and Spiegal 1970) Core actors within Asian-Pacific geopolitics include the People's Republic of China (PRC), Japan, and the Association of Southeast Asian Nations (ASEAN). ASEAN members include Brunei, Indonesia, Malaysia, the Philippines, Singapore, and Thailand. The PRC and Japan have cohesive and fairly long-standing political infrastructures as well as their own identifiable worldviews. ASEAN is just now emerging along similar unified lines at the regional level. The nation-states constituting ASEAN, however, may still be regarded as more vulnerable and fragmented than either China or Japan because the potential for domestic political instability in these countries is still high. Any future global economic recession could affect them more severely and lastingly than the Asian-Pacific core states. These core states have the ability to withstand such socioeconomic disruptions on the basis of their greater size and resources.

Asian-Pacific geopolitics must also be distinguished from the more narrow concept of "geostrategy," which more often than not drives the worldviews of both superpowers. Geostrategy encompasses images of "heartlands," "world islands," and other components of classical geopolitics. Unlike geopolitics, geostrategy often tends to ignore or discount the realities of systemic change either at the regional or at the global level of analysis. (Cohen 1982, Taylor 1985, and Johnson 1985-1986) Systemic change must be considered as a key geostrategic variable when assessing the Asian-Pacific's effect on the global power balance and when considering that region's own stability in terms of economic growth and political cohesion. Robert H. Johnson has aptly described the basic conceptual problem at hand: "geostrategic concepts [often] lack clear meaning. . . . Concepts that emphasize the importance of geographic position [alone] often represent an inappropriate transposition of ideas relating military tactics to the realm of geopolitics." (1985-1986, 34–35) Are the Straits of Malacca, for example, best viewed in terms of being a global strategic variable, integral to evaluating the vortex of superpower naval competition, or are the straits better understood as integral to Indonesian-Malaysian regional policy, underscoring ASEAN's determination to realize the resources and commercial benefits of critical waterways?

Most international relations analysts contend that elements of both the "globalist" and "regionalist" worldviews are applicable to a geopolitical assessment of Asian-Pacific strategy and politics. The types of problem areas concerning both internal and external actors who have been and are now determined to set regional priorities during the postwar era are applicable to the concerns of either faction. What is obvious to both schools of thought, however, is that challenges are now emerging in the Asian-Pacific that, if left unaddressed, could radically alter the course of Asian-Pacific development along lines inimical to Western security interests. The failure of key Asian-Pacific actors to endure such challenges from Soviet-backed Marxists or from indigenous anti-Western sources, moreover, would transform large sectors of the region in unpredictable but clearly dangerous ways. It could well be that the region would drift toward an anarchical state of affairs, perhaps far removed from orthodox superpower competition, but also detached from the mainstream of global economic and political dynamics. The USSR's continued backing of Vietnam and Soviet naval presence in the Pacific present security challenges to the Western Alliance. Mikhail Gorbachev's speech in Vladivostok (July 28, 1986) affirmed that Asia and the Pacific were as important to the Soviets as any other region of the world. Furthermore, the growth of the Soviet fleet in the region has some Asian leaders suggesting that the Soviets are looking to build a permanent presence in both the Pacific and Indian oceans.

Western security interests have also been challenged by New Zealand's efforts to create a South Pacific nuclear-free zone and similar movements within ASEAN to establish a Zone of Peace, Freedom, and Neutrality (ZOPFAN). Supporters of these common-security proposals represent actors in the Asian-Pacific who are pressing for an overall regional-security agenda. These highly idealistic visions of security and geopolitics seem to overlook the importance of this region to many outside powers, and seek to establish an independent security area within the Pacific that is also removed from global geopolitical conflicts. (Graham, 1986)

What follows is a brief discussion of some key issues that have generated concern and debate between the United States and its Asian-Pacific allies system maintainers, the Soviet Union and its regional proxies as would-be system reformers, and a new wave of system transformers as represented by the Asian-Pacific region's nuclear-disarmament and neutrality advocates. One such issue is the future role of U.S. military power—and especially its nuclear components—as the ultimate guarantor of Asian-Pacific nations' ability to pursue pro-Western lines of political and economic development. Another problem relates to the long-term viability of economic-development programs now under way in China (with its Four Modernizations program) and in pro-Western Taiwan, South Korea, ASEAN, and the South Pacific. Can these countries be successful in generating and sustaining satisfied middle classes within their societies and thus avoid social polarization or new forms of violent internal revolution? This problem, in turn, leads into the third basic question of concern. How will the Asian-Pacific's development experience coincide or contrast with an increasingly uncertain and volatile global environment? Again, how the United States shapes its own geopolitics within the international arena will most likely have a critical impact upon the Asian-Pacific region's overall strategic and political identity.

U.S. Policies in the Asian-Pacific

Following the enunciation of the Nixon Doctrine in 1969 and the withdrawal of U.S. ground forces from South Vietnam during the early 1970s, the United

States returned to its traditional approach of sustaining an active maritime strategy in the Asian-Pacific in conjunction with its reinforcement strategy directed toward North Atlantic Treaty Organization (NATO) Europe. Nixon reaffirmed U.S. alliance commitments in the Pacific theater on the condition that those Asian-Pacific allies benefitting from U.S. extended deterrence become more self-sufficient in defending against their internal security threats. What he could not foresee was the degree to which the Soviet Union, long regarded as the world's premier land-based power, would build up its naval capabilities as a direct threat to U.S. maritime assets. Previously, Washington was able to capitalize on the Asian-Pacific's ambiguous lines of political and military demarcation to compensate for its own "contradictory pulls of continuing [Asian] interests with a changable public mood at times inclined to minimize an American security presence and at other times prepared to support a forceful intervention in regional affairs." (Soloman 1980, 19) By the late 1970s, however, the Soviet Union had moved successfully toward achieving greater strategic reach in the Pacific through its naval presence in Vietnam's Cam Ranh Bay and through its deployment of the SS20, the "Backfire" bomber, and other theater nuclear-weapons systems designed to match if not exceed U.S. offshore capabilities in the Pacific.

The U.S. strategic presence in the Pacific region was drawn into even greater question during the later years of the Carter administration. The president clearly misread the Northeast Asian balance of power in 1977, prematurely withdrawing part of the U.S. ground-force contingent from South Korea. This action seemed to ignore rising Chinese and ASEAN concerns that gradual U.S. dissociation from its long-standing postwar containment posture in Southeast Asia represented a decreased capacity for all other Asian-Pacific actors to remain outside the Soviet orbit. The short-lived yet much publicized "swing strategy," which envisioned a further decrease of U.S.-force presence in Asia in favor of defending NATO during a future West European security crisis, also tended to undermine Japan's, China's, and the ASEAN states' confidence in ultimate U.S. intentions to check Soviet military power in the Far East. It gradually became clear to most of the Asian-Pacific's important regional-security actors that the United States was still prepared to use its defense resources in flexible and responsive ways to preserve the overall regional-power equilibrium in the Asian-Pacific without necessarily provoking the USSR or blocking its legitimate search for economic and cultural ties in the region. U.S. forces would remain deployed "over the horizon" at their bases in the Philippines, Okinawa, Guam, and in the western United States. These forces would have sufficient mobility and firepower to gain access to Asian-Pacific locales should the need arise, even in the absence of more formal collective-defense commitments.

Geostrategic Goals
This policy course of strategic calibration changed when President Reagan assumed office. Under his leadership, the United States moved quickly to em-

brace a more overt geostrategy rather than adhere to the broader geopolitical approach toward the Asian-Pacific security system pursued by the Nixon and Carter administrations. Within the past few years, the U.S. Pacific Command (USPACOM), which deploys roughly half of all U.S. naval power, has added a number of nuclear-capable weapons to its inventories. As significantly, U.S. defense planners have introduced what has become labeled the "Doctrine of Maritime Supremacy": an offensively oriented naval strategy concentrating on the imperative of taking the battle to the opponent from the beginning of hostilities and emphasizing "aggressive surveillance," stepped-up naval exercises, and constant enhancement of naval firepower during peacetime. (Arkin and Chapell 1985, Arkin and Fieldhouse 1985)

The Buildup of U.S. Nuclear Forces
Specifically, the acceleration of the USPACOM force buildup under President Reagan has involved six measures:

1. An extensive introduction of sea-launched Tomahawk cruise missiles as the key nuclear-delivery system in USPACOM for selected strikes against both fixed and maritime targets in either a land-war support or sea-control operational environment
2. The nuclear replenishment of USPACOM's six operational aircraft carriers and supporting naval elements to deploy over 700 nuclear warheads for delivery against targets in the Soviet Far Eastern Command up to 1,900 miles from launch points or for use in antisubmarine warfare (ASW) operations
3. The addition of a number of nuclear-powered Los Angeles-class attack submarines to interdict and destroy Soviet naval units attempting to break out of Northeast Asia's key straits and chokepoints into open waters
4. The insertion of the Ohio-class ballistic missile Trident I submarine with alleged "counterforce" (war-fighting/precision target) capabilities into the U.S. Seventh Fleet (ten Tridents will eventually be homeported in Bangor, Washington)
5. The arming of U.S. B-52 strategic bombers stationed in Guam with stand-off air-launched cruise missiles (ALCMs) capable of reaching distant Soviet targets in the Far Eastern Command
6. The placement of F/A-18 nuclear-capable Hornet tactical attack aircraft in U.S. Marine units supporting USPACOM (Arkin and Fieldhouse 1985)

There can be little doubt remaining among Washington's Asian-Pacific allies that the United States has decided to match Soviet military growth in their region, even though the USSR has little other than its own military capabilities in the way of enduring means of influence to project into this region. The U.S. nuclear buildup progressed, moreover, despite obvious and inherent limitations in the type of strategic forces the Soviets were able to deploy in the Pacific. Soviet Typhoon and Delta III nuclear-ballistic-missile submarines, for example, while capable of striking a number of U.S. targets, are highly vulnerable to U.S. (and to a lesser extent, Japanese) ASW operations, because they usually operate so close to the USSR's home territory (i.e., in the Sea of Okhotsk). This cuts down the effective roaming area available to such Soviet vessels for evading USPACOM detection and neutralization from U.S. or allied attack-submarine barriers set up off the coast from Petropavlovsk and Vladivostok—the two major base complexes of the Far East Command. Moscow also faces two formidable nuclear opponents adjacent to its territory in the Asian-Pacific theater: the United States and the People's Republic of China. (IISS 1986) Even with the latest Soviet force-modernization efforts, the Soviet Far Eastern Command may have some problems. (Arkin and Fieldhouse 1985) A Western strategic analyst notes that "without mobilization and considerable reinforcement of forces from the western USSR, the present Pre-War Readiness Potential (PRP) of Soviet forces in the Far East is insufficiently high to ensure successful operations, even against Red China alone." (Sadykiewicz 1983, 189)

In more comprehensive geopolitical terms, the United States seems to have not only maintained its regional strategic (especially offshore or maritime) advantage over the Soviets, but by coalescing with China (a significant and growing nuclear continental power in its own right) and Japan (the economic giant of the region and a potential maritime guardian of Asian-Pacific sea lanes), the United States has demonstrated to other regional actors the limitations of Soviet military strength. The Soviets can only intimidate the United States and its allies during limited war conditions over short periods of time as opposed to credibly dominating their theater during conditions of general warfare. The regional military balance can thus be summarized in a geopolitical framework along the following lines: The best Moscow can hope for in a region-wide Asian military confrontation is to neutralize China while holding the line against inherently superior U.S. maritime power, reinforcable from the U.S. mainland. Moscow does not, and cannot, enjoy a force-posture asymmetry in the Asian-Pacific's predominantly maritime environment in the same way as it can apply superior land forces to a strategic confrontation in Central Europe.

U.S. strategic advantages in the Pacific region are underscored even more by Japanese, South Korean and (to a lesser extent) Australian contributions to the West's overall deterrence capabilities. Secretary of State George Shultz recently outlined U.S. defense burden-sharing expectations (July 1985); he noted that each U.S. regional ally in the Asian-Pacific has a responsibility to supplement U.S. nuclear and conventional military power in order to sustain effective anti-Soviet deterrence in the theater. Japan has responded to such U.S. appeals by embarking upon a number of expanded defense commitments, including expanding its air and naval capabilities to patrol 1,000 nautical miles, transferring advanced electronics and computer technology to the U.S. military-industrial complex, and agreeing to participate in research for the building of a "non-nuclear" U.S. Strategic Defense Initiative (SDI). (Langdon 1985) South Korea, also, has modernized its military forces while continuing to host the only nuclear-weapons deployment that is maintained by a foreign power on Asian-Pacific soil: approximately 150 U.S. tactical nuclear weapons (TNWs) at Kun-san airbase. In 1983, Australia reviewed its security relationship with the United States and reaffirmed its contribution to the U.S. global strategic deterrent by permitting the United States to operate strategic tracking installations on Austra-lian soil. This endorsement was forthcoming despite Australia's recent cutbacks in its own forward-defense maritime forces and ground-force presence because of budgetary problems. (Dibb 1986)

"Alternative Security": Nuclear Free Zones

The ongoing superpower nuclear-arms competition in the Asian-Pacific region and the steady development of China's nuclear forces have provided the most visible rationale for those who would transform that region's security framework. As early as 1975, the South Pacific Forum (SPF) had endorsed an initiative forwarded by the New Zealand Labour government to create a South Pacific Nuclear Free Zone (SPNFZ). The proposal was dropped when Conser-vative governments returned to power in both New Zealand and Australia by the end of that year. In August 1984, a new Australian Labour government revived SPNFZ in a somewhat modified form (each SPF member could decide on the question of nuclear-ship visits, on a case-by-case basis) to head off a far more radical plan advanced by the re-elected Labour Party government in New Zea-land, which called for the banning of all nuclear weapons or nuclear-capable systems from the South Pacific. The Australian proposal generally complies with the stipulations found in Latin America's Treaty of Tlatelolco. The Austra-lian SPNFZ version "constitutes the prohibiting of the permanent land-based presence of weapons rather than the passing of weapons through a region aboard ships and planes." (Fry 1985, 16)

The Australian government was able to push through its SPNFZ draft with a strong majority during the SPF's 1985 annual meetings. The resulting Treaty of Rarotonga was resisted only by Papua New Guinea, the Solomon Islands, Vanuatu, and New Zealand. These states favored banning *all* types of nuclear activity in the South Pacific. However, these states were overruled by Australia and a voting majority of SPF members, who believed that any agreement should be somewhat consistent with U.S. defense objectives in their region. Australia was determined to minimize any impact a nuclear-free-zone position statement might have on its existing security relations with Washington. Australia's posi-tion was supported by Fiji, Tonga, the Cook Islands, Western Samoa, and sev-eral other SPF members.

It is interesting to note that the "poles of opinion" concerning how strong nuclear reform in the South Pacific should be tend to vary between Polynesian and Melanesian countries. The Polynesians have tended to adopt a more rigid stance because of their proximity to French nuclear-weapons testing in Moruroa Atoll. Their understandable revulsion against French activities has brought them into line with New Zealand's strong antinuclear position. The Melanesians, by contrast, have desired to retain the right to host U.S. naval units. They do not, however, enthusiastically support the prospect of future U.S. bases emerging in South Pacific waters if Washington's military presence at Clark Air Force Base and the Subic Bay naval installation in the Philippines is terminated when the present leasing agreements for those installations expire in 1991. (Fry 1985)

The United States has expressed its gratitude to the Australian government for its South Pacific diplomacy, but has yet to lend its formal support to the Australian version of the SPNFZ. However, it may be to U.S. advantage to lend greater support to the more pragmatic Australian plan. A supportive U.S. government might discourage Soviet penetration of selected South Pacific island-state economies through limited economic-assistance programs (e.g., in 1985 a Soviet fishing agreement with Kiribati was signed), or through Moscow's cultivation of political factions in newly emerging island-states. A decision by Washington to engage in limited political and economic trade-offs with SPF elites, in the form of attractive economic-assistance packages and more liberal fishing-rights agreements, seems to be the most effective means currently available for encouraging South Pacific island-states to continue some form of strategic relations with the United States.

New Zealand, a system transformer in the nuclear-weapons area, will continue to lead a small but committed antinuclear faction within the SPF in defining security formulas alternative to traditional Western extended deterrence. In a few instances, would-be system reformers at the interregional level, such as the USSR or its proxies, will coalesce with system-reformist elements within the region to confront the United States, France, Australia, and other system maintainers more effectively. By way of example, both Cuba and Libya have been recently involved in attempting to shape Vanuatu's domestic politics. (Premdas and Hammond 1985) The USSR also offered military intelligence-sharing and "friendship treaty" arrangements to New Zealand. (Long 1986) In general, the transformers have declined such offers of cooperation, yet have been ineffective in offering viable explanations of exactly how regional security could be better served by the adoption of their positions.

The System Transformer's Position
The essence of the system transformer's lines of argument in New Zealand is articulated by the "Committee of Just Defense" and similar organizations. Their views are presented below:

1. The South Pacific's geography provides an appropriate setting for the countries of this area to move gradually toward armed neutrality, as long as the democratic institutions and values underwriting New Zealand's and the Pacific

Island states' governance can remain intact. This is the same way that Austria, Sweden, and Switzerland maintain democratic institutions and government outside any formal alliance system.

2. Regional threats, as anticipated by the West's original postwar collective-defense and extended-deterrence arrangements, really have not materialized. Collective defense was misconstrued, both in its anticipation of situations inevitably materializing to justify its continued existence (e.g., an expansionist PRC) and in its anticipation of the imperative for sustaining extended deterrence.

3. South Pacific repudiation of extended deterrence on the nuclear level will not only be a better policy avenue toward regional security than traditional approaches, but will gradually earn the respect of otherwise potentially belligerent outsiders. It will also, over time, reduce the costs of defense to New Zealand and other system-transformer states. The idea of "common security" should be adopted because the costs of nuclear miscalculation or resource deprivation over large parts of the world are becoming too great to continue pursuing nuclear means for international systemic maintenance. (Kidson 1985, 6)

These propositions represent the particular worldview that is held by those who seek to transform the present security priorities in this region. These same propositions are subject to equally forceful counterarguments. In an era of long-range strategic nuclear forces, geographic distance can no longer be regarded as a very likely variable in modern warfare. Additionally, United States naval operations in a wartime environment, by their very nature, would be all-encompassing in terms of covering the wider Pacific Ocean. No geographic barriers or indigenously produced modes of political expression now appear credible enough to restructure the scope of either U.S. Seventh Fleet or Soviet Pacific Fleet operations in a general war. In sum, the system transformers' appeals for geographic autonomy are irrelevant in the age of modern geopolitics governed by nuclear deterrence and defense.

Those Pacific states seeking to create a non-aligned or neutral zone in the Pacific need to consider that democratic neutral countries such as Austria, Sweden, and Switzerland, which they present as models, are allowed to remain neutral because their independent defense assets are perceived as adding to the non-Communist world's forward-defense network. In reality, both superpowers tacitly recognize that Sweden's sea and air forces are primarily geared against Soviet encroachments along Western Europe's northern flank, that Switzerland's formidable self-defense forces would never be directed against a NATO power but very well could be used in a Central European defense against advancing Warsaw Pact forces, and that German-Austrian historicocultural ties are just too strong to envision Vienna remaining neutral if West Germany were ever to suffer the effects of a full-scale Soviet onslaught. The realities of the contemporary international system would likewise most probably preclude the United States from standing by if New Zealand were ever threatened with external invasion, despite the moribund status of the Australia, New Zealand, and United States defense pact. Prime Minister Lange of New Zealand has acknowledged this likelihood on several different occasions. Ramesh Thakur summarized such realities involved in the New Zealand case:

> The credibility paradox is related to a country's multidimensional affinities. . . . Simply put, it is dubious in the extreme whether New Zealand's neutrality could be sustained if the survival of America or Britain were at stake [because] New Zealand society would almost certainly be convulsed if its government tried to maintain neutrality under such circumstances; . . . we delude ourselves if we believe that the destructive aftermath of a nuclear holocaust would not reach out to consume us, simply because we are neutrals. (1986, 144)

STRATEGIC DIMENSIONS OF MIDDLE-CLASS DEVELOPMENT

There is little question about the appeal that market economics has for most nation-states throughout East and Southeast Asia. After years of internal political turmoil, the People's Republic of China has structured its recent economic-reform programs in a dramatic, pro-Western direction. ASEAN countries have also pursued Western economic-development models for the most part and have grown accustomed to annual real-economic growth rates of around 7 or 8 percent. Such economic growth has led to relative internal political stability in these states (with the possible exception of the Philippines) since the end of the Vietnam War.

Future Threats to Economic Stability

However, the ongoing economic stability of ASEAN societies is about to be challenged. First, disruptions will be brought about by "stagflation," a slowdown in economic growth and an increase in inflation. Second, problems will result from intensified disputes over political succession brewing in almost every ASEAN state. Third, leaders in these states will be forced to deal with external pressures emanating from the Asian-Pacific's overall dependence upon an industrialized Western community. The West may prove to be singularly indifferent if not openly opposed to continued ASEAN development. U.S. sentiments for trade protectionism have risen; Japanese investment patterns have adjusted in response. If Organization for Economic Cooperation and Development (OECD) members do not exercise a more sensitive and imaginative collective approach toward the growth and stability of emerging Pacific nations, inevitable strains between the developed world and the increasingly resentful Asian-Pacific actors could well rend the already delicate fabric of interdependence that has fueled regional progress. This, in turn, could provide the Soviet/Marxist system reformers with the geopolitical openings they need to supplant U.S. regional influence. To avoid this, the United States, along with the rest of the industrialized world, needs to direct more attention to some of the regional political and social issues threatening military and economic priorities. This is the only way for the United States to retain its traditional postwar access to and influence within the Asian-Pacific region.

China

China, historically the region's most dominant cultural force, must achieve what it regards as acceptable success levels in its Four Modernizations program. Deng Xiaoping's regime has gambled in moving against Marxist ideological and political orthodoxy by adopting liberal economic methods to reach what one respected Western analyst has characterized as a "balance between central political and economic control on the one hand, and individual initiative and reliance on market forces on the other." (Romberg 1986, 522) As evidenced by the Chinese Communist Party's crackdown on recent student demonstrations, there is still significant opposition to Deng's policy course within his country's bureaucracy. Many in China would be ideologically more comfortable with raising the state's relatively stagnant defense budget (about 40 billion yuan per annum since 1977) in order to overtly challenge the superpowers' regional military presence. Such a move might also work to discredit Deng's premise that greater Chinese economic and technological prowess can eventually be converted into more credible and enduring Chinese military power. The PRC's movement toward at least a partial economic rapprochement with the USSR and the spectacular increase in trade volumes between the world's two largest Marxist states over the past few years (capped by the July 1985 signing of a five-year, $14 billion trade agreement) serves as evidence that China's "tilted non-alignment" toward the West could well be tentative.

ASEAN

China's identity crisis over its future national development course is matched by ASEAN's concern that it can survive the rest of this decade as an integrated economic community. While senior ASEAN officials tend to be self-congratulatory about how these diverse Southeast Asian states have prospered through collective action, what actually binds these nations together is based as much on negative incentives as on common interests:

> At the heart of ASEAN's desire to prosper as a grouping of good neighbors is a very real fear that the existence of Communist powers on the region's doorstep [in Indochina] and the potential for Communist-inspired dissidence in each [ASEAN country] constitutes a major threat to ASEAN stability. . . . Each ASEAN government has to prove that its non-Communist system, with a shared emphasis on market-oriented and export-oriented economy, brings more benefits to its people than a socialist system. And this concept is bolstered if it is treated collectively, on a regional basis, given geographic realities. (Far Eastern Economic Review 1984, 94)

By the end of 1985, however, the combined economic outlook for ASEAN was anything but promising. Malaysia's national debt, for example, had approached 60 percent of its gross national product (GNP) and its commodities prices (offshore oil, rubber, palm oil, and pepper) slumped, perhaps irretrievably, on the world market. Ethnic discontent among the country's Chinese and Indian minorities accelerated against the central government's *Bumiputra* (Malay-first) policies. Indonesia has suffered as its oil exports, which account for 73 percent of that country's total export earnings, have slumped in value. The average Indonesian still earns less than $600 per year in a nation where bureaucratic corruption is institutional and up to 20 percent of the GDP is squandered through various illegal or semi-legal enterprises. During his country's celebration of the twentieth anniversary of its independence, Singapore's Prime Minister Lee Kuan Yew compared that city-state's economy to Great Britain's "economic disease" and warned of dire economic consequences if worker demands continued to outstrip actual economic performance. Thailand's debt-service ratio, in the meantime, had reached $15 billion and strict, unpopular economic-austerity measures seemed inevitable for that country's population. The Philippines' internecine strife has been on the front pages of the world's press, but the most fundamental weaknesses include a 20 percent unemployment rate and a GNP that has dropped on the average of 4 percent a year since 1983 (a slight rise of 0.3 percent was recorded in 1986). As a result, the New People's Army has expanded by a yearly rate of 20 percent and now claims to have over 23,000 active forces. (Romberg 1986, 530)

All of this economic downturn in the ASEAN region has occurred at a time when the U.S. Congress has weighed passage of laws calling for sharp cuts in textile imports and similar measures designed to cut U.S. imports of other Asian products. Ironically, ASEAN has been lumped in with Japan and the other Asian newly industrialized countries (NICs) for protectionist legislation, despite being responsible for only a small proportion of the overall U.S. trade-deficit problem. Other Asian-Pacific industrial powers have fared no better in their efforts to relate to ASEAN politically or economically.

Japan still seems an impenetrable culture to most Southeast Asians, whose memories of Japanese occupation during World War II are still fresh. These memories are accentuated by intermittently rash or inappropriate comments offered by Japanese education ministers, who tend to dismiss their own country's wartime behavior as self-defense. The Japanese "dumping" of products in Southeast Asian markets without any built-in economic reciprocity is also despised by ASEAN societies. Recent schemes advanced by Tokyo to bankroll its oft-stated intent to forge "heart-to-heart" relations with ASEAN at an institutional level (originally called for in 1977 by the Fukuda Doctrine) have been frustrated by countervailing Japanese and ASEAN bureaucratic interests. Australia also has inadvertently worsened its ties with ASEAN. The Australian government's willingness to conduct at least limited diplomacy with Vietnam, over ASEAN objections or without its input, is a case in point. Tensions between Australia and Indonesia remain strong over the latter's alleged territorial designs on Papua New Guinea and over its administrative practices relating to East

Timor. A recently leaked Australian defense document identified Indonesia as the only possible external threat now confronting the antipodean state.

It is perhaps most important to system maintainers' concerns about Southeast Asian economic problems that each ASEAN country, with the possible exception of Singapore, is developing an industrial sector from little or no initial foundation or infrastructure, necessitating continued, steady flows of external capital (through trade or investment) from developed countries. ASEAN countries also suffer from generally narrow, and largely redundant, ranges of export commodities with which to compensate, thus limiting their potentials for economic diversification. As they are largely complementary in their overall development and trade patterns, only more effectively coordinated intraregional measures for trade with the outside world can make up the difference. While ASEAN foreign ministers have energetically pursued such formulas in their collective gatherings, the impetus of their efforts tends to break down at the regional level:

> Member states . . . vigorously [exploit] presumed national advantages which could coincidentally be detrimental to their ASEAN neighbors—for example, establishing national trade promotion offices overseas alongside ASEAN trade centers, while national airlines compete in scheduling and advertising and preferential oil sales are made to "old customers" rather than to ASEAN partners. . . .
> Unfortunately, the effort that went into obtaining recognition for the external dimension of ASEAN was at the expense of internal operational progress. (Indorf 1984, 8–9)

RECONCILING REGIONAL SECURITY
WITH INTERNATIONAL INSECURITY

Leaders in the United States and Western Europe have seen the Asian-Pacific region as "one among a number of geographically linked regions through which ran the main fault line of demarcation between the communist and noncommunist worlds" during the immediate postwar era. (Jorgensen-Dahl 1982, 3) Unlike Europe, the Asian-Pacific countries, having emerged from decolonization at the height of the Cold War, perceive the United States' predominant focus on the Soviet threat to be restrictive and, at times, even diametrically opposed to their own interpretations of desirable security approaches. The legacy of regional dissent to Western global strategy was thus imprinted almost from the outset of the Cold War itself. As superpower competition throughout Southeast Asia intensified during the Vietnam War, regional elites sought viable policy alternatives to Western containment and extended-deterrence prescriptions.

ASEAN
Policy alternatives were articulated in ASEAN's ZOPFAN, which was approved at the regional associations conference in Kuala Lumpur during

November 1971. The Kuala Lumpur Declaration establishing ZOPFAN as a regional security alternative sought to remove the member-states' territories from the vortex of great-power competition over international security. The strategy was to elicit great-power guarantees for the region's unencumbered socioeconomic development. (Gurtov and Marsot 1974, 145–146)

If allowed to pursue ZOPFAN in the manner prescribed by the Kuala Lumpur Declaration, most ASEAN states very likely would embrace some form of Western political- and economic-development strategy. In anticipation of this, the Soviet Union advanced its own preferred version of systemic reform for the Asian-Pacific with its Asian collective security (ACS) proposal. The Soviet ACS proposal envisions the minimizing of great-power presence in the region as an initial means to achieve true regional neutrality, followed by the implementation of Soviet as well as (presumably) U.S. guarantees for the security of the region's indigenous national actors. The difference between Soviet ACS and ZOPFAN revolves largely around the timing as well as the actual implementation of neutrality. That is, ZOPFAN allows for a gradual dismantling of Western military bases and military ties, in accordance with each ASEAN state's national prerogatives. The Soviet formula insists that no situation of regional neutrality can exist as long as such bases or assistance relations are still in effect. The Soviet ACS proposal was recently given new attention by Mikhail Gorbachev in a landmark speech delivered in Vladivostok in 1986. (Novosti Press Agency, July 29, 1986, 25–27) Contemporary Soviet diplomacy in the Asian-Pacific seems to have been restructured along more subtle and less "reformist" lines so as to engender a favorable response from ASEAN members and other Asian-Pacific nations. Most of these states have been highly skeptical of previous Soviet ACS representations. (Horelick 1974)

External Forces on ASEAN
The apparent direction of present ASEAN security positions toward the strategic interests of the United States and other system maintainers, however, does not guarantee continued convergence. The Soviet Union's determination to compete for political and strategic influence in the Asian-Pacific area is and will remain a regional fact of life. Continued Soviet-U.S. competition (along with the possible exercise of higher profiles by both China and Japan, politically as well as economically and culturally) promises to ensure a dynamic process of systemic interaction between regional and extraregional actors throughout the Asian-Pacific for years to come. Increasingly, policymakers in Southeast Asia are giving more attention to the need to forge their own theoretical and policy approaches to security problems as an alternative to the region's implicit reliance on the good will of outside powers. Security specialists from this region have focused on how ASEAN members might coalesce more effectively despite lingering ethnic and territorial disputes, which still exist between them, in an effort to present a more convincing image of "regional resiliency" against great-power intrusion. By weighing its identity and the impact of its collective be-

havior on both the Southeast Asian area and the greater Asian-Pacific region, ASEAN has moved toward providing its member-states a greater sense of self-confidence in confronting external challenges. In addition, these efforts have encouraged multilateral consultation and policy implementation within the organization, giving members a greater sense of power and capability and a greater respect for regional cooperation. (Choy 1981)

It remains uncertain to what extent the major powers that shape the global balance of power will allow ASEAN to function in its present, somewhat autonomous fashion. Both China and Japan could move to play much more extensive intraregional Asian-Pacific roles in the future. China, in particular, while obviously a key element of a regional-power system, chooses for now to remain somewhat apart from regional affairs. The Chinese seem to be focusing their energies on implementing their domestic course of economic and political development. During the late 1970s, China's concerns over increased Soviet military activity along its borders and in neighboring regions led Japanese and U.S. officials to believe that China would become a more active system maintainer in the region. Certainly the Ford and Carter administrations interpreted the PRC's short-lived "united front" strategy in such a way. But China has since taken care to downplay its anti-Soviet posture in favor of what it labels an independent foreign policy. In reality, the ASEAN states' political ties with Beijing remain correct or even cool. Only Thailand, which sets China as a counterweight to Vietnamese expansionism, seems receptive to a great role for China. As one respected Western observer has concluded: "ASEAN's views of China are much less unified and benevolent than the Americans [initially] believed; and the Association's perceptions of the Soviets are probably less negative in the long term than the Americans had hoped." (Simon 1985, 93)

In its pursuit of the role of a system maintainer, the United States has not always been viewed by its supposed beneficiaries as the best candidate to restore the Asian-Pacific's balance-of-power equilibrium. Indeed, U.S. preemptive behavior, as exemplified by its launching of the 1975 Mayaguez rescue operations from Thailand without consulting Thai leaders, and by its current policy of transferring military weapons and technology to China, has caused many ASEAN leaders to question the U.S. commitment to their goals. U.S. leaders have been accused in a number of ASEAN quarters as being short-sighted and as taking policy positions that potentially destabilize the overall regional security. ASEAN is still far away from achieving the levels of economic and political cohesion originally envisioned by international integration theorists as needed to form a "pluralistic security community." Nonetheless, the ASEAN states have collectively established themselves as a core security actor in their region, an actor to be taken into account by system maintainers and reformers. In addition, those who would transform the region's entire political agenda through nuclear-free-zone politics or through introducing some other predominant value system into the Asian development process must also consider the growing importance of ASEAN as a regional and global actor.

CONCLUSION

The Asian-Pacific regional-security environment is characterized by increasing fluctuations in composition as well as by the increasingly independent strategic-policy interests and behavior of its participants. The United States remains the primary system maintainer within this environment. The ASEAN states and China are more willing now than at any time since the early days of postwar containment to defend the region's adherence to a pro-Western economic-development model. These states seem to be willing to act alone if they perceive U.S. actions in the region to be too bellicose or indifferent to serve their own national or collective defense interests. ASEAN often criticizes Washington for extending security support for China at their long-term strategic expense, while China goes to some lengths in order to distance itself from intermittent U.S. efforts to represent them as a supplementary system maintainer in support of U.S. anti-Soviet containment policies in the Pacific region. Japan is only just beginning to emerge as a regional security actor in its own right. Any hard conclusions about its future identity as a system maintainer in a geopolitical sense would be premature.

The Soviet Union is intent on reforming the security agenda of states within this region. It hopes to encourage the Pacific states to support an increased U.S. strategic withdrawal from Asian-Pacific bases and a general decrease in U.S. military involvement in the region. During the late 1960s, the Soviets also pressed for an ACS arrangement that would isolate China from the rest of the area. However, recent moves by both the USSR and the PRC toward renewed economic ties and efforts aimed at easing persistent political differences have allowed the present Soviet leadership to advertise the Soviet ACS in a more subtle, and perhaps more appealing, framework vis-à-vis would-be Asian-Pacific collaborators. Vietnam's continued military presence in Cambodia and the uncertain future of the Korean peninsula, however, render projections about the long-term effectiveness of the Soviet ACS campaign tenuous at best.

System transformers, led by nuclear-free-zone advocates, contend that as long as the Soviet Union, United States, China, France, or any other power conducts nuclear politics or strategy in the Asian-Pacific, the outlook for achieving long-term regional peace and stability remains bleak. The arguments advanced by those backing the SPNFZ movement and advocating its expansion to a region-wide dimension have not been supported by the majority of Asian-Pacific leaders and their respective constituents. The nuclear-free-zone idea is not currently seen as adequate to replace extended deterrence. Until such an alternative is identified and implemented throughout the region, prospects are not very likely for the systemic transformation of Asian-Pacific security.

Continued research and evaluation of Asian-Pacific geopolitics, with the intention of broadening the scope of inquiry itself or of pursuing new strategies that might lead to less competitive and ambiguous debates among internal and external powers, should be pursued. It may well also be true that more appealing means of welfare and security can be realized by the end of this century and that prospects for both global and Asian-Pacific regional conflict will be reduced in the process.

REFERENCES

Arkin, William M. and David Chapell. "Forward Defensive Strategy: Raising the Stakes in the Pacific." *World Policy Journal* 2 (Summer 1985):481–500.

Arkin, William M. and R. W. Fieldhouse. *Nuclear Battlefields: Global Links in the Arms Race*. Cambridge, MA: Ballinger, 1985.

Ayoob, Mohammed, editor. *Regional Security in the Third World*. Boulder, CO: Westview Press, 1986.

Buss, Claude. "The Pacific Theater: Key to Global Stability." In *National Security Interests in the Pacific Basin*. Edited by Buss. Stanford, CA: Hoover Institution, 1985.

Cantori, Louis J. and Steven Spiegal. *The International Politics of Regions: A Comparative Approach*. Englewood Cliffs, NJ: Prentice Hall, 1970.

Chawla, Suderchan, Melvin Gurtov, and Alain-Gerard Marsot. *Southeast Asia Under the New Balance of Power*. New York: Praeger, 1974.

Choy, Chong Li. *Open Self-Reliant Regionalism*. Singapore: Institute of Southeast Asian Studies, 1981.

Clark, Ian. "Collective Security in Asia: Toward a Framework of Soviet Diplomacy." *The Round Table*. October 1973: 473–481.

Cohen, Saul. "A New Map of Global Political Equilibrium: A Developmental Approach." *Political Geography Quarterly*. (March 1982):223–242.

Crome, Donald. *The ASEAN States: Coping With Dependence*. New York: Praegar, 1983.

Dibb, Paul. *Review of Australia's Defense Capabilities*. Canberra: Australian Government, March 1986.

Far Eastern Economic Review. *Asia 1985 Yearbook*. Hong Kong: South China Morning Post, 1984.

Fry, Greg. "Toward a South Pacific Nuclear Free Zone." *Bulletin of the Atomic Scientists* 41 (June/July 1985):16–21.

Goldbat, J. and S. Lodgaard. "The South Pacific Nuclear Free Zone: Variation on a Latin American Theme." *New Zealand International Review* 11 (May/June 1986):12–16.

Graham, Ken. "Common Security—A Link to the Global Age," *New Zealand International Review* 11, No. 4 (July/August 1986):12–16.

Horelick, Arnold. "The Soviet Union's Asian Collective Security Proposal: A Club in Search of Members." *Pacific Affairs* 47 (Fall 1974):269–285.

Indorf, Hans. *Impediments To Regionalism In Southeast Asia*. Singapore: Institute of Southeast Asian Studies, 1984.

International Institute for Strategic Studies. *1986–1987 Military Balance*. London: IISS, 1986.

Johnson, Robert H. "Exaggerating America's Stakes in Third World Conflicts." *International Security* 10 (Winter 1985–1986):33–38.

Jorgenson-Dahl, A. *Regional Organization and Order in Southeast Asia*. London: MacMillan, 1982.

Kidson, Jim. "Wellington Labor Group Proposes Alternative Defense Policy." *The Evening Post* (May 27, 1985):68–70.

Langdon, Frank. "The Security Debate in Japan." *Pacific Affairs* 58 (Fall 1985):397–410.

Long, Richard. "PM Rejects Soviet Information Offer." *The Dominion* (August 28, 1986).

Macky, Roger. "Dibb Report Conference Issue." *The Evening Post* (May 14, 1986):4.

Nations, Richard. "Moscow's New TACT." *Far Eastern Economic Review* (August 14, 1986):30–35.

Novosti Press Agency. "Text of Vladivostok Speech." July 29, 1986.

Park, Jae Kyn, and Joseph M. Ha, editors. *The Soviet Union and East Asia in the 1980's*. Seoul: Kyungnow, 1983.

Perry, Peter. "Neutrality and New Zealand." *New Zealand International Review* 11 (May/June 1986):15–16.

Premdas, Ralph, and Michael Hammond. "Vanuatu's Foreign Policy: Contradictions and Constraints." *Australian Outlook* 39 (December 1985):177–186.

Romberg, Alan D. "New Stirrings in Asia." *Foreign Affairs—America and the World* 64 (1986):515–538.

Sadykiewicz, Michael. "Soviet Far East High Command: A New Developmental Factor in the USSR Military Strategy Toward East Asia," in *The Soviet Union and East Asia in the 1980s*. Edited by Jae Kyn Park and Joseph M. Ha. Seoul: Kyung now Press, 1983.

Shultz, George. "On Alliance Responsibility." *Current Policy* 724 (July 17, 1985):1–4.

Simon, Sheldon. "China and Southeast Asia: Protector or Predator?" *Australian Outlook* 39 (August 1985):93–98.

Sigur, Gaston J. "The Strategic Importance of the Emerging Pacific." *Current Policy* 871 (September 1986):1–4.

Solomon, Richard. "American Defense Planning and Asian Security: Policy Choices for A Time of Transition." In *Asian Security in the 1980's*. Edited by Solomon. Cambridge, MA: Oelgeschlinger, Gunn and Hain, 1980.

Sopiee, Noordin. "ASEAN and Regional Security." In *Regional Security in the Third World*. Edited by Mohammed Ayoob. Boulder, CO: Westview, 1986.

Taylor, Peter J. *Political Geography: World Economy Nation State and Locality*. London: Longman, 1985.

Thakur, Ramesh. *In Defense of New Zealand*. Boulder, CO: Westview Press, 1986.

Index

ABM. *See* Antiballistic missile system
ABM Treaty. *See* Anti-Ballistic Missile Treaty
Acid rain, 179
ACS. *See* Asian collective security
Aden, 35
Advanced industrial countries (AICs), 82;
    trade, 77, 84, 87, 88, 91-92, 93-94, 96. *See*
    also various countries
Afghanistan, 145, 151; Soviets in, 37, 43, 52,
    190, 194; war, 29, 36
Africa, 1, 44, 109, 110, 113, 114, 117, 165,
    205, 219, 238; arms purchases, 41, 42;
    development, 116-117; ethnicity, 231, 236,
    238, 243; per capita income, 108, 181; wars,
    36, 53. *See also various countries*
African Charter on Human and Peoples'
    Rights, 146
Agence-France Presse, 217
Agriculture, 106; Central America, 265-267,
    268, 269, 275; preindustrial society, 163-
    164. *See also* Cash crops; Food
AI. *See* Amnesty International
AICs. *See* Advanced industrial countries
Aid programs, 9, 125, 127, 267. *See also*
    Development; Economic development;
    Military
Aircraft, 61
Air-launched cruise missiles (ALCMs), 61
ALASEI, 219
ALCMs. *See* Air-launched cruise missiles
Algeria, 35, 42
Algiers Economic Declaration, 114-115
Alien Tort Claims Act (1789), 147
Allende, Salvador, 7
Alliance for Progress, 267
Allies, 32
American Civil Liberties Union, 145
Amin, Idi, 150, 157
Amnesty International (AI), 148-149, 153, 157
ANTEL, 268

Antiballistic missile system (ABM), 61, 69
Anti-Ballistic Missile (ABM) Treaty, 193
Anti-communism: Central America, 272, 276,
    277, 279; U.S. views, 39, 42, 188
AP. *See* Associated Press
Apartheid, 139
Arab-Israeli War (1973), 32
Arafat, Yasir, 239
Arbenz Guzmán, Jacobo, 264, 271, 275; coup,
    274, 284; election, 277-278
Arévalo, Juan José, 271, 275, 276
Argentina, 107, 151, 152, 157, 215; Falklands/
    Malvinas war, 32, 36; nuclear power, 8, 65;
    trade system, 91, 92
Armas, Carlos Castillo, 278
Arms. *See* Arms control; Arms race; Arms
    sales; Weapons
Arms control, 74; negotiations, 45-46; system
    reformers, 71-72; U.S.-Soviet, 193-194.
    See also Arms race; Nuclear weapons
Arms race, 1, 37, 122, 190; factors, 62-63, 64,
    69-70, 72. *See also* Arms control; Nuclear
    weapons
Arms sales, 29, 41-42, 278; consequences, 46-
    47. *See also* Arms race; Weapons
ASEAN. *See* Association of Southeast Asian
    Nations
Asia, 53, 108, 114, 165, 181, 219; arms
    purchases, 41, 42; ethnicity, 231, 243;
    security, 300-302. *See also* Association of
    Southeast Asian Nations; *various countries*
Asian collective security (ACS), 301, 303
ASIN, 219
Associated Press (AP), 217, 252
Association of Southeast Asian Nations
    (ASEAN), 289, 290, 291; economic
    development, 297-300; security policy, 300-
    302. *See also various countries*
Australia, 102, 214, 216, 293; defense, 294,
    297; and Indonesia, 299-300; nuclear free

About the Book

Designed for global education and international relations programs, this innovative textbook investigates seven international policy issues and examines five areas of regional tension and their impact on international relations.

The authors employ a contending-worldviews analytical framework in their consideration of international conditions and events: the reader is provided with information that encourages critical analysis from the points of view of system maintainers, system reformers, and system transformers. This framework encourages an exploration of competing worldviews and requires the weighing of evidence from differing ideological, cultural, and gender perspectives. For example, the chapter on international inequality compares free trade solutions (system maintenance) with interventionary strategies proposed by such groups as the Brandt Commission (system reform) and more radical proposals for a new international economic order (system transformation).

Each chapter provides a thorough description of the issues being examined, a review of theoretical explanations that account for the development of particular problems; a review of predictions about the future; and a discussion of possible policy responses.